Issues in Hispanic and Lusophone Linguistics (IHLL)
ISSN 2213-3887

IHLL aims to provide a single home for the highest quality monographs and edited volumes pertaining to Hispanic and Lusophone linguistics. In an effort to be as inclusive as possible, the series includes volumes that represent the many sub-fields and paradigms of linguistics that do high quality research targeting Iberian Romance languages. IHLL considers proposals that focus on formal syntax, semantics, morphology, phonetics/phonology, pragmatics from any established research paradigm, as well as psycholinguistics, language acquisition, historical linguistics, applied linguistics and sociolinguistics. The editorial board is comprised of experts in all of the aforementioned fields.

For an overview of all books published in this series, please see *benjamins.com/catalog/ihll*

Editors

Patrícia Amaral
Indiana University

Megan Solon
Indiana University

Editorial Board

Jennifer Cabrelli
University of Illinois at Chicago

Sonia Colina
University of Arizona

João Costa
Universidade Nova de Lisboa

Inês Duarte
Universidade de Lisboa

Daniel Erker
Boston University

Timothy L. Face
University of Minnesota

Sónia Frota
Universidade de Lisboa

Ángel J. Gallego
Universitat Autònoma de Barcelona

María del Pilar García Mayo
Universidad del País Vasco

Anna Gavarró
Universitat Autònoma de Barcelona

Michael Iverson
Indiana University

Matthew Kanwit
University of Pittsburgh

Juana M. Liceras
University of Ottawa

John M. Lipski
Pennsylvania State University

Gillian Lord
University of Florida

Jairo Nunes
Universidade de São Paulo

Acrisio Pires
University of Michigan, Ann Arbor

Pilar Prieto
Universitat Pompeu Fabra

Jason Rothman
UiT The Arctic University and Universidad Nebrija

Liliana Sánchez
Rutgers University

Ana Lúcia Santos
Universidade de Lisboa

Scott A. Schwenter
Ohio State University

Naomi Lapidus Shin
University of New Mexico

Carmen Silva-Corvalán
University of Southern California

Miquel Simonet
University of Arizona

Juan Uriagereka
University of Maryland

Elena Valenzuela
University of Ottawa

Bill VanPatten
Michigan State University

Volume 43

Research at the Intersection of Second Language Acquisition and Sociolinguistics. Studies in honor of Kimberly L. Geeslin
Edited by Megan Solon, Matthew Kanwit and Aarnes Gudmestad

Research at the Intersection of Second Language Acquisition
and Sociolinguistics

Research at the Intersection of Second Language Acquisition and Sociolinguistics

Studies in honor of Kimberly L. Geeslin

Edited by

Megan Solon
Indiana University

Matthew Kanwit
University of Pittsburgh

Aarnes Gudmestad
Virginia Polytechnic Institute and State University

John Benjamins Publishing Company
Amsterdam / Philadelphia

The paper used in this publication meets the minimum requirements of the American National Standard for Information Sciences – Permanence of Paper for Printed Library Materials, ANSI z39.48-1984.

DOI 10.1075/ihll.43

Cataloging-in-Publication Data available from Library of Congress:
LCCN 2025011524 (PRINT) / 2025011525 (E-BOOK)

ISBN 978 90 272 2197 1 (HB)
ISBN 978 90 272 4481 9 (E-BOOK)

© 2025 – John Benjamins B.V.
No part of this book may be reproduced in any form, by print, photoprint, microfilm, or any other means, without written permission from the publisher.

John Benjamins Publishing Company · https://benjamins.com

*To Sean, Logan, and Hayden McGuire, Elaine
and the late Bill Geeslin, Patty Gildea McGuire
and the late Clifford "Kippy" McGuire, and Melissa Snodgrass
for generously sharing Kim Geeslin with us and for helping
inspire the wonderful work she did for so many.*

Table of contents

Introduction: The acquisition of variation and the legacy
of Kimberly L. Geeslin   1
   Megan Solon, Matthew Kanwit & Aarnes Gudmestad

SECTION 1. Furthering established lines of inquiry

CHAPTER 1. A study of lexical bases and variation of progressive
constructions in the Spanish of English-speaking learners   10
   Stephen Fafulas, Jingyi Guo, Juan Berríos & Kimberly L. Geeslin

CHAPTER 2. What frequency, regularity, and form avoidance tell us about
strategic competence: The case of L2 Spanish future variation   35
   Irene Soto-Lucena & Matthew Kanwit

CHAPTER 3. Implicit bias and the L2 perception of the Peninsular Spanish
interdental fricative /θ/   65
   Carmen Fernández Flórez & Bret Linford

CHAPTER 4. Revisiting the acquisition of the variable perfective past in L2
Spanish during short-term study abroad   89
   Nicholas M. Blaker & Thomas Goebel-Mahrle

CHAPTER 5. Acquiring sociolinguistic competence: A comparison of subject
pronoun expression in L2 and L3 Spanish   116
   *Chelsea Escalante, Rebecca Pozzi, Robert Bayley, Xiaoshi Li
& Xinye Zhang*

SECTION 2. Breaking new ground

CHAPTER 6. University Spanish instructors' trill production within
and outside of the language classroom   144
   Sara L. Zahler, Danielle Daidone & Emily Kuder

CHAPTER 7. Interlocutor perceptions of regional phone use in L2 Spanish:
The Castilian Spanish /θ/   178
   Stacey Hanson & Elena Schoonmaker-Gates

CHAPTER 8. Sociopragmatic variation and identity construction
in L2 Spanish: An analysis of context and group membership   203
   Shana Scucchi & Paul A. Malovrh

CHAPTER 9. Dialectal variation in secondary Spanish classrooms in the United States: A sociolinguistically informed pedagogical approach to teaching and learning the *usted, tú*, and *vos* forms of address   230
Francisco Salgado-Robles, Angela George & Brisilda Ndreka

CHAPTER 10. Acquisition of sociolinguistic variation: The case of filled pauses in L2 Spanish   260
Megan Solon, Travis Evans-Sago & Kaitlin Moen

CHAPTER 11. An exploration of L1 attitudes and individual characteristics in the study of sociolinguistic perception in additional-language Spanish   289
Ian Michalski & Aarnes Gudmestad

CHAPTER 12. Theoretical, methodological, and computational perspectives on immersive virtual reality in variationist SLA: Insights from user experience   317
Mason A. Wirtz & Simone E. Pfenninger

Epilogue   344
Robert Bayley, Kristen Kennedy Terry, Laura Gurzynski-Weiss & Eliza Pavalko

Index   369

Acknowledgements

First, we want to acknowledge our deep gratitude for the numerous ways that Kim Geeslin truly excelled in every portion of her life as a researcher, teacher, mentor, colleague, friend, and confidante, not to mention as a mother, sister, and daughter. We provide more detailed accounts of the manifold ways that Kim has forever shaped us in the introductory chapter, as do other colleagues (Bob Bayley, Laura Gurzynski-Weiss, Kristen Kennedy Terry, and Eliza Pavalko) in the epilogue.

We are incredibly grateful to the numerous scholars who supported this project from its initial proposal stages to its publication. We are thankful for the diligent work and spirit of collaboration of the contributing authors who made this volume possible. We would also like to recognize the following individuals for their help in reviewing the chapters in this volume: Grant Berry, Whitney Chappell, Jenny Dumont, Chelsea Escalante, Stephen Fafulas, Angela George, Amanda Huensch, Tiffany Judy, Stephanie Knouse, Xiaoshi Li, Bret Linford, Ian Michalski, María Elena Placencia, Rebecca Pozzi, Ana de Prada Pérez, Brendan Regan, Lauren B. Schmidt, Naomi Shin, Virginia Terán, Trish Thrasher, Nicole Tracy-Ventura, Mason Wirtz, and Sara Zahler. We are also grateful to Patrícia Amaral and Ymke Verploegen for editorial support.

Finally, we would like to acknowledge the late Robert Bayley, who contributed to this volume as a co-author on both a chapter and the volume's epilogue. Bob was an ardent and generous supporter of this project and of all of the scholars who participated. He championed the idea for the volume, participated fully (despite his own ailing health), and encouraged wider dissemination through a conference panel at NWAV 52 in Miami, Florida in November 2024. Like Kim Geeslin, Bob Bayley was a kind, generous, and supportive mentor to so many. He made an indelible mark on the fields of Hispanic linguistics and sociolinguistics and on innumerable scholars and mentees. He is dearly missed.

Introduction
The acquisition of variation and the legacy of Kimberly L. Geeslin

Megan Solon, Matthew Kanwit & Aarnes Gudmestad
Indiana University | University of Pittsburgh | Virginia Polytechnic Institute and State University

Learning a language involves acquiring more than categorical rules regarding the use of grammatical forms or lexical items. Critically, it also requires knowledge about forms whose use varies systematically according to linguistic, geographical, social, and contextual factors. In comprehension and in production, learners' knowledge of variable patterns of language use can help them successfully navigate communicative and social situations (e.g., to understand implied meanings, gain entrance into social groups, establish friendships, and respond politely). Research on the acquisition of sociolinguistic variation in a second or additional language (L2) works to capture learners' developing L2 sociolinguistic repertoires, their understanding of sociolinguistic variants (e.g., what they "mean" or index, where/when they "should" be used), and the processes by which learners come to display and attach meaning to variants in the L2. For instance, for the variable (ING) in L2 English, learners may develop a preference for the reduced (i.e., alveolar) variant, as in "runnin'", with familiar interlocutors in informal settings and for the nonreduced (i.e., velar) variant, seen in "running", with unfamiliar interlocutors in more formal settings.

Kimberly L. Geeslin was a pioneer in research on L2 sociolinguistic variation. In the early 2000s, Kim's work on variation in the Spanish copula system brought together and extended ongoing research in second language acquisition (SLA) on the acquisition of the copulas *ser* and *estar* 'to be' (e.g., Ryan & Lafford, 1992; VanPatten, 1985, 1987) and in sociolinguistics on changes in the use of *ser* and *estar* among US Spanish speakers (e.g., Silva-Corvalán, 1986, 1994). Geeslin's work examined patterns of copula selection and use by native (i.e., expert) and L2 users of Spanish and explored the influence of numerous linguistic, social, and contextual factors. Her research laid the foundation for a subfield of investigation that explores how interlanguage Spanish varies in systematic and socially meaningful ways across various levels or modules of language (e.g., phonetics/phonology, morphosyntax, lexicon); how variation in learner Spanish is related to the speakers, contexts, and experiences that learners are in contact with; and how learners' knowledge and use of variable features develop over the course of their learning trajectories.

Kimberly Geeslin passed away unexpectedly in January 2023 with a robust research agenda still ahead of her and a community of students, mentees, and colleagues who feel her loss daily in ways both professional and deeply personal. In Kim's honor, this volume brings together work by scholars that advances research at the intersection of SLA and sociolinguistics. The chapters in this volume explore established avenues of investigation with new questions, additional factors worth consideration, and novel approaches. The included studies also break ground on new avenues of inquiry, investigating under-explored linguistic features and testing innovative methodologies that have the potential to expand our understanding of learners' interlanguage systems and acquisitional trajectories. The volume, thus, is organized around these two approaches to advancing the field: meaningfully revisiting established lines of inquiry and breaking new ground. Contributions focus on a wide range of variable features spanning lexical, morphosyntactic, phonetic/phonological, and pragmatic levels of language. Although the focus of most chapters is on Spanish as an additional language, the volume also includes a methodologically focused chapter that explores L2 German but makes connections to Spanish. The latter chapter and the myriad citations to variationist work on numerous L2s throughout the volume demonstrate the widespread relevance, impact, and influence of Kim's work, as the volume lays the groundwork for the next stage of innovative research on L2 sociolinguistic variation.

In addition to her immense scholarly contributions, Kimberly Geeslin was widely recognized for her exemplary and generous mentorship, which extended well beyond her own students and advisees. Thus, in addition to its topical cohesion, this volume honors Kim's legacy in its intentional orientation toward the promotion of the work of early-career scholars and toward the fostering of collaboration and mentorship. Readers will note that each chapter is authored by teams of at least two scholars who have been purposefully connected to enhance on-going work and to foster the development of up-and-coming scholars in this area. Taken together, this volume aims to continue the scholarly and professional work of Kimberly Geeslin. We follow Kim's lead in advancing the agenda within research on L2 sociolinguistic variation, and we aim to do so in a way that cultivates and supports the next generation of Hispanic linguists and other linguists focused on the intersection of SLA and sociolinguistics.

The first section of the book collects five chapters that meaningfully revisit well-established lines of inquiry in research on the intersection of Spanish sociolinguistics and SLA. To begin, Fafulas, Guo, Berríos, and Geeslin advance an on-going line of research on the L2 Spanish expression of progressive aspect (e.g., Fafulas, 2015; Geeslin & Fafulas, 2012, 2022). Whereas previous research has focused on the most common progressive construction (i.e., *estar* 'to be' + present progressive participle), this chapter investigates the range of lexical bases that L1 and L2 Spanish speakers accept to form the progressive and identifies changes in the lexical bases accepted across different learner proficiency levels. The chapter shows that, even though *estar* was the most frequently selected progressive lexical base, learners at all proficiency levels accepted all five of the lexical bases tested.

Soto-Lucena and Kanwit offer a novel look at the acquisition of future-time expression by examining not just how learners vary systematically in expressing the future but also by investigating whether and why learners may avoid certain forms as relates to frequency and regularity. Soto-Lucena and Kanwit argue that form avoidance can be closely linked to awareness and may signal strategic competence on the part of the learner in that learners strategically avoid forms that might negatively impact successful communication (e.g., due to the learner being uncertain of an irregular or infrequent future form).

One of two chapters in the volume exploring acquisition of Spanish /θ/, Fernández Flórez and Linford examine learners' perception of the /θ/ from the lens of implicit bias. Using an Implicit Association Test and a sample of beginning-level learners of Spanish, they find significant implicit bias against /θ/, which may help to provide some empirically-based explanatory evidence for the low rates of adoption of /θ/ in the speech of L2 learners across previous studies (e.g., Geeslin & Gudmestad, 2008a; George, 2014; Grammon, 2021; Knouse, 2012; Ringer-Hilfinger, 2012).

Blaker and Goebel-Mahrle revisit the acquisition of variable perfective past states and events in L2 Spanish (i.e., use of present perfect versus preterite in hodiernal perfective contexts) during study abroad in Spain. Blaker and Goebel-Mahrle build on prior research by introducing a contextualized verb elicitation task (to complement previous research using contextualized *preference* tasks). In contrast to previous findings, Blaker and Goebel-Mahrle do not observe increases in hodiernal present perfect when students must conjugate verbs themselves (as compared to selecting from provided verb forms).

Subject pronouns have received wide-ranging attention in both L1 and L2 Spanish sociolinguistic research (e.g., Bayley et al., 2017; Cameron, 1995; Flores-Ferrán, 2004; Geeslin & Gudmestad, 2008b; Guy et al., forthcoming; Linford & Geeslin, 2022; Long, 2021; Otheguy & Zentella, 2012; Silva-Corvalán, 1994). Escalante, Pozzi, Bayley, Li, and Zhang extend this research by exploring Spanish subject pronoun use by L1 Mandarin learners of Spanish. Their findings contribute to a growing body of research that investigates under-explored language pairings, advancing our understanding of this oft-studied variable phenomenon by examining its patterning among populations of learners underrepresented in the literature on this topic.

The second section of this book collects chapters that break new ground in some way within research on the acquisition of L2 sociolinguistic variation. Zahler, Daidone, and Kuder document the variable input available to L2 learners by investigating the realization of the Spanish trill by instructors of Spanish in speech samples from within and outside of the classroom. Although they find that instructors vary in their trill production in both situational contexts, Zahler et al.'s study provides evidence that instructors modify their speech, producing more canonical Spanish trills in their classroom speech, thus affecting the range and frequency of variants (and overall amount of variation) present in classroom input.

As the second chapter in the volume to examine /θ/, Hanson and Schoonmaker-Gates also explore perception of this regionally marked phone. They use a matched guise technique to explore how L1 and L2 Spanish listeners evaluate L2 Spanish speakers in terms of nativeness, naturalness of speech, solidarity, and prestige when they produce the /θ/ and when they do not (i.e., when they produce /s/ instead). Findings suggest that evaluations vary based on L2 speakers' overall nativelikeness in pronunciation and that L1 and L2 speakers may evaluate learners' adoption of /θ/ differently. As with Fernández Flórez and Linford, Hanson and Schoonmaker-Gates's chapter provides empirical evidence to help explain L2 /θ/ adoption patterns and proffers new information about how the use of this phone by L2 speakers may be differentially perceived depending on interlocutors' characteristics.

Scucchi and Malovrh's chapter offers an innovative combination of sociopragmatic and variationist sociolinguistic approaches to learner language by exploring how one Spanish learner constructs her speaker identity in response to varying dynamics related to native speaker status and situational expertise. The study examines interactions between the same learner and several combinations of other speakers (i.e., other L2 learners versus L1 Spanish speakers) in different contexts (i.e., in the US versus during study abroad in Spain) with varying degrees of expertise (i.e., prior experience with/knowledge of the shared context: a board game). Their analysis illustrates the fluidity of speaker identity and the potential influence of situational and sociopragmatic factors.

Salgado-Robles, George, and Ndreka bring the volume back to the classroom to explore the use of Spanish second-person singular pronouns *usted*, *tú*, and *vos*, following sociolinguistically informed input and instruction on all three forms. Results from two tasks suggest increased use of all three forms post-instruction. In addition to examining L2 learners, this chapter also extends the growing body of work on the additional-language sociolinguistic variation of heritage speakers.

Solon, Evans-Sago, and Moen explore filled pauses in L2 Spanish as a potential rich locus for the study of L2 sociolinguistic and, in particular, sociophonetic development. Whereas many sociophonetic variants — especially those that index regional or social information — appear sparingly in learner speech, filled pauses are a frequent and intrinsic component of human speech that exhibit systematic variation. Solon and colleagues explore filled pause use in various ways and document changes in L2 filled pause patterns as learners' Spanish proficiency increases.

Michalski and Gudmestad tackle the native-speaker bias in L2 sociolinguistic research by proposing an approach to exploring learner attitudes toward sociophonetic variants that does not consist of a comparison to native speaker attitudes toward the same variants. Instead, Michalski and Gudmestad compare learners' evaluations of L2 (Spanish) sociophonetic variants with their evaluations of sociophonetic variants in their L1 (English), and they examine learners' L2 attitudes in relation to a series of language-experience variables. Informed by their findings, the authors offer targeted recommendations for future research.

Finally, Wirtz and Pfenninger — focused on an additional language other than Spanish — detail an innovative experimental procedure that can help increase the ecological validity of L2 sociolinguistic research while maintaining needed experimental control regardless of the language under study. Wirtz and Pfenninger's chapter provides results from an exploratory study of L2 German learners in an immersive virtual reality environment. Findings suggest rich potential for virtual reality experimental contexts, especially with regard to what these contexts can reveal about intra-individual variation.

The volume closes with a detailed accounting of and heartfelt tribute to the scholarly work and academic as well as personal impact of Kimberly Geeslin, written by Robert Bayley (Professor Emeritus, University of California at Davis) and Kristen Kennedy Terry (Assistant Professor, Arizona State University) with contributions from Kim's Indiana University colleagues Laura Gurzynski-Weiss (Indiana University Professor of Spanish) and Eliza Pavalko (former Indiana University Vice Provost for Faculty Affairs).

We would like to acknowledge that an edited volume, by nature, has to limit the contributions it collects, but the mentees, supporters, colleagues, and friends of Kim Geeslin were numerous. So many others have contributed to this volume and its goal of celebrating Kim's scholarly work and personal and professional impact by reviewing the volume's proposal and its individual chapters, by encouraging and supporting its progress and that of other projects, and by carrying on Kim's work in their own research, teaching, mentorship, and personal and professional lives. Of course, this volume does not include everyone whom Kim guided and supported as a professor, advisor, informal mentor, or colleague. The number of individuals who consider Kim's role in their academic careers and scholarly development to be absolutely central is extraordinary. We also recognize and direct the reader to the compelling tributes shared by family, friends, and colleagues on a virtual memorial board following Kim's passing (available here: https://www.kudoboard.com/boards/gBVZdANO).

With this volume, we hope to honor (in an admittedly small way) Kimberly Geeslin, the role she played in our lives, and the scholarly impact she has had on the fields of Hispanic linguistics, second language acquisition, and sociolinguistics. We (Megan, Matt, and Aarnes) could undoubtedly fill a complete volume with our own reflections, memories, anecdotes, and tributes to illustrate Kim's impact on our careers, perspectives, and lives. Instead, we hope this volume pays tribute to that immeasurable impact, while also contributing to the subfield Kim nurtured and highlighting the work of several of the scholars she mentored, collaborated with, or influenced. We intend for this volume to provide a heartfelt and loving look back at the work, contributions, and impact of an incredible person, scholar, teacher, and mentor, and to look forward to avenues of investigation for which Kim's foundation has laid a path.

References

Bayley, R., Greer, K. A., & Holland, C. L. (2017). Lexical frequency and morphosyntactic variation: Evidence from U.S. Spanish. *Spanish in Context, 14*, 413–439.

Cameron, R. (1995). The scope and limits of switch reference as a constraint on pronominal subject expression. *Hispanic Linguistics, 6*(7), 1–28.

Fafulas, S. (2015). Progressive constructions in native-speaker and adult-acquired Spanish. *Studies in Hispanic and Lusophone Linguistics, 8*(1), 85–133.

Flores-Ferrán, N. (2004). Spanish subject personal pronoun use in New York City Puerto Ricans: Can we rest the case of English contact? *Language Variation and Change, 16*, 49–73.

Geeslin, K., & Fafulas, S. (2012). Variation of the simple present and present progressive forms: A comparison of native and non-native speakers. In K. Geeslin & M. Díaz-Campos (Eds.), *Selected proceedings of the 14th Hispanic Linguistics Symposium* (pp. 179–196). Cascadilla Proceedings Project.

Geeslin, K., & Fafulas, S. (2022). Linguistic variation and second language Spanish: A study of progressive and habitual marking by English-speaking learners. In R. Bayley, D. R. Preston, & X. Li (Eds.), *Variation in second and heritage languages: Crosslinguistic perspectives* (pp. 159–198). John Benjamins.

Geeslin, K. L., & Gudmestad, A. (2008a). The acquisition of variation in second-language Spanish: An agenda for integrating studies of the L2 sound system. *Journal of Applied Linguistics, 5*(2), 137–157.

Geeslin, K. L., & Gudmestad, A. (2008b). Variable subject expression in second-language Spanish: A comparison of native and non-native speakers. In M. Bowles, R. Foote, & S. Perpiñán (Eds.), *Selected proceedings of the 2007 Second Language Research Forum* (pp. 69–85). Cascadilla Proceedings Project.

George, A. (2014). Study abroad in central Spain: The development of regional phonological features. *Foreign Language Annals, 47*(1), 97–114.

Grammon, D. (2021). Consequential choices: A language ideological perspective on learners' (non-)adoption of a dialectal variant. *Foreign Language Annals, 54*(3), 607–625.

Guy, G. R., Adli, A., Bayley, R., Beaman, K. V., Erker, D., Orozco, R., & Zhang, X. (forthcoming). *Subject pronoun expression: A cross-linguistic variationist sociolinguistic study*. Cambridge University Press.

Knouse, S. M. (2012). The acquisition of dialectal phonemes in a study abroad context: The case of the Castilian theta. *Foreign Language Annals, 45*(4), 512–542.

Linford, B., & Geeslin, K. L. (2022). The role of referent cohesiveness in variable subject expression in L2 Spanish. *Spanish in Context, 19*(3), 508–536.

Long, A. Y. (2021). Korean learners' acquisition and use of variable first-person subject forms in Spanish. *Languages, 6*(4), 208.

Otheguy, R., & Zentella, A. C. (2012). *Spanish in New York: Language contact, dialectal leveling, and structural continuity*. Oxford University Press.

Ringer-Hilfinger, K. (2012). Learner acquisition of dialectal variation in a study abroad context: The case of the Spanish [θ]. *Foreign Language Annals, 45*(3), 430–446.

Ryan, J. M., & Lafford, B. A. (1992). Acquisition of lexical meaning in a study abroad environment: Ser and estar and the Granada experience. *Hispania, 75*(3), 714–722.

Silva-Corvalán, C. (1986). Bilingualism and language change: The extension of estar in Los Angeles Spanish. *Language, 62*(3), 587–608.

Silva-Corvalán, C. (1994). *Language contact and change: Spanish in Los Angeles*. Clarendon Press.

VanPatten, B. (1985). The acquisition of ser and estar by adult learners of Spanish: A preliminary investigation of transitional stages of competence. *Hispania, 68*(2), 399–406.

Van Patten, B. (1987). Classroom learners' acquisition of ser and estar: Accounting for developmental patterns. In B. VanPatten, T. R. Dvorak, & J. F. Lee (Eds.), *Foreign language learning: A research perspective* (pp. 19–32). Newbury House.

SECTION 1

Furthering established lines of inquiry

CHAPTER 1

A study of lexical bases and variation of progressive constructions in the Spanish of English-speaking learners

Stephen Fafulas,[1] Jingyi Guo,[2] Juan Berríos[3]
& Kimberly L. Geeslin[2]
[1] University of Mississippi | [2] Indiana University | [3] California State University, Fresno

> We investigated allowance of five common lexical bases used to form Spanish progressive constructions: *estar, andar, ir, venir,* and *seguir.* In a written contextualized acceptability task, five identical sentences appeared after a given context, the only difference being the lexical base used. Participants evaluated each sentence as *possible* or *not possible.* There were 80 sentences (4 verbal aspectual categories × 4 adverbial types × 5 lexical bases), producing a corpus of 7,600 responses. We compared learners from four different proficiency levels ($n=75$), and a first-language Spanish ($n=20$) baseline. Results indicate that *estar* was the most accepted lexical base, and learners allowed all five lexical bases from the lowest Spanish proficiency level. Relevant pedagogical implications are discussed.
>
> **Keywords:** progressive constructions, Spanish, lexical bases, sociolinguistic variation, second language acquisition

In the growing field of variationist approaches to second language acquisition (SLA; see Geeslin, 2022), the necessity of considering the full range of forms that fulfill a certain function has been acknowledged in order to fully account for the complexity of learners' interlanguage, particularly when the multiple forms are closely related (Geeslin & Gudmestad, 2010). The acquisition of progressive aspectual marking in Spanish provides a productive test case in this sense since one key difference between first language (L1) and second language (L2) speakers of Spanish is related to the range of lexical bases (e.g., *estar* 'to be', *andar* 'to go around', etc.) used to form the progressive (Fafulas, 2015). The present study investigates a range of lexical bases that speakers may use to form the progressive, and it tracks development across multiple L2 proficiency levels. Specifically, we ana-

https://doi.org/10.1075/ihll.43.01faf
© 2025 John Benjamins Publishing Company

lyze the acceptability of progressive constructions in contexts of progressive and habitual action by L1 and L2 speakers of Spanish. Following Klein (1980), most of this work has focused on the alternation between the simple present and the *estar* present progressive (Table 1, examples a–b).

Table 1. Alternation between the simple present and the *estar* present progressive (data from Fafulas, 2021)

Form	Spanish	English gloss
a. Simple present	*Y los tres* **caminan** *satisfechos*	'And the three happily **walk**'
b. *Estar* present progressive	*Aquí el niño* **está caminando** *en el...*	'Here the boy **is walking** in the...'

Prior research (e.g., Dumont & Wilson, 2016; Torres Cacoullos, 2011) conducted with monolinguals and bilinguals, including diachronic and synchronic analyses, shows that these two forms can "neutralize in discourse" (Berry, 2017, p. 206). Studies have shown that L2 Spanish speakers move toward a path of acquiring the linguistic constraints that determine L1 speaker use of each form, although they employ the simple present at significantly lower rates than L1 speakers when describing 'ongoing action' (see Geeslin & Fafulas, 2012). Much less work has been conducted on the L2 acquisition of different progressive constructions in Spanish. However, Sedano (2000) and Fafulas (2021) show that Spanish speakers across dialects employ a range of progressive constructions in the domain of imperfective aspect (Table 2, examples a–d), making this a productive test case for L2 acquisition of these forms.

Table 2. Progressive construction variation (data from Fafulas, 2021)

Progressive construction	Spanish	English gloss
a. *Estar* present progressive	*que* **está caminando** *con sombrerito el señor*	'that the man with the hat **is walking**'
b. *Ir* Present Progressive	*ahora* **va caminando** *con la bicicleta*	'now (he) **goes walking** with the bike'
c. *Continuar* Present Progressive	*Ahora* **continúan** *las tres personas* **caminando**	'now the three people **continue walking**'
d. *Seguir* Present Progressive	*... y luego* **sigue caminando** *con la bicicleta*	'... and then (he) **keeps on walking** with the bike'

Grammaticalization theory (Hopper & Traugott, 2003), along with evidence from typological research (Bybee et al., 1994), points to similar paths of diachronic development for simple present and present progressive forms in both

English and Spanish (Torres Cacoullos, 2000). For example, the Spanish *estar* progressive originated as a locative construction composed of the verb *stare* 'to stand' and a gerund indicating that the action was happening in that specific location. Over time, the locative function of the form was slowly lost, and a construction with aspectual import emerged, similar to the modern-day English *be* progressive construction (Berry, 2017). However, currently, both languages are at different points along the grammaticalization cline, resulting in cross-linguistic variation. That is, the *estar* Spanish progressive still exhibits variation with the simple present, while the English *be* progressive is more widespread across lexical aspectual classes (including stative predicates; e.g., the McDonald's slogan "I'm lovin' it!") and is essentially the obligatory means of expressing an *event in progress* in English. The target-like use of patterns of variation — morphosyntactic and phonological alike — such as those attested in the formation of progressive constructions is considered to be a key factor in sociolinguistic competence (i.e., rules of language use and discourse in context, itself a component of communicative competence along with grammatical and strategic competence; Canale & Swain, 1980). In the present study, we address how L2 learners attend to variation and the acquisition of multiple progressive constructions in Spanish. We now turn to a greater explanation of the results of previous research conducted with L1 and L2 Spanish speakers.

Previous studies

Spanish progressive constructions

In Spanish, the simple present has a wide variety of possible meanings, including habitual, futurate, narrative, and reportative interpretations (e.g., Alarcos-Llorach, 1994; Torres Cacoullos, 2000). It is therefore not always interchangeable with the present progressive. However, the forms have previously been studied among L1 speakers with a focus on ongoing actions, which is a context in which the two forms can be neutralized. The primary linguistic factors that have been shown to consistently constrain variation are adverbial type and the lexical aspect of the verbal predicate (see Tasks Section 5.2 for examples), with the use of the present progressive generally being favored with achievements, accomplishments, and activities (i.e., dynamic predicates) and when the adverbial present in the utterance denotes simultaneity with speech time (Berry, 2017; Fafulas, 2012, 2021; Torres Cacoullos, 2000).

As regards diachronic development, Torres Cacoullos (2000, 2012) argues that the predominant *estar* "to be" + V-*ndo* progressive participates in a progressive-to-imperfective grammaticalization path; a cyclical grammaticalization shift that has been attested for several constructions cross-linguistically (Bybee et al., 1994; Deo, 2015). Thus, it has expanded from a locative meaning (an agent doing something while located in a particular place) to the progressive meaning it primarily holds nowadays and slowly to contexts of habituality, where the simple present is preferred. Changes attested for *estar* + V-*ndo* and other progressive constructions are also in accordance with the cross-linguistic trend of analytic forms increasingly fulfilling functions formerly filled only by synthetic forms (Hopper & Traugott, 2003), investigated priorly for Spanish morphosyntactic variable structures such as future-in-the-past expression (Swain et al., 2023).

L2 Spanish progressive research

Previous studies have investigated how variation in Spanish progressive expression is acquired by L1 English learners of L2 Spanish. Most of these studies dealt entirely with the acquisition of the *estar* + V-*ndo* form and its grammaticality or acceptability in contexts of 'action in progress' and 'habituality'. In the current section, we focus specifically on variationist accounts and the few studies that have explicitly targeted L2 development of multiple progressive constructions, in addition to *estar* + V-*ndo*.

Geeslin and Fafulas (2012) compared oral film retelling produced by advanced L2 Spanish learners and L1 Spanish speakers. The authors included in their analysis all finite verbs that indicated the present time frame and focused on variation between *estar* + V-*ndo* and simple present forms. Results showed that advanced L2 learners produced more *estar* + V-*ndo* forms than L1 speakers. For both groups, the *estar* + V-*ndo* form was favored with activity predicates, in subordinate clauses and with plural, full noun phrase direct objects. Using an oral simultaneous film narration task, Fafulas (2015) examined the acquisition of variation in the production of simple present forms and present progressive forms considering the full range of lexical bases + present participle progressive constructions (e.g., *estar, andar, venir, ir, seguir* + V-*ndo*). Fafulas (2015) found that L2 learners did not produce lexical bases other than *estar* "to be" until they reached a higher level of Spanish proficiency (i.e., fourth-year Spanish). Fafulas (2015) also employed a contextualized judgment task where participants selected whether the different lexical base + present participle progressive constructions were possible in a given context. Results indicated that L1 Spanish speakers' judgments were constrained by two linguistic factors: adverbial type and the lexical aspect of the predicate. As learners' Spanish proficiency level increased, they first developed sensitivity to adverbial type and then additionally to lexical aspect, gradually converging towards the target. More recently, Geeslin and Fafulas (2022) elicited preference selection data using a contextualized preference task, where participants indicated in each habitual or ongoing context whether they preferred the simple present form, the *estar* + V-*ndo* form, or that both were equally preferable. The authors found that learners' acquisitional paths were influenced by two aspects of the English and Spanish baseline groups' preference patterns: first, the degree of difference between the two baseline groups; second, the extent to which the baseline groups displayed categorical preference towards one form. The acquisitional trends in the prior studies were all found to be influenced in part by lexical aspect, in line with the predictions of the Aspect Hypothesis (Andersen, 2002; Andersen & Shirai, 1996), one of the most widely tested hypotheses in the study of the acquisition of tense-aspect morphology. The main tenet of the Aspect Hypothesis is that aspectual classes have an influence on the way tense and aspect are marked, as there are prototypical associations between a class and a marker (e.g., atelic predicates and the imperfect) which learners might overgeneralize at first and use in a more sophisticated manner with increases in proficiency. In the developmental sequence proposed by Andersen and Shirai (1996), for instance, it is proposed that progressive constructions are initially associated with dynamic predicates and at later stages are not overextended to stative predicates. However, there is limited work on the Aspect Hypothesis and the development of various progressive constructions in present-time contexts, which is a focus of the current study.

To test how the impact of factors such as lexical aspect extends to oppositions in past (e.g., imperfect and imperfect progressive) or future temporalities (e.g., synthetic future or future progressive), Berríos and Kanwit (2024) also used a contextualized preference task completed by L1 English learners of Spanish. The results mirrored prior research regarding *estar* + V-*ndo* forms being favored in dynamic contexts, whereas co-occurring adverbs (limited to an adverb of immediacy or none) did not condition selection significantly. Berríos and Kanwit (2024) also reported that temporality was a relevant factor for selection, as *estar* + V-*ndo* forms, for instance, were strongly disfavored in contexts with future-time temporality even when co-occurring with dynamic predicates. In the same manner as in Fafulas (2015) and Geeslin and Fafulas (2022), the authors also found that learners generally patterned with the L1 baseline with increases in proficiency.

In summary, prior research on progressive aspectual marking in L2 Spanish has provided ample evidence of the influence of factors such as the lexical aspect of the predicate and the semantic value of adverbials, among others (Berríos & Kanwit, 2024; Fafulas, 2015; Geeslin & Fafulas, 2012, 2022). Nevertheless, it is necessary to conduct a more fine-grained analysis of the potential effects of the multiple lexical bases of the progressive constructions, as noted in Fafulas (2015). This analysis is important for understanding L2 variation because it acknowledges a wider range of lexical forms that fulfill the same progressive function. Thus, the analysis serves to reveal the complexity of learners' evolving interlanguage as they navigate multiple interrelated forms that participate in variation and to which they are potentially exposed in the input (Geeslin & Gudmestad, 2010). In doing so, we seek to go beyond the individual form-meaning association of focus in prior research (i.e., *estar* + V-*ndo*) to arrive at a potentially more complex understanding of how a number of competing forms fit together into the learner's tense-aspect system more generally (Bardovi-Harlig, 2017). We now turn to the research questions of the current study, followed by a detailed description of our experimental task and analysis.

Current study

Our review of prior work on the L2 acquisition of Spanish progressive constructions shows that, with the exception of Fafulas (2015), there is little evidence of how learners come to incorporate lexical bases other than *estar* as their proficiency increases. Equally as important, while there is growing literature on how learners incorporate the variation between the *estar* progressive and simple present and on the factors that predict use of these forms by L1 and L2 speakers, we do not yet have a clear picture as to how learners' patterns of *estar* and the other potential lexical bases used in Spanish progressive constructions compare to L1 speakers of Spanish. Considering a wider range of lexical bases may reveal important differences between L1 and L2 Spanish (Geeslin & Gudmestad, 2010) thereby offering further understanding of the L2 development of morphosyntactic variation. Thus, the present investigation sets out to establish how learners at different levels of proficiency compare to L1 speakers who were residing in the same community. We targeted their acceptability of multiple lexical bases on a task that was designed to test a range of progressive constructions in Spanish, as well as the influence of lexical aspect and adverbial phrase type as linguistic factors. Our study is guided by the following research questions:

1. On a written contextualized acceptability task, what are speakers' acceptability rates for each of the five progressive constructions:
   a. *estar* + V-*ndo*   "to be + V-ing"
   b. *andar* + V-*ndo* "to go around + V-ing"
   c. *seguir* + V-*ndo* "to keep on + V-ing"
   d. *venir* + V-*ndo*   "to come along + V-ing"
   e. *ir* + V-*ndo*   "to go + V-ing"?

2. What is the relationship between these rates and the lexical base of the progressive construction, the lexical aspect of the verbal phrase, and the adverbial phrase type embedded in each sentence on the elicitation task?
3. What changes can be observed as learners increase in Spanish proficiency?

Method

Participants

All participants were living in southern Indiana, United States of America, a region that has experienced an increase in its Latinx population over the past two decades. The participants in this study were affiliated with a large university in the region. We included a baseline group to establish a sample of selection rates on the written contextualized acceptability task. Their demographic information can be seen in Table 3. The Spanish baseline is comprised of L1 speakers from Mexico and Spain.[1] The L1 Spanish speakers were living in the same community as the learners, with an average of 4.8 years in the US, and, as confirmed by self-reporting in the background questionnaire, represented the diversity of input that learners were exposed to. All L1 Spanish speakers were born and educated through the secondary level in their home country and have L1 Spanish-speaking parents. Our motivation to include local L1 Spanish speakers of the community as an appropriate target for the L2 speakers is rooted in calls to compare L2 speakers to late bilinguals (Ortega, 2013).

Table 3. Demographic information of the Spanish baseline group

Group	n	Gender	Mean proficiency score (SD)	Mean age (SD)	Description
Spanish L1	20	9M/11W	24.5 (0.6)	31.7 (5.2)	Born and educated in Mexico or Spain, US 4.8 years average

Note. Max score for proficiency test was 25

---

1. Preliminary results showed that both groups had the same ordering of preference for the progressive constructions and did not differ significantly on the task. The supplementary corpus search also showed similar results thereby justifying our decision to combine the groups for inferential analyses.

The learners in the current study received formal education through classroom instruction and were exposed to varieties of L1 and L2 Spanish both within and outside of the classroom. The first group of learners is from an intact class, the last course necessary to complete the undergraduate foreign-language requirement in Spanish. The next learner level includes data from an *Introduction to Hispanic Linguistics* class, designed for beginning majors and minors of Spanish. The next group was formed from students in a course on Spanish SLA for advanced undergraduate students. The last learner group includes graduate students and instructors of university-level Spanish. As expected, the mean score on a standardized grammar test (see Tasks Section 5.2 below) increased with each learner level, as did the amount of study abroad experience. The summary of the learner profiles is displayed in Table 4.

Table 4. Demographic information of the L2 learners of Spanish

Group	n	Gender	Mean grammar score (SD)	Mean age (SD)	3+ months experience abroad
2nd Year	20	8M/12W	9.9 (2.4)	19.8 (1.2)	5.0%
3rd Year	19	6M/13W	14.4 (2.6)	20.7 (0.9)	31.6%
4th Year	17	7M/10W	18.7 (3.1)	22.5 (3.8)	64.7%
Graduate	19	8M/11W	23.5 (1.6)	28.1 (4.4)	100%

Note. Max score for grammar test was 25

Tasks

Before the written contextualized acceptability task, participants completed a 12-item written task that targeted selection/acceptability of simple present and *estar* progressive forms. The results from that task are presented in Geeslin and Fafulas (2022). Before data elicitation, each instrument was piloted with L1 speakers from different countries of origin to verify comprehensibility and sociopragmatic appropriateness. All L2 learners and the L1 Spanish baseline received tasks and instructions in Spanish.

The written contextualized acceptability task used in this study focused on Spanish progressive constructions formed with the *estar, andar, ir, venir,* and *seguir* base forms. These five progressive constructions are among the most commonly cited in previous investigations (e.g., Torres Cacoullos, 2000). The task design ensured that all combinations of the independent variables were presented. These variables were: (i) lexical aspectual category (stative, activity, accomplishment, achievement) and (ii) semantic value of the adverb which rendered contexts as:

(a) initiated before speech time and continuing into the moment of speech (e.g., *desde el año pasado* 'since last year'), (b) simultaneous with speech time (e.g., *ahora* 'now'), (c) habitually occurring (e.g., *siempre* 'always'), or (d) no additional adverb. Tables 5 and 6 show the lexical aspectual classes and adverbs used in the written contextualized acceptability task. Following each of these contexts, five identical sentences appeared, differing only in the lexical base of the progressive construction.

Instructions required participants to evaluate each individual response as *possible* or *not possible*. Each participant evaluated 80 sentences (four lexical aspectual categories x four adverbial types x five progressive constructions). The storyline situated the participant in a scenario in which he/she returned to their childhood neighborhood and interacted with known acquaintances. An example from the instrument can be seen in (1).

(1) *Ustedes entran y la Sra. Rodríguez sale de la cocina para saludarte. Ella te dice:*
   a. *Llegaron justo a tiempo. En este momento ando preparando una torta para el postre. Va a estar lista pronto.*
   b. *Llegaron justo a tiempo. En este momento vengo preparando una torta para el postre. Va a estar lista pronto.*
   c. *Llegaron justo a tiempo. En este momento estoy preparando una torta para el postre. Va a estar lista pronto.*
   d. *Llegaron justo a tiempo. En este momento sigo preparando una torta para el postre. Va a estar lista pronto.*
   e. *Llegaron justo a tiempo. En este momento voy preparando una torta para el postre. Va a estar lista pronto.*

'You all enter and Mrs. Rodriguez comes out of the kitchen to say hello. She says to you:
   a. You arrived right on time. At this moment I go around preparing a cake for dessert. It will be ready soon.
   b. You arrived right on time. At this moment I come along preparing a cake for dessert. It will be ready soon.
   c. You arrived right on time. At this moment I am preparing a cake for dessert. It will be ready soon.
   d. You arrived right on time. At this moment I keep on preparing a cake for dessert. It will be ready soon.
   e. You arrived right on time. At this moment I go preparing a cake for dessert. It will be ready soon.'

This item was coded as [accomplishment verb: *preparar una torta* 'prepare a cake'] and [immediate adverb: *en este momento* 'at this moment']. Progressive constructions were not used in the storyline or instructions, and the progressive constructions were randomized across the contexts.

Chapter 1. Variation of progressive constructions in L2 Spanish   19

Table 5. Lexical aspectual classes used in instrument

Lexical aspect	Spanish	English translation
Stative	*creer, querer, pensar, sentirse*	believe, want, think, feel
Activity	*tocar música, jugar tenis, jugar póker, buscar trabajo*	play music, play tennis, play poker, look for work
Accomplishment	*caminar 5 km, comer dos manzanas, preparar una torta, construir un nuevo edificio*	walk 5 km, eat two apples, prepare a cake, build a new building
Achievement	*salir, llegar, recordar, desaparecer*	leave, arrive, remember, disappear

Table 6. Adverbs used in instrument

Adverbial reading of event	Spanish	English translation
Initiated before speech time and continuing into moment of speech	*desde hace mucho tiempo, desde el año pasado, desde el mes pasado*	since a while ago, since last year, since last month
Simultaneous with speech time	*en este momento, ahora*	at this moment, now
Repetitive action	*todos los días, típicamente por las noches, siempre*	every day, typically at night, always
None		

To ensure that our instrument was ecologically valid and sentences resembled speech that participants might encounter in everyday communication with Spanish speakers, we made corpus searches for all possible combinations of the lexical bases *estar, andar, ir, venir,* and *seguir* with verbs included in the instrument listed in Table 3 when used as a present participle (i.e., a progressive construction). For this purpose, we used the Web/Dialects section of *Corpus del español*, a 2-billion-word corpus covering a total of 21 varieties of Spanish (Davies, 2016-). To make sure our searches reflected our participant pool as closely as possible, we only extracted tokens from the Peninsular and Mexican Spanish subcorpora. Table 7 provides the results of the searches, including the total tokens found for each lexical base and the percentage of the data they represent relative to the other four bases. Each progressive construction appeared at least once, which means that there was at least one possible combination of each lexical base with a present participle. As expected, and in accordance with the literature (Torres Cacoullos, 2000), *estar* was the most commonly employed base, encompassing 57.27% of the data in Peninsular Spanish and 61.95% in Mexican Spanish, followed by *seguir, ir, andar,* and *venir* in descending order. Bolded cells indicate the most common combination of a lexical base and present participle relative to the other four lexical bases.

Table 7. Progressive constructions in Mexican and Peninsular Spanish in Davies (2016-)

Lemma	*Estar* k	*Estar* %	*Seguir* k	*Seguir* %	*Ir* k	*Ir* %	*Andar* k	*Andar* %	*Venir* k	*Venir* %
Buscar	**15819**	**70.91**	2899	12.99	1274	5.71	2093	9.38	224	1
Caminar	678	21.89	1000	32.28	**1277**	**41.22**	43	1.39	100	3.23
Comer	**2315**	**69.88**	667	20.13	285	8.6	23	0.69	23	0.69
Construir	**2389**	**56.38**	546	12.89	1212	28.61	7	0.17	83	1.96
Creer	228	9.15	**2149**	**86.24**	62	2.49	34	1.36	19	0.76
Desaparecer	572	30.85	26	1.4	**1245**	**67.15**	2	0.11	9	0.49
Jugar	**5637**	**72.03**	1781	22.76	174	2.22	95	1.21	139	1.78
Llegar	**3444**	**60.45**	622	10.92	1551	27.22	6	0.11	74	1.3
Pensar	**14529**	**70.25**	4852	23.46	908	4.39	192	0.93	200	0.97
Preparar	**5985**	**82.67**	237	3.27	876	12.1	59	0.81	83	1.15
Querer	639	35.64	**1031**	**57.5**	58	3.23	56	3.12	9	0.5
Recordar	**427**	**41.42**	387	37.54	195	18.91	6	0.58	16	1.55
Salir	**3707**	**56.79**	964	14.77	1733	26.55	28	0.43	96	1.47
Sentir	**1494**	**50.94**	981	33.45	401	13.67	6	0.2	51	1.74
Tocar	**1700**	**71.01**	327	13.66	304	12.7	40	1.67	23	0.96

The next task that the Spanish L1 and L2 speakers completed was a 25 discrete-item, multiple-choice grammar test covering commonly taught structures. This proficiency measure has been used previously and identified as a reliable means of grouping learners (e.g., Geeslin & Fafulas, 2012). Results of the mean scores on the grammar test confirmed the divisions based on level of enrollment. Finally, each participant completed a questionnaire eliciting social and language learning background characteristics, including information on contact with L1 speakers outside of class and travel abroad.

Analysis

We analyzed our data using SPSS Statistics (version 29) and the R statistical environment (R Core Team, 2023). We examined data for normality using cross-tabulations as well as visualizations. We present our results in terms of response rates across participant groups and lexical bases, and the results of a generalized mixed-effects linear model (GLM) performed using the R lme4 package (Bates et al., 2015), followed by generalized additive models (GAM) for each lexical base using the R mgcv package (Wood, 2021).

Results

Rates of form selection by group

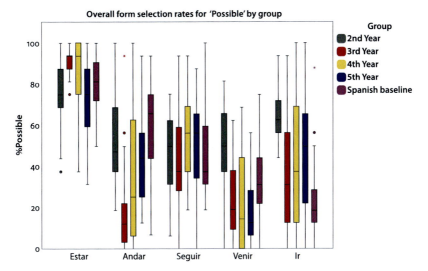

Figure 1. Boxplots of selection rates by group on written contextualized acceptability task
Note: Median values are represented by the horizontal line inside each box. The bottom edge of the box indicates the lower quartile, and the uppermost part of the box shows the upper quartile. The minimum and maximum values are indicated by the lower and upper 'whiskers' respectively. Outliers appear as circles or stars outside the boxes.

As can be seen in Figure 1, *estar* was the most commonly accepted lexical base for all the groups. Observing only the L1 Spanish baseline, the *andar* lexical base was the next most common form, followed by *seguir, venir,* and *ir*. Although L2 speakers showed different orderings of the four lexical bases, they allowed all four lexical bases from the lowest Spanish proficiency level examined. We also observe that the L2 speakers maintained more consistent *estar* 'possible' rates across proficiency levels, while their 'possible' rates for the other bases was more varied, a finding we address in the Developmental trends Section.

GLM results

We now present the results of a GLM measuring how independent variables conditioned the selection of a *possible* or *not possible* response, our dependent variable, for the Spanish speakers. Therefore, in our model we include data from all four learner groups along with the L1 Spanish baseline. We used a mixed-effects GLM with a logit link function. The choice of model responds to the binary response variable and the wish to account for individual variation at the participant and experimental item level, given that data points could be clustered by both grouping factors. Given the focus and scope of our study, we chose to test lexical base, adverbial phrase type, and lexical aspect as fixed effects, whereas the participant and item were considered as random effects. We present the results of the best-fit model, containing only variables that significantly increased the model's predictive power, as indicated by lower Akaike information criterion (AIC) scores and analysis of variance (ANOVA) comparisons. In the model's output, presented in Table 8, reference levels for each independent variable are specified first, with predicted levels and corresponding estimates following. Positive estimates (β) indicate a higher likelihood of the predicted response (i.e., that the sentence is deemed to be *possible*) compared to *not possible* responses. Negative estimates indicate a lower likelihood of *possible* responses compared to *not possible* responses. We also report standard errors (SEs) and 95% confidence intervals (CIs) between brackets to indicate variability within each category, along with statistical significance (i.e., $p < 0.05$).

All three independent linguistic variables entered as fixed effects yielded significance and aided the model's predictive power. To begin, when compared to the predominant *estar* '"to be"' progressive, participants were significantly less likely to select a *possible* response when the lexical base used was *venir* ($\beta = -2.71$, $p < .001$), *andar* ($\beta = -2.05$, $p < .001$), *ir* ($\beta = -2.01$, $p < .001$), and *seguir* ($\beta = -1.82$, $p < .001$). In this sense, all four bases were significantly different from *estar*, which was the reference level and the most commonly used lexical base reported in the literature as well as our corpus searches in Davies (2016-). Moreover, the model also showed that participants were significantly less likely to select a *possible* response when the adverbial included in the experimental item was one denoting simultaneity with speech time ($\beta = -0.64$, $p < .001$). However, when the adverbial denoted that the event was repetitive or occurred before speech time, there was not a significant difference with the reference level (no adverbial included in the

Table 8. GLM of allowance in written contextualized acceptability task (Reference level: Possible)

Variable	β	SE	95% CI	z	p
(Intercept)	1.71	0.22	[1.27, 2.15]	7.65	<0.001
Lexical base					
Estar 'To be'	Reference				
Andar 'To go around'	−2.05	0.20	[−2.44, −1.67]	−10.36	<0.001
Ir 'To go'	−2.01	0.20	[−2.40, −1.62]	−10.15	<0.001
Seguir 'To keep on'	−1.82	0.20	[−2.20, −1.43]	−9.16	<0.001
Venir 'To come along'	−2.71	0.20	[−3.11, −2.32]	−13.56	<0.001
Temporal reference					
None	Reference				
Before speech time	−0.25	0.17	[−0.59, 0.09]	−1.44	0.150
Repetitive	−0.19	0.17	[−0.53, 0.15]	−1.07	0.283
Simultaneous	−0.64	0.18	[−0.98, −0.29]	−3.63	<0.001
Lexical aspect					
Stative	Reference				
Accomplishment	0.29	0.17	[−0.05, 0.63]	1.67	0.094
Achievement	0.28	0.17	[−0.06, 0.62]	1.61	0.107
Activity	0.46	0.17	[0.12, 0.80]	2.62	0.009
Random Effects					
Participant			N 95 τ$_{00}$ 0.62 SD 0.79		
Item			N 80 τ$_{00}$ 0.24 SD 0.49		
Observations			7600		
Marginal R^2 / Conditional R^2			0.180 / 0.350		
AIC			8803.534		
log-Likelihood			−4388.767		

experimental item). In addition, the results of the model showed a significant comparison regarding lexical aspect, as participants were significantly more likely to select a *possible* response when the predicate was an activity as compared to a state (β = 0.46, p < .001). The accomplishment and achievement categories of the lexical aspect variable likewise had positive estimates, although they missed the significance threshold.

Developmental trends

We now turn to developmental trends, as evidenced in 'possible' selection rates for each lexical base by L2 learners across four different levels of Spanish proficiency. As we observed more items showing a non-linear developmental pattern than a linear one, we fit a GAM for each base to determine whether the observed developmental curvature was statistically significant. A GAM is a flexible generalization of linear regression models that allows for the modeling of nonlinear relationships between the dependent and independent variables. In each GAM, the 'possible' selection rate is the dependent variable; group is the independent variable (containing four levels of learners); the interaction of lexical aspect and temporal reference is also included to assess how different combinations of these two factors affect the selected percentage. A smooth term is applied to group to capture non-linear trends in the data. Figures 2a–e demonstrate the estimated effect of group on the selected percentage based on the GAMs. For *estar*, the smooth term for group (*edf* = 2.70) was highly significant ($p = .001$), indicating a non-linear relationship. As can be seen from Figure 2a, the estimated effect of group on percentage peaked around Group 2 (i.e., third-year learners) and decreased thereafter, indicating a reverse U-shaped developmental pattern. Similarly, for *andar*, a significant non-linear relationship is also detected (*edf* = 2.93, $p < .001$). Figure 2b shows that for items with *andar*, the estimated effect of group on percentage dipped around Group 2 (i.e., third-year learners) and increased thereafter, indicating a U-shaped developmental pattern. Regarding *venir*, the non-linear relationship is also significant (*edf* = 2.76, $p < .001$). Figure 2c reveals a downward trend as group increases from 1 to 4. For *ir*, there is also a significant non-linear relationship with group and selected percentage (*edf* = 2.80, $p < .001$). Figure 2d shows an initial decline in the effect as group increases from 1 (second-year learners) to 2 (third-year learners), followed by a rise and a subsequent leveling off, indicating a U-shaped pattern. Lastly, for *seguir*, the smooth term for group did not reach statistical significance (*edf* = 1, $p = .255$), suggesting that group has a minimal non-linear impact on selected percentage, which is demonstrated in Figure 2e. For *seguir* only, because the non-linear pattern was not significant, a subsequent model comparison among a null model, a linear model ($p = .250$, Residual Deviance = 8873.0), and this GAM (a non-linear model, $p < .001$, Residual Deviance = 8873.0) showed that neither the non-linear model nor the linear model significantly improved the null model, suggesting that for *seguir*, neither a non-linear nor a linear pattern existed for the relationship between group and percentage.

For lexical bases that demonstrated a clear non-linear developmental pattern (i.e., *estar, andar, venir,* and *ir*), we additionally checked whether learners moved towards the target (i.e., Spanish baseline). For both *estar* and *andar*, in 13 out of 16 items, learners moved towards the target. Regarding *venir* and *ir*, learners in general moved away from the target; a pattern we observed in nine out of 16 of the items for each lexical base.

Discussion

Answers to research questions

The present study was designed to answer three research questions regarding the acquisition of multiple lexical bases in progressive constructions by L1 English, L2 Spanish learners. The first research question addressed the acceptability rates for each of the five lexical bases in progressive constructions in a written contextualized acceptability task. Overall, all the groups allowed *estar* 'to be' at the highest rate. This result provides evidence from a contextualized acceptability task that is in support of prior research on both L1 and L2 Spanish with regards to *estar* as the most widespread lexical base in progressive constructions (Fafulas 2015, 2021; Geeslin & Fafulas, 2012; Torres Cacoullos, 2000), further supported by the supplementary corpus data presented in Table 7. There was variation with respect to the remaining four lexical bases, as the second most frequently allowed lexical base among L1 Spanish participants was *andar*, followed by *seguir, venir*, and *ir*. As for L2 learners of Spanish, the ordering of the rest of the four Spanish lexical bases in terms of allowed percentage differed across the four levels, as depicted in Figure 1.

The second research question examined the role of three independent linguistic variables (lexical base, adverbial phrase type, and lexical aspect) on acceptability rates. The results of the GLM model showed that, when considering all participant groups, all three independent variables were significant in predicting responses. More specifically, *estar* 'to be' as opposed to the other four lexical bases was the most significantly likely to be allowed as possible. The finding that *estar* was significantly different from all other lexical bases provides further evidence for the strong association between the base and imperfective meaning, which could be attributed in part to the generalization of *estar* 'to be' + V-*ndo* as it advances in the progressive-to-imperfective grammaticalization path (Bybee et al., 1994; Deo, 2015). The estimates, however, indicate different effect sizes. The implication is that, whereas all four bases are different from *estar*, participants did not treat them as a uniform group. Participants were also more likely to select *possible* in items without adverbial phrases than in items with an adverbial phrase indicating simultaneity with speech time. This finding might be explained by the robustness of *estar* as a marker of progressiveness (hence not necessarily needing an adverb of simultaneity), on the one hand, as well as the semantic nuances

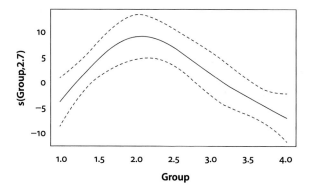

a. Estar

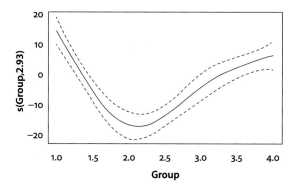

b. Andar

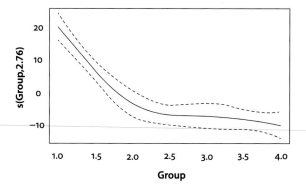

c. Venir

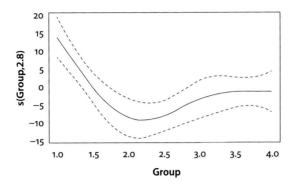

d. Ir

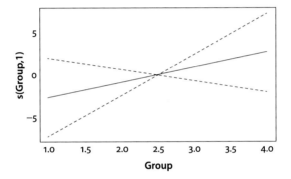

e. Seguir

Figure 2. Estimated effect of group on percentage using a GAM

Note. In each figure, the horizontal axis represents the variable group, which ranges from 1 to 4; 1 corresponds to second-year learners, 2 represents third-year learners, 3 indicates fourth-year learners, and 4 refers to graduate students. The numbers between the integers (e.g., 1.5) do not hold any meaningful value but were included in the figures by default because a smooth rather than discrete term is applied to group to capture non-linear trends in the data. The vertical axis represents how much the selected percentage changes as group changes relative to the baseline percentage of each model. The solid line represents the estimated effect, while the dashed lines indicate 95% CIs.

of bases such as *seguir* 'to keep on', which make them less likely candidates for allowance in contexts of simultaneity as opposed to those denoting habituality. Lastly, lexical aspect was also significant in the model, as participants were significantly more likely to select a possible response when the predicate was an activity rather than a state. This finding is in line with prior research, which has generally found that dynamic predicates (i.e., activities, accomplishments, and achievements) tend to allow progressive morphology to a greater extent than stative predicates (Berríos & Kanwit, 2024; Fafulas, 2015; Geeslin & Fafulas, 2012, 2022) as well as the predictions of the Aspect Hypothesis that learners of languages with overt progressive markers first use such devices with activities and at later stages do not incorrectly extend them to states (Andersen & Shirai, 1996). The results of the GLM analysis presented in Table 8 show that activities indeed had the strongest association with the selection of a *possible* response—that is, that participants considered the use of progressive constructions as allowable in such contexts. This adds to prior work on the Aspect Hypothesis by showing that the predictions hold for a wider range of lexical bases as well as in the present tense, which is important because most prior studies focus on past-tense marking (Bardovi-Harlig, 2000)

The third research question was concerned with changes observed as learners increase in Spanish proficiency. Based on the GAM results, we found that for *estar* 'to be' and *andar* 'to go around', the two most frequently allowed lexical bases by the L1 Spanish baseline, L2 learners moved towards the target with a reverse U-shaped or U-shaped development pattern, respectively. As for *seguir* 'to keep on', the third most frequently allowed base by the L1 Spanish baseline, we did not find any uniform developmental trends, and learners mostly did not move towards the target. Regarding *venir* 'to come along' and *ir* 'to go', the two least frequently allowed bases by the L1 Spanish baseline, L2 learners in general moved away from the target in a downward direction or with a U-shaped pattern, respectively. Altogether, the L2 acquisitional paths and the overall acceptability rates of lexical bases suggest that L2 learners can approximate target-like allowance of lexical bases that L1 Spanish speakers allow at relatively high rates (i.e., *estar* 80%, *andar* 59%). By contrast, in the case of lexical bases infrequently allowed by L1 Spanish speakers, L2 learners did not appear to move towards the target. The preceding findings highlight the contribution of our approach in considering different lexical bases, as the general progression towards the target with increases in proficiency seen in studies focusing only on *estar* (e.g., Berríos & Kanwit, 2024; Fafulas, 2012; Geeslin & Fafulas, 2022) is not uniform when the envelope of variation is expanded to include less frequent yet viable progressive constructions. Thus, our study adds to L2 variation research in Spanish which has shown that when expanding the envelope of variation, for example with subject expression (Gudmestad, House, & Geeslin, 2013) and future-time expression (Geeslin & Gudmestad, 2010), a more nuanced picture of interlanguage development emerges as compared to analyses limited to a binary dependent variable consisting of only two of the potentially variable forms.

Implications for pedagogy

Our findings may be of interest to language professionals teaching Spanish for several reasons. This study shows that learners follow different developmental trajectories depending on the frequency of the lexical base allowed in Spanish progressive constructions by L1 speakers, and possibly the strength of its association with the main verb (i.e., as a collocation), even if the latter point is a matter for future exploration. Although further work and training using corpora will be necessary, our study's findings suggest that teachers could use corpora to call attention to the different progressive constructions as well as the adverbial phrases with which they co-occur. Davies (2000), for instance, has detailed his success in incorporating corpus-based approaches to teaching advanced linguistics courses. Including examples from readily available corpora (e.g., Davies, 2016-) might help move learners along in their acquisition of progressive constructions or at least make them aware of the variation that may be present in the input to which they are exposed, whether through authentic media or conversations in the community or classroom. This also ties in with their development of lexical diversity and vocabulary acquisition more generally (see Gudmestad, 2022 highlighting prior work on corpus-based research and lexical acquisition). Further, instruction, whether implicit or explicit, on progressive constructions and their variation can also be a valuable path for showing learners how tense and aspect interact in Spanish (in language or linguistics classes) as well as how forms vary depending on contextual factors. This could be complemented by corpus-based research that shows how learners develop tense-aspect-mood constructions and follow the tenets of the Aspect Hypothesis (e.g., Domínguez et al., 2013). Based on our findings, teachers might do well to start by teaching the most frequent lexical bases used in progressive constructions (i.e., *estar* and *andar*) along with the most frequent participles and only later move to less frequent lexical bases (such as *ir* and *venir*) and their associated participles. Thus, our study makes implications for the teaching of Spanish progressive constructions, though, as Gudmestad (2022) observes, the next step would be to develop an 'application' and test how a pedagogical intervention using this corpus-based research actually aides in the development of learner knowledge of these forms over time.

This study also shows that for those learners who wish to approximate local or L1 patterns (although this might not be the goal of all L2 speakers), incorporating variation and the full range of Spanish progressive constructions is necessary for development. In turn, this means that the pedagogy community, including instructors of the language as well as publishers, need to incorporate variation of linguistic forms as a necessary feature of their instructional materials in order to make available to learners the realities of the Spanish-speaking world, rather than only presenting them with the most commonly used or standardized forms of the language (Schoonmaker-Gates, 2017; Shin & Hudgens Henderson, 2017). For example, research has shown the overwhelming tendency for instructors in US Spanish classrooms to employ *tú* at the expense of *vos* when teaching and practicing second-person singular subject pronouns (LeLoup & Schmidt-Rinehart, 2018), although the reality is that *vos* predominates in many regions of the Spanish-speaking world. This is likely reinforced by textbooks for adults learning Spanish, which overemphasize the use of *tú* in depictions of L1 speaker interactions. By incorporating variation in the classroom and in learner course materials, practitioners can help learners acquire sociolinguistic competence, as the use of patterns of variation in a contextually appropriate manner is one of its key components (Canale & Swain, 1980). Our view is also consistent with recent calls to incorporate Spanish as a local, rather than a foreign, language in U.S. classrooms (Brown & Thompson, 2018). As Mattson-Prieto and Showstack (2022) explain, "Teachers can examine and modify the ways in which their classroom language use positions different kinds of speakers of the target language, how communities of speakers are represented in classroom activities, and in what kinds of target-language interactions they are preparing their students to engage" (p. 265). By including bilingual L1 Spanish speakers living in the same mid-western U.S. community as our learners, we have established the local target that L2 speakers may be in contact with both within and outside of the classroom.

Conclusion and future directions

This study has taken a step forward in our understanding of how learners incorporate a range of progressive constructions, beyond the most commonly studied *estar* 'to be' lexical base, in their developing L2. In addition, we have learned more about the development of morphosyntactic and tense-aspect variation in Spanish. One general pattern emerged in our study whereby L2 learners more consistently followed a developmental trajectory (either U-shaped or reverse U-shaped) with those lexical bases that were the most frequently allowed (*estar* and *andar*) by the L1 Spanish bilinguals. Future research within and outside the classroom context will need to determine if these are in fact the forms that most commonly occur in the input to which L2 speakers are exposed. Relatedly, we have also made a call consistent with recent methodological trends to include local baselines to establish the potential path by which learners develop (Ortega, 2016). Moreover, our study is an example of how the results of quasi-experimental and corpus-based research may be useful for language education (e.g., Gudmestad, 2022).

Our study also takes a step in the direction of supplementing corpus-based research when designing grammaticality judgments and instruments directed at tapping learners' knowledge of morphosyntactic forms. This practice is becoming more readily possible with the many freely available corpora and tools for collecting data and scraping the web. For example, Egbert and Baker (2019) highlight how corpora can be used to triangulate data and increase rigor in linguistic research while also furthering our understanding of the phenomena under investigation by offering multiple perspectives on their analysis and discovery. Future research on progressive constructions, for instance, could further investigate the role that the co-occurrence of certain present participles with a lexical base play on variation (e.g., *venir* frequently co-occurs with *caminar* in corpus data), as with pairings of copulas and adjectives (Kanwit & Geeslin, 2020). Thus, moving forward, future studies might do well to take a deeper dive into available corpora as well as in designing instruments to prompt oral production of multiple progressive constructions. Researchers employing judgment tasks could also explore continuous outcome variables (e.g., Likert scale) rather than the binary choices of 'possible' vs. 'not possible' when tapping learners' knowledge of progressive constructions. In exploring the range of forms available in the domain of imperfective aspect in Spanish, studies will also want to include the simple present to see how development of this form works in tandem with acquisition of the various progressive constructions in Spanish. This will offer a more complete view of how learners come to incorporate simple present and present progressive forms and the acquisition of variable structures in Spanish.

Acknowledgements

Kimberly Geeslin was instrumental in this project through the project inception, data collection, and in the early stages of the analysis and discussion. She was part of the team that presented the initial findings at NWAV 50 (Fafulas et al., 2022), and we are grateful to be able to complete the manuscript in her honor. We also note that the first three authors were equally responsible for the write up and analysis and all contributed to the final version of this paper.

References

Alarcos Llorach, E. (1994). *Gramática de la lengua española*. Espasa Calpe.
Andersen, R. W. (2002). Dimensions of "pastness". In M. R. Salaberry & Y. Shirai (Eds.), *Tense-aspect morphology in L2 acquisition* (pp. 79–105). John Benjamins.

Andersen, R.W., & Shirai, Y. (1996). The primacy of aspect in first and second language acquisition: The pidgin-creole connection. In W.C. Ritchie & T.K. Bhatia (Eds.), *Handbook of second language acquisition* (pp. 527–570). Academic Press.

Bardovi-Harlig, K. (2000). *Tense and aspect in second language acquisition: Form, meaning, and use.* Oxford: Blackwell.

Bardovi-Harlig, K. (2017). Beyond individual form-meaning associations in L2 Tense-Mood-Aspect research. In M. Howard & P. Leclercq (Eds.), *Tense-Aspect-Modality in a Second Language* (pp. 27–52). John Benjamins.

Bates, D., Mächler, M., Bolker, B., & Walker, S. (2015). Fitting linear mixed-effects models using lme4. *Journal of Statistical Software, 67*(1), 1–48.

Berríos, J., & Kanwit, M. (2024). Progressive aspect across temporalities: Variation between synthetic and analytic forms in L1 and L2 Spanish. *Studies in Hispanic and Lusophone Linguistics 17*(2), 1–35.

Berry, G.M. (2017). Structural autonomy and aspectual import: A new(er) Spanish progressive. *Probus, 29*(2), 205–232.

Brown, A.V. & Thompson, G.L. (2018). *The changing landscape of Spanish language curricula: Designing higher education programs for diverse students.* Georgetown University Press.

Bybee, J., Perkins, R., & Pagliuca, W. (1994). *The evolution of grammar: Tense, aspect, and modality in the languages of the world.* University of Chicago Press.

Canale, M., & Swain, M. (1980). Theoretical bases of communicative approaches to second language teaching and testing. *Applied Linguistics, 1,* 1–47.

Davis, M. (2000). Using multi-million word corpora of historical and dialectal Spanish texts to teach advanced courses in Spanish linguistics. In L. Burnard & T. McEnery (Eds.), *Rethinking language pedagogy from a corpus perspective* (pp. 173–85). Peter Lang.

Davies, M. (2016–). Corpus del Español: Web/Dialects. http://www.corpusdelespanol.org/web-dial/

Deo, A. (2015). The semantic and pragmatic underpinnings of grammaticalization paths: The progressive to imperfective shift. *DeSemantics and Pragmatics, 8,* 1–52.

Domínguez, L., N. Tracy-Ventura, M.J. Arche, R. Mitchell, and F. Myles. (2013). The Role of Dynamic Contrasts in the L2 Acquisition of Spanish Past Tense Morphology. *Bilingualism: Language and Cognition, 16,* 558–577.

Dumont, J., & Wilson, D.V. (2016). Using the variationist comparative method to examine the role of language contact in synthetic and periphrastic verbs in Spanish. *Spanish in Context, 13*(3), 394–419.

Egbert, J., & Baker, P. (Eds.). (2019). *Using corpus methods to triangulate linguistic analysis.* Routledge.

Fafulas, S. (2012). Nuevas perspectivas sobre la variación de las formas presente simple y presente progresivo en español y en inglés. *Spanish in Context, 9*(1), 58–87.

Fafulas, S. (2015). Progressive constructions in native-speaker and adult-acquired Spanish. *Studies in Hispanic and Lusophone Linguistics, 8*(1), 85–133.

Fafulas, S. (2021). Variation of the simple present and present progressive: Peruvian Spanish, 'Pear Story,' and language contact, oh my! In M. Díaz-Campos (Ed.), *The Routledge handbook of variationist approaches to Spanish* (pp. 328–344). Routledge.

Fafulas, S., Geeslin, K., & Guo, J. (2022, October 13–15). *A study of lexical bases and variation of progressive constructions in the Spanish of English-speaking learners* [Conference presentation]. New Ways of Analyzing Variation 50, Stanford, CA, United States.

Geeslin, K. (Ed.). (2022). *The Routledge handbook of second language acquisition and sociolinguistics*. Routledge.

Geeslin, K., & Fafulas, S. (2012). Variation of the simple present and present progressive forms: A comparison of native and non-native speakers. In K. Geeslin & M. Díaz-Campos (Eds.), *Selected proceedings of the 14th Hispanic Linguistics Symposium* (pp. 179–196). Cascadilla Proceedings Project.

Geeslin, K., & Fafulas, S. (2022). Linguistic variation and second language Spanish: A study of progressive and habitual marking by English-speaking learners. In R. Bayley, D. R. Preston, & X. Li (Eds.), *Variation in second and heritage languages: Crosslinguistic perspectives* (pp. 159–198). John Benjamins.

Geeslin, K. L., & Gudmestad, A. (2010). An exploration of the range and frequency of occurrence of forms in potentially variable structures in second-language Spanish. *Studies in Second Language Acquisition, 32*(3), 433–463.

Gudmestad, A. (2022). Development of grammar, vocabulary, and pragmatics in an additional language: Insights from Spanish learner corpus research. *Journal of Spanish Language Teaching, 9*, 161–173.

Gudmestad, A., House, L., & Geeslin, K. L. (2013). What a Bayesian analysis can do for SLA: New tools for the sociolinguistic study of subject expression in L2 Spanish. *Language Learning, 63*(3), 371–399.

Hopper, P., & Traugott, E. C. (2003). *Grammaticalization* (2nd ed.). Cambridge University Press.

Kanwit, M., & Geeslin, K. (2020). Sociolinguistic competence and interpreting variable structures in a second language: A study of the copula contrast in native and second-language Spanish. *Studies in Second Language Acquisition, 42*(4), 775–799.

Klein, F. (1980). A quantitative study of syntactic and pragmatic indications of change in the Spanish of bilinguals in the U.S. In W. Labov (Ed.), *Locating language in time and space* (pp. 69–82). Academic Press.

LeLoup, J. W., & Schmidt-Rinehart, B. C. (2018). Forms of address in the Spanish language curriculum in the United States: Actualities and Aspirations. *Hispania, 101*(1), 10–24.

Mattson-Prieto, R., & Showstack, R. (2022). "Are there any Mexicans listening?" Stancetaking and language ideologies in a Spanish L2 classroom. *Language Learning, 72*(s1), 240–274.

Ortega, L. (2013). SLA for the 21st century: Disciplinary progress, transdisciplinary relevance, and the bi/multilingual Turn. *Language Learning, 63*(s1), 1–24.

Ortega, L. (2016). Multi-competence in second language acquisition: inroads into the mainstream? In V. Cook & L. Wei (Eds.), *The Cambridge handbook of linguistic multi-competence* (pp. 50–76). Cambridge University Press.

R Core Team. (2023). R: A language and environment for statistical computing, vers. 4.3.0. https://www.r-project.org/

Schoonmaker-Gates, E. (2017). Regional variation in the language classroom and beyond: Mapping learners' developing dialectal competence. *Foreign Language Annals, 50*(1), 177–194.

Sedano, M. (2000). La perífrasis de gerundio en Caracas y otras ciudades hispanohablantes. *Nueva Revista de Filología Hispánica, 48*(2), 253–274.

Shin, N. L., & Hudgens Henderson, M. (2017). A sociolinguistic approach to teaching Spanish grammatical structures. *Foreign Language Annals, 50*(1), 195–213.

Swain, A., Berríos, J., & Kanwit, M. (2023). Exploring future-in-the-past variation in Seville and Caracas: ¿Cambiaría o Iba a Cambiar? In S. Fernández Cuenca, T. Judy, & L. Miller (Eds.), *Innovative approaches to research in Hispanic linguistics: Regional, diachronic, and learner profile variation* (pp. 58–80). John Benjamins.

Torres Cacoullos, R. (2000). *Grammaticization, synchronic variation, and language contact: A study of Spanish progressive-ndo constructions*. John Benjamins.

Torres Cacoullos, R. (2011). Variation and grammaticalization. In M. Díaz-Campos (Ed.), *The handbook of Hispanic sociolinguistics* (pp. 148–167). Wiley-Blackwell.

Torres Cacoullos, R. (2012). Grammaticalization through inherent variability. *Studies in Language, 36*(1), 73–122.

Wood, S. N. (2021). *mgcv: Mixed GAM Computation Vehicle with Automatic Smoothness Estimation.* R package version 1.8-33. Retrieved from https://CRAN.R-project.org/package=mgcv

CHAPTER 2

What frequency, regularity, and form avoidance tell us about strategic competence
The case of L2 Spanish future variation

Irene Soto-Lucena & Matthew Kanwit
University of Pittsburgh

Avoidance behavior is under-investigated in research on the acquisition of variation, although it may contribute to variability. Learners, uncertain about infrequent or irregular combinations, may avoid a certain future-time variant as part of strategic competence. Sixty-one intermediate Spanish learners completed open-ended writing prompts and a form-avoidance questionnaire. Learners used less morphological future (MF) and more lexical and periphrastic futures later in course sequencing. MF was favored with distant temporality, lack of negation, and frequent, regular verbs. Thus, the regular pattern's high type frequency was bolstered by forms of high token frequency. Similarly, learners reported avoiding MF due to concerns regarding accuracy, especially with irregulars. We provide novel data on strategic competence demonstrated through form avoidance based on infrequency and irregularity.

Keywords: strategic competence, form avoidance, future-time expression, frequency, regularity, polarity

Future-time expression in Spanish provides an ideal test case for the study of language variation, as multiple forms convey futurity, which is conditioned by a range of contextual factors (e.g., temporal distance, regional origin; for an overview, see Orozco, 2021). For learners and expert (i.e., native) speakers of Spanish, the morphological future (MF; *hablaré* 'I will talk') is generally declining in favor of the periphrastic future (PF; *voy a hablar* 'I am going to talk') and the present indicative (PI; *hablo* 'I talk') (see Blas Arroyo, 2008; Kanwit, 2017;

Orozco, 2021; Sedano, 1994; Silva-Corvalán & Terrell, 1989).[1] Although variationist research first focused on MF and PF forms, more recent studies have also considered the PI (e.g., de Prada Pérez et al., 2021; Gudmestad & Geeslin, 2013; Kanwit, 2017; Orozco, 2021). Some have also noted that lexical futures (LFs; Bardovi-Harlig, 2005), constructions containing a verb conjugated in the PI that semantically denote futurity (e.g., desire, obligation) in combination with an infinitival form (e.g., *quiero hablar* 'I want to talk'), are among the most common forms of future-time expression in Spanish (Kanwit, 2017).

The present study investigates variation of future-time expression in second-language (L2) Spanish via written production, which has received less attention than oral production and written preference (cf. Solon & Kanwit, 2014). On the one hand, task type has been shown to play an important role in constraining learner variation (see Geeslin & Gudmestad, 2008), meaning that conclusions about rates and predictors of future-time variants that are largely built on oral production (e.g., Gudmestad & Geeslin, 2011; Kanwit, 2017) and written preference data (e.g., Gudmestad & Geeslin, 2011; Kanwit & Solon, 2013) should be supplemented with other forms of data. Moreover, as described in the two paragraphs that follow, if learners indeed avoid infrequent and irregular combinations as part of their strategic competence, finding evidence of such behavior even in a setting where learners are free of time, interlocutor, and pronunciation pressure (i.e., when providing an open-ended written response rather than speaking) may reinforce how potent such a strategy may be. Consequently, fourth-semester and third-year learners were assessed via a series of open-ended writing prompts targeting future temporality.

Based on concept-oriented approaches (Bardovi-Harlig, 2020), the present study accounts for all verb forms and devices (such as adverbial phrases, expressions related to time, etc.) that learners employ to express future meaning. While future-time variation is conditioned by numerous linguistic and extralinguistic predictors (Gudmestad & Geeslin, 2013; Kanwit, 2017; Orozco, 2021), additional factors likely also contribute to learner variation (Bybee, 2008; Hubert, 2015). Therefore, informed by usage-based approaches to language development (Brown, 2018), our analysis also considers morphological regularity (Collentine, 1997; Gudmestad, 2006, 2012; Kanwit & Geeslin, 2014; Quesada, 1998) and the frequency of verb forms (e.g., Bybee, 2007, 2008, 2017; Fratini et al., 2014; Giancaspro et al., 2022; Goldberg, 2013), which have generally been absent from the study of L2 future-time variation.[2]

---

[1]. Nevertheless, the MF is especially viable in regions in contact with Catalan, and usage tends to be higher in Spain than Latin America (Blas Arroyo, 2008; for a recent overview, see Table 1, p. 63 of Swain et al., 2023, which summarizes oral production and written preference data).

Beyond considering a series of independent predictors, this study applies to future-time expression the consideration of under-investigated strategies of form avoidance (Alonso-Vázquez, 2004; Hubert, 2015). In viewing avoidance behavior as a communication strategy (CS), we aim to learn more about learners' strategic competence, or the strategies learners use for successful communication (Canale & Swain, 1980; Kanwit & Solon, 2023). Because avoidance behavior is closely tied to the notion of awareness, an avoidance questionnaire was included to investigate motives in avoiding particular forms. Little attention has been paid so far to the construct of avoidance with respect to whether learners may avoid a certain future variant based on uncertainty regarding knowledge of or ability to produce relevant forms. However, this issue is important because L2 proficiency may correspond with the employment of CSs (e.g., avoidance), and because previous research has found L2 learners to rely on avoidance strategies when communicating (Hubert, 2015). The current study connects form-avoidance responses to the factors of frequency and regularity in the production data, hypothesizing that infrequent and irregular forms would be better candidates for avoidance than their frequent, regular counterparts, which should have stronger memory representations (Bybee, 2008). Thus, we contribute an analysis of frequency/regularity and form avoidance to the study of the written production of a variable structure where these constructs and this modality have lagged. Together, these novel considerations help demonstrate how language variation can illuminate a critical aspect of learners' communicative competence: their evolving strategic competence.

Research context

Future-time expression in first-language (L1) and L2 Spanish

Future-time expression refers to a temporal relation posterior to the moment of speech (Silva-Corvalán & Terrell, 1989). Given displacement from the present, future is often conveyed via temporal marking (Bardovi-Harlig, 2004). Because multiple forms can convey futurity (e.g., MF, PF, PI, LF forms), it is a good candidate for variationist analysis (i.e., ascertaining which contextual factors favor which variants). Moreover, future-time expression involves tense, mood, and aspect, indicating that form-meaning connections made by learners are likely to

---

[2]. Although our focus is on L2 grammars, frequency plays a foundational role in usage-based accounts of L1 grammars (e.g., Bybee, 2017; Goldberg, 2013), and regularity has also been shown to constrain L1 variation (e.g., Bybee, 2007; Gudmestad, 2012).

be complex (Bardovi-Harlig, 2004; Gudmestad & Geeslin, 2011; Kanwit, 2017) and learners may need to pursue form-specific CSs in the face of such complexity (Hubert, 2015). L2 learners at lower proficiency levels generally employ PI (as a base form) to convey future, and as learners' proficiency increases, so does the tendency to employ PF. Following a brief spike during the semester when MF is a focus of instruction, use of the MF variant tends to decrease as learners move toward the general, expert-like preference of employing PF seen in many varieties of Spanish (Gudmestad & Geeslin, 2011, 2013; Kanwit, 2017; Kanwit & Solon, 2013; Solon & Kanwit, 2014).

Factors such as person/number, temporal distance, clause type, and the presence of temporal adverbials often predict the future variants that relatively advanced learners and experts use. PF is favored over MF in immediate future distances, main clauses, and in the absence of temporal adverbials (Blas Arroyo, 2008; Gudmestad & Geeslin, 2011; Kanwit, 2017; Orozco, 2021). First person has also served as a favorable context for the frequent PF (Kanwit, 2017). PI is favored in third person (for scheduling, as in *la fiesta es el viernes* 'the party is on Friday'), close temporal distances, main clauses, and accompanied by temporal adverbials (Gudmestad & Geeslin, 2011; Kanwit & Solon, 2013; Orozco, 2021). LFs are less temporally restricted than the PI for future, require less adverbial modification, and occur more in first person, as speakers know their own obligations and desires more than those of others (Bardovi-Harlig, 2005; Kanwit, 2019, 2021). Although polarity has tended to be absent from past studies of L2 futurity, negation contributes further complexity to a clause, so it is important to consider among the factors that may constrain the use of variants. Simpler future variants may be favored in the presence of negation, whereas variants such as the multisyllabic, complex MF, with its numerous morphemes per word, should be comparatively favored in the absence of negation (Mondorf, 2014).

As a result, having numerous options makes learner development of future-time expression complex. The MF contains its own inflectional paradigm to learn, adding to the difficulty for learners, whereas the other three variants all contain elements of the early-acquired PI. Namely, PF only requires conjugating *ir* 'to go' in the present; the first (i.e., finite) verb in any LF construction is conjugated in the present; and, of course, PI usage in future-time contexts maintains the present conjugation. Furthermore, the lack of a one-to-one relationship between form and function (i.e., multifunctionality) presents challenges not only because multiple forms can convey futurity but also because individual forms may fulfill multiple functions, such as PI as present or future (Bardovi-Harlig, 2004).

The roles of frequency and form regularity

As informed by usage-based approaches to the emergence of linguistic structure, a speaker's grammar is extracted from use and experience, highlighting the importance of lexical frequency, as well as likely contexts of occurrence (Brown, 2018; Goldberg, 2013; Kanwit & Berríos, 2023; Langacker, 2015). Learners are therefore likely to demonstrate early usage of new structures vis-à-vis frequent word-forms, with lexical frequency facilitating the acquisition of linguistic forms (e.g., Bybee, 2007, 2008; Fratini et al., 2014; Giancaspro et al., 2022; Goldberg, 2013; Tomasello, 2009). Highly frequent forms (i.e., forms with high token frequency) build stronger mental representations, due to repeated usage and presence in the input, resulting in higher activation strength and easier access (Brown, 2018; Bybee, 2008; Tomasello, 2009). Forms with high token frequency effectively block potential competitors (i.e., alternative variants) when a speaker selects a form for use. High token frequency also may result in the greater reduction or irregularity of a form over time, with high memory strength permitting a form to pattern differently from its counterparts (i.e., to withstand irregularity; Bybee, 2007). A past form like English 'was', for instance, is highly frequent and can withstand that it is formed differently from most past verbs (i.e., ending in '-ed'). Alternatively, forms with low token frequency have weaker representations, making speakers more likely to assign them to patterns of high type frequency (e.g., more verbs form the English past through '-ed' than through suppletion or vowel changes). This means that if a speaker is uncertain of the past form of a verb like 'hypothesize', '-ed' would be a more likely candidate than the alternatives. Because patterns with high type frequency affect many lexemes, they are often described as regular, default, or productive (Bybee, 2007). While these terms are not synonymous, for our purposes, note that speakers turn to default patterns when uncertain or when "all else fails", that productive patterns affect numerous lexemes and can be used to coin neologisms, and that regular patterns show lesser allomorphy (i.e., changes to the base or affix; Bybee, 2007; Haspelmath & Sims, 2010). Accordingly, patterns such as the English '-ed' past or the MF formed with the full infinitive in Spanish can be classified as regular, productive, and having high type frequency. On the other hand, patterns with lower type frequency are often described as irregular, are later acquired, and often consist of just a few word-forms with high token frequency (Bybee, 2007, 2008, 2017; Tomasello, 2009). Two examples are English vowel changes for the past (e.g., 'fell') and the Spanish reduced MF pattern (e.g., *haré* 'I will do').

Consequently, one of the main predictions in the current study is that frequent, regular verb forms will most favor the MF variant, as this is a complex, multi-syllabic, relatively late-acquired variant. The high type frequency of the regular MF pattern, applied to more frequent verb forms predicts a stronger mental representation for this combination for learners, which should make for a more reliably produced form, accessed either via whole-form storage or through the application of a reliable schema (i.e., paradigmatic pattern; Bybee, 2007, 2017; Haspelmath & Sims, 2010). Contrastingly, forms of lower token (i.e., infrequent forms) or type frequency (i.e., irregular forms) are predicted to be less reliably produced by learners. Given possible uncertainty about such combinations, learners may instead implement combinations of greater certainty, instead selecting a verb conjugated in the present (i.e., PI, PF, or a LF).

Although frequency and regularity are generally absent from the study of future-time variation in L2 Spanish, these constructs have been considered for other morphosyntactic variables, such as mood contrast. Learners have shown sensitivity, for instance, to verbal morphological regularity in favoring production and selection of the subjunctive with (frequent) irregular verbs, which are especially salient to learners (Collentine, 1997; Gudmestad, 2006, 2012; Quesada, 1998). Interpretation results have also shown that (frequent) irregular verbs lend themselves to meanings associated with the subjunctive (i.e., that an action has not yet occurred), standing out due to the heightened salience of their irregularity (Kanwit & Geeslin, 2014). Nevertheless, these studies on the subjunctive tended to consider (ir)regularity while not necessarily teasing apart frequency; thus, favoring of the indicative with regular forms may also be considered favoring by infrequent forms, which would match the prediction that the later-acquired or more complex variant (i.e., the subjunctive) would appear later with forms of low token frequency.

In fact, more recent research has shed further light on the role of regularity in L2 Spanish, investigating mood variation and controlling for verb frequency. Irregular forms were found to favor use of the subjunctive mood (Giancaspro et al., 2022). Although irregular forms tend to have higher token frequency, we can also find regular and frequent forms. That is, though irregular verb forms are significantly more frequent than regular forms in Spanish according to mean frequencies, correlations between frequency and regularity are tenuous across frequency bands and can be skewed by highly frequent verbs (Fratini et al., 2014). Whereas frequent forms tend to be shorter and irregular forms more frequent, note the existence of high-frequency regular forms and infrequent irregular forms. The aforementioned subjunctive research supports the claims that verbal morphological regularity can play an important role in constraining learner use and interpretation of variable structures. Even so, the need to tease apart the roles of frequency and regularity for learners and to do so across morphosyntactic structures remains.

Communication strategies, form avoidance, and strategic competence

Acquisitionists continue to endeavor to better understand learners' strategies when using the L2, along with the nature of CSs and strategic language devices. CSs were emphasized among five central processes in L2 learning (Dörnyei & Scott, 1997) and similar notions such as coping strategies have informed communicative language teaching since early works (Selinker, 1972). These strategies have been discussed as first-aid devices that help compensate for gaps in speakers' L2 proficiency and as tools used to overcome crises when a language structure is inadequate for conveying one's thoughts (Tarone, 1977). Thus, CSs help learners solve a problem while trying to reach a specific communicative goal.

These interpretations of CSs closely relate to the notion of communicative competence, formed by grammatical, sociolinguistic, and strategic competences (Canale & Swain, 1980; Kanwit & Solon, 2023). The latter term refers to learners' strategies to overcome difficulties when unsuccessful communication or breakdowns occur, such as the implementation of a known form when doubts arise regarding a more uncertain form. Given the importance of strategic competence, it is no wonder that this construct is invoked in nearly all conceptualizations of communicative competence (Bachman & Palmer, 2010; Canale, 1983; Canale & Swain, 1980; Celce-Murcia, 2008; Celce-Murcia et al., 1995; Kanwit & Solon, 2023).

Most definitions of CSs assume that consciousness/awareness is part of the concept of strategy, which generally refers to the willful planning or explicit course of action to accomplish a communication goal, suggesting intentionality or learner awareness. In fact, CSs have been defined as "every potentially intentional attempt to cope with any language-related problem of which the speaker is aware during the course of communication" (Dörnyei & Scott, 1997, p. 13). Learners employ a series of strategies, including reduction and evasive behavior (Alonso-Vázquez, 2004), such as topic avoidance, which occurs when "the learner avoids any mention of a particular topic, word, or grammatical structure" (Hubert, 2015, p. 145).

Despite a growing body of research on the acquisition of future-time expression, this variable structure has received little attention in L2 empirical studies on avoidance, regardless of the L2. L2 learners' avoidance behavior remains a relevant issue to investigate, due to the relationship and possible correspondence between L2 proficiency and the employment of CSs. Research on CSs, moreover, has rarely addressed avoidance behavior among L2 learners of Spanish, with exceptions of previous research focusing on past-time and present subjunctive forms (Hubert, 2011, 2015), which found L2 learners to rely on avoidance strategies.

Previous work focusing on avoidance in L2 English found that phrasal verbs were avoided regardless of equivalency to the L1 (e.g., Liao & Fukuya, 2004), with proficiency level and verb type constraining avoidance. Given the role of proficiency, avoidance has been interpreted as revealing an earlier interlanguage stage (Laufer & Eliasson, 1993; Liao & Fukuya, 2004). Moreover, research investigating the acquisition of the negation system by elementary Spanish-speaking learners of English found that all participants employed avoidance strategies and highlighted the cyclical character of such behavior (Alonso-Vázquez, 2004). These studies are evidence of the importance of avoidance strategies and strengthen the need for investigating L2 learners' avoidance behavior.

Assuming a correspondence between the employment of CSs and L2 proficiency level, more recent work has investigated overreliance on avoidance strategies in relation to awareness (Hubert, 2015). Two communicative writing tasks were completed (eliciting the use of the preterit/imperfect aspectual distinction and the use of the subjunctive) by university students of L2 Spanish at elementary and intermediate levels. During follow-up interviews (1–24 hours after completing the writing tasks) participants were asked to reflect retrospectively on whether their avoidance was a conscious strategy. This was done via a series of questions designed to measure awareness of the reasons behind each participant's choices in their use or avoidance of grammar, as the researcher reviewed the learners' writing samples with them. Participants self-reported a significant amount of active and intentional avoidance of both targeted grammatical forms (Hubert, 2015). This connection between the (non)usage of linguistic structures and avoidance strategies critically informs the present study as a possible indicator of learners' strategic competence seen in language variation.

Remaining gaps, research questions, and hypotheses

Integrating the construct of avoidance as a common phenomenon in interlanguage that illustrates L2 learners' strategic competence, the current study investigates L2 variation in future-time expression and analyzes the possible relationships among frequency, regularity, and form avoidance. The present study examines L2 Spanish in written production in order to determine whether learners report form avoidance even when free of pronunciation pressure or an in-person interlocutor and with reduced time pressure.

Informed by gaps in the literature regarding (a) future-time expression in relation to avoidance strategies and (b) the possible relationships among frequency, regularity, and form avoidance in L2 Spanish future-time variation, the following questions guided this research:

1. In open-ended writing prompts, at what rates do fourth-semester and third-year learners of Spanish employ different devices to express future time?
2. What linguistic factors predict the use of one form over another?

3. To what extent do learners self-report avoiding specific future-time forms?

We hypothesized that, consistent with the principle of multifunctionality (Andersen, 1990), learners would rely less on a dominant variant and make greater use of multiple variants later in the course sequence (e.g., Bardovi-Harlig, 2004; Gudmestad & Geeslin, 2011; Solon & Kanwit, 2014), including reduced preference for MF later in the sequence (Gudmestad & Geeslin, 2013; Kanwit, 2017).

We also anticipated that PF would be favored over MF in immediate future distances, with first-person subjects, in main clauses, and without temporal adverbials (Blas Arroyo, 2008; Gudmestad & Geeslin, 2011; Kanwit, 2017; Orozco, 2021). We hypothesized that PI would be favored with third person, close temporal distances, main clauses, and temporal adverbs (Gudmestad & Geeslin, 2011; Kanwit & Solon, 2013; Orozco, 2021), and that LFs would be less temporally restricted than PI, require less adverbial modification, and occur more with first person (Bardovi-Harlig, 2005; Kanwit, 2019, 2021). As negation contributes further complexity to a clause, we predicted that the multi-syllabic, complex MF should be favored in the absence of negation, whereas simpler future variants may be favored with negation (Mondorf, 2014). Because MF contains its own inflectional paradigm, we anticipated that it would be favored by frequent, regular verbs based on the strong mental representations for forms of high token and type frequency (Brown, 2018; Bybee, 2008), with infrequent and irregular word-forms thus more favorable contexts for the variants that included verbs from earlier-acquired present conjugations (PI, LFs, and PF). Finally, we hypothesized that learners would report avoiding specific forms (Hubert, 2011, 2015) and that for future-time reference, the MF would be especially reported as avoided, given that it has its own inflectional paradigms, including lengthy, multi-syllabic forms extended from the infinitive, and numerous irregular forms (Bybee, 2007; Haspelmath & Sims, 2010; Mondorf, 2014).

Method

Participants

Sixty-one university-level undergraduate learners of Spanish participated in this study. Participants were enrolled in a high intermediate Spanish course (fourth-semester) or in one of two low-advanced courses (third-year): conversation or grammar and composition. All reported English as their L1, and none were heritage speakers of Spanish. In order to ensure course groupings, participants completed a grammar test and background questionnaire before engaging in the writing task. All tasks can be found in their entirety at https://osf.io/hncs3/

Table 1 shows the number of participants per level along with grammar test average scores and ranges (see *Grammar Test* Section). Given the proximity of the two levels, mean scores were quite similar; the lower and upper ranges were in fact slightly higher for the fourth-semester students. Two participants were excluded from the final analysis due to categorical use of MF.

Table 1. Participants' grammar test scores (out of 25) by course level

Grammar test score	Fourth-semester ($n=24$)	Third-year ($n=37$)
M	13.1	13.9
Range	8–24	6–20

Materials and procedure

Written personal prompt task

Participants completed a communicative writing task in which they responded to four brief, open-ended writing prompts, including one distractor. The writing prompts were created for this project, based on prior research on avoidance behavior (adapted from Hubert, 2011, 2015) and prior prompts to elicit oral future-time reference (Kanwit, 2017). The task offers ecological validity, as it mirrors writing activities that these learners have encountered before and can form part of classroom practice and assessment tools. Instructions reminded participants to write approximately 5–7 sentences per prompt, that participation was voluntary, and that they could opt out at any time. Learners who opted out could instead practice with other in-class activities. Participants responded to these brief writing prompts during the same class period.

The first prompt inquired in detail about immediate plans for that same day after class, the weekend, and winter break. The second prompt inquired about plans for spring/summer break (i.e., further into the future relative to participation; the task was adapted to the specific time of the year, as data collection took place during two different semesters). The third prompt asked participants to describe a relative or friend. The last prompt asked about how participants envision their lives in 20 years. The prompt for the more immediate future was expected to favor other variants over MF. Similarly, the greater temporal distances of the prompts inquiring about spring/summer break and especially the 20-year distance were predicted to favor MF.

Follow-up questionnaire

Immediately after completing the writing task, participants were given a follow-up questionnaire asking about their performance and whether they were aware of having avoided any particular forms (questionnaire adapted from Hubert, 2015). Participants were asked whether they thought they avoided the use of a specific form to express future-time, and if so, what the reasons were. The questionnaire also included several questions targeting whether learners reported avoiding any additional linguistic forms or concepts in Spanish.

Grammar test

To confirm course groupings and aid the generalizability of findings, participants completed a 25 discrete-item, multiple-choice grammar test targeting a range of structures and implemented in prior research on the acquisition of variation (e.g., Gudmestad & Geeslin, 2013). Recent work has reported the Cronbach's Alpha for the test as 0.868 (Geeslin et al., 2023), based on over 500 expert and learner participants who have completed the test across several studies. This reliability rating indicates 'good' internal consistency (see George & Mallery, 2012).

Background questionnaire

Participants completed the Language Experience and Proficiency Questionnaire prior to the elicitation tasks (Marian et al., 2007). This questionnaire provided the basic demographics and language learning histories for the participants, revealed that English was participants' L1, and provided additional information for subsequent individual analyses beyond the current study.

Coding and analysis

The written samples were analyzed for any devices that learners employed to express future-time expression, regardless of well-formedness, as long as future meaning was unambiguous (Bardovi-Harlig, 2004). The main forms identified were MF, PF, PI with future-time value, and LF. The conditional, which uses the same base as the MF, was the fifth most frequent variant.

Predictors found to be significant in previous research were coded for each future predicate (Table 2). Given the relevance of adverbs in constraining temporal expression, the presence of temporal adverbials (or lack thereof) was coded for each clause. Coding also included clause type (main/subordinate) and temporal distance (originally with six categories, ranging from immediate reference, to that same day, within the same week, over one week, over one month, and over one year away). Based on similar patterning in the data, immediate and same-day distances were later combined, as were the week and month distances, yielding

Table 2. Predictors

Alternate options (where relevant)	Predictor	Categories
	Person	First Third
	Number	Singular Plural
	Presence of temporal adverbial	Yes No
	Temporal distance	Today (immediate or later the same day) Intermediate (within the same week, over one week away, or over one month away) Over one year away
	Clause type	Main Subordinate
	Sentence polarity	Affirmative Negative
Option 1	Verb frequency/regularity	Frequent regular Infrequent regular Irregular (frequent)
Option 2: Interaction of:	Verb frequency (continuous)	Logarithmic transformation of the verb's frequency in *Corpus del español: News on the Web*
	Verb regularity	Regular Irregular
Option 1	Course level	Fourth-semester Third-year
Option 2	Grammar score (continuous)	Score on grammar test (6–24)

three categories of same day (immediate), week/month (intermediate), and year (distant). Each token was also coded for person (first/third; participants did not use second person) and number (singular/plural),[3] as well as polarity (negated/affirmative clause).

---

3. We first coded person/number as one variable, but third-person plural yielded small cells (i.e., < 5 tokens) for two variants and third-person singular did so for one. Thus, the two needed to be combined into third person.

We also coded the frequency and regularity of the future-time verb. Due to encountering few infrequent irregular verb forms in the data (17 total tokens) and given the nonorthogonal relationship between frequency and regularity, the variables were collapsed into three categories: frequent regular, infrequent regular, and (frequent) irregular.[4] Frequency information was based on data from the 7.6-billion-word *Corpus del español: News on the Web* (Davies, 2018). Verbs that yielded more than 100,000 results were coded as frequent. These frequency data were also coded as a continuous variable and, because frequency has an exponential (i.e., Zipfian) distribution, values were logarithmically transformed. This continuous variable was considered in interaction with the regularity of the verb form. Finally, we coded the learner's course level.[5] The independent predictors were then considered in a multinomial mixed-effect regression, with the two operationalizations of frequency/regularity compared in separate models. The participant and verb lexeme were entered as random effects.

Sample coding is found in (1), an unedited use of PI as part of a response to the third prompt (spring break plans), which elicited an intermediate distance (more than one month away):

(1) Durante la   vacacione de primavera **voy**   a Vancouver
     During ART.DEF vacation of spring   go.1SG.PI to Vancouver
     'During spring break I go to Vancouver'

Coding: First-person singular; temporal adverb present; intermediate distance; main clause; affirmative polarity; (frequent) irregular verb (4,436,097 corpus results); fourth-semester learner

For the follow-up questionnaire on avoidance behavior, answers were considered descriptively and qualitatively (i.e., the number of learners who provided a particular response and the qualitative content of responses). Based on the notion of idea units, comments were organized according to question and thematic similarity (Krippendorff, 2004). Both tasks were coded by the first author, who raised any questions to the second author, who then confirmed or revised any cases of doubt in further discussion with the former.

---

[4] Here, we refer to the combined category as (frequent) irregular because 97.5% (669/686) of the irregulars were frequent.

[5] We also considered the learner's grammar score as a continuous predictor. It was not significant overall and it did not interact with any of the linguistic predictors or with course level. For reference, a plot of the probability of form usage by grammar score is included in the Appendix (Figure A1, designed using Jamovi for R Version 2.3.28).

Results

Written production task

Learners employed six variants to express 1,341 total tokens of future meaning, although conditional (*k*=63, 4.7%) and present subjunctive forms (*k*=48, 3.6%) each constituted less than 5% of the data. To avoid small token counts, these 111 tokens were excluded from the multinomial regression. Table 3 reveals the relative percentages of the main four variants (*k*=1,230): MF (46.7%), PF (20.7%), LF (18.1%), and PI (14.5%).

Table 3. Most common forms used in written production task

Morphological Future		Periphrastic Future		Lexical Future		Present Indicative		Total
k	%	*k*	%	*k*	%	*k*	%	*k*
574	46.7	255	20.7	223	18.1	178	14.5	1,230

Although the fourth-semester and third-year learners were close in course proximity, the latter group indeed used MF at lower rates (42.5% compared to 53.3%), while using the other three variants at slightly higher rates than the earlier group (Figure 1). Nevertheless, course level was not significant in our mixed-effects regression, nor did it interact with the other predictors, so we consider the two learner groups together for the remainder of the study.

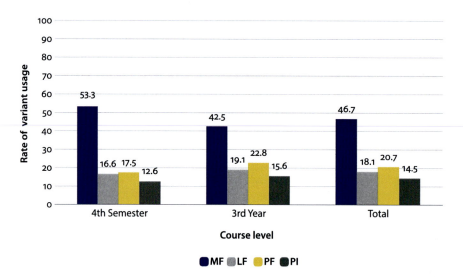

Figure 1. Rates of variant usage by course level

Table 4. Summary of mixed-effects multinomial regression

Significant main effects			Significant interaction
Temporal distance	Person	Polarity	Verb frequency: Regularity
<.001***	<.001***	<.001***	0.005**

** $p<.01$, *** $p<.001$

Table 4 summarizes the mixed-effects multinomial regression (performed in IBM SPSS Statistics Version 28), presenting the overall *p*-values associated with each independent predictor in the regression. Given the multiple data points from each learner and the fact that a different verb could be used at different rates across the categories of the other predictors, the participant and verb were entered as random effects. Additional *p*-values are reported for each future-time variant within the multinomial regression, and those and other model values are provided in greater detail in Table 5. Overall, temporal distance, person, and polarity were significant predictors. The interaction of verb frequency (log transformation) and regularity was also significant. Presence of a temporal adverbial, clause type, and course level were not significant, nor did course level interact with any other variables.

We now consider which comparisons within the regression contributed to the significance reported in the prior table. Table 5 summarizes one multinomial regression that included multiple comparisons (formatted following Gries, 2021). In each comparison, a future variant (i.e., PF, PI, or LF) was compared to MF, which was selected as the reference category because it occurred at the highest rate. Positive coefficients and *t*-values indicate favoring of that variant over MF, whereas negative values indicate disfavoring of that variant (i.e., favoring of MF). *P*-values below 0.05 indicate significant comparisons and correspond with 95% confidence intervals whose range does not include 0. The standard error indicates the level of variability in the category. Within each independent variable, one category serves as a reference category for the other categories and is placed in the subscript to the left of the arrow, preceding the category being predicted. All significant comparisons have been bolded. For the continuous variable verb frequency, which revealed a significant interaction with regularity, negative coefficients indicate that an increase in frequency corresponds with lesser use of the variant in question (e.g., the negative value −0.46 indicates lesser use of PF over MF as verb frequency increased [for regular verbs]).[6]

---

6. Because frequency and regularity are nonorthogonal, we considered the two operationalizations presented in Table 2. The interaction of the continuous log-transformed operationalization of frequency with regularity was included in the best-fit model.

Table 5. Mixed-effects multinomial regression of use of PF, PI, and LFs versus MF (reference category)

Variable	Coefficient	95% CI	Std. error	t value	p value
PF versus MF					
(Intercept)	2.09	[−0.37, 4.22]	1.05	1.93	0.054
Temp. Dist._Today→Year	−1.23	[−1.87, −0.59]	0.33	−3.76	<.001
Temp. Dist._Today→Interm.	−0.46	[−0.93, 0.01]	0.24	−1.91	0.057
Person_First→Third	−1.11	[−2.07, −0.15]	0.49	−2.26	0.024
Polarity_Positive→Negative	0.39	[−1.19, 1.96]	0.80	0.48	0.630
Verb Freq.: Regular	−0.46	[−0.84, −0.09]	0.19	−2.41	0.016
Verb Freq.: Irregular	−0.43	[−0.75, −0.10]	0.17	−2.58	0.010
PI versus MF					
(Intercept)	−4.13	[8.12, −0.13]	2.04	−2.03	0.043
Temp. Dist._Today→Year	−1.76	[−2.42, −1.11]	0.33	−5.30	<.001
Temp. Dist._Today→Interm.	−0.64	[−1.15, −0.12]	0.26	−2.41	0.016
Person_First→Third	0.99	[0.24, 1.74]	0.38	2.60	0.010
Polarity_Positive→Negative	1.80	[0.71, 2.88]	0.55	3.25	0.001
Verb Freq.: Regular	0.42	[−0.31, 1.14]	0.37	1.13	0.259
Verb Freq.: Irregular	0.53	[−0.09, 1.16]	0.32	1.67	0.095
LFs versus MF					
(Intercept)	−16.50	[−28.59, −4.41]	6.16	−2.68	0.008
Temp. Dist._Today→Year	−2.62	[−3.71, −1.52]	0.56	−4.70	<.001
Temp. Dist._Today→Interm.	−1.23	[−2.19, −0.27]	0.49	−2.51	0.012
Person_First→Third	−2.22	[−4.78, 0.34]	1.31	−1.70	0.087
Polarity_Positive→Negative	−2.09	[−4.16, −0.02]	1.06	−1.98	0.048
Verb Freq.: Regular	1.43	[−0.61, 3.46]	1.04	1.38	0.169
Verb Freq.: Irregular	1.32	[−0.48, 3.12]	0.92	1.44	0.150

Random effects: Participant, *SE* 0.80 (PF), 0.39 (PI), 0.49 (LFs)

Verb, *SE* 0.09 (PF), 0.48 (PI), 2.44 (LFs)

Model summary: Intercept: $p < .001$, AIC: 17846.37, $R^2_{marginal} = 0.80$, $k = 1{,}230$

We now summarize each predictor's effect in the regression. Learners were significantly less likely to use PF, PI, or LFs over MF when the temporal distance was one year away rather than today/immediate. Learners were also significantly less likely to use PI or LFs over MF at the intermediate (week/month) distance compared to the today distance; the same pattern held for PF, although that comparison just missed significance ($p = 0.057$).

With respect to person, two comparisons were significant. When the subject was third person, learners used significantly less PF over MF and more PI over MF. LF usage was also lesser in third person, although that comparison missed significance ($p = 0.087$). For polarity, two comparisons also yielded significance. When negation occurred, learners used significantly more PI over MF and less LF over MF.

The interaction between regularity and the natural log of frequency revealed two significant comparisons. As verb frequency increased, learners were less likely to use PF over MF with regular verbs. Similarly, as verb frequency increased, learners were also less likely to use PF over MF with irregular verbs. This is visualized in Figure 2, where verbs whose frequency was one *SD* lower than the mean (i.e., less frequent verbs) appear at the top of the figure, with verbs within one *SD* of the mean in the center, and verbs one *SD* higher than the mean (i.e., more frequent) at the bottom of the figure. For instance, high usage of the MF with frequent, regular verbs can be seen at the bottom right of the figure. Alternatively, usage of LFs with infrequent, irregular verbs can be noted at the top left of the figure.[7]

---

7. Although we ultimately used the continuous operationalization of frequency based on our best-fit model, we had also considered a categorical operationalization of the possible combinations of frequency and regularity (Figure A2), revealing that the MF was used above its baseline (i.e., overall) rate with frequent, regular verbs and below this rate with irregular verbs and infrequent verbs. Alternatively, PI and LFs were used above their baseline rates with irregular verbs and below these rates with frequent, regular verbs.

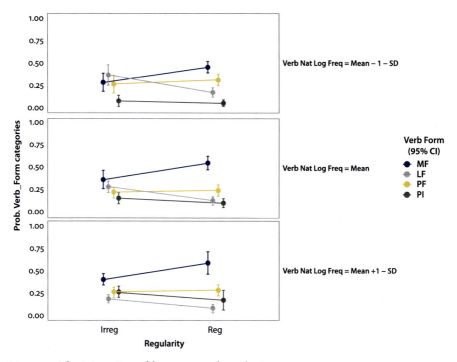

Figure 2. The interaction of frequency and regularity

Self-report questionnaire

In the questionnaire inquiring about avoidance behavior, when reporting that they avoided a particular form, learners' most typical comment was choosing forms with which they were most comfortable or knew very well. Nineteen responses contained explicit mention of feeling scared of making mistakes and/or wishing to avoid being "incorrect" or "wrong".

Responses to Question 1 ("To your knowledge, did you avoid using a particular form in your writing task? If so, why?") illustrate how learners reflect on their avoidance strategies and the forms to which these may apply. For instance, there were numerous mentions of avoiding the subjunctive due to its difficulty and trouble remembering its conjugations correctly. Mentions of avoiding perfect tenses were also common, along with fewer mentions of conditional and "the future" (i.e., the MF). The trend observed highlights learners not feeling comfortable using a specific form/structure, being unsure of conjugations, and trying to use only what they knew how to conjugate. Unedited representative responses include the following:

Yes, I avoided using future tense for my verbs because I am unsure of all the conjugations. (Third-year learner)

I was avoiding the future tense. I preferred using the present tense as I am more comfortable with it simply because I've spent more time on it. (Third-year learner)

I tried to only use present or conditional because it is the easiest to remember. (Third-year learner)

I did not intentionally avoid any form, however I know that I default to tenses that I am more comfortable with. (Third-year learner)

I don't use subjunctive frequently because it is more difficult to remember the irregular + each tense's conjugations [...] (Third-year learner)

Figure 3 summarizes the results to Question 2 ("Do you think avoiding this was a conscious decision you made?"), which echoes the findings of Question 1.

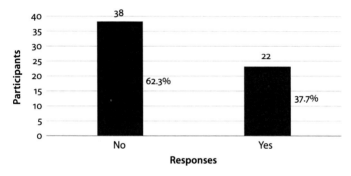

Figure 3. Follow-up questionnaire: Responses to question 2 (conscious decision)

With respect to Question 3 ("In your writing task, if you avoided using a particular form to express future, what did you use in its place? Briefly explain why."), learners showed preference for conjugating a verb in the present, including when this meant using the PF, as in: "I used simple future like *voy a hacer algo*. Or I just tried to explain it in the present" (fourth-semester learner). Many learners also mentioned choosing to use the conditional and "the future" (i.e., MF). Explicit references to making the decision to avoid different forms were also quite common, along with choosing forms to which learners were more accustomed. Additionally, a few learners noted resorting to the quickest or easiest way to express an idea and complete an activity. Overall, responses reflected how these learners avoided some specific forms and that most reported consciously making strategic decisions in a variety of manners. Representative responses to Question 3 include the following:

> [I used the] present tense because it is the form I have the most practice with [...]
> (Third-year learner)

> I was not very confident in my ability to use future the correct way, therefore I simply avoided using it.
> (Third-year learner)

From a more general point of view, Figure 4 shows responses to Question 5 ("To what extent do you think you avoided using a particular form or structure in today's writing practice when writing in Spanish?"). Five participants reported that they avoided a particular form all the time, and the majority of participants (54%) did so "sometimes".

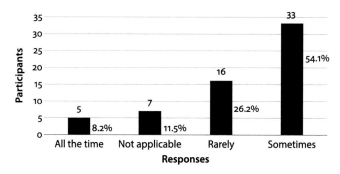

Figure 4. Follow-up questionnaire: Responses to question 5 (avoidance)

Discussion

Rates and predictors of usage

The first two research questions guiding the study related to the rates and predictors of usage of future-time variants. The principal variants used in the written samples were MF (46.7%), PF (20.7%), LF (18.1%), and PI (14.5%). Fourth-semester learners used MF roughly 10% more than third-year learners, who used the other three variants slightly more than the earlier group. Nevertheless, the two groups were not significantly different in our mixed-effects regression, likely due to multiple factors including proximity of the two courses, overlap in the range of grammar scores, and individual variability within each group. Namely, learners showed considerable individual variability within each course in terms of the range of grammar scores, prior research has shown that individual learners may specialize in the usage of particular future variants (Kanwit, 2017; Solon & Kanwit, 2014), and individual variability is thought to be particularly robust at intermediate course levels (see the generally greater within-group consistency of advanced learners described in Geeslin, 2018). Decreased preference for MF as learners move across intermediate and advanced course levels is consistent with prior findings (Gudmestad & Geeslin, 2013; Kanwit, 2017; Kanwit & Solon, 2013). Moreover, part of the slight preference for MF in the fourth semester may be related to instruction on the future perfect that had occurred earlier in the semester. The future perfect uses the MF of *haber* as its auxiliary (e.g., *habré cantado* 'I will have sung'), though rates of this form itself were low. Although MF instruction did not occur in-semester, fourth-semester learners were also closer to the earlier semesters of MF instruction.

Several predictors helped explain learner choice of variants. In a mixed-effects multinomial regression, significant variables were temporal distance, person, polarity, and the interaction between regularity and the continuous value (log transformation) of verb frequency. Temporal distance followed past literature, with learners generally favoring MF at greater distances and the other variants at closer distances (de Prada Pérez et al., 2021; Gudmestad & Geeslin, 2013; Kanwit, 2017). Person also followed previous trends, with first person favoring PF, third person favoring PI, and higher rates of LFs in first person, relative to MF. The default status of PF as the main variant in most varieties and our knowledge of our obligations, needs, and desires more than those of others help explain why first person fosters PF and LF usage (Bardovi-Harlig, 2005; Kanwit, 2019; Orozco, 2021). Third person and PI are linked in the future of scheduling (e.g., *el examen es mañana* 'the exam is tomorrow').

Polarity has tended to receive less attention in L2 future-time expression. Relative to MF, learners favored PI with negated predicates, while disfavoring LFs. This may be explainable in that negation adds to the clause's complexity (Mondorf, 2014). PI is the shortest/simplest of the variants, so it may be an especially strong candidate for accommodating the added complexity of negation for learners at this level. Alternatively, because LFs include a conjugated verb plus an infinitive, they may not accommodate negation as well for these learners structurally. Moreover, semantically, speakers may be more inclined to speak about the existence of obligations, needs, and desires rather than the lack thereof.

Roles of frequency, regularity, and form avoidance in revealing strategic competence

Our third research question related to whether learners reported avoiding any forms. Before we interpret learner responses regarding form avoidance, recall that the interaction between frequency and regularity was significant in our written production task. As verb frequency increased, learners were significantly less likely to use PF over MF with regular verbs, and the same was true for irregular verbs. In other words, MF was especially favored with more frequent verbs. An earlier analysis also revealed that learners were significantly less likely to use PI over MF with frequent, regular verbs, and significantly more likely to use PF over MF with infrequent, regular verbs, as compared to irregular verbs. Accordingly, learner usage of MF was above its baseline rate with frequent, regular verbs (where PI was disfavored), but it was below this rate with irregular verbs (where PI and LFs were used at rates above their baselines) and infrequent, regular verbs (where PF was favored). The connection between the MF and frequent, regular verb forms supports the usage-based prediction that the high type frequency of the regular (MF) pattern and its application to high token frequency forms would yield a favorable context for frequent, regular forms (Brown, 2018; Bybee, 2007; Giancaspro et al., 2022). The low type frequency of the irregular MF pattern (i.e., its application to few verb lexemes) contributes to the disfavoring of MF with irregular verbs, which would support the claim that less typical combinations are less activated (thus, less likely to be stored) and should require more effort to be constructed (Bybee, 2007; Tomasello, 2009).

Both PF and LFs were used above their baseline rates with infrequent verbs, which makes sense given that the verb conjugated for each of these variants is reliable. On the other hand, for PI or MF, the infrequent verb itself would have to be conjugated, which may help explain why those two forms showed usage below their baseline rates with infrequent verbs. If learners are uncertain whether an infrequent verb is irregular, they can use it with PF or a LF and avoid conjugating the verb altogether (e.g., *voy a predecir* 'I am going to predict' or *quiero predecir* 'I want to predict', as opposed to *predigo* 'I predict' or *prediciré* 'I will predict'). We moreover see effects for frequency and regularity even in a written task in which the pressure to communicate is less time-sensitive than in oral production (Geeslin & Gudmestad, 2008; Solon & Kanwit, 2014), supporting the potential strength of these constructs. We will see connections to learner reports of form avoidance later in the discussion.

Results on avoidance behavior support previous findings (Hubert, 2011, 2015), as the vast majority of learners in the present study claimed, for instance, to avoid the subjunctive. This aligns with Hubert (2015), where most participants (28 of 31) reported conscious avoidance of subjunctive forms. Learners in the present study credited their avoidance behavior mostly to feeling uncomfortable with grammar or lacking confidence.

The lack of use of a (target-like) variant has long received attention in the field of L2 acquisition (as problematized, for instance, in Canale & Swain, 1980; Corder, 1967; Selinker, 1972). Consequently, one imagines that form avoidance and the admission of consciously performing such a practice could be viewed negatively by teachers, learners, and scholars alike. When applied to MF, negative attitudes may be exacerbated, as Spanish learners may think this variant is the "real" or "more correct" future form. This is because it contains its own conjugations and receives more attention in curricular materials, even though it is less frequent than PF in most varieties (Gutiérrez & Fairclough, 2006; Kanwit, 2017; Orozco & Thoms, 2014). Nevertheless, we note an important aspect of form avoidance: our tasks reveal that learners avoid a variant when uncertain about a particular conjugational combination and instead implement a more reliable combination. We argue that this reveals two important pieces of information.

On the one hand, learner usage of a form for which there is greater certainty or comfort enables the learner to continue communicating. Such a practice precisely reveals strategic competence, even in the face of inadequate or developing resources (Canale & Swain, 1980). In our data, learners turned to PF, PI, or LFs, all of which are expected in future contexts and interpretable as futures by expert and L2 interlocutors. Accordingly, learners can continue their response with the desired temporality. Strategically using a more certain form when resources lag, as when facing the greater complexity of negated contexts (Mondorf, 2014) or when using an infrequent or irregular form, is an important part of the L2 learner's arsenal. This illuminates why, beyond grammatical competence (e.g., ability to conjugate verbs) or sociolinguistic competence (e.g., sensitivity to contextual factors), strategic competence has recurred as a critical component of the types of knowledge and skills that a L2 learner must possess (Bachman & Palmer, 2010; Canale, 1983; Canale & Swain, 1980; Celce-Murcia, 2008; Celce-Murcia et al., 1995; Kanwit & Solon, 2023).

Secondly, the relationship among form avoidance, frequency, and regularity provides useful information for L2 variationism. Namely, choice is affected by the forms that learners can capably use in a particular moment of speech, in addition to the range of independent predictors shown to favor one variant over others (e.g., temporal distance, presence of adverbs, person/number). In the face of limited resources, learners can be predicted to avoid more complex or uncertain combinations, adding to the probabilistic likelihood of using simpler or more familiar variants, which further "weight the coin" of which variant will be selected (Preston, 1993). Such avoidance supplements the other contextual factors that have been more robustly studied. Faced with an infrequent or irregular verb, our learners are more likely to use variants other than MF, and this speaks to their strategic competence in using whatever future variant is available to them in a given moment of language use in a particular linguistic and social context.

Regardless of whether expert speakers may be affected by, for instance, the regularity of a given verb in constraining future-time variation, we know that factors that affect learners need not be identical to those that condition expert speech (Bayley & Tarone, 2012; Geeslin, 2018; Preston, 1993). In early (i.e., pragmatic) stages of expressing and interpreting temporality, for example, learners tend to impose chronological ordering on the clauses they interpret and produce (Bardovi-Harlig, 2020). Consequently, although expert language users may not necessarily glean information about event realization from clause ordering, this can be a relevant factor for learners. Research on the study of the interpretation of verbal moods illustrates this observation. Fifth-semester learners in Kanwit and Geeslin (2014) perceived the order of main and adverbial clauses as a relevant cue to event interpretation, but more proficient learners and expert speakers did not exhibit the same pattern. Similarly, the regularity of a verb's subjunctive form has tended to be especially relevant for learners (Collentine, 1997; Gudmestad, 2006; Kanwit & Geeslin, 2014; Quesada, 1998), even in cases when it does constrain expert speaker usage or interpretation. This study has provided support for frequency/regularity as important contributors to learner variation of future-time expression, showing greater favoring of MF over simpler variants (i.e., PI, LFs, and PF: those conjugated in the present and with fewer morphemes per word) in contexts that are more frequent and regular, whereas the other, simpler variants are favored with less reliable combinations and in contexts of greater complexity (e.g., accompanied by negation). Such a system speaks to learners' strategic competence in still providing a viable future-time variant across different cognitive loads.

Limitations and future directions

Although the present study has considered the existing body of research on form avoidance and on avoidance as a CS in L2 learning as a point of departure, the design presents limitations that bear noting. Self-report data of L2 behavior offers a window into learner insights, although there may be misalignment between what learners do and what they think/say they do. For instance, learners may answer in accordance to what they think they "should" say, which could entail reporting preferences for a form that they think is more "correct" or prestigious; noting avoidance rather than responding "no" to such a question, in a possible attempt to be a dutiful study participant; or simply attempting to indicate certainty instead of doubt or a lack of memory (Gass & Mackey, 2000). Of course, learners may not be aware of reliance on avoidance strategies, especially for phenomena that may be unconscious.

Future research will do well to consider the role of learner individual differences (Zahler, 2022) in constraining CSs and variant usage. For instance, such work could investigate links between working memory and form avoidance, reported use of Spanish outside the classroom or intention to major/minor in Spanish and strategies used, and avoidance responses and individual usage. Our dataset can be explored for some of these links in subsequent studies.

Conclusion

Departing from predecessors on the acquisition of future-time expression, the present study considered the roles that frequency and regularity play in constraining L2 variable futurity. Although learners were sensitive to predictors that have repeatedly conditioned particular variants (e.g., temporal distance, person), the study revealed that part of the learner's choice in what form to use relates to how frequently occurring the form is and its regularity. Frequent, regular verbs were shown to favor MF relative to the other variants, whereas infrequent and irregular verbs were more favorable contexts for the other variants (i.e., PF, PI, LFs), likely because those variants only require the verb to be conjugated in the present. The study supplemented this information with a form avoidance questionnaire, indicating that learners reported strategic decisions of avoiding certain variants. Rather than viewing this admission as a deficiency on the part of the learner, we note that such a strategy is an important part of the learner's communicative competence. Namely, learners avoid uncertain combinations to instead use a form they know will provide the necessary complex meaning of [base + future temporality]. This demonstrates one way in which learners ensure successful communication within the repertoire of forms and meanings available to them in the moment of speech — it reveals their strategic competence.

Acknowledgements

This project was greatly informed by Kim Geeslin's work on sociolinguistic competence, the acquisition of variation, and variable future-time expression. We are honored to dedicate this small study to her memory as a scholar and, more importantly, as a generous mentor and friend. We're grateful to handling editors Aarnes Gudmestad and Megan Solon and two anonymous reviewers for their helpful comments and to Amanda Huensch for feedback on a prior version of the project. All errors are our own.

References

Alonso-Vázquez, M. (2004). Avoidance as a learning strategy. *Estudios Ingleses de la Universidad Complutense, 13*, 67–83.

Andersen, R. W. (1990). Models, processes, principles and strategies: Second language acquisition inside and outside the classroom. In B. VanPatten, & J. F. Lee (Eds.), *Second language acquisition–Foreign language learning* (pp. 45–78). Multilingual Matters.

Bachman, L. F., & Palmer, A. S. (2010). *Language assessment in practice: Developing language assessments and justifying their use in the real world*. Oxford University Press.

Bardovi-Harlig, K. (2004). The emergence of grammaticalized future expression in longitudinal production data. In M. Overstreet, S. Rott, B. VanPatten, & J. Williams (Eds.), *Form and meaning in second language acquisition* (pp. 115–137). Erlbaum.

Bardovi-Harlig, K. (2005). The future of desire: Lexical futures and modality in L2 English future expression. In L. Dekydtspotter, R. A. Sprouse, & A. Liljestrand (Eds.), *Proceedings of the 7th Generative Approaches to Second Language Acquisition Conference (GASLA 2004)* (pp. 1–12). Cascadilla Proceedings Project.

Bardovi-Harlig, K. (2020). One functional approach to second language acquisition: The concept-oriented approach. In B. VanPatten, G. Keating, & S. Wulff (Eds.), *Theories in second language acquisition* (3rd ed., pp. 40–62). Routledge.

Bayley, R., & Tarone, E. (2012). Variationist perspectives. In S. Gass & A. Mackey (eds.), *Handbook of Second Language Acquisition* (pp. 41–56). Routledge.

Blas Arroyo, J. L. (2008). The variable expression of future tense in Peninsular Spanish: The present (and future) of inflectional forms in the Spanish spoken in a bilingual region. *Language Variation and Change, 20*, 85–126.

Brown, E. L. (2018). Usage-based approaches to Spanish linguistics. In K. Geeslin (Ed.), *The Cambridge Handbook of Spanish Linguistics* (pp. 52–71). Cambridge University Press.

Bybee, J. L. (2007). Regular morphology and the lexicon. In J. Bybee (Ed.), *Frequency of use and the organization of language* (pp. 167–193). Oxford University Press.

Bybee, J. L. (2008). Usage-based grammar and second language acquisition. In P. Robinson & N. C. Ellis (Eds.), *The Routledge handbook of cognitive linguistics and second language acquisition* (pp. 216–236). Routledge.

Bybee, J. L. (2017). Grammatical and lexical factors in sound change. *Language Variation and Change, 29*(3), 273–300.

Canale, M. (1983). From communicative competence to communicative language pedagogy. In J. Richards & R. Schmidt (Eds.), *Language and communication* (pp. 2–27). London Group Ltd.

Canale, M., & Swain, M. (1980). Theoretical bases of communicative approaches to second language teaching and testing. *Applied Linguistics, 1*, 1–47.

Celce-Murcia, M. (2008). Rethinking the role of communicative competence in language teaching. In E. A. Soler & M. P. S. Jordà (Eds.), *Intercultural language use and language learning* (pp. 41–57). Springer.

Celce-Murcia, M., Dörnyei, Z., & Thurrell, S. (1995). Communicative competence: A pedagogical model with content specifications. *Issues in Applied Linguistics, 6*(2), 5–25.

Collentine, J. (1997). The effects of irregular stems on the detection of verbs in the subjunctive. *Spanish Applied Linguistics*, 1, 3–23.

Corder, P. (1967). The significance of learners' errors. *International Review of Applied Linguistics*, 5(4), 161–170.

Davies, M. (2018). Corpus del Español: 7.6 billion words, 21 countries. Available online at https://www.corpusdelespanol.org/now/

de Prada Pérez, A., Gómez Soler, I., & Feroce, N. (2021). Variable future-time expression in Spanish: A comparison between heritage and second language learners. *Languages*, 6, 206.

Dörnyei, Z. & Scott, M.L. (1997). Communications strategies in a second language: definitions and taxonomies. *Language Learning*, 47(1), 173–210.

Fratini, V., Acha, J., & Laka, I. (2014). Frequency and morphological irregularity are independent variables. Evidence from a corpus study of Spanish verbs. *Corpus Linguistics and Linguistic Theory*, 10(2), 289–314.

Gass, S.M., & Mackey, A. (2000). *Stimulated recall methodology in second language research*. Erlbaum.

Geeslin, K.L. (2018). Variable structures and sociolinguistic variation. In P. Malovrh & A. Benati (Eds.), *The handbook of advanced proficiency in second language acquisition* (pp. 547–565). Wiley.

Geeslin, K.L., Goebel-Mahrle, T., Guo, J., & Linford, B. (2023). Variable subject expression in second language acquisition: The role of perseveration. In P. Posio & P. Herbeck (Eds.), *Referring to discourse participants in Ibero-Romance languages* (pp. 69–104). Language Science Press.

Geeslin, K.L., & Gudmestad, A. (2008). Comparing interview and written elicitation tasks in native and non-native data: Do speakers do what we think they do? In J. Bruhn de Garavito & E. Valenzuela (Eds.), *Selected proceedings of the 10th Hispanic linguistics symposium* (pp. 64–77). Cascadilla Proceedings Project.

George, D. & Mallery, P. (2012). *IBM SPSS statistics 19 step by step: A simple guide and reference*. Pearson.

Giancaspro, D., Pérez-Cortes, S., & Higdon, J. (2022). (Ir)regular mood swings: Lexical variability in heritage speakers' oral production of subjunctive mood. *Language Learning*, 72(2), 456–496.

Goldberg, A. (2013). Constructionist approaches. In T. Hoffmann & G. Trousdale (Eds.), *The Oxford handbook of construction grammar* (pp. 15–31). Oxford University Press.

Gries, S. Th. (2021). (Generalized linear) mixed-effects modeling: A learner corpus example. *Language Learning*, 71(3), 757–798.

Gudmestad, A. (2006). L2 variation and the Spanish subjunctive: Linguistic features predicting mood selection. In C.L. Klee & T.L. Face (Eds.), *Selected proceedings of the 7th Conference on the Acquisition of Spanish and Portuguese as First and Second Languages* (pp. 170–184). Cascadilla Press.

Gudmestad, A. (2012). Toward an understanding of the relationship between mood use and form regularity: Evidence of variation across tasks, lexical items, and participant groups. In K. Geeslin & M. Díaz-Campos (Eds.), *Selected proceedings of the 14th Hispanic Linguistics Symposium* (pp. 214–227). Somerville, MA: Cascadilla Press.

Gudmestad, A., & Geeslin, K. (2011). Assessing the use of multiple forms in variable contexts: The relationship between linguistic factors and future-time reference in Spanish. *Studies in Hispanic and Lusophone Linguistics, 4*, 3–33.

Gudmestad, A., & Geeslin, K. (2013). Second-language development of variable future-time expression in Spanish. In A. M. Carvalho & S. Beaudrie (Eds.), *Selected proceedings of the 6th Workshop on Spanish Sociolinguistics* (pp. 63–75). Cascadilla Proceedings Project.

Gutiérrez, M., & Fairclough, M. (2006). Incorporating linguistic variation into the classroom. In R. Salaberry & B. Lafford (Eds.), *The art of teaching Spanish* (pp. 173-191). Georgetown University Press.

Haspelmath, M., & Sims, A. D. (2010). *Understanding morphology*. 2nd ed. Hatchette.

Hubert, M. D. (2011). Foreign language production and avoidance in US university Spanish language education. *International Journal of Applied Linguistics, 21*(2), 222–243.

Hubert, M. D. (2015). Avoidance behavior in US university Spanish-language instruction. *International Journal of Applied Linguistics, 25*(2), 141–159.

Kanwit, M. (2017). What we gain by combining variationist and concept-oriented approaches: The case of acquiring Spanish future-time expression. *Language Learning, 67*(2), 461–498.

Kanwit, M. (2019). Beyond the present indicative: Lexical futures as indicators of development in L2 Spanish. *The Modern Language Journal, 103*(2), 481–501.

Kanwit, M. (2021). Allowable temporal distances for future-time forms: The case of advanced L2 Spanish learners. In M. Menke & P. Malovrh (Eds.), *Advancedness in second language Spanish: Definitions, challenges, and possibilities* (pp. 116–141). John Benjamins.

Kanwit, M., & Berríos, J. (2023). Corpora, cognition, and usage-based approaches. In M. Díaz-Campos & S. Balasch (Eds.), *The handbook of usage-based linguistics* (pp. 269–286). Wiley-Blackwell.

Kanwit, M., & Geeslin, K. L. (2014). The interpretation of Spanish subjunctive and indicative forms in adverbial clauses. *Studies in Second Language Acquisition, 36*, 487–533.

Kanwit, M., & Solon, M. (2013). Acquiring variation in future-time expression abroad in Valencia, Spain and Mérida, Mexico. In J. E. Aaron, J. Cabrelli Amaro, G. Lord, & A. de Prada Pérez (Eds.), *Selected proceedings of the 16th Hispanic Linguistics Symposium* (pp. 206–221). Cascadilla Proceedings Project.

Kanwit, M., & Solon, M. (Eds.). (2023). *Communicative competence in a second language: Theory, method, and applications*. Routledge.

Krippendorff, K. (2004). *Content analysis: An introduction to its methodology*. Sage.

Langacker, R. W. (2015). Cognitive grammar. In B. Heine & H. Narrog (Eds.), *The Oxford handbook of linguistic analysis* (2nd ed., pp. 1–22). Oxford University Press.

Laufer, B. & Eliasson, S. (1993). What causes avoidance in L2 learning. *Studies in Second Language Acquisition, 15*, 35–48.

Liao, Y. & Fukuya, Y. J. (2004). Avoidance of phrasal verbs: the case of Chinese learners of English. *Language Learning, 54*(2), 193–226.

Marian, V., Blumenfeld, H. K., & Kaushanskaya, M. (2007). The Language Experience and Proficiency Questionnaire (LEAP-Q): Assessing language profiles in bilinguals and multilinguals. *Journal of Speech, Language, and Hearing Research, 50*, 940–967.

Mondorf, B. (2014). Apparently competing motivations in morphosyntactic variation. In B. MacWhinney, A. L. Malchukov, & E. A. Moravcsik (Eds.), *Competing motivations in grammar and usage* (pp. 209–228). Oxford University Press.

Orozco, R. (2021). The expression of futurity in Spanish: An empirical investigation. In M. Díaz-Campos (Ed.), *The Routledge handbook of variationist approaches to Spanish* (pp. 315–327). Routledge.

Orozco, R., & Thoms, J. J. (2014). The future tense in Spanish L2 textbooks. *Spanish in Context*, *11*(1), 27–49.

Preston, D. (1993). Variationist linguistics and second language acquisition. *Second Language Research*, *9*(2), 153–172.

Quesada, M. L. (1998). L2 acquisition of the Spanish subjunctive mood and prototype schema development. *Spanish Applied Linguistics*, *2*, 1–23.

Sedano, M. (1994). El futuro morfológico y la expresión ir a + infinitivo en el español hablado en Venezuela. *Verba*, *21*, 225–240.

Selinker, L. (1972). Interlanguage. *IRAL*, *10*, 209–230.

Silva-Corvalán, C. & Terrell, T. (1989). Notas sobre la expresión de futuridad en el español del Caribe. *Hispanic Linguistics*, *2*, 191–208.

Solon, M., & Kanwit, M. (2014). The emergence of future verbal morphology in Spanish as a foreign language. *Studies in Hispanic and Lusophone Linguistics*, *7*, 115–148.

Swain, A., Berríos, J., & Kanwit, M. (2023). Exploring future-in-the-past variation in Seville and Caracas: ¿*Cambiaría o iba a cambiar?* In S. Fernández Cuenca, T. Judy, & L. Miller (Eds.), *Innovative approaches to research in Hispanic linguistics: Regional, diachronic, and learner profile variation* (pp. 58–80). John Benjamins.

Tarone, E. (1977). Conscious communication strategies in interlanguage: A progress report. In H. D. Brown, C. A. Yorio & R. C. Crymes (Eds.), *TESOL '77* (pp. 194–203). TESOL.

Tomasello, M. (2009). The usage-based theory of language acquisition. In E. L. Bavin (Ed.), *The Cambridge handbook of child language* (pp. 69–87). Cambridge University Press.

Zahler, S. (2022). Measuring individual differences: A look at working memory. In K. Geeslin (Ed.), *The Routledge handbook of second language acquisition and sociolinguistics* (pp. 30–44). Routledge.

Appendix

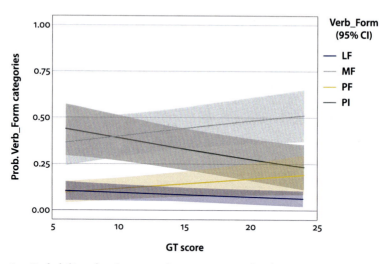

Figure A1. Probability of variant usage by grammar test (GT) score

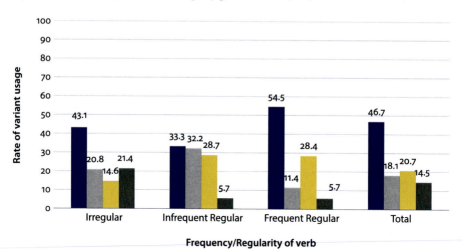

Figure A2. Rate of variant usage by frequency/regularity of verb

CHAPTER 3

Implicit bias and the L2 perception of the Peninsular Spanish interdental fricative /θ/

Carmen Fernández Flórez & Bret Linford
Grand Valley State University | Brigham Young University — Idaho

Research on second language acquisition of regional variation shows that learners' adoption of regionally variable forms depends on various (extra)linguistic factors (Schoonmaker-Gates, 2020). Only some regional features are adopted by L2 learners (Ringer-Hilfinger, 2012). Explicit learner attitudes have been examined to understand this discrepancy (Schmidt, 2020). However, explicit attitudes may not align with implicit biases. This study investigates implicit biases toward the Peninsular Spanish interdental fricative, /θ/, among beginner-level L2 learners. An Implicit Association Test with auditory stimuli reveals a significant implicit negative bias against /θ/. Factors such as motivation for studying Spanish and explicit opinions about /θ/ constrain this bias. These findings enhance our understanding of the relationship between language attitudes, sociolinguistic competence, and L2 acquisition.

Keywords: implicit bias, L2 Spanish acquisition, interdental fricative, sociolinguistic competence, language attitudes

Linguistic attitudes — perceptions and evaluations of different languages, dialects, or linguistic features — influence social interactions and cultural dynamics. These attitudes impact language policy, educational practices, and individual language choices, making their understanding crucial for addressing language discrimination, preservation, and change. For example, in the United States, Southern American English often evokes stereotypes about speakers' education and intelligence, despite evidence that contradicts these views (Lippi-Green, 2011). Such negative attitudes can lead to social and economic disadvantages for those with stigmatized accents.

In bilingual and multilingual contexts, attitudes towards minority languages can create pressures to assimilate. In Catalonia, Spain, for instance, using Catalan instead of Spanish can reflect broader societal views regarding regional identity and autonomy. Catalan speakers may see their language as vital to cultural identity, while some Spanish speakers may view the focus on Catalan as unnecessary or divisive (Pujolar, 2009). Similarly, English learners in Japan face ambivalent attitudes: while English proficiency is linked to global opportunities, there is concern it may undermine native language and culture (Seargeant, 2009).

These linguistic attitudes can be conscious and reportable or unconscious and uncontrollable (Devos, 2008; McKenzie & Carrie, 2018; Rydell & McConnell, 2006). Research over the past 60 years has examined favorable and unfavorable language attitudes across different contexts, revealing their complexity and the influence of factors like age, gender, social status, and education level (Baker, 1992). Although most research has focused on native (i.e., expert) speakers' attitudes toward other native speakers' speech (Díaz-Campos & Killam, 2012; Madariaga et al., 2016), recent studies are investigating second language (L2) learners' attitudes toward regional varieties of Spanish (Schmidt & Geeslin, 2022).

This study expands on research regarding learners' attitudes toward their L2 by exploring L2 learners of Spanish and their attitudes toward the Peninsular Spanish interdental fricative /θ/, a salient dialectal feature that has proven challenging for learners to acquire. By examining both explicit and implicit attitudes, we aim to provide a more comprehensive understanding of the factors influencing the acquisition of this sociolinguistic variable.

Literature review

L2 learners' acquisition of dialect-specific variable features

Language learners encounter diverse linguistic input, especially in study-abroad contexts, where they often face non-standard language that may differ from classroom instruction. For instance, in North-Central Spain, in contrast to the normative use of the third-person singular clitic pronoun *le* for indirect objects, learners may encounter *leísmo*, where *le* is used as a direct object (Geeslin et al., 2012). Research shows that even when learners comprehend variable structures, they often use them less frequently than native speakers (Starr, 2022; Tse, 2022; Zhang et al., 2022).

In Spanish, research on the L2 acquisition of dialectal features has led to mixed results. Whereas some studies have shown significant L2 adoption of certain features after extended exposure to the variants, such as L2 learners adopting the Argentine prepalatal fricatives — [ʃ] and [ʒ] — and second-person singular pronoun *vos* instead of *tú* after a semester abroad (Pozzi & Bayley, 2021), others have found little adoption of features that are prevalent but often stigmatized in the Spanish-speaking world or that could be considered phonologically complex, such as /s/-weakening (Linford et al., 2021; Pozzi, 2022).

Overall, these studies indicate that extended exposure to dialectal features during study abroad may — but does not always — lead to the adoption of said features (Baker, 2008; Raish, 2015; Ringer-Hilfinger, 2012). Furthermore, studies examining the perception of dialectal features indicate that learners can acquire the ability to recognize, interpret, and understand phonological constraints without necessarily producing the variant (Chappell & Kanwit, 2022; Escalante, 2018; Schmidt, 2018). Thus, similar to extended exposure, developing a receptive knowledge of dialectal variation does not always lead to L2 learners employing the variation.

L2 acquisition of the Peninsular Spanish /θ/

In North-Central Spain, native speakers produce the interdental fricative /θ/ ('theta') for the orthographic 'z' and 'c' when followed by 'i' or 'e.' Research on the L2 acquisition of Spanish /θ/ has primarily examined its production. For instance, Geeslin and Gudmestad (2008) investigated /θ/ usage among L2 learners at various proficiency levels. They found that in an oral role-play task, only nine of the 130 participants produced /θ/, with production significantly higher at the three highest proficiency levels. In a study involving U.S. university students studying abroad in Madrid, Ringer-Hilfinger (2012) found that learners produced /θ/ only six times out of 209 contexts where it could have occurred during oral tasks. Additionally, a matched-guise test showed no learner preference for /s/ over /θ/, but despite a positive attitude towards /θ/, not all learners with this attitude used /θ/ in practice. Reported use exceeded actual use in oral tasks, suggesting that factors such as linguistic insecurity influenced production.

Knouse (2012) compared /θ/ production in two groups: students studying abroad for six weeks in Salamanca, Spain and those taking a six-week U.S. course with a Peninsular Spanish professor. Data were collected via reading a newspaper article aloud and responding to open-ended questions, before and after the instructional experience. The Pronunciation Attitude Inventory (PAI) was also used. Among students abroad, /θ/ occurred 36 times out of 2,119 possible contexts, with no occurrences among U.S. students. Those studying in Spain and majoring in Spanish were more likely to produce /θ/, suggesting influences of exposure and personal motivation. Also, higher PAI scores were not found to significantly increase /θ/ realization among learners, leading Knouse to propose that non-production of /θ/ could stem from communication not being hindered by /s/ or the high cognitive load of acquiring a regional variant.

George (2014) explored the development of /θ/ and /χ/ in students participating in a semester-long study abroad in Toledo, Spain and also found limited production of /θ/. Data from a read aloud task, a word list task, and a spontaneous speech task showed minimal /θ/ production, with no significant increase over the semester. Higher use of /θ/ and /χ/ occurred in reading tasks than in spontaneous speech, indicating an orthographic influence in reading. Stevens (2017) also analyzed the production of /θ/ by intermediate L2 learners studying abroad in Úbeda, Spain. After six weeks, /θ/ use increased by 12% and was more frequent in stressed syllables, among women learners, and among those who had a greater desire for native-like pronunciation. However, as with previous studies, frequency of use remained low, and no learner approached native-speaker levels.

Finally, Grammon (2021) examined the non-adoption of the /θ/ by students enrolled in a third-year Spanish pronunciation undergraduate course taught by a native speaker from Northern Spain. Employing a language ideological framework, he examined language attitudes and beliefs through qualitative analyses of pedagogical materials, classroom discourse, and participant interviews to discover language ideologies of "shared conceptualizations of language that are mobilized in interaction as meaning-making resources in ways that serve particular social interests" (p. 609). He found that the beliefs of the learners' professor regarding the use of the /θ/ influenced their choice to avoid using it in their Spanish. The instructor's beliefs, which favored a Latin American Spanish variety and discouraged mixing dialects, shaped the students' development of sociolinguistic competence (Canale & Swain, 1980; van Compernolle & Williams, 2012) despite their personal attitudes towards using /θ/.

In summary, despite variables such as L2 proficiency and time abroad (Geeslin & Gudmestad, 2008; Stevens, 2017), learner gender (Stevens, 2017), instructor beliefs (Grammon, 2021), and task type (George, 2014) characterizing the use of /θ/ by L2 learners, factors such as positive attitudes toward the feature have not been shown to constrain its production (Ringer-Hilfinger, 2012), and no factor has been shown to lead to widespread adoption of this feature. Given the apparent lack of influence of positive evaluations of the /θ/ on its use, questions remain regarding whether the measurements of attitudes in previous research reveal everything about students' attitudes. Indeed, George (2014) and Stevens (2017) suggested that the non-acquisition of /θ/ among L2 learners studying in Spain may be due to the perception of this sound as a lisp, but no study has clearly shown this quantitatively. In addition, although Ringer-Hilfinger (2012) employed a matched-guise test, previous research has tended to rely on learners' self-reported attitudes towards dialectal features instead of more implicit measures.

Measuring attitudes toward language

Decades of research show that a speaker's accent impacts how listeners perceive the speaker's social identity, with standard accents typically rated more favorably (Giles, 1970; Gluszek & Dovidio, 2010). L2 speakers often face negative consequences due to their foreign accents (Kinzler et al., 2009; Pantos & Perkins, 2012). Most studies have used explicit methods, like questionnaires, to gauge language attitudes (Cigliana & Serrano, 2016). Implicit methods, such as matched- and verbal guise techniques, can reveal attitudes indirectly by having listeners rate speakers on personality traits (Ciller & Fernández-Flórez, 2016; Lambert et al., 1960).

Recently, sociolinguists have incorporated advances in attitude theory from social psychology, differentiating explicit attitudes (i.e., conscious awareness) from implicit ones (formed through repeated exposure) (Petty et al., 2009). Techniques like the Implicit Association Test (IAT) measure implicit biases by recording reaction times to paired concepts (Greenwald et al., 2011; Pantos & Perkins, 2012). The IAT is a computer-based sorting task that measures relative reaction times between distinct pairings of concepts or attributes. A feature is paired with a negative or positive word, and participants must categorize the concept and the positive/negative word as quickly as they can (see Appendix A). If a pairing is well established in memory, the participant is expected to respond accurately and quickly when that pairing is presented, while responding more slowly and less accurately indicates that the pairing is less well-established in memory (Pantos & Perkins, 2012, p. 4). In their study, Pantos and Perkins found that participants implicitly favored U.S. accents over foreign ones but expressed more favorable explicit attitudes towards the latter, indicating a divergence between implicit and explicit attitudes. It also shows that there can be an oppositional relationship between the two attitude modalities in which listeners might report a more socially acceptable (tolerant) attitude if they suspect their implicit attitudes might reveal a socially unacceptable bias. Such hypercorrection in attitude reporting has been shown to occur when participants are concerned about how their self-presentation may be perceived (Baron & Banaji, 2006; de Jong et al., 2003; Lane et al., 2007).

Traditional research has focused on native speakers' perceptions of first language (L1) forms, but some studies have explored L2 learners' attitudes toward L1 varieties, influenced by factors like experience abroad (Abreu, 2016; Lindemann, 2003; Schmidt & Geeslin, 2022). Results from these studies showed that L2 speakers' attitudes are similar in several ways to the attitudes of their L1 counterparts but seem to be more heavily influenced by external factors such as the learners' experience abroad and length of contact with the variety in question. In terms of the use of an IAT to measure implicit attitudes toward Spanish, we are aware of only one previous study, Ianos et al. (2023), who used the IAT to examine implicit attitudes of adolescents in a Spanish/Catalan context in Catalonia, Spain. They found significant implicit bias overall in favor of Catalan over Spanish. However, when external factors (e.g., home language) were taken into account, participants showed a significant implicit bias in favor of the language used at home. The home language influence aligns with the concept that implicit attitudes can be understood as resulting from past experiences and feelings (Álvarez-Mosquera & Marín-Gutiérrez, 2018).

Although some studies on the L2 acquisition of Spanish have employed implicit measures such as the matched-guise technique (e.g., Chappell & Kanwit, 2022; Ringer-Hilfinger, 2012; Schmidt & Geeslin, 2022), perception studies that gauge learners' attitudes toward and ideologies about specific linguistic items have been rare. Our study contributes to the field of Spanish language acquisition and attitudes by exploring L2 learners' perceptions of /θ/ using an IAT, an instrument that has not been used for this feature before.

Method

Research questions

This study aims to answer the following research questions:

1. To what extent do English-speaking L2 learners of Spanish show implicit negative bias toward the Peninsular Spanish /θ/? What factors constrain this bias?
2. To what extent do L2 learners' implicit biases align with their explicit attitudes for this regional variable form?

Participants

A total of 123 undergraduate students (106 women, 14 men, three non-binary/preferred not to answer) at an American university participated in this study. The participants' ages ranged from 18 to 22 years ($M=20.2$ years; $SD=1.2$ years). All were enrolled in a Spanish class at the time of participation and placed at the beginner proficiency level based on an adaptation of the *Diploma de Español como Lengua Extranjera* [Spanish as a Foreign Language Diploma] (DELE) test. Participants were US American nationals, reported English as their L1, and had no Latinx heritage. In addition, 62 participants indicated that they had had at least one Spanish teacher from Spain, but only 20 indicated they had family or friends from Spain. Additionally, only 15 students indicated that they had spent three or more weeks in a Spanish-speaking country, and of those participants, only three indicated having spent this time in Spain. Also, only 10 students indicated that the Spanish they spoke was most similar to Spain (i.e., Peninsular) Spanish.

Procedure and tasks

Participants completed three tasks in the following order:

1. IAT
2. Language proficiency test
3. Language background questionnaire

Prior to all tasks, researchers described to the students the production and use of the /θ/ by describing the orthographic contexts in which it is used and the regions where it is produced, and by showing audio samples of its pronunciation.

Task 1. *IAT*

For the current study, the IAT was developed in Qualtrics using a modified version of the IAT code provided by Carpenter et al. (2019) in order to allow for auditory stimuli. It consisted of five blocks of trials: three practice blocks and two test blocks (see Appendix A). In each block, participants were asked to categorize every stimulus as belonging to the category that appeared in the upper left or upper right of the computer screen by pressing the computer key "E" for left or "I" for right. Participants were instructed to answer as quickly as possible and told that there were no penalties for mistakes. Block I was a practice stage where participants only categorized the evaluative words as either positive (Good) or negative (Bad). Participants were presented with each of these 16 stimuli twice, for a total of 32 trials. Block II was also a practice one in which participants were shown the target words and heard the audio stimuli and had to categorize the audio with /θ/ as *'th' sound*[1] and the audio with /s/ as *'s' sound*. Each of the 8 audio stimuli appeared twice (4 for the /θ/, and 4 for the /s/), for a total of 16 trials. Block III was a testing block where participants had to categorize the positive/negative words and the audio stimuli with either /θ/ or /s/ into randomized combinations of the categories 'th sound' and 's sound' with 'Bad' and 'Good'. This test block included a total of 32 trials. Block IV was another practice block and the same as Block II, but the *th* sound and *s* sound labels were reversed on the sides of the screen. The final Block V was the other testing block and was identical to Block III, except that the positive/negative attribute categories were now categorized with the opposite sound from Block III. In order to avoid the effects of combination order or screen

---

1. We used *'th' sound* instead of 'theta' or "/θ/" to avoid any misunderstandings of what the latter meant.

sides, the order of the trials within each block were randomized and the location on the screen (left or right) of the combinations ('*th sound*' or '*s sound*' with 'Bad' or 'Good') were counterbalanced. Additionally, if an incorrect answer was given by a participant, a red X appeared on the screen and the participant needed to correct it before moving on (see Appendix B for an example screenshot of what a student would see while completing Blocks III and V).

The audio stimuli for the IAT were four words: *cele* 'unripe', *cipo* 'milestone', *zapa* 'spade', *zulo* 'hideout', which were 4-letter, 2-syllable paroxytone words that began with the orthographic "z" or "ci,ce." All words were infrequent (i.e., not within the 5,000 most-frequent words of Spanish; Davies & Davies, 2017) to minimize the effects of semantic bias (see Guasch et al., 2016; Stadthagen-Gonzalez et al., 2017). Each word was produced twice in a soundproof booth, once with /θ/ and once with /s/, by a woman native speaker from Northern Spain. The evaluative words, presented in written English, consisted of eight positive (marvelous, superb, pleasure, beautiful, joyful, glorious, lovely, wonderful) and eight negative (tragic, horrible, agony, painful, terrible, awful, humiliate, nasty) valence words taken from Pantos and Perkins (2012).

Task 2. *Proficiency test*

Participants completed an adapted version of the DELE (Montrul, 2012) to provide a standardized measure of proficiency. This test assessed grammatical and semantic knowledge using multiple-choice questions and a cloze test. It has been used in a variety of investigations to assess learner proficiency (e.g. Czerwionka & Olson, 2020; Montrul et al., 2008; Slabakova et al., 2012; White et al., 2004). Following Montrul (2012), learners who scored between 40–50 were classified as advanced, those who scored between 30–39 were classified as intermediate, and those who scored below 30 as beginners.

Task 3. *Language background questionnaire*

The final task that participants completed was a background questionnaire that was also administered online. This questionnaire included items that were created specifically for the current study but were based heavily on the Language Contact Profile (Freed et al., 2004) as well as questionnaires found in Cohen et al. (2005), Dörnyei and Taguchi (2010), and Linford (2014). The questionnaire included 27 questions that elicited participants' demographic information, previous Spanish course enrollment (K–12 and university), previous experience with linguistics courses/content, experience living in a Spanish-speaking country, exposure to Spanish in their daily lives, other languages and self-reported proficiency in them, previous experience with Spanish from Spain, scaled rating of items regarding the students' attitude toward the language/people/culture, learning preferences, anxiety in the L2, explicit beliefs about the Spanish /θ/, and scaled rating of items regarding the students' attitude toward the Spanish /θ/.

Analysis

Dependent variable

We examined the dependent variable in two ways: First, we determined the total time it took each student to complete the /θ/+good; /s/+bad blocks (henceforth "/θ/+good") and the /θ/+bad; /s/+good blocks (henceforth "/θ/+bad"). A longer overall duration with the /θ/+good blocks than the /θ/+bad blocks would suggest a negative implicit bias against /θ/ because it would reveal that it was more difficult for participants to associate positive words with words produced with /θ/ than with words produced with /s/. Second, for the regression analysis, we calculated the percent difference in duration between the /θ/+good versus the /θ/+bad blocks to minimize the potential effects of completion rate variability across learners.

Independent variables

The independent variables considered in this study came from the attributes of the IAT task, the results of the IAT, and information gathered from the background questionnaire.[2]

Statistical analyses

For the analysis, we used SPSS 28 (IBM Corp., 2021) to compare the overall completion duration and the total number of errors for the /θ/+good versus the /θ/+bad blocks using a paired samples t-test.[3] In addition, we examined the results of several items on the background questionnaire related to the students' use of the /θ/ and their attitudes and beliefs related to various aspects of the Spanish language, cultures, and the /θ/. Finally, again we used SPSS 28 (IBM Corp., 2021) to run a linear regression to determine which factors significantly constrained the percent difference in duration between the /θ/+good versus the /θ/+bad blocks.

---

2. Not all of the information gathered on the background questionnaire led to the creation of independent variables. In most cases, this was because there was negligible representation for the categories of the variable considered (e.g., very few participants had spent time abroad, had taken a linguistic course, or were men).

3. The dependent variable is the time students took to complete each of the testing blocks, instead of the individual response times to categorize each stimuli. We acknowledge that not including individual response times may limit the robustness of the statistical results.

Table 1. Independent variables and their categories

Independent variable	Description	Categories
IAT /θ/ side	Side in which the label '*th sound*' appeared on the screen	1. Right 2. Left
/θ/+good/bad order	The order in which the combinations of /θ/+good and /θ/+bad appeared in the task	1. /θ/+good first 2. /θ/+bad first
Number of errors	Overall number of errors in each Block (i.e., when the participant categorized stimuli/valence words into the wrong category)	Continuous
Spanish level	Combination of proficiency score level, Spanish Class level, and Grades in Spanish classes	Continuous
Language contact	Combined reported frequency of reading, writing, speaking, and listening to Spanish outside of class	Continuous
Teacher from Spain	Reported having Peninsular Spanish instructors or not	1. "Yes" 2. "No" or "Not sure"
Opinions of dialect and culture from Spain	Derived from scaled ratings of statements related to Spanish dialect and culture of Spain (see Table 3 for statements)	Continuous
Opinions of /θ/	Derived from scaled ratings of statements related to the /θ/ (see Table 4 for statements)	Continuous
/θ/ awareness	Derived from answers to the question "Before participating in this study, were you aware that Spanish speakers from Spain pronounce the letters 'z' and 'c' (when followed by 'e' or 'i') like the English 'th' as in 'thin'?"	1. "Yes" or "I had heard about it, but didn't know the specifics" 2. "No"

Table 1. *(continued)*

Independent variable	Description	Categories
/θ/ use	Answer selected to the question "Do you use the Spanish 'theta' when you speak Spanish?"	Five categories (see Table 2 for specific responses)
Spanish variety	Reported variety of Spanish used by the participant	1. Spain (i.e., Peninsular) Spanish 2. Latin American Spanish; Not sure/Neither
Reasons for studying Spanish	For this variable, each individual reason was examined separately as either selected or not (students were allowed to select up to four primary reasons)	1. Communicate with more people 2. Fulfill a degree requirement 3. Benefit my future career 4. It is fun/interesting 5. I have a knack for learning languages 6. I love learning about foreign cultures 7. Travel the world 8. Learn more about my heritage 9. Expand my circle of friends
Level of intrinsic motivation to learn Spanish	Calculated by adding up the number of intrinsic reasons (4, 6, 8, 9) students selected for studying Spanish minus the number of selected extrinsic reasons (1–3, 5, 7) (see list in the prior row of categories)	Continuous

Results

We begin by presenting the results of the overall difference between the /θ/+good and /θ/+bad block response times. It was found that the /θ/+good blocks took an average of 40.99 seconds to complete ($SD=8.54$ sec.) whereas the /θ/+bad blocks took 37.34 seconds to complete ($SD=9.26$). In other words, the /θ/+good blocks took, on average, 3.65 seconds ($SD=6.76$ sec.) longer than /θ/+bad blocks. This is an average duration difference of 11.37% ($SD=19.7\%$) per participant between blocks. According to the results of the paired samples t-test, this difference was significant and had a moderate effect size ($t_{122}=5.992$, $p<0.001$, 95% CI [2.45, 4.86], Cohen's $d=.540$). Moreover, out of the 123 participants, over three quarters ($n=95$) had a slower response time with the /θ/+good blocks than the /θ/+bad blocks. Figure 1 displays these results visually as boxplots.

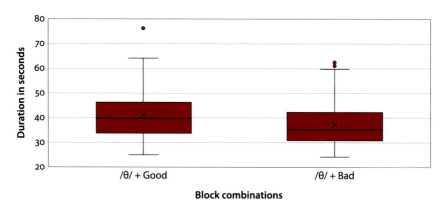

Figure 1. Box and whisker plot of block combinations and duration

In line with the overall longer duration to complete the /θ/+good blocks, although it only had a small effect size, it was found that participants committed significantly more categorization errors within the /θ/+good blocks ($M=3.77$) than /θ/+bad blocks ($M=3.00$) ($t_{122}=-3.083$, $p=0.03$, 95% CI [−1.268, −.276], Cohen's $d=-.278$).

Questionnaire results

In this section, the results of several items on the background questionnaire are reported, beginning with the participants' self-reported /θ/ use, followed by their attitudes and beliefs regarding pronunciation and the Peninsular Spanish language and culture in comparison to Latin American language and culture in general. We conclude the section by presenting the participants' attitudes and beliefs regarding Peninsular Spanish /θ/ in particular.

With regard to the students' self-reported use of the Peninsular Spanish /θ/, the responses to the question "Do you use the Spanish 'theta' when you speak Spanish?" show that over two-thirds of the students (71.5%) indicated that they do not use it (see Table 2 below). However, only 17.1% indicated that they didn't think they would ever use it, and nearly half of the students (46.4%) indicated that they either use the /θ/ to some degree or would like to learn to use it.

Table 2. Self-reported use of the Peninsular Spanish /θ/

Response	k	%
No, and I don't think I ever will	21	17.2
No, but it's possible in the future	44	36.1
No, but I want to learn to use it	22	18.0
Yes, but not always	29	23.8
Yes, as much as I can	6	4.9
Total	122	100.0

In Table 3, we see the students' overall ratings for the statements regarding Peninsular Spanish language and culture and, in some cases, how it compares to Latin American language and culture. For the presentation of the results, the responses were converted into numerical form using the following scale: Scale: −2 Strongly disagree, 0 Neither Agree/Disagree, +2 Strongly Agree.

Table 3. Opinions of dialect and culture from Spain

Attitude/belief statements	M rating	SD
I think Spanish spoken in Spain is beautiful	+.83	.81
I like Latin American Spanish more than Spain Spanish	+.43	.90
I think Latin American culture tends to be more interesting than Spain culture	+.23	.94
The world would be a better place if everyone lived like people from Spain	−.45	.89
Native speakers from Spain are easier to understand than native speakers from Latin America	−.47	.77
The Spanish spoken in Spain is more pure than Latin American Spanish	−.56	.85

Students overall agreed that the Spanish spoken in Spain is beautiful. However, they slightly agreed that they liked Latin American Spanish better and thought that Latin American culture was more interesting than Spain's culture. They also slightly disagreed that the world would be better if people lived like Spaniards, that native speakers from Spain were easier to understand than Latin Americans, and that the Spanish spoken in Spain was purer than the Spanish in Latin America.

In Table 4, the results for the ratings of the statements regarding the students' attitudes/beliefs related to the Peninsular Spanish /θ/ are presented.

The only statement that the students generally agreed with was that they love to hear native speakers use the Peninsular Spanish /θ/, a statement that they over-

Table 4. Attitude/belief statements regarding the Peninsular Spanish /θ/

Attitude/belief statements	M rating	SD
I love to hear a native speaker use the 'theta'	+.48	.88
I have a more difficult time understanding native speakers who use the 'theta'	+.15	.96
I think it sounds great when non-native speakers use the 'theta' in Spanish	+.04	.73
The Spanish 'theta' sounds like a lisp or speech impediment	+.02	1.12
I think it sounds weird when non-native speakers use the 'theta' in Spanish	−.31	.96
The Spanish 'theta' sounds feminine	−.49	.86
The Spanish 'theta' sounds masculine	−.59	.78

all slightly agreed with. In addition, students overall neither agreed nor disagreed with the statement that they had a more difficult time understanding speakers who employed the /θ/, that it sounded great when non-native speakers used the /θ/, and that the /θ/ sounded like a speech impediment. Finally, students slightly disagreed overall that it was weird to hear non-native speakers use the /θ/ as well as that it sounded feminine or masculine.

Correlations between block completion durations and independent variables

In order to determine which factors significantly constrained participants' performance on the IAT task, we calculated the mean percent difference between the /θ/+good blocks and the /θ/+bad blocks to normalize the results across participants since each participant completed the task at a different rate. Then a linear stepwise regression was run with the dependent variable being percent difference of duration between the /θ/+good and /θ/+bad blocks and the independent variables listed in Table 1.

The results of the regression were significant ($F(1,81) = 7.925$, $p < 0.001$, with an R^2 of .144) and revealed that two independent variables significantly constrained percent difference between /θ/+good and /θ/+bad blocks: Selecting "Expand my circle of friends" as a primary reason for studying Spanish and students' overall opinions of the /θ/ (see Table 5).

However, an R^2 of .144 indicates that only 14.4% of the variation was explained by the model.

The first factor that was included was whether students reported that one of the primary reasons for studying Spanish was to expand their circle of friends. For this factor, those who reported this reason had a significantly higher percentage change between θ/+good versus the /θ/+bad blocks; that is, they had significantly longer duration in the /θ/+good versus the /θ/+bad blocks.

Table 5. Stepwise regression of duration between /θ/+good and /θ/+bad blocks

Variable	Unstandardized coefficients B	Std. error	Standardized coefficients Beta	95% confidence interval Lower bound	Upper bound	p value
Expand my circle of friends	.305	.119	.270	.068	.541	.012
Overall opinions of the /θ/	−.056	.024	−.246	−.104	−.008	.022

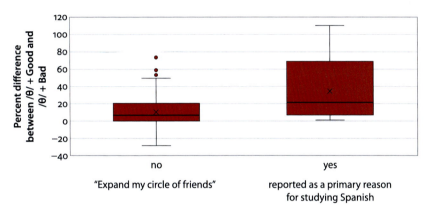

Figure 2. Box and whisker plot of expand circle of friends by percent difference between /θ/+good vs. /θ/+bad blocks

The other factor that was included in the model was the students' opinions of the /θ/, that is, the total score of the positive minus negative ratings of the /θ/. In this case, higher overall positive opinions led to significantly lower percent change between blocks, or in other words, the students with higher overall ratings of the /θ/ varied less in the overall duration between /θ/+good and /θ/+bad blocks.

The factors that were not significant and as such excluded from the model were IAT /θ/ side, /θ/+good/bad order, number of errors, Spanish level, language contact, teacher from Spain, opinions of dialect and culture from Spain, opinions of /θ/, /θ/ awareness, /θ/ use, Spanish variety, and level of intrinsic motivation to learn Spanish.

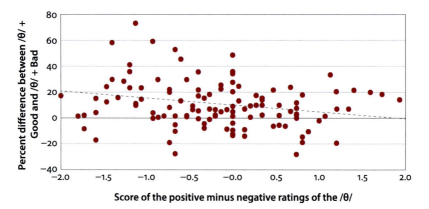

Figure 3. Scatter plot of the positive minus negative ratings by percent difference between /θ/+good vs. /θ/+bad blocks
Note. Scale: −2 Strongly Disagree, 0 Neither Agree/Disagree, +2 Strongly Agree

Discussion

This study aimed to investigate implicit biases toward the Peninsular Spanish interdental fricative /θ/ among L2 learners of Spanish and to examine factors constraining these biases. Our findings offer new insights into the complex relationship among language attitudes, sociolinguistic competence, and L2 acquisition.

Implicit bias toward /θ/

Our results revealed an implicit negative bias against the Peninsular Spanish /θ/ among beginner-level L2 learners. Participants demonstrated significantly longer response times and more errors when associating /θ/ with positive words compared to negative words in the IAT. This finding aligns with previous research suggesting learners' reluctance to produce the /θ/ (Geeslin & Gudmestad, 2008; Knouse, 2012; Ringer-Hilfinger, 2012) but provides novel evidence that this reluctance may stem from unconscious negative associations rather than solely explicit attitudes.

The presence of implicit bias at early stages of acquisition is particularly noteworthy. It suggests that even before extensive exposure to the target language, learners have already formed meaningful sociolinguistic categories (Lindemann, 2003) and associated implicit attitudes with specific phonological features. This may be due to the formation of negative biases through repeated past exposure (Petty et al., 2009) or personal experiences and feelings towards a given variant (Álvarez-Mosquera & Marín-Gutiérrez, 2018). These biases can develop even if the exposure was not in the L2 but rather related to stigmatized uses of the variant in the native language (e.g., the /θ/ being considered a lisp). This early development of implicit attitudes may help explain the persistent difficulty learners face in acquiring and producing the /θ/, even after extended exposure and instruction (Stevens, 2017).

Factors constraining implicit bias

Contrary to our expectations, many factors included in the study did not significantly constrain implicit bias, including proficiency level (e.g. Geeslin & Gudmestad, 2008), contact with Spanish, exposure to Peninsular Spanish teachers, or explicit opinions about Spanish dialects and cultures. This lack of significance across multiple factors may be an artifact of the participant pool being rather homogenous (e.g., all participants were beginner level learners) or the lack of variation in certain responses in the questionnaire (participants generally had positive opinions about the Peninsular Spanish dialect and culture). Whatever the cause may be, this finding underscores the strength and persistence of the implicit bias against /θ/ for our participants.

However, two factors did emerge as significant predictors of implicit bias in the regression model: (1) selecting "Expand my circle of friends" as a primary motivation for studying Spanish, and (2) overall explicit opinions of /θ/. Interestingly, those who reported expanding their social circle as a motivation showed stronger negative implicit bias against the /θ/. This counterintuitive finding may reflect a desire to acquire a more "neutral" or widely-accepted accent to facilitate broader social connections (Pekarek Doehler, 2019). On the other hand, unlike previous research (Pantos & Perkins, 2012), more positive explicit opinions of /θ/ significantly correlated with reduced implicit bias against the /θ/ on the IAT task, suggesting some alignment between explicit and implicit attitudes. However, the predictiveness of the regression model was low given that these two factors only explained 14.4% of the variation. The lack of a clear and strong correlation between implicit and explicit attitudes may be a result of students' desire to report a more socially tolerant attitude and avoid revealing a more socially unacceptable bias, as suggested in previous research (Baron & Banaji, 2006; de Jong et al., 2003; Lane et al., 2007).

The fact that proficiency level and language contact did not significantly impact implicit bias also warrants further investigation. While our study focused on beginner-level learners with limited exposure to Spanish, future research should examine whether implicit biases persist or change among intermediate and advanced learners with substantially more exposure to Spanish. Just as learners at higher levels of proficiency/exposure have been shown to produce the /θ/ more frequently (Geeslin & Gudmestad, 2008; Knouse, 2012), it is possible that increased exposure and mastery of Spanish could lead to shifts in implicit attitudes over time.

Theoretical implications

Our findings contribute to ongoing discussions in both second language acquisition (SLA) and sociolinguistics regarding the role of attitudes in language learning. The lack of a strong connection between explicit and implicit attitudes toward /θ/ supports dual-process models of cognition (Petty et al., 2009) and highlights the need to consider both types of attitudes in SLA research. This study also reinforces the importance of examining specific linguistic features, rather than only general language attitudes, to understand the nuanced ways in which sociolinguistic competence develops in L2 learners.

The persistence of implicit bias across various learner characteristics challenges simplistic notions of exposure leading directly to acquisition. Instead, it suggests a complex interplay between cognitive, social, and affective factors in the development of sociolinguistic competence (Schmidt et al., 2022). Our results indicate that internal factors, such as attitudes and implicit biases, may play a more significant role in the acquisition of regional variants than previously recognized.

Pedagogical and programmatic implications

Attitudes towards the language, its speakers, and the culture associated with it can significantly impact language learning as they shape the learner's experience and outcomes in acquiring the new language (Kersten & Winsler, 2023). Positive attitudes towards the target language often foster greater motivation and a deeper investment in learning, leading to improved linguistic outcomes (Gardner, 1985; Ushioda, 2009). Conversely, negative attitudes can result in diminished interest and effort, potentially hindering the acquisition process and limiting proficiency (Dörnyei, 2001).

Pedagogical approaches in SLA often seek to address and positively shape learners' linguistic attitudes. Instructional practices that validate and incorporate learners' existing linguistic identities and experiences can mitigate negative attitudes and build a more inclusive and supportive learning environment (Norton, 2000). Learners often develop preferences for certain dialects or registers based on perceived prestige or familiarity, which can influence their language use and acquisition (Dragojevic et al., 2017). Understanding these preferences allows educators to design more effective curricula that address learners' attitudes and encourage the acquisition of a broader linguistic repertoire. Additionally, addressing any biases or negative attitudes towards a certain variety can promote a more holistic and flexible approach to language learning and enhance learners' ability to connect with speakers from different regions through addressing the diverse ways in which the target language is used globally (Garrett, 2010). Study abroad programs, in particular, may need to reassess their approaches. While immersion experiences may facilitate the acquisition of certain regional variants (Pozzi & Bayley, 2021), our findings suggest that pre-existing implicit biases could hinder this process, as suggested in previous research (e.g., Linford et al., 2021). Thus, pre-departure orientation programs might benefit from activities designed to uncover and address these biases before students encounter the target dialect in situ.

Limitations and future directions

Although this study provides valuable insights into implicit attitudes toward /θ/, several limitations should be addressed in future research. First, the IAT is only one way to measure implicit attitudes. Future studies could employ the IAT alongside additional measures of implicit attitudes, such as matched-guise tasks, to provide a more robust assessment. Additionally, the current study only analyzed students' self-reported use of the /θ/, which may not be an accurate representation of what they actually produce when speaking Spanish, as Ringer-Hilfinger (2012) discovered. Hence, incorporating production data alongside attitudinal measures would allow for a direct examination of how implicit biases impact learners' willingness to adopt the /θ/ in their own speech.

Finally, our study focused specifically on the implicit attitudes towards one specific dialectal feature: the Peninsular Spanish /θ/. Employing the IAT to examine implicit biases toward other sociolinguistic variables in Spanish and other languages would help determine whether the patterns observed here are specific to this feature or reflect broader trends in L2 sociolinguistic development.

Conclusion

This study provides evidence of the presence of implicit biases against the Peninsular Spanish /θ/ among U.S. L2 learners of Spanish, even at early stages of acquisition. These biases persist across various learner characteristics and demonstrate some alignment with explicit attitudes. Our findings underscore the complex nature of the development of sociolinguistic competence in L2 learners and highlight the need for a more nuanced approach to examining linguistic variation in SLA contexts. By addressing both explicit and implicit attitudes, language educators and programs can better support learners in developing the sociolinguistic competence necessary for effective communication across diverse Spanish-speaking contexts.

References

Abreu, L. (2016). Awareness of racial diversity in the Spanish-speaking world among L2 Spanish speakers. *Foreign Language Annals*, 49(1), 180–190.

Álvarez-Mosquera, P., & Marín-Gutiérrez, A. (2018). Implicit language attitudes toward historically white accents in the South African context. *Journal of Language and Social Psychology*, 37(2), 238–248.

Baker, C. (1992). *Attitudes and language*. Multilingual Matters.

Baker, W. (2008). Social, experiential and psychological factors affecting L2 dialect acquisition. In M. Bowles, R. Foote, S. Peripiñán, & R. Bhatt (Eds.), *Selected proceedings of the 2007 second language research forum* (pp. 187–198). Cascadilla Proceedings Project.

Baron, A. S., & Banaji, M. R. (2006). The development of implicit attitudes: Evidence of race evaluations from ages 6 and 10 and adulthood. *Psychological Science*, 17(1), 53–58.

Canale, M., & Swain, M. (1980). Theoretical bases of communicative approaches to second language teaching and testing. *Applied Linguistics*, 1(1), 1–47.

Carpenter, T. P., Pogacar, R., Pullig, C., Kouril, M., Aguilar, S., LaBouff, J., … & Chakroff, A. (2019). Survey-software implicit association tests: A methodological and empirical analysis. *Behavior Research Methods*, 51, 2194–2208.

Chappell, W., & Kanwit, M. (2022). Do learners connect sociophonetic variation with regional and social characteristics?: The case of L2 perception of Spanish aspiration. *Studies in Second Language Acquisition*, 44(1), 185–209.

Cigliana, K. A., & Serrano, R. (2016). Individual differences in US study abroad students in Barcelona: A look into their attitudes, motivations and L2 contact. *Study Abroad Research in Second Language Acquisition and International Education*, 1(2), 154–185.

Ciller, J. F., & Fernández-Flórez, C. (2016). On attitudes toward Spanish varieties: A bilingual perspective. *Todas as Letras-Revista de Língua e Literatura*, 18(2), 98–116.

Cohen, A. D., Paige, R. M., Shively, R. L., Emert, H. A., & Hoff, J. G. (2005). Integrating language and culture learning strategies into the classroom at home and abroad. In L. C. Anderson (Ed.), *Internationalizing undergraduate education: Integrating study abroad into the curriculum* (pp. 103–108). Learning Abroad Center, University of Minnesota.

Czerwionka, L., & Olson, D. J. (2020). Pragmatic development during study abroad: L2 intensifiers in spoken Spanish. *International Journal of Learner Corpus Research*, 6(2), 125–162.

Davies, M., & Davies, K. H. (2017). *A frequency dictionary of Spanish: Core vocabulary for learners*. Routledge.

De Jong, P. J., van den Hout, M. A., Rietbroek, H., & Huijding, J. (2003). Dissociations between implicit and explicit attitudes toward phobic stimuli. *Cognition & Emotion*, 17, 521–545.

Devos, T. (2008). Implicit attitudes 101: Theoretical and empirical insights. In W. D. Crano & R. Prislin (Eds.), *Attitudes and attitude change* (pp. 61–86). Psychology Press.

Díaz-Campos, M., & Killam, J. (2012). Assessing language attitudes through a matched-guise experiment: The case of consonantal deletion in Venezuelan Spanish. *Hispania*, 95(1), 83–102.

Dörnyei, Z. (2001). *Motivational strategies in the language classroom*. Cambridge University Press.

Dörnyei, Z. & Taguchi, T. (2010). *Questionnaires in second language research: Construction, administration, and processing.* Routledge.

Dragojevic, M., West, K. J., & DeBono, K. (2017). The role of language and accent in the communication of social identity. *Journal of Language and Social Psychology, 36*(1), 5–28.

Escalante, C. (2018). The acquisition of a sociolinguistic variable while volunteering abroad: S-weakening among heritage- and L2 learners in coastal Ecuador. University of California, Davis dissertation.

Freed, B., Dewey, D., Segalowitz, N., & Halter, R. (2004). The Language Contact Profile. *Studies in Second Language Acquisition, 26*(2), 349–356.

Gardner, R. C. (1985). *Social psychology and second language learning: The role of attitudes and motivation.* Edward Arnold.

Garrett, P. (2010). *Attitudes to language.* Cambridge University Press.

Geeslin, K. L., & Gudmestad, A. (2008). The acquisition of variation in second-language Spanish: An agenda for integrating studies of the L2 sound system. *Journal of Applied Linguistics, 5*(2), 137–158.

Geeslin, K. L., García-Amaya, L. J., Hasler-Barker, M., Henriksen, N. C., & Killam, J. (2012). The L2 acquisition of variable perfective past time reference in Spanish in an overseas immersion setting. In K. Geeslin & M. Díaz-Campos (Eds.), *Selected proceedings of the 14th Hispanic Linguistics Symposium* (pp. 197–213). Cascadilla Proceedings Project.

George, A. (2014). Study abroad in central Spain: The development of regional phonological features. *Foreign Language Annals, 47*(1), 97–114.

Giles, H. (1970). Evaluative reactions to accents. *Educational Review, 22,* 211–227.

Gluszek, A., & Dovidio, J. (2010). The way they speak: A social psychological perspective on the stigma of nonnative accents in communication. *Personality and Social Psychology Review, 14,* 214–237.

Grammon, D. (2021). Consequential choices: a language ideological perspective on learners' (non-)adoption of a dialectal variant. *Foreign Language Annals, 54*(3), 607–625.

Greenwald, T., Banaji, M., & Nosek, B. (2011). About the IAT — Project Implicit. Project Implicit. Retrieved August 5, 2024, from https://www.projectimplicit.net/resources/about-the-iat/

Guasch, M., Espunya, A., & Pujol, D. (2016). Linguistic identity and language attitudes in bilingual families with young children. *Journal of Multilingual and Multicultural Development, 37*(2), 165–179.

Ianos, M. A., Rusu, A., Huguet, À., & Lapresta-Rey, C. (2023). Implicit language attitudes in Catalonia (Spain): investigating preferences for Catalan or Spanish using the Implicit Association Test. *Journal of Multilingual and Multicultural Development, 44*(3), 214–229.

IBM Corp. Released 2021. *IBM SPSS Statistics for Windows, Version 28.0.* IBM Corp.

Kersten, K., & Winsler, A. (2023). *Understanding variability in second language acquisition, bilingualism, and cognition.* Routledge.

Kinzler, D., Shutts, K., DeJesus, J., & Spelke, E. S. (2009). Accent trumps race in guiding children's social preferences. *Social Cognition, 27,* 623–634.

Knouse, S. M. (2012). The acquisition of dialectal phonemes in a study abroad context: The case of the Castilian 'theta'. *Foreign Language Annals, 45*(4), 512–542.

Lambert, W. E., Hodgson, R. C., Gardner, R. C., & Fillenbaum, S. (1960). Evaluational reactions to spoken languages. *The Journal of Abnormal and Social Psychology, 60*(1), 44–51.

Lane, K. A., Banaji, M. R., Nosek, B. A., & Greenwald, A. G. (2007). Understanding and using the Implicit Association Test: IV. What we know (so far) about the method. In B. Wittenbrink & N. Schwarz (Eds.), *Implicit measures of attitudes* (pp. 59-102). Guilford Press.

Lindemann, S. (2003). Koreans, Chinese or Indians? Attitudes and ideologies about nonnative English speakers in the United States. *Journal of Sociolinguistics, 7*, 348-364.

Linford, B. (2014). Self-reported motivation and the L2 acquisition of subject pronoun variation in Spanish. In R. Miller, K. Martin, C. Eddington, A. Henery, N. Marcos Miguel, A. Tseng, A. Tuninetti, & D. Walter (Eds.), *Selected proceedings of the 2012 Second Language Research Forum: Building bridges between disciplines* (pp. 193-210).

Linford, B., Harley, A., & Brown, E. K. (2021). Second language acquisition of /s/-weakening in a study abroad context. *Studies in Second Language Acquisition, 43*(2), 403-427.

Lippi-Green, R. (2011). *English with an accent: language, ideology and discrimination in the United States* (2nd ed.). Routledge.

Madariaga, J. M., Huguet, Á., & Janés, J. (2016). Language attitudes in Catalan multilingual classrooms: educational implications. *Language and Intercultural Communication, 16*(2), 216-234.

McKenzie, R. M., & Carrie, E. (2018). Implicit–explicit attitudinal discrepancy and the investigation of language attitude change in progress. *Journal of Multilingual and Multicultural Development, 39*(9), 830-844.

Montrul, S. (2012). DELE proficiency test. *Unpublished instrument*. Retrieved from http://international.ucla.edu/nhlrc/data/example

Montrul, S., Foote, R., & Perpiñán, S. (2008). Gender agreement in adult second language learners and Spanish heritage speakers: The effects of age and context of acquisition. *Language Learning, 58*(3), 503-553.

Norton, B. (2000). *Identity and language learning: Gender, ethnicity and educational change*. Longman/Pearson Education.

Pantos, A. J., & Perkins, A. W. (2012). Measuring implicit and explicit attitudes toward foreign accented speech. *Journal of Language and Social Psychology, 32*(1), 3-20.

Pekarek Doehler, S. (2019). L2 interactional competence and L2 education. In S. Kunitz, N. Markee, & O. Sert (Eds.), *Classroom-based conversation analytic research: Theoretical and applied perspectives on pedagogy*. Springer.

Petty, R. E., Brinol, P., & Priester, J. R. (2009). Mass media attitude change: Implications of the elaboration likelihood model of persuasion. In J. Bryan & M. B. Oliver (Eds.), *Media effects* (pp. 141-180). Routledge.

Pozzi, R. (2022). Acquiring sociolinguistic competence during study abroad: US students in Buenos Aires. In R. Bayley, R., D. R. Preston, & X. Li (Eds), *Variation in second and heritage languages* (pp. 199-222). John Benjamins.

Pozzi, R., & Bayley, R. (2021). The development of a regional phonological feature during a semester abroad in Argentina. *Studies in Second Language Acquisition, 43*(1), 109-132.

Pujolar, J. (2009). Immigration and language education in Catalonia: Between national and social agendas. *Linguistics and Education, 20*(4), 229-243.

Raish, M. (2015). The acquisition of an Egyptian phonological variant by U.S. students in Cairo. *Foreign Language Annals, 48*(2), 267-283.

Ringer-Hilfinger, K. (2012). Learner acquisition of dialect variation in a study abroad context: The case of the Spanish [θ]. *Foreign Language Annals, 45*(3), 430-446.

Rydell, R. J., & A. R. McConnell. (2006). Understanding implicit and explicit attitude change: A systems reasoning analysis. *Journal of Personality and Social Psychology*, 91(6), 995–1008.

Schmidt, L. B. (2018). L2 development of perceptual categorization of dialectal sounds: A study in Spanish. *Studies in Second Language Acquisition*, 40(4), 857–882.

Schmidt, L. B. (2020). Role of developing language attitudes in a study abroad context on adoption of dialectal pronunciations. *Foreign Language Annals*, 53(4), 785–806.

Schmidt, L. B., & Geeslin, K. L. (2022). Developing language attitudes in a second language: Learner perceptions of regional varieties of Spanish. *Revista Española de Lingüística Aplicada/Spanish Journal of Applied Linguistics*, 35(1), 206–235.

Schmidt, L. B., Linford, B., & Fafulas, S. (2022). Regional variation. In K. Geeslin (Ed.), *The Routledge handbook of second language acquisition and sociolinguistics* (pp. 126–137). Routledge.

Schoonmaker-Gates, E. (2020). The acquisition of dialect-specific phonology, phonetics, and sociolinguistics in L2 Spanish: Untangling learner trends. *Critical Multilingual Studies*, 8(1), 80–103.

Seargeant, P. (2009). *The idea of English in Japan: Ideology and the evolution of a global language.* Multilingual Matters

Slabakova, R., Kempchinsky, P., & Rothman, J. (2012). Clitic-doubled left dislocation and focus fronting in L2 Spanish: A case of successful acquisition at the syntax–discourse interface. *Second Language Research*, 28(3), 319–343.

Stadthagen-Gonzalez, H., Imutan, T., & Szecsi, T. (2017). Attitudes towards different varieties of spoken English in an international context. *Journal of Multilingual and Multicultural Development*, 38(4), 331–346.

Starr, R. L. (2022). Production and evaluation of sociolinguistic variation in Mandarin Chinese among children in Singapore. In R. Bayley, D. R. Preston, & X. Li (Eds.), *Variation in second and heritage languages* (pp. 43–70). John Benjamins.

Stevens, J. (2017). The acquisition of Spanish 'theta' in a study abroad context. *MIFLC Review*, 18, 177–205.

Tse, H. (2022). What can Cantonese heritage speakers tell us about age of acquisition, linguistic dominance, and sociophonetic variation?. In R. Bayley, D. R. Preston, & X. Li (Eds.), *Variation in second and heritage languages* (pp. 97–126). John Benjamins.

Ushioda, E. (2009). A person-in-context relational view of emergent motivation, self and identity. In Z. Dörnyei & E. Ushioda (Eds.), *Motivation, language identity and the L2 self* (pp. 215–228). Multilingual Matters.

van Compernolle, R. A., & Williams, L. (2012). Teaching, learning, and developing L2 French sociolinguistic competence: A sociocultural perspective. *Applied Linguistics*, 33(2), 184–205.

White, L., Valenzuela, E., Kozlowska–Macgregor, M., & Leung, Y. K. I. (2004). Gender and number agreement in nonnative Spanish. *Applied Psycholinguistics*, 25(1), 105–133.

Zhang, P., Li, J., & Zhuang, H. (2022). The effect of Chinese perfective aspect marker *le* on the simple past use in English interlanguage. In R. Tong, Y. Lu, M. Dong, W. Gong, & H. Li (Eds.), *2022 International Conference on Asian Language Processing (IALP)* (pp. 329–334). IEEE.

Appendix A. Description of each block in the IAT

Block	# of trials	Function	Labels: left of screen	Stimuli	Labels: right of screen
1	32	Practice	Good	marvelous, superb, pleasure, beautiful, joyful, glorious, lovely, wonderful, tragic, horrible, agony, painful, terrible, awful, humiliate, nasty.	Bad
2	16	Practice	'th' sound	cele_s, cipo_s, zapa_s, zulo_s cele_z, cipo_z, zapa_z, zulo_z	's' sound
3	32	Test	Good + 'th' sound	Evaluative traits + s/z word-audios	Bad + 's' sound
4	16	Practice	's' sound	cele_s, cipo_s, zapa_s, zulo_s cele_z, cipo_z, zapa_z, zulo_z	'th' sound
5	32	Test	Bad + 'th' sound	Evaluative traits + s/z word-audios	Good + 's' sound

Note. The side of the screen and the order in which the combinations appeared in Blocks III and V were randomized for each participant.

Appendix B. Image of what participants saw on the screen on the testing blocks while listening to the different words (in this case, *cele*)

Good
or
'th' sound

Bad
or
's' sound

cele

Press E or I to advance to the next word/image. Correct mistakes by pressing the other key.

CHAPTER 4

Revisiting the acquisition of the variable perfective past in L2 Spanish during short-term study abroad

Nicholas M. Blaker & Thomas Goebel-Mahrle
Indiana University

This study investigates the acquisition of past-time in L2 Spanish, focusing on variation between the preterite and present perfect (PP) through a combined variationist/concept-oriented approach. Learners before and after study abroad (SA) in León, Spain, and native speakers (NSs) from the same region completed a contextualized verb elicitation task, examining influence of temporal reference and telicity on written verb forms. Participants used various verb forms, and learners increased their preterite use, but they did not use the PP after SA. Mixed-effects models indicated that telicity and time of data collection constrained learners' past-time use; only temporal reference influenced NSs' use of the preterite and PP. Results suggest general development of past-time expression in L2 Spanish rather than acquisition of the variation between the preterite and PP.

Keywords: L2 Spanish, L2 variation, study abroad, present perfect, tense and aspect, variationist sociolinguistics, Leonese Spanish, language attitudes

Research into second language (L2) acquisition of variable morphosyntactic structures in the short-term study abroad (SA) context has expanded substantially over the last decade (Geeslin, 2022). Several studies have investigated the acquisition of variation between the preterite and present perfect (hereafter PP) in L2 Spanish during short-term SA given that both forms can express perfectivity in Peninsular Spanish (Geeslin et al., 2012; Kanwit et al., 2015; Linford, 2016; Zahler & Whatley, 2023). In Peninsular Spanish, the PP is moving into the semantic domain of the preterite and is favored in hodiernal contexts (i.e., eventualities that occur the same day as speech time) while also appearing in indeterminate past-time contexts and to a lesser degree in hesternal and pre-hesternal contexts (e.g., Schwenter, 1994; Schwenter & Torres Cacoullos, 2008; Serrano, 1994).

Prior studies into the acquisition of preterite and PP variation during SA have shown that learners were able to adjust frequency of selection/use of the preterite and PP and develop sensitivity to the linguistic factors (e.g., temporal reference) that constrained selection/use of these forms in line with native speakers (NSs; Geeslin et al., 2012; Kanwit et al., 2015; Linford, 2016). Nonetheless, Zahler and Whatley (2023) found evidence that when at-home learners and SA learners were compared, both groups behaved similarly regardless of learning context. Despite divergent findings, what unites these previous accounts is near exclusive use of a contextualized preference task (CPT) in which learners indicate a preference between given options within a specific context. While CPTs have multiple benefits (see Kanwit, 2022 for an overview), they do not provide insights into learner production. There are other tasks (e.g., contextualized verb elicitation tasks) that can provide the researcher with similar benefits while also obtaining learner production albeit controlled (Gudmestad, 2012).

This investigation explores what L2 Spanish learners do when they are not asked to select between predetermined options but rather to provide their own preferred written form. We adopt a combined variationist/concept-oriented approach to second language acquisition (SLA; Kanwit, 2017) to investigate not only L2 Spanish learners' acquisition of preterite and PP variation, but also their acquisition of past-time more generally. Our results can be examined in relation to previous findings from studies that have used a CPT under similar SA learning conditions (Geeslin et al., 2012; Kanwit et al., 2015; Whatley & Zahler, 2023) to provide a more comprehensive view of what has been observed in both production and selection.

Background

A combined approach to SLA

The variationist approach to SLA

Based on the foundations of variationist sociolinguistics (Labov, 1972), the variationist approach to SLA investigates the frequency of use of a given form and the (extra)linguistic factors that constrain this form with learners (Geeslin, 2020). The influence of (extra)linguistic variables and the intricate connection between them are revealed through use of multivariate statistical analyses to uncover the constraints that govern learners' language patterns and how these constraints compare to NSs' (Bayley & Tarone, 2012; Geeslin, 2020; Gudmestad, 2014). The variationist approach to SLA distinguishes between Type 1 and Type 2 variation (Rehner, 2002). Type 1 variation refers to variation between a targetlike and nontargetlike form, and Type 2 variation refers to variation between grammatical forms by and among NSs (i.e., sociolinguistic variation). The acquisition of Type 2 variation can contribute to learners' sociolinguistic competence (Canale & Swain, 1980; Rehner, 2002).

The concept-oriented approach and the combined variationist/concept-oriented approach to SLA

The concept-oriented approach "identifies one function, concept, or meaning and investigates how it is expressed" (Bardovi-Harlig, 2020, p. 41). The primary construct within the concept-oriented approach is the concept, which can be understood broadly (e.g., temporality) or narrowly (e.g., past-time; Bardovi-Harlig, 2020). A concept-oriented approach "seeks to explain how meanings within a larger concept are expressed at a given time, and how the expression of the concept changes over time" (Bardovi-Harlig, 2020, p. 42). The importance of examining all forms that express a similar function (e.g., past-time) as opposed to two or three forms has been highlighted in the variationist approach to SLA. For example, Geeslin and Gudmestad (2010, p. 437) stated that "overlooking the full range of forms that occurs in a given context is in direct conflict with the conceptualization of interlanguage as a complex system".

Therefore, a combined variationist/concept-oriented approach to SLA permits an examination of the acquisition and use of not only the preterite and PP but all possible forms that form part of the functional domain of past-time (Kanwit, 2017). While previous studies (i.e., Geeslin et al., 2012; Kanwit et al., 2015; Linford, 2016; Zahler & Whatley, 2023) focus specifically on the acquisition of the preterite and PP variation, additional work on the acquisition of past-time in L2 Spanish has shown that learners use a variety of forms to express past-time (e.g., Terán, 2020). Thus, adopting the combined approach permits us to explore not only the acquisition of variation between preterite and PP, but all forms used to express past-time before and after SA.

Tense and aspect in Spanish

Following Comrie (1976), tense "relates the time of the situation referred to (…) some other time" (pp. 1–2). Comrie (1976) distinguishes between the present (the moment of speaking), past (prior to the moment of speaking), and future (subsequent to the moment of speaking). Contrastingly, aspect refers to "different ways of viewing the internal temporal constituency of a situation" (Comrie, 1976, p. 3). The term *aspect* can be further partitioned into grammatical and lexical aspect (De Miguel, 1999). Grammatical aspect is primarily expressed through verbal morphology. In Spanish, aspectual distinctions in the past are primarily expressed via the preterite and imperfect opposition. The preterite expresses perfective aspect in which the situation is viewed as temporally bounded as in (1), while the imperfect denotes imperfective aspect, and the situation is not viewed as bounded (Bybee et al., 1994). The imperfect also expresses a range of additional meanings in the past such as continuous as in (2), progressive as in (3), and habitual as in (4) (Fábregas, 2015).

(1) *Juan tomó un café.*
Juan drank-PFV a coffee.
'Juan drank a coffee.'

(2) *Juan era alto.*
Juan was-IPFV tall.
'Juan was tall.'

(3) *En ese momento, Juan tomaba un café.*
In that moment, Juan was drinking-IPFV a coffee.
'In that moment, Juan was drinking a coffee.'

(4) *Todos los días, Juan tomaba un café.*
Every day, Juan drank-IPFV a coffee.
'Every day, Juan drank a coffee.'

Lexical aspect is related to the underlying semantic properties of verbs or verbal predicates (Comrie, 1976; De Miguel, 1999; Smith, 1991; Vendler, 1957). Vendler (1957) classified verbal predicates into four types based on the properties of telicity, dynamicity, and punctuality. Telicity refers to whether the verbal predicate is telic (e.g., *correr una milla* 'to run a mile') and possesses an inherent endpoint, or is atelic and does not possess an inherent endpoint (e.g., *correr* 'to run'). Atelic verbs are divided into states (e.g., *estar* 'to be'), which are not dynamic and do not require energy, while activities (e.g., *correr* 'to run') are dynamic and lack an inherent endpoint. Telic verbs are partitioned into accomplishments (e.g., *escribir un ensayo* 'to write an essay'), requiring time to carry out the event, while achievements (e.g., *llegar* 'to arrive') are punctual and have no or minimal duration (Smith, 1991).

Grammaticalization of the preterite and present perfect in Spanish

A present perfect is a verbal form used to denote a past event that has current relevance. Comrie (1976) describes the perfect as "indicat[ing] the continuing present relevance of a past situation" (p. 52). Within the Romance family, perfects are not only used to express their canonical perfect meaning, but in many languages have also developed a perfective meaning resulting in variation between the PP and simple past (e.g., the preterite in Spanish) where the PP is supplanting simple past forms. The movement of the PP into the semantic domain of the preterite has been termed *aoristic drift* (Squartini & Bertinetto, 2000) and is common cross-linguistically.

It has been argued that Romance languages can be described as sitting at one of four distinct stages of grammaticalization which roughly align with Comrie's four 'types' of perfects (Comrie, 1976). These stages and the languages whose perfect meanings are closest to Comrie's perfects are exemplified in Figure 1 below, adopted from Schwenter and Torres Cacoullos (2008). As seen in Figure 1, different varieties of Spanish (e.g., Latin American and Peninsular Spanish) are at different stages (Harris, 1982; Howe, 2013). For example, the Latin American perfect is said to be between stages II and III. Perfects at stage II may have an iterative reading or be used for durative situations (i.e., a past situation that continues into the present). The PP at Stage III is represented by Peninsular Spanish and denotes a past event with current relevance. Furthermore, Peninsular Spanish also sits between Stages III and IV (i.e., the PP is used with its prototypical perfect meaning and perfective meaning; Harris, 1982; Schwenter, 1994).

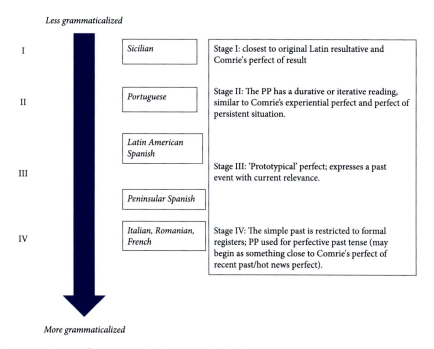

Figure 1. Stages of present perfect grammaticalization

Given that the PP is at various stages on the cline of grammaticalization in different Spanish varieties, this has led to variation between the preterite and PP forms. For instance, in Latin American Spanish, it is common for the preterite to be used in hodiernal perfective contexts, as in (5), while in Peninsular Spanish, the PP is employed in this context, as in (6).

(5) *Esta mañana corrí cinco millas.*
    This morning I ran-PFV five miles.
    'This morning, I ran five miles.'

(6) *Esta mañana he corrido cinco millas.*
    This morning I have run-PRF five miles.
    'This morning, I ran/have run five miles.'

Research into individual varieties of Spanish, especially in Latin America (e.g., Howe, 2013), has shown divergent paths of development, highlighting the importance of not treating Spanish varieties as a monolith.

Use and variation of the preterite and PP in Peninsular Spanish with focus on León, Spain

Early work on preterite and PP variation in Peninsular Spanish noted that although the PP was favored in hodiernal contexts, it was also observed in hesternal and, to a lesser degree, in pre-hesternal contexts (Schwenter, 1994; Serrano, 1994). More recently, Schwenter and Torres Cacoullos (2008) compared use of the preterite and PP in Mexico City and Madrid to determine whether the PP was constrained similarly across varieties. The PP was favored in hodiernal, indeterminate, and irrelevant contexts in Madrid while in Mexico City, it was disfavored in hodiernal and hesternal/pre-hesternal contexts. These scholars concluded that it was through indeterminate contexts where the PP was expanding and becoming the preferred marker of perfectivity within Peninsular Spanish.

Speakers in Galicia, Asturias, and León have been shown to use the preterite more than the PP in hodiernal contexts contra other Peninsular varieties as detailed in Pato and Heap (2008). These scholars investigated the geographic distribution of preterite and PP variation in oral Peninsular Spanish through a comparison of linguistic atlases and corpora (Pato & Heap, 2008). They examined verbal forms produced in main clauses with temporal adverbials (e.g., *esta tarde* 'this afternoon') and without temporal adverbials. Results across datasets demonstrated a clear preference for the preterite over the PP in hodiernal and pre-hesternal/hesternal contexts in Leonese Spanish, while this was different for other provinces. Despite a preference for the preterite in hodiernal contexts in Leonese Spanish, Kempas (2002) observed that the PP may also be expanding into hesternal/pre-hesternal contexts given that Leonese Spanish speakers self-reported some or exclusive use of the PP in hesternal/pre-hesternal contexts.

The acquisition of past-time in L2 Spanish

The acquisition of past-time in L2 Spanish has primarily focused on testing the predictions of the Aspect Hypothesis, the Default Past Tense Hypothesis, or the Discourse Hypothesis. However, the investigation of multiple factors on the acquisition of the preterite and imperfect (Blaker, 2024; Salaberry, 2011) and past-time more generally (Terán, 2020; Whatley, 2013) is a burgeoning area of research. The Aspect Hypothesis predicts that the emergence and use of past-time morphology is influenced by the lexical aspect of the verbal predicate (Andersen, 1991). Andersen (1991) observed that in L2 Spanish the preterite emerged first with telic predicates (achievements then accomplishments) and later with atelic predicates (activities then states), while the opposite trend was observed for imperfect marking (i.e., the imperfect emerged first with atelic predicates [states then activities] and later with telic predicates [accomplishments then achievements]). The Aspect Hypothesis has been supported in L2 Spanish studies (Hasbún, 1995; Ramsay, 1990), and lexical aspect has been observed to influence L2 Spanish learners even into advanced levels of proficiency (Cadierno, 2000; Liskin-Gasparro, 2000).

Contrary to the findings of the Aspect Hypothesis in L2 Spanish, Salaberry (1999) found that first-language (L1) English/L2 Spanish learners at lower proficiency levels were not influenced by lexical aspect and instead used high rates of the preterite regardless of lexical aspect. Salaberry (1999) proposed the Default Past Tense Hypothesis and argued that the preterite "acts as a default marker of past tense during the beginning stages of acquisition among classroom L2 learners" (p. 171). The hypothesis has been substantiated by L2 Spanish research (Camps, 2005; Terán, 2020). Nonetheless, Bardovi-Harlig and Comojoan-Colomé (2020) explain that the Default Past Tense Hypothesis does not contradict the Aspect Hypothesis, but explains the acquisition of the preterite and imperfect in certain language pairs (e.g., L1 English and L2 Spanish), primarily with beginners and in the classroom context.

The Discourse Hypothesis asserts that "learners use emerging verbal morphology to distinguish foreground from background in narratives" Bardovi-Harlig (1994, p. 43). Specifically, the preterite is used more in the foreground and the imperfect in the background of narratives. Since the establishment of the Discourse Hypothesis, studies have not only shown that both lexical aspect and discourse grounding influence L2 Spanish learners (Liskin-Gasparro, 2000), but also that what distinguishes learners from NSs is that learners are influenced more by lexical aspect whereas NSs appeared to be influenced more by discourse grounding in narratives. (Salaberry, 2011; Whatley, 2013).

The acquisition of the preterite and present perfect variation in L2 Spanish

Geeslin et al. (2012) examined the acquisition of the preterite and PP variation with L2 Spanish learners living and studying Spain during a seven-week immersion program. Learners completed three different versions of a CPT, while NSs from León completed the CPT once. The CPT controlled and systematically combined the linguistic variables temporal reference, telicity, anteriority (i.e., does the predicate have consequences in the present), and background information (i.e., is the predicate used with the imperfect). Participants selected their preferred verb form (i.e., preterite, PP, or *both*). The researchers analyzed the *both* response as acceptance of the PP. Learners' selection of the PP increased from Time 1 (T1) to Time 2 (T2), but decreased at Time 3 (T3) to a rate below the NSs'. Regression analyses revealed that NSs' selection of the PP was constrained only by temporal reference. Learners' selection of the PP at T1 and T2 was constrained by telicity and years of study while background information was also significant at T2. Learners' selection of the PP at T3 was constrained by temporal reference and a range of extralinguistic predictors. The researchers concluded that the learners gained sensitivity to dialectal constraints on variable perfective past expression due to their senstivitity to temporal reference at T3.

Kanwit et al. (2015)[1] investigated the acquisition of variation between the preterite and PP by L1 English-speaking learners of Spanish living and studying in Valencia, Spain during a seven-week Spanish immersion program. Native Spanish speakers from Valencia, Spain served as a comparison group. Learners completed a CPT at the beginning and at the end of the SA program, while NSs completed it once. The linguistic variables temporal reference, telicity, and frequency (i.e., presence or absence of a frequency adverbial) were systematically controlled across the task. The Spanish NSs selected the preterite and PP at similar rates and the option *both* only minimally. Learners decreased their selection of the preterite and the option *both* and increased their selection of the PP. The PP was favored with hodiernal and indeterminate contexts and telic predicates. Learners' selection of the PP was not constrained by any factors at the onset, but the PP was favored in hodiernal and indeterminate contexts in line with NSs at the end of SA.

Linford (2016)[2] investigated the acquisition of the preterite and PP with L2 Spanish learners living and studying in Madrid, Spain for four months. Native Spanish speakers from Madrid served as a comparison group. Learners completed an oral interview and a CPT that investigated the influence of temporal

---

1. See Kanwit et al. (2015) for information regarding the learners in Mexico.
2. See Linford (2016) for information regarding the learners in the Dominican Republic.

reference and (direct) object plurality at the beginning and end of SA, and NSs completed these tasks once. For the oral interview, learners increased their use of the PP and decreased their use of the preterite from T1 to T2 in line with NSs. The NSs use of the preterite and PP was constrained by temporal reference, lexical aspect, and clause type. Learners were only constrained by temporal reference at T1 and T2. Learners increased their use of the PP in hodiernal and irrelevant contexts. For the CPT, learners' selections were governed by object plurality at T1 and were constrained by temporal reference in line with NSs and object plurality contra NSs at T2. Learners increased their selection of the PP in hodiernal contexts in line with NSs, but overshot NS selection rates while preterite selection increased in the hesternal and pre-hesternal contexts.

Zahler and Whatley (2023) analyzed SA learners in Chile and Spain compared to at-home learners from multiple levels of proficiency. A control group of NSs (i.e., 11 residing in the US, seven from Chile, and five from León, Spain) was included. All participants completed a CPT. Learners in the SA groups completed the task at the beginning and end of SA. Results showed that the SA learners decreased their frequency of PP selection and developed similarly regardless of SA site. That is, learners in both Chile and Spain demonstrated similar behavior, despite being exposed to different varieties of input, as reflected by differences in constraints favoring the PP identified in the NS analysis. The authors found that both groups of SA learners performed similarly to the at-home learners. Zahler and Whatley (2023) concluded that the L2 participants showed development of past-time along an acquisitional path common to L1 English speakers, regardless of learning context, and the SA learners did not approximate regional norms of preterite and PP selection.

Building on prior research, we investigate the acquisition of past-time in L2 Spanish with a focus on the acquisition of preterite and PP variation through adoption of a combined variationist/concept-oriented approach (Kanwit, 2017). We use a controlled production task to compare learners' past-time expression before and after SA and compare these results to NSs from the same city as the SA program. Our controlled production task differs from and complements previous accounts on the acquisition of this variable structure. The present study is guided by the following research questions:

1. What forms do L2 Spanish learners use in past-time contexts before and after SA? In particular, if the preterite and PP are used, does the frequency of use of these forms change during SA, and how does this compare to NSs?
2. What linguistic and extralinguistic factors constrain forms used in a past-time context by L2 Spanish learners before and after SA, and how does this compare to NSs?

Method

Participants

A total of 23 L2 Spanish learners participated in the current study. The L2 learners were high school Spanish students from the Midwestern United States and were enrolled in a six-and-a-half-week home-stay immersion program in León, Spain. The L2 learner group was comprised of 17 women and six men with an average age of 17.3 years old. Only three participants indicated knowledge of an additional spoken language (Italian and Urdu) or language system (American Sign Language). There were three participants who indicated that at least one of their parents spoke Spanish as a native language. An independent samples *t*-test was conducted in the Statistical Package for the Social Sciences (SPSS) to determine if these three participants differed significantly on the grammar test at T1 from the other participants. There was no statistical difference between these groups ($t(21) = -.288$, $p = .776$), and all participants remained in the analysis.

Prior to participation in the immersion program, participants signed a contract that required them to use Spanish for all communication needs while abroad. All participants enrolled in the program completed Spanish courses on grammar/communication, linguistics/phonetics, and culture/literature; engaged in afternoon activities; and spent their evenings and weekends with their host families. While learners were not instructed on preterite and PP variation, learners were instructed on a range of grammatical structures (e.g., the preterite, the imperfect, the present subjunctive, etc.), and they received instruction on Spanish orthography (i.e., rules of accentuation and changes in meaning between verb forms and lexical items).

A total of 24 Spanish NSs who were born, raised, and living in León, Spain at the time of the data collection participated in the study. The NS group was comprised of 15 women and nine men with an average age of 46.8 years old. Within the NS group, 66.6% (16/24) had completed some form of post-secondary education (e.g., professionalization programs, university courses/degrees, etc.). The remaining 33.3% (8/24) of participants only completed secondary education. Among the NSs, 70.8% (17/24) indicated knowledge of one or more languages, while 29.1% (7/24) only possessed knowledge of Spanish. Additionally, 41.6% (10/24) had lived for some period outside of León with a range of two to 22 years ($M = 7.50$ years outside of León, Spain, $SD = 6.28$), but all participants had spent more than half of their lives in León.

Data elicitation

The learners completed a contextualized verb elicitation task (CVET), a grammar test, and a background questionnaire. Only the CVET and the grammar test were completed twice: T1 (day of departure to Spain) and T2 (the last week of the program). The NSs only completed the CVET and the background questionnaire. The grammar test was an 11-item discrete point test that tested learners' general knowledge of Spanish grammar structures (e.g., prepositions, mood, etc.) and served to measure changes in their general Spanish grammar knowledge from T1 to T2. This grammar test has been effectively employed in other L2 studies to measure learner general grammatical knowledge (Geeslin et al., 2012; Gudmestad, 2012; Woolsey, 2006).

The CVET was based on Gudmestad (2012) and consisted of 20 items where 12 items focused exclusively on past-time. The remaining eight items served as distractors with a focus on mood distinction. Participants read a paragraph-length discourse context in Spanish that formed a story about two Spanish-speaking friends living in León, Spain. After participants read the discourse context, they were presented with a cloze-style sentence that formed dialogue between characters in the story. Participants were asked to write in a form of the infinitive verb provided for that context. They were not instructed to write in a past-time verb form, but to provide a verb form that they preferred. This is different from a traditional CPT, which provides participants with two identical sentences that only differ by verb form and participants select their preferred sentence or they can select a *both* option. The CVET is considered a controlled production task (i.e., it is not free production) given that participants do not generate their own sentences but write-in a verb form.

The task investigated the interaction of two linguistic variables (i.e., temporal reference and telicity) because they have been found to be significant for both NSs (e.g., Schwenter & Torres Cacoullos, 2008) and L2 Spanish learners (Geeslin et al., 2012; Kanwit et al., 2015; Linford, 2016) in the selection/use and acquisition of the preterite and PP variation. *Temporal reference* consisted of three levels (i.e., hodiernal, hesternal, and pre-hesternal) given the focus on these categories in previous L2 Spanish studies (Geeslin et al., 2012; Kanwit et al., 2015; Linford, 2016) and also investigations into Peninsular (Schwenter, 1994; Serrano, 1994) and Leonese Spanish (Kempas, 2002; Pato & Heap, 2008). Telicity was comprised of two levels (i.e., atelic and telic predicates). Regarding telicity, there were an equal number of states, activities, accomplishments, and achievements used throughout the task to investigate the potential influence of lexical aspect on past-time use. Each lexical aspectual category had the same number of each of the four verb types. The diagnostics in Shirai (2013) were employed for determining lexical aspect, and interrater reliability reached 100% between researchers. These factors were equally combined (i.e., temporal reference and telicity) and resulted in six items, which were doubled and resulted in 12 target items. A NS of Spanish checked the final task for grammatical accuracy and general naturalness. A sample item from the task is provided in (7); the coding matrix is hodiernal + telic (accomplishment). The entire task is available for download in the IRIS depository.

(7) *Son las 9:45 de la noche y los dos se sientan en la mesa del salón para cenar y ver las noticias. Hugo le pregunta a Víctor: ¿Qué me cuentas?*
Víctor dice:
Esta tarde yo _____ (leer) dos capítulos de una novela para mi clase de literatura hispánica.
'It is 9:45 at night and the two sit at the dining room table to eat and watch the news. Hugo asks Victor: "What's up?"
Victor says:
This afternoon I _____ (to read) two chapters of a novel for my Hispanic literature class.'

Analysis

The analysis consisted of (1) classification and frequency of verb forms for learners and NSs, (2) generalized linear mixed-models (GLMMs) in SPSS for both groups, and (3) cross-tabulations of significant predictors for each group.

First, all verb forms used by learners at T1 and T2 and by NSs were classified and tabulated. Both researchers coded the verb forms based on tense/aspect. Orthographic marks were considered because they can be necessary for identifying verb forms. For example, if a participant supplied *hablé*, it was coded as preterite whereas *hable* was coded as ambiguous because the verb form could be considered preterite (i.e., without an orthographic mark) or the present subjunctive. If a participant supplied *(yo) habló* (i.e., a mismatch between the subject and the verb), this was counted as preterite given that acquisition of tense/aspect and person/number are separate acquisitional processes (Bardovi-Harlig, 2000). However, if a participant supplied *(yo) hablo,* this was counted as ambiguous because it was impossible to determine if the participant used the present[3] or the preterite (i.e., in 3rd person singular). With these criteria in place, interrater reliability for the coding of T1 verbs reached a rate of 90.9% while T2 verbs reached a rate of 98.9%. Any disagreements were discussed and resolved between

---

3. The term *present* indicates present indicative; if we refer to subjunctive, we use the term *present subjunctive.*

researchers. These same measures were applied to the NSs data, and 100% agreement was reached. Then, frequency tabulations for all forms were conducted for learners and NSs.

Next, we created two different statistical models (i.e., one for the NSs and one for the learners). For the NSs, we ran a binomial GLMM; the dependent variable consisted of two levels (i.e., the preterite and PP) given that these were the two forms used with the highest frequency and permitted statistical analysis. The preterite served as the reference category (i.e., a positive coefficient > 1 favors the PP to the preterite). Participant was run as a random effect while telicity and temporal reference were run as fixed effects. For the learners, we ran a multinomial GLMM given that the dependent variable consisted of three levels (i.e., the preterite, imperfect, and present). The reason that only these forms were selected for statistical analysis was based on their higher rate of use; the lower frequency of the other forms would not permit statistical analysis. The preterite served as the reference category (i.e., a positive coefficient > 1 favors the imperfect or the present to the preterite). The participant was run as a random effect and telicity, temporal reference, and time of data collection were run as fixed effects. Based on recommendations within SPSS, we selected the Kenward-Roger approximation instead of the Residual method given its appropriateness for smaller sample conditions. Lastly, cross-tabulations were created for each group's significant predictors and past-time use.

Results

Learners grammar scores at T1 and T2

The results of the grammar scores at T1 and T2 demonstrate improvement in general Spanish grammar knowledge. At T1 learners scored an average of 6.86 ($SD=2.92$, range: 2–11). At T2, learners' average increased to 8.56 ($SD=1.22$, range 4–11). A paired samples t-test was conducted and indicated a statistical difference between scores at T1 and T2, $t(22)=-3.690, p=<.001$.

Rates of verb forms used

Table 1 presents the rates of form suppliance for the L2 group at T1 and T2 and for the NS group.

As can be seen in Table 1, the NS group used the preterite at a rate of 78.0%, whereas the PP was only used at a rate of 10.8%. This group also supplied preterite progressive (3.1%), imperfect (2.7%), future (0.6%), and present (0.3%) forms.

Table 1. Frequency of verb forms used by learners at T1 and T2 and NSs

Verb form	T1 #	T1 %	T2 #	T2 %	NSs #	NSs %
Preterite	135	48.9	203	73.5	224	78.0
Imperfect	38	13.7	48	17.3	8	2.7
Present indicative	38	13.3	6	2.1	1	0.3
PP	1	0.3	0	0	31	10.8
Preterite progressive	0	0	0	0	9	3.1
Future	10	3.6	5	1.8	2	0.6
Conditional	1	0.3	0	0	0	0
Present subjunctive	0	0	1	0.3	0	0
Infinitive	4	1.4	1	0.3	0	0
Ambiguous	49	17.7	12	4.3	12	4.1
Total	276	100	276	100	287	100

Note: A NS supplied both the preterite and PP in a single context. This token was excluded from the analysis.

Approximately 4% of NSs' forms were considered ambiguous due to lack of orthographic marks. Learners at T1 used the preterite most often (48.9%) followed by the imperfect (13.7%) and present (13.3%). At T1, learners used ambiguous forms (17.1%) and other forms (e.g., future, conditional, etc.) at lower rates. At T2, learners' use of the preterite increased to 73.5% and the imperfect increased to 17.3% while present use decreased to 2.1% and ambiguous forms decreased to 4.3%. Only one PP form was supplied by the L2 group at T1, and no PP forms were produced at T2.

Results of generalized linear mixed-models

The results of the binomial GLMM for the NSs are provided in Table 2. The only factor that was significant for NSs was temporal reference. For temporal reference, pre-hesternal contexts served as the base category and were compared to hesternal and hodiernal contexts. The pre-hesternal and hesternal comparison was not significant while the hodiernal and pre-hesternal comparison was significant. For this comparison, the PP was more likely to occur in a hodiernal context when compared to a pre-hesternal context.

The results of the multinomial GLMM for the L2 Spanish learners are presented in Table 3. Different from the NS model, the multinomial GLMM compared the preterite to the imperfect and the preterite to the present. Overall,

Table 2. Results of the binary generalized linear mixed model (GLMM) for NSs predicting PP

Effect	Coefficient	SE	t value	p value	CI
(Intercept)	−3.74	0.72	−5.21	<.001	[−5.16, −2.33]
Telicity [Telic]					
Atelic	−0.17	0.47	−0.36	.717	[−1.10, 0.76]
Temporal ref. [Pre-hesternal]					
Hesternal	−1.15	1.18	0−.98	.331	[−3.46, 1.17]
Hodiernal	2.81	0.66	4.23	<.001	[1.50, 4.12]
Random Effect Covariance	**Estimate**	**SE**	**z value**	**p value**	**CI**
Participant	1.91	1.02	1.86	.059	[0.67, 5.41]

Note. Model summary: Overall Percent Correct = 92.5%; AIC = 1522.48; BIC = 1525.99; −2 log likelihood = 1520.4; log likelihood = 760.2

telicity and time of data collection constrained use of the preterite, imperfect, and present while temporal reference did not. Regarding the preterite and imperfect comparison (Table 3), atelic predicates were more likely to be used with the imperfect than the preterite when compared to telic predicates. Although temporal reference was not significant in the overall model, hodiernal contexts were more likely to favor the preterite than the imperfect when compared to pre-hesternal contexts. Time of data collection was not significant for the preterite and imperfect comparison.

Table 3. Results of the multinomial GLMM preterite vs. imperfect comparison for L2 learners

Effect	Coefficient	SE	t value	p value	CI
(Intercept)	−2.10	0.37	−5.72	<.001	[−2.84, −1.38]
Telicity [Telic]					
Atelic	1.49	0.29	5.07	<.001	[0.92, 2.08]
Temporal ref. [Pre-hesternal]					
Hesternal	−0.36	0.31	−1.18	.237	[−0.97, 0.24]
Hodiernal	−0.84	0.33	−2.51	.012	[−1.49, −0.18]
Time of data collection [Time 2]					
Time 1	0.18	0.27	0.66	.511	[−0.35, 0.71]
Random Effect Covariance	**Estimate**	**SE**	**z value**	**p value**	**CI**
Participant	0.78	0.36	2.15	<.031	[0.32, 1.94]

Note. Model summary: Overall Percent Correct = 76.1%; AIC = 4389.74; BIC = 4397.97; −2 log likelihood = 4385.72; log likelihood = −2192.86

Regarding the preterite and present comparison (Table 4), only time of data collection was significant for this comparison; the present was more likely to occur than the preterite at T1 than at T2.

Table 4. Results of the multinomial GLMM preterite vs. present comparison for L2 learners

Effect	Coefficient	SE	t value	p value	CI
(Intercept)	−4.56	0.72	−6.31	< .001	[−5.99, −3.13]
Telicity [Telic]					
Atelic	−0.72	0.39	−0.19	0.85	[−0.83, 0.69]
Temporal ref. [Pre-hesternal]					
Hesternal	0.10	0.48	0.19	0.84	[−0.86, 1.04]
Hodiernal	0.20	0.48	0.42	0.68	[−0.75, 1.15]
Time of data collection [Time 2]					
Time 1	2.96	0.54	5.47	< .001	[1.89, 4.02]
Random Effect Covariance	Estimate	SE	z value	p value	CI
Participant	2.96	1.25	2.35	< .019	[1.29, 6.81]

Note. Model summary: Overall Percent Correct=76.1%; AIC=4389.74; BIC=4397.97; −2 log likelihood=4385.72; log likelihood=−2192.86

Cross-tabulations of significant factors

Figure 2 shows cross-tabulations for temporal reference and preterite and PP use for NSs. For hodiernal eventualities, the NSs provided the preterite in 68.2% of contexts and the PP at a rate of 31.7%. For hesternal contexts, the preterite was almost categorical at 98.8%, versus 1.17% PP, while pre-hesternal eventualities favored the use of preterite at 96.4%. Moreover, the PP was used sparingly at 3.52%. Although the PP was used at a rate of 31.7% in hodiernal contexts, the Leonese speakers used the preterite in the majority of these contexts, suggesting that the preterite is the preferred form to express perfectivity.

The cross-tabulations for time of data collection, telicity, and past-time for learners are presented in Figure 3. The preterite increased with atelic and telic predicates from T1 to T2 (i.e., in the direction of the NSs). The preterite increased with telic predicates from 48.8% at T1 to 68.9% at T2. The preterite was used more with telic predicates at T1 (70.5%), and use of the preterite increased to 88.0% at T2. The use of the imperfect increased with atelic predicates from 26.6% at T1 to 28.7%, while the imperfect was used minimally (8.8%) with telic predicates at T1 and decreased to 8.0% at T2. The present was used more with telic predicates than

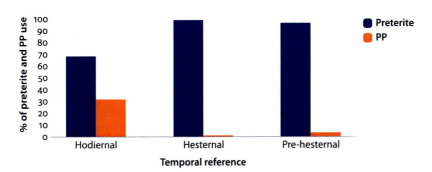

Figure 2. Cross-tabulation for temporal reference and preterite and PP use with NSs

atelic predicates at T1, but the use of the present decreased from 15.5% with atelic predicates to 2.27% at T2, and the same trend was observed for telic predicates (i.e., 20.5% at T1 to 2.4% at T2).

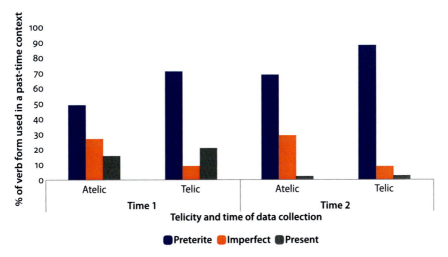

Figure 3. Cross-tabulations for telicity, time of data collection and verb form used

Post-hoc within-category analyses with learners and NSs

To further inquire into the influence of lexical aspect from T1 to T2, a within-category analysis was conducted (Bardovi-Harlig & Comajoan-Colomé, 2020). This within-category analysis is the proportion of the total number of times a verbal lexical aspectual class occurred in the CVET divided by the total number of times these classes appeared with specific verbal morphology (e.g., preterite, imperfect, etc.). The within-category analysis for lexical aspect and verb form used denoting past-time is presented in Table 5 for NSs and Table 6 for learners at T1 and T2.

NSs used the preterite more than any other verb form with all verb classes, but they used the preterite more with achievements at a rate of 83.3%, then accomplishments at a rate of 80.2%, followed by states at a rate of 77.7%, and lastly with activities 70.8%. NSs used the preterite progressive at a rate of 12.5% with only activities, while the imperfect was used only with states at a rate of 11.1%. The PP was used more with accomplishments at a rate of 15.4% followed by states and activities at a rate of 9.72% and lastly with achievements at a rate of 8.3%.

Table 5. Results of the within-category analysis for verb forms and lexical aspect for NSs

Verb form	State #	State %	Activity #	Activity %	Accomplishment #	Accomplishment %	Achievement #	Achievement %
Preterite	56	77.7	51	70.8	57	80.2	60	83.3
Imperfect	8	11.1	0	0.0	0	0.0	0	0.0
Present	1	1.38	0	0.0	0	0.0	0	0.0
Present perfect	7	9.72	7	9.72	11	15.4	6	8.3
Preterite progressive	0	0.0	9	12.5	0	0.0	0	0.0
Future	0	0.0	1	1.38	1	1.41	0	0.0
Ambiguous	0	0.0	4	5.5	2	2.8	6	8.3
Total	72	100	72	100	71	100	72	100

In the within-category analysis, learners increased their use of the preterite across verb classes, but this was most notable with dynamic predicates. Learners used the preterite at a rate of 52.1% for achievement and accomplishment verbs at T1, and these rates increased to 81.5% for both verb types at T2. Learners used the preterite at a rate of 50.7% with activities at T1 and 79.7% at T2 while the preterite was used at a rate of 40.5% with states and this increased to 52.1%. This increased use of the preterite across verb classes was in line with NSs. Learners' use of the imperfect increased from T1 to T2, and this was most notable with states where the imperfect increased from 31.8% at T1 to 43.4% at T2. Learners also increased their use of the imperfect with activities, but this was only minimal from 10.1% to 11.5%. Learners decreased their use of the imperfect with accomplishments from 11.5% to 10.1%, while they increased their use of the imperfect with achievements from 1.4% to 4.3%. Learners increased use of the imperfect at T2 was a movement away from the NSs in particular with dynamic predicates. A single learner used the PP with a state at T1 and this was lost at T2.

Table 6. Results of within-category analysis for verb forms and lexical aspect for learners at Time 1 and Time 2

Verb form	State T1 #	State T1 %	State T2 #	State T2 %	Activity T1 #	Activity T1 %	Activity T2 #	Activity T2 %	Accomplishment T1 #	Accomplishment T1 %	Accomplishment T2 #	Accomplishment T2 %	Achievement T1 #	Achievement T1 %	Achievement T2 #	Achievement T2 %
Preterite	28	40.5	36	52.1	35	50.7	55	79.7	36	52.1	56	81.5	36	52.1	56	81.1
Imperfect	22	31.8	30	43.4	7	10.1	8	11.5	8	11.5	7	10.1	1	1.4	3	4.3
Present	13	18.8	2	2.8	4	5.7	1	1.4	9	13.0	1	1.4	12	17.3	2	2.8
Present perfect	1	1.4	0	0.0	0	0.0	0	0.0	0	0.0	0	0.0	0	0.0	0	0.0
Future	0	0.0	0	0.0	2	2.8	1	1.4	6	8.6	1	1.4	2	2.8	3	4.3
Conditional	0	0.0	0	0.0	0	0.0	0	0.0	0	0.0	0	0.0	1	1.4	0	0.0
Present subjunctive	0	0.0	0	0.0	0	0.0	0	0.0	0	0.0	0	0.0	0	0.0	1	1.4
Infinitive	2	2.8	0	0.0	0	0.0	0	0.0	0	0.0	1	1.4	2	2.8	0	0.0
Ambiguous	3	4.3	1	1.4	21	30.4	4	5.7	10	14.4	3	4.3	15	21.7	4	5.7
Totals	69	100	69	100	69	100	69	100	69	100	69	100	69	100	69	100

At T1, learners used the present more with states (18.8%) followed by achievements (17.3%), accomplishments (13.0%) and then activities (5.7%). At T2, the present was redistributed mostly in line with the lexical aspect of the verbal predicate. That is, of those 38 present forms at T1, 57.8% (22/38) of those were redistributed as the preterite. Of those 22 redistributed preterite forms at T2, 45% (10/22) were achievements, 22.7% (5/22) were accomplishments, whereas 18.1% (4/22) were states and 13.6% were activities. In addition, those 38 present forms at T1, 23.6% (9/38) were redistributed as imperfect at T2 and 66.6% (6/9) were states, 22.2% (2/9) were accomplishments and one (11.1%) was an activity. The remaining 18.4% (7/38) of present forms at T1 were redistributed as other forms: 42.8% (3/7) were ambiguous, 28.5% (2/7) remained present, one (14.2%) was used with the future, and one (14.2%) with the present subjunctive. Learners' use of ambiguous forms decreased across all verb classes. Learners used additional verb forms (e.g., infinitives, conditional, etc.), but these verb forms do not show a clear pattern of use in relation to lexical aspect.

Discussion

We first set out to identify all forms that learners employed in a past-time context, with particular interest in the preterite and PP, and how these forms changed during SA and compared to NSs (RQ1). Regarding the NSs, the preterite form was produced more than any other past-time form at a rate of 78.0%, while the PP was only produced at a rate of 10.8%. These results corroborate Pato and Heap (2008) who observed that regardless of temporal reference, NSs from León favored the preterite to the PP, distinguishing it from other Peninsular varieties (e.g., Madrid Spanish). When these rates for the preterite and PP are compared to previous studies that employed a CPT with NSs from León, (i.e., Geeslin et al., 2012; Zahler & Whatley, 2023) higher rates of PP selection were noted (i.e., 21% in Geeslin et al. 2012, and 26% in Zahler & Whatley, 2023). It may be that when NSs from León are asked to select between the preterite and PP in a CPT, they may consider the PP the prescriptively correct form in hodiernal contexts, which results in higher selection of the PP. This hypothesis is bolstered by evidence from a NS participant who reached out to the first author after completing the study and stated the following:

> in León when we talk about past we don't differentiate really good between past and present perfect (...) for example, in León we say *esta mañana fui a comprar* and the **correct thing** [emphasis added] would be like *esta mañana he ido a comprar,* so I tried to answer the questionnaire in the León version, and I just wanted

you to take that into account because probably there are some verbs that are not really good conjugated. (*sic*, Susana, Leonese participant)

Additionally, it is worth mentioning that studies on the use/selection of the preterite and PP in León have also incorporated not only different linguistic variables (cf. Geeslin et al., 2012 who incorporated *backgrounding*; Zahler & Whatley, 2023 who manipulated *sequencing*) but also different numbers of categories of each variable, both of which may influence NS patterns of use/selection (i.e., task variation; see Geeslin 2006). For instance, Geeslin et al. (2012) included a category for events that occurred *today* as well as a category for *one hour ago*, whereas we only looked at events that occurred *today* without further distinction. These differences may also account for the lower rates of use of the PP in the current study and the observed higher rates of PP selection in previous work for León (see Geeslin et al. 2012; Zahler & Whatley, 2023).

Learners increased their rate of use of the preterite in line with NSs, but also increased their use of the imperfect from T1 to T2 contra the NSs. A single learner used the PP at T1, and no learner used the PP at T2. The increased rate of the imperfect with learners appears to be related to the influence of lexical aspect, and in particular stative verbs. Whatley (2013) observed that all learners in her study increased their selection of the imperfect while the preterite did not show this trend for all learner groups. Similarly, in the current study, learners' increased use of the imperfect and decreased use of the present in reference to past-time is reflective of an increase in proficiency over the course of SA. This trend has been observed across L2 Spanish studies in which learners begin with higher rates of present tense forms, and, as proficiency increases, they begin to incorporate more preterite and imperfect forms in production (Camps, 2005; Hasbún, 1995; Lubbers Quesada, 2006; Ramsay, 1990; Salaberry, 1999; Terán, 2020). Learners decreased their use of ambiguous forms, which was likely related to instruction during the SA program supporting the observation that instructed L2 learners often supply appropriate verb morphology before appropriate use when compared to naturalistic learners (Bardovi-Harlig & Bofman, 1989).

Additionally, we investigated (extra)linguistic predictors that constrain past-time use with learners and how these compared to NSs (RQ2). NSs' use of the preterite and PP was constrained only by temporal reference; the PP was favored in hodiernal contexts while the preterite was favored in hesternal and pre-hesternal contexts (Geeslin et al., 2012; Zahler & Whatley, 2023). Although the PP was more likely to occur in hodiernal contexts as compared to pre-hesternal contexts, the preterite was the most common form supplied across all contexts, supporting Pato and Heap's (2006) description of Leonese Spanish past-time expression. Learners' use of the preterite, imperfect, and present was constrained by lexical aspect and time of data collection. The imperfect was more likely to be used with atelic predicates as compared to the preterite, whereas telicity was not significant for the preterite and present comparison. These findings were further supported in the cross-tabulations and correspond to previous L2 Spanish studies (e.g., Blaker, 2024; Terán, 2020; Whatley, 2013) where lexical aspect guides learners use of past-time forms. Interestingly, hodiernal contexts favored the preterite when compared to the imperfect, and this appeared to be due to learners' increased use of the preterite in this context from T1 to T2 (i.e., 64.7% to 86.3%). The time of data collection was significant with the preterite and present comparison where the present was more likely to occur at T1 than at T2 supporting increased use of past-time forms with increased proficiency (Lubbers Quesada, 2006; Terán, 2020).

Although lexical aspect did not constrain NSs' use of the preterite and PP, the within-category analysis demonstrated that NSs used different past-time forms that appeared to be in relation to lexical aspect. For example, while NSs favored the preterite with states, they also used the imperfect, even though it was isolated to *tener* 'to have' and *sentirse* 'to feel', while *estar* 'to be' was categorically preterite. This aligns with previous accounts that have also observed NS variation between the preterite and imperfect with states in Spanish (see Blaker, 2024; Knouse, 2009). On the other hand, learners used the imperfect more with stative verbs suggesting that they are assigning grammatical aspect, at least with states, based on the congruence and prototypicality between states and the imperfect (Andersen, 1991; Andersen & Shirai, 1994). Furthermore, learners demonstrated an increase in preterite use with all verb classes over time in line with NSs, but this was most notable with dynamic predicates. Thus, while it appears that learners are influenced by lexical aspect, they are influenced more by the state versus dynamic distinction within the CVET where the imperfect was primarily associated with states and the preterite with dynamic predicates (Domínguez et al., 2013).

We also inquired into how our results with a CVET would compare to studies that employed a CPT (i.e., Geeslin et al., 2012; Kanwit et al., 2015; Linford, 2016; Zahler & Whatley, 2023). With the exception of Zahler and Whatley (2023), these researchers generally found evidence for an increased preference for the PP for the PP after SA. Conversely, in the current study, only one learner used the PP at T1, and the PP was not used at T2. There are a number of possible reasons why our results diverge from previous work. First, the NSs did not produce the PP at a high rate in hodiernal contexts as observed in selection, which suggests that learners may have received higher rates of preterite in the input in hodienal contexts during SA. Second, as previously mentioned, prior L2 Spanish studies (Geeslin et al., 2012; Kanwit et al., 2015; Linford, 2016; Zahler & Whatley, 2023) have included not only different linguistic variables but also different categories within each variable, complicating comparisons between studies (Geeslin & Gudmestad, 2008). Therefore, it may be the case that with more hodiernal contexts in the CVET that L2 learners would have produced the PP. However, given that NSs only produced it in 10.8% of contexts (31/287), we find this argument less convincing. Third, it may be that length of stay (i.e., more time in the SA context) promotes the acquisition of sociolinguistic competence. For example, Linford's (2016) learners were in Madrid for four months while our learners were only in the SA context for six-and-a-half weeks. Nevertheless, within the context of the CVET, we find evidence that our learners developed their ability to use past-time, with increased rates of the preterite (i.e., in line with NSs) and imperfect (i.e, not entirely against NSs), and a concomiant decrease in present and amigiguous forms (i.e., in line with NSs). These findings reaffirm the the importance of SA in the acquisition of morphosyntax (Collentine, 2003). However, we do not find evidence to support acquisition of preterite and PP variation contra previous work with CPT's (i.e., Geeslin et al., 2012; Kanwit et al., 2015; Linford, 2016).

Conclusion

Our results from a CVET found evidence for development of past-time expression more generally (i.e., increased use of the preterite like a NS comparison group), but we did not find support for acquisition of variation between the preterite and PP like previous work (Geeslin et al., 2012; Kanwit et al., 2015; Linford, 2016). Furthermore, we observed that not only is the preterite preferred in León, Spain, even in hodiernal contexts (Pato & Heap, 2008), but NSs also used a range of forms (e.g., preterite, imperfect, PP, preterite progressive) suggesting a larger variable context that must be taken into account for both NSs and L2 Spanish learners use/acquisition of past-time. (Geeslin & Gudmestad, 2010; Kanwit, 2017). Regarding learners, their use of past-time, particularly the preterite, imperfect, and present, was guided by lexical aspect, especially the state versus dynamic distinction within our CVET. (Domínguez et al., 2013).

Future research will benefit from incorporating multiple data elicitation tasks (i.e., a CVET and CPT) that systematically control linguistic predictors across both tasks to provide a more detailed account of the acquisition of the preterite and PP variation (Geeslin, 2010; Geeslin & Gudmestad, 2008). Researchers are encouraged to incorporate similar variables that have been investigated across studies on the preterite and PP variation in L2 Spanish (i.e., telicity and temporal reference). Within the CVET, instead of using first/third-person singular forms, controlled production tasks would benefit from using 3rd person plural forms to avoid syncretism between different TMA forms. For temporal reference, more work is needed on the acquisition of the preterite and PP variation in irrelevant, specific, and indeterminate contexts (see Kanwit et al., 2015, but also, Schwenter & Torres Cacoullos, 2008) because it may be the case that Leonese Spanish speakers do use higher rates of the PP in irrelevant and indeterminate contexts than in temporally specific contexts. Also, it may be important to include the individual verbs or items from the task as random effects in the GLMM to control for a possible influence on past-time use in L2 Spanish and with NSs. Given the lower rates of PP use in hodiernal contexts in León, Spain, it may be important to compare not only learners' exposure to different Spanish varieties across countries, but within the same country (e.g., Madrid vs. León). Lastly, more work on NS attitudes towards the preterite and PP variation may be important to interpret findings with NSs from different varieties of Spanish.

References

Blaker, N. M. (2024). The influence of temporal adverbials and lexical aspect on variable preterite and imperfect selection in native and second language Spanish: A variationist account. In M. Gradoville & S. Mckinnon (Eds.), *Recent developments in Hispanic linguistics: Studies in structure, variation, and bilingualism* (pp. 222–244). John Benjamins Publishing Company.

Andersen, R. W. (1991). Developmental sequences: The emergence of aspect marking in second language acquisition. In T. Huebner & C. A. Ferguson (Eds.), *Crosscurrents in second language acquisition and linguistic theories* (pp. 305–324). John Benjamins Publishing Company.

Andersen, R. W., & Shirai, Y. (1994). Discourse motivations for some cognitive acquisition principles. *Studies in Second Language Acquisition*, 16, 133–156.

Bardovi-Harlig, K. (1994). Anecdote or evidence? Evaluating support for hypotheses concerning the development of tense and aspect. In S. Gass, A. Cohen, & E. Tarone (Eds.), *Research methodology in second language acquisition* (pp. 41–60). Erlbaum.

Bardovi-Harlig, K. (2000). *Tense and aspect in second language acquisition: Form, meaning, and use.* Wiley/Blackwell.

Bardovi-Harlig, K. (2020). One functional approach to L2 acquisition: The concept-oriented approach. In B. VanPatten, G. D. Keating, and S. Wulff (Eds.), *Theories in Second Language Acquisition* (pp. 40–62). Routledge.

Bardovi-Harlig, K., & Bofman, T. (1989). Attainment of syntactic and morphological accuracy by advanced language learners. *Studies in Second Language Acquisition*, 11(1), 17–34.

Bardovi-Harlig, K., & Comajoan-Colomé, L. (2020). The aspect hypothesis and the acquisition of L2 past morphology in the last 20 years: A state-of-the-scholarship review. *Studies in Second Language Acquisition*, 42(5), 1137–1167.

Bayley, R., & Tarone, E. (2012). Variationist perspectives. In S. Gass & A. Mackey (Eds.), *Handbook of Second Language Acquisition* (pp. 41–56). Routledge.

Bybee, J. L., Perkins, R. D., & Pagliuca, W. (1994). *The evolution of grammar: Tense, aspect, and modality in the languages of the world* (Vol. 196). University of Chicago Press.

Cadierno, T. (2000). The acquisition of Spanish grammatical aspect by Danish advanced language learners. *Spanish Applied Linguistics*, 4, 1–53.

Camps, J. (2005). The emergence of the imperfect in Spanish as a foreign language: The association between imperfective morphology and stative verbs. *International Review of Applied Linguistics*, 43, 163–192.

Canale, M., & Swain, M. (1980). Theoretical bases of communicative approaches to second language teaching and testing. *Applied Linguistics*, 1, 1–47.

Collentine, J. G. (2003). The effects of study abroad and classroom contexts on the acquisition of Spanish as a second language: From research to application. In B. Lafford & J. G. Collentine (Eds.), *Spanish Second Language Acquisition: State of the Science* (pp. 169–182). Georgetown University Press.

Comrie, B. (1976). *Aspect: An introduction to the study of verbal aspect and related problems* (Vol. 2). Cambridge University Press.

De Miguel, E. (1999). El aspecto léxico. In I. Bosque & V. Demonte (Eds.), *Gramática Descriptiva de la Lengua Española Volumen 2* (pp. 2977–3060). Espasa.

Domínguez, L., Tracy-Ventura, N., Arche, M. J., Mitchell, R., & Myles, F. (2013). The role of dynamic contrasts in the L2 acquisition of Spanish past tense morphology. *Bilingualism: Language and Cognition*, 16(3), 558–577.

Fábregas, A. (2015). 'Imperfecto' and 'indefinido' in Spanish: what, where and how. *An International Journal of Hispanic Linguistics*, 4, 1–70.

Geeslin, K. L. (2006). Task design, discourse context and variation in second language data elicitation. In C. A. Klee & T. L. Face (Eds.), *Selected Proceedings of the 7th Conference on the Acquisition of Spanish and Portuguese as First and Second Languages* (pp. 74-85). Cascadilla Proceedings Project.

Geeslin, K. L. (2010). Beyond "naturalistic": On the role of task characteristics and the importance of multiple elicitation methods. *Studies in Hispanic and Lusophone Linguistics*, 3, 501–520.

Geeslin, K. L. (2020). Variationist perspective(s) on interlocutor individual differences. In L. Gurzynski-Weiss (Ed.), *Cross-theoretical explorations of interlocutors and their individual differences* (pp. 127–157). John Benjamins Publishing Company.

Geeslin, K. L. (Ed.). (2022). *The Routledge handbook of second language acquisition and sociolinguistics*. Routledge.

Geeslin, K. L., García-Amaya, L. J., Hasler-Barker, M., Henriksen, N. C., & Killam, J. (2012). The L2 acquisition of variable perfective past time reference in Spanish in an overseas immersion setting. In K. L. Geeslin & M. Díaz-Campos (Eds.), *Selected proceedings of the 14th Hispanic Linguistics Symposium* (pp. 197–213). Cascadilla Proceedings Project.

Geeslin, K. L., & Gudmestad, A. (2008). Comparing interview and written elicitation tasks in native and non-native data: Do speakers do what we think they do? In J. Bruhn de Garavito, & E. Valenzuela (Eds.), *Selected proceedings of the 10th Hispanic linguistics symposium* (pp. 64–77). Cascadilla Proceedings Project.

Geeslin, K. L., & Gudmestad, A. (2010). An exploration of the range and frequency of occurrence of forms in potentially variable structures in second-language Spanish. *Studies in Second Language Acquisition*, 32(3), 433–463.

Gudmestad, A. (2012). Acquiring a variable structure: An interlanguage analysis of second language mood use in Spanish. *Language Learning*, 62(2), 373–402.

Gudmestad, A. (2014). Variationist approaches to second language Spanish. In K.L. Geeslin (Ed.), *The handbook of Spanish second language acquisition* (pp. 80–95). Wiley Blackwell.

Harris, M. (1982). The 'past simple' and the 'present perfect' in Romance. In N. Vincent & M. Harris (Eds.), *Studies in the Romance Verb* (pp. 42–70). Croom Helm.

Hasbún, L.M. (1995). The role of lexical aspect in the acquisition of the tense/aspect system in L2 Spanish (Publication No. 9608574) [Doctoral dissertation, Indiana University]. Proquest Dissertations & Theses Global.

Howe, C. (2013). *The Spanish perfects: Pathways of emergent meaning*. Palgrave Macmillan.

Kanwit, M. (2017). What we gain by combining variationist and concept-oriented approaches: The case of acquiring Spanish future-time expression. *Language Learning, 67*(2), 461–498.

Kanwit, M. (2022). Sociolinguistic competence: What we know so far and where we're heading. In K.L. Geeslin (Ed.), *The Routledge handbook of second language acquisition and sociolinguistics* (pp. 30–44). Routledge.

Kanwit, M., Geeslin, K.L., & Fafulas, S. (2015). Study abroad and the SLA of variable structures: A look at the present perfect, the copula contrast, and the present progressive in Mexico and Spain. *Probus, 27*(2), 307–348.

Kempas, I. (2002). Sobre las actitudes de estudiantes españoles hacia el uso del pretérito perfecto prehodiernal en comparación con las de estudiantes santiagueños (Argentina). *Neuphilologisch Mitteilungen, 103*, 435–447.

Knouse, S. (2009). Variation in Aspectual Morphology: Stative verbs in the Spanish of Salamanca (Publication No. 3400274) [Doctoral dissertation, University of Florida]. Proquest Dissertations & Theses Global.

Labov, W. (1972). *Sociolinguistic patterns*. University of Pennsylvania Press.

Linford, B.G. (2016). The second-language development of dialect-specific morpho-syntactic variation in Spanish during study abroad (Publication No. 10130845) [Doctoral dissertation, Indiana University]. Proquest Dissertations & Theses Global.

Liskin-Gasparro, J. (2000). The use of tense-aspect morphology in Spanish oral narratives: Exploring the perceptions of advanced learners. *Hispania, 83*, 831–844.

Lubbers Quesada, M. (2006). L2 acquisition of temporal reference in Spanish and the interaction of adverbials, morphology, and clause structure. In N. Sagarra & A.J. Toribio (Eds.), *Selected proceedings of the 9th Hispanic Linguistics Symposium* (pp. 157–68). Cascadilla Proceedings Project.

Pato, E., & Heap, D. (2008). La organización dialectal del castellano: La distribución de *he cantado* vs. *canté* en el español de la Península Ibérica. In C. Company Company & J.G. Morendo de Alba (Eds.), *Actas del VII Congreso Internacional de Historia de la Lengua Española volumen 1* (pp. 927–941). Arco/Libros

Ramsay, V. (1990). Developmental stages in the acquisition of the perfective and the imperfective aspects by classroom L2 learners of Spanish (Publication No. 9111134) [Doctoral dissertation, University of Oregon]. Proquest Dissertations & Theses Global.

Rehner, K.A. (2002). The development of aspects of linguistic and discourse competence by advanced second language learners of French (Publication No. NQ74623) [Doctoral dissertation, University of Toronto]. Proquest Dissertations & Theses Global.

Salaberry, M.R. (1999). The development of past tense verbal morphology in classroom L2 Spanish. *Applied Linguistics, 20*, 151–178.

Salaberry, M. R. (2011). Assessing the effect of lexical aspect and grounding on the acquisition of L2 Spanish past tense morphology among L1 English speakers. *Bilingualism: Language and Cognition, 14*(2), 184–202.

Schwenter, S. A. (1994). The grammaticalization of an anterior in progress: Evidence from a peninsular Spanish dialect. *Studies in Language, 18*(1), 71–111.

Schwenter, S. A., & Torres Cacoullos, R. (2008). Defaults and indeterminacy in temporal grammaticalization: The 'perfect' road to perfective. *Language variation and change, 20*(1), 1–39.

Serrano, M. (1994). Del pretérito indefinido al pretérito perfecto: Un caso de cambio y gramaticalización en el español de Canarias y Madrid. *Lingüística Española Actual, 16,* 37–57.

Shirai, Y. (2013). Defining and coding data: Lexical aspect in L2 studies. In M. R. Salaberry & L. Comajoan-Colomé (Eds.), *Research design and methodology in studies on L2 tense and aspect.* (pp. 271–308). De Gruyter.

Smith, C. (1991). *The parameter of aspect.* Kluwer.

Squartini, M., & Bertinetto, P. M. (2000). The simple and compound past in Romance Languages. *Empirical Approaches to Language Typology,* (6), 403–440.

Terán, V. (2020). The acquisition of variable past-time expression in L2 Spanish: combining concept-oriented, form-oriented, and variationist research traditions within functionalism (Publication No. 27834326) [Doctoral dissertation, University of Pittsburgh]. Proquest Dissertations & Theses Global.

Vendler, Z. (1957). Verbs and times. *The Philosophical Review, 66,* 143–160.

Whatley, M. (2013). The acquisition of past tense variation by L2 learners of Spanish in an abroad context. In J. Cabrelli Amaro, G. Lord, A. de Prada Pérez, & J. E. Aaron (Eds.), *Selected proceedings of the 16th Hispanic Linguistics Symposium* (pp. 190–205). Cascadilla Proceedings Project.

Woolsey, D. S. (2006). Second language acquisition of the Spanish verb estar with adjectives: An exploration of contexts of comparison and immediate experience (Publication No. 3215174) [Doctoral dissertation, Indiana University]. Proquest Dissertations & Theses Global.

Zahler, S. L., & Whatley, M. (2023). Learning context and the development of second language Spanish: Past-time perfective marking at home and abroad. In S. Zahler, A. Y. Long, & B. Linford (Eds.), *Study abroad and the second language acquisition of sociolinguistic variation in Spanish* (pp. 321–349). John Benjamins.

CHAPTER 5

Acquiring sociolinguistic competence
A comparison of subject pronoun expression in L2 and L3 Spanish

Chelsea Escalante,[1] Rebecca Pozzi,[2] Robert Bayley,[3] Xiaoshi Li[4] & Xinye Zhang[3]
[1] University of Wyoming | [2] California State University, Monterey Bay | [3] University of California, Davis | [4] Michigan State University

> This paper compares the acquisition of subject pronoun expression in written Spanish by first-language (L1) speakers of English learning Spanish as a second language and L1 speakers of Chinese learning Spanish as a third language. A mixed-effects regression indicated that learners' choices between null and overt forms are constrained by many of the factors that affect native (i.e., expert) Spanish speakers: switch reference, reflexivity, person/number, and verb type. Although both groups of speakers decreased their rates of overt pronouns over time, Chinese L1 speakers began to use significantly fewer pronouns after two quarters of Spanish study, but English L1 participants did not demonstrate significant drops until quarter 5. We also noted more individual variability in Chinese-speaking participants.
>
> **Keywords:** subject pronoun expression, L2/L3 variation, Spanish, English, Mandarin

Like many of the world's languages, Spanish and Chinese exhibit variation between null and overt pronominal subjects, for example:

Yo pienso   我想   (wǒ xiǎng)   I think
Ø pienso   Ø 想   (xiǎng)   *think

As is the case with other sociolinguistic variables, research on native speaker (NS) subject pronoun expression (SPE) has shown that a speaker's choice between a null or overt pronoun is not random but rather is constrained by a rich array of constraints, many of which are found cross-linguistically, including co-reference with the subject of the preceding verb, person/number, clause type, discourse genre, semantic features of the verb, tense-mood-aspect (TMA), and potential ambiguity of the verb form (Barrenechea & Alonso, 1973; Bayley et al., 2017; Cameron, 1995; Flores-Ferrán, 2004; Guy et al., forthcoming; Otheguy & Zentella, 2012; Silva-Corvalán, 1994; inter alia).

In addition to studies on SPE among NSs, research has addressed this phenomenon among second-language (L2) learners to determine the rates of occurrence of null subjects as well as the factors related to these rates according to proficiency level. Most of this research to date focuses on SPE of a L2 (e.g., Spanish or Mandarin Chinese) among speakers of English as a first language (L1). However, recent research (Cherici, 2021) has also examined the role of a L1 and a L2 as sources of transfer based on typological (or structural) similarities in the acquisition of a third language (L3). This study compares the acquisition of the constraints on SPE in Spanish by L1 speakers of Mandarin Chinese, which allows null subjects, and L1 speakers of English, which only allows null subjects in a few rare contexts (Nagy, 2024; Wagner, 2016). In addition, it compares when these learners begin to acquire the constraints on SPE.

A majority of SPE variation studies in L2 have been conducted in oral discourse (e.g., Geeslin & Gudmestad, 2008, 2011; Gudmestad & Geeslin, 2010; Li, 2014, 2017). However, research has shown that oral and written language are different. Compared with oral language, written language tends to be more formal and features "integration" of a sequence of ideas into a structurally complex and coherent linguistic production due to longer planning time and absence of immediate interaction with audiences (e.g., Biber & Conrad, 2001; Christensen, 2000). Studies of Chinese have shown that sociolinguistic variation is different in oral and written discourses (e.g., Christensen, 2000; Li, 2017). For example, Li (2017) found higher use of the Chinese morphosyntactic particle DE in written texts than in oral conversations, but less use of subject pronouns in writing than in conversations. Christensen (2000) found Chinese speakers produced significantly fewer overt subject pronouns in narrative writing than in oral narratives, which corroborated Li's results.

To have a full understanding of SPE in learners' interlanguage, research needs to investigate the written modality and oral use. In recent years, Geeslin and collaborators have made important contributions in expanding the body of L2 SPE variation research by investigating L2 Spanish written forms (e.g., Geeslin & Linford, 2012; Geeslin et al., 2015; Geeslin et al., 2023; Linford & Geeslin, 2022). For example, they examined the effect of certain constraints on subject-form selection by different levels of learners on highly controlled written contextualized tasks. Fernández Flórez (2023) investigated first-person SPE by Spanish heritage speakers in essays and found the overall rate of overt SPE was much lower than in previous studies of Spanish oral discourse. To expand on this research, the current study is designed to investigate SPE in learner-produced essays by L2 and

L3 Spanish learners at different levels, which will further contribute to the understanding of SPE variation in written discourse by Spanish learners and the importance of exploring written modality to understand L2 variation and acquisition in general.

In addition to furthering the study of written language, this investigation contributes to a growing body of research on additional-language acquisition by speakers who already speak more than one language. Increasingly, multilingualism is becoming the norm. Recent estimates suggest that approximately 7,000 languages are currently spoken worldwide in only 196 countries (Simons & Fennig, 2018), meaning that the vast majority of the world's population is multilingual (Marian & Shook, 2012). In the European Union, 56 percent of residents are functionally bilingual, and in the U.S. and Canada, 20% speak a language at home other than English (Maher, 2017). The U.S. currently has more Spanish speakers than any other country except for Mexico, and there are approximately 46 million ethnic Chinese living outside China, Hong Kong, Taiwan, and Macau (Liu & Van Dongen, 2013). Given the increasing linguistic diversity of the U.S., we can expect language classes to become more like those that provided the data for this study, where many of the students have already successfully learned a L2 and are in the process of acquiring a third or nth language.

Literature review

SPE in Spanish

Spanish permits the subject pronoun of a verb to be expressed (overt) or unexpressed (null). Variationist sociolinguistic studies on the topic show that overt SPE rates vary widely across dialects of Spanish, with the lowest levels of overt SPE occurring in European Spanish (15–23%), followed by mainland Latin American Spanish (23–37%), and lastly, Caribbean Spanish (34–43%; Guy et al., forthcoming). In US Spanish in particular, overt pronoun rates vary, with greater rates among Spanish speakers of Caribbean descent (36–45%) and lower rates among those of Mexican descent (20–28%, see Bayley & Pease-Alvarez, 1997; Cameron, 1992; Flores-Ferrán, 2004; Otheguy & Zentella, 2012; Silva-Corvalán, 1994).

This body of work on SPE in Spanish has largely been based on oral rather than written data (Flores-Ferrán, 2007). Studies on the latter are limited to examinations of historical documents in Spanish (see Cerrón-Palomino et al., 2023; Ramos, 2016), which show that, while historical written SPE rates exhibit some variation, they are quite similar to SPE rates of the Spanish spoken today in those regions. Despite variability in SPE rates across dialects, historical time periods, and modality, overall, constraints on SPE have been found to be relatively stable (Cameron, 1995). Some of the most prominent constraints found in SPE studies are switch reference, TMA, reflexivity, person/number, clause type, ambiguity of the verb, and semantic verb type (Abreu, 2009; Bayley et al., 2017; Carvalho & Child, 2011; Erker & Guy, 2012; Michnowicz, 2015; Otheguy & Zentella, 2012).

SPE in Mandarin Chinese

As with Spanish, pronominal subjects in Mandarin Chinese can be expressed overtly or omitted. However, SPE has received much less attention in Mandarin Chinese than in Spanish (see Jia & Bayley, 2002; Li, 2017; Li & Bayley, 2018; Li et al., 2012; Zhang, 2021). Nevertheless, previous and ongoing research (Guy et al., forthcoming; Li, 2017) has shown differences in oral SPE rates in different communities. For example, Guy et al. (forthcoming) found that Mandarin speakers in Shanghai chose the overt option at a rate of 69% while speakers in Taipei chose it at a rate of 62.9%. Mandarin heritage students in California also exhibited a high rate of overt subject pronoun use (62.7%, Zhang, 2021). These high rates of overt SPE are in sharp contrast to the rather low rate of 35.9% reported by Li et al. (2012) for young people in Harbin, China. However, given the paucity of variationist studies of Mandarin SPE, we cannot provide an explanation for the disparity.

To move beyond oral SPE rates, Li (2017) explored how SPE differs across and within modalities. With respect to differences in SPE rates in oral communication, Li found that overt pronouns were used more by Chinese language teachers during classroom instruction (58.9%) than by NSs in colloquial speech (35.9%). This difference may be due to teachers' efforts to make their speech more comprehensible to learners by using more overt pronouns. In addition, overt pronouns were found in advanced-level Chinese textbooks (which included authentic written Chinese from magazines, newspapers, and literary works) 29.9% of the time, demonstrating lower SPE rates in writing than in speech (Li, 2017). As Li (2017) notes, these SPE rates may differ across modalities for several reasons. One potential reason is the difference between oral and written use of anaphoric reference (i.e., employing a word or phrase to relate to something previously mentioned in the discourse). While oral discourse tends to be more spontaneous (Beaman, 1982; Chafe, 1982), written discourse allows for more time and planning, resulting in greater use of topic chains (Li, 2004) and thus an increase in pronoun omission (Christensen, 2000) in written as opposed to spoken Chinese.

Despite these differences in SPE rates across modalities, the constraints on SPE have been found to be similar in Mandarin Chinese and other languages, including Spanish. As seen with Spanish, in Mandarin Chinese, the two most prevalent linguistic constraints on SPE include coreference and person/number

(Jia & Bayley, 2002; Li & Bayley, 2018; Li et al., 2012). Numerous other linguistic (genre, sentence type, and verb type) and social (age and gender) constraints on SPE have also been identified in the literature on Mandarin (Guy et al., forthcoming; Jia & Bayley, 2002; Li & Bayley, 2018).

Acquisition of SPE

Acquisition of SPE in Spanish

In addition to the sociolinguistic literature on SPE among Spanish NSs, a growing body of research (Geeslin et al., 2023; Geeslin & Gudmestad, 2008; Geeslin et al., 2015; Linford & Geeslin, 2022; Zahler, 2018) has examined how L2 learners acquire this phenomenon. Overall, findings suggest that, as proficiency increases, learners move toward using more null subjects and constraints similar to those that condition NS SPE, such as person/number, TMA, switch reference, and frequency. This acquisitional trajectory, however, does not seem to be linear, but rather U-shaped, as L2 learners first exhibit lower, more targetlike overt SPE rates in the lowest proficiency levels, followed by greater overt SPE rates that move beyond targetlike norms in the next proficiency levels, and finally decreased overt SPE rates again in the highest proficiency levels, thus approximating NS norms (Geeslin et al., 2015). Geeslin and Gudmestad (2008) and Zahler (2018) found that the same constraints relevant to NSs, such as person/number, TMA, and change of reference, also constrained L2 SPE.

The aforementioned studies on L2 acquisition of SPE from a variationist perspective (Geeslin & Gudmestad, 2008; Gudmestad & Geeslin, 2011) generally rely on oral data obtained through sociolinguistic interviews and similar methods. Some recent research on the topic (Geeslin et al., 2023; Geeslin & Linford, 2012; Geeslin et al., 2015; Linford & Geeslin, 2022) has focused on subject selection using written contextualized tasks (WCTs) or written contextualized preference tasks (WCPTs). These tasks typically involve a fictional dialogue where participants choose the most natural-sounding option, varying only by the subject form. They allow researchers to manipulate constraints evenly across items and facilitate data collection among large groups of participants, contributing to understanding L2 Spanish subject pronoun variation. However, further research using learner-produced written data is warranted to examine variation in "natural writing" as opposed to the "vernacular", or less monitored speech, traditionally elicited orally in sociolinguistic interviews. Learner-produced writing data can provide real-time snapshots of interlanguage development in written discourse, and variability in this production can serve as an indicator of L2 writing proficiency (Huang et al., 2021). That said, this study aims to address this gap in our understanding of SPE in writing by examining L2 and L3 learners' essays in Spanish.

Acquisition of SPE in Mandarin Chinese

In contrast to the substantial research on the acquisition of Spanish SPE, studies on the topic in Mandarin Chinese are rare. These studies (Li, 2014, 2017) show that learners tend to use overt pronouns more than NSs, but that the constraints on SPE rates are similar. The most prevalent of the constraints are in line with those found in previous literature across languages, including person/number and switch reference.

In Li's (2014) study of high intermediate and advanced L2 learners of Chinese who spoke English, Korean, Japanese, or Russian as an L1, she found that learners used overt pronouns 59.4% of the time. The constraints of person/number and switch reference were the strongest predictors of SPE rates, followed by sentence type, native language, length of residence in China, gender, discourse context, proficiency level, and specificity. In a subsequent study, Li (2017) examined the same data set and found that although L2 learners used more overt pronouns than NSs, L2 overt SPE rates were similar to but slightly higher than those of their teachers. As such, learners seem to mirror SPE production of the input to which they are exposed (i.e., that of their teachers).

Acquisition of SPE: Relationship between L1, L2, and L3

Despite the numerous studies conducted on SPE rates among NSs and the growing body of literature on the acquisition of SPE, to date, researchers have been unable to clearly determine the role of the L1 in the acquisition of sociolinguistic competence. This question is related to crosslinguistic influence, which is made up of three types of transfer (linguistic, semantic, and conceptual) that are difficult to tease apart and likely work together (Jarvis, 2016). Although several studies suggest that language typology alone does not fully explain crosslinguistic influence (Jarvis, 2016), substantial debate remains with respect to the role of linguistic transfer in this process. While some studies suggest that learners transfer structures from their L1 to their L2 (Dewaele, 1999; Mougeon et al., 2004; Trevise & Noyau, 1984), others indicate that the L1 does not play a significant role in this process (Dewaele, 1998; Li, 2010).

One recent study that sheds light on this question with respect to SPE in typologically similar languages is that of Long (2021), who examined SPE rates among Korean-speaking learners of Spanish (Korean is also pro-drop) in four different instructional levels (first, second, third, and fourth year). She found that learners at each level primarily used null subjects (70% of the time), which is similar to null subject rates in speech among NSs of Korean. However, she also found that, with each level of Spanish instruction, the rate of use of null pronouns decreased while that of overt pronouns increased. This is different than what previous research has found for English-speaking learners of Spanish in which an increase in null subjects has been observed as proficiency increases as well as a higher rate of null pronoun use among English-speaking learners as opposed to NSs (Geeslin et al., 2015). In addition, Long found that verb number, verb-form regularity, verb semantics, and use of Spanish outside of class significantly predicted learner use of overt subject pronouns. She concluded that future studies might explore learner SPE rates from different L1 backgrounds to examine the role of typological similarity in SPE acquisition.

Regarding typological similarities and differences in terms of SPE, Li (2014) expected that L2 learners of Chinese who spoke English as an L1 would be more likely to use overt pronouns than those learners who spoke Russian, Korean, or Japanese (pro-drop languages) as L1s. Although she found that L1 English speakers favored overt pronouns, producing them more than the other speakers, L1 Russian speakers also favored overt pronouns (albeit less than L1 English speakers). Upon further analysis, Li determined that L2 learners' SPE rates in Mandarin Chinese were similar to the SPE rates found among NSs of each of their L1s, respectively, and thus suggested that SPE use in one's L1 can be transferred to the L2, in this case to Mandarin. These results regarding L1-L2 transfer were corroborated in Zhang (2021), who found that heritage learners of Mandarin who had acquired English first or who had acquired English and Mandarin at the same time used more overt pronouns than their counterparts who acquired Mandarin first.

In addition to exploring the role of the L1 in L2 acquisition, research on crosslinguistic influence also examines how L1 experiences and L2 learning relate to learning another language (McManus, 2022). Several recent models seek to explain L3 acquisition, and many take typological similarity into account. For example, the Full Transfer/Full Access model (Schwartz & Sprouse, 1996) suggested that the grammar of the L1 or the L2 is transferred depending on which is typologically most similar to the L3. The Typological Primacy Model (Rothman, 2011, 2015) proposed that the L1 or L2 is selected as the basis for L3 grammar. Rothman (2015) proposed that, according to a linguistic hierarchy (lexicon > phonology > morphology > syntax), the typologically more similar language would be determined and the grammar from that language would be transferred to the L3 in the first stages of acquisition. Most recently, the Scalpel Model (Slabakova, 2017) suggested that aspects of the L1 or L2 can be transferred selectively, as needed, according to the task at any time during L3 acquisition. As such, neither the L1 nor the L2 has privileged status in L3 acquisition, and aspects of the L1 and the L2 can be selected with "scalpel-like precision" when acquiring a L3. Similarly, the Linguistic Proximity Model (Westergaard et al., 2017) proposed that the L1 and L2 are available for transfer at any point in L3 acquisition, depending on the feature at hand.

Some recent studies have investigated L3 acquisition of SPE, focusing on transfer from an L1 and/or a L2 to an L3, as opposed to that from an L1 to an L2. For example, Clements and Domínguez (2018) examined the written use and interpretation of null and overt subjects by L1 speakers of English who were learning Chinese as an L3. These speakers were divided into two groups: those who had an pro-drop language (Spanish) as an L2 and those who had an non-pro-drop language as an L2. Null subjects were not difficult to acquire for either learner group, as both groups exhibited targetlike use of null subjects. Both groups had more problems with the use and interpretation of overt pronouns, however, suggesting that they are more difficult to acquire than null subjects. Moreover, there was transfer from both background languages, but for different properties. For example, there was a small advantage for learners who had a pro-drop language as a L2 in acquiring L3 Chinese, which suggests L2 transfer occurred. In addition, there were significant differences for both groups in the interpretation of overt pronouns when compared to a control group of Chinese NSs, which could indicate transfer from the L1 (English). The authors suggested that these results are in line with the Scalpel Model (Slabakova, 2017), which states that the L1 and the L2 can be transferred to the L3 depending on the property at hand. The authors concluded that partial transfer is possible in L3 acquisition and that structural similarities between the background and the target languages are important in this transfer.

Another recent study, Cherici (2021), investigated SPE among L1 speakers of Mandarin Chinese with different levels of L2 proficiency in English when acquiring Italian (a pro-drop language) as an L3. Using an acceptability judgment task, she found that learners with lower L2 English proficiency rejected overt subjects more accurately than learners with higher L2 English proficiency. In other words, learners with lower L2 English proficiency seemed to exhibit more SPE transfer from the L1 to the L3, whereas learners with higher L2 English proficiency seemed to exhibit more SPE transfer from the L2 to the L3. She concluded that SPE patterns can be transferred from the L1 and the L2 to the L3 and that proficiency level in the L2 may affect learners' ability to transfer patterns from the L2 to the L3.

Research questions

While previous literature has established NS norms for SPE rates and constraints in both Spanish and Mandarin Chinese, and research on the acquisition of SPE in these languages has generally shown that learners approximate NS rates and constraints as proficiency increases, little is known about SPE rates and constraints in written discourse among both NSs and learners. Moreover, while L1 norms seem to transfer to L2 SPE rates, it is not clear to what extent the typological similarity of an L1 might transfer to an L3. As such, the present study aims to answer the following research questions:

1. Do L1 speakers of English (a non-pro drop language) and L1 speakers of Mandarin Chinese (a pro-drop language) pattern similarly or differently in their use of overt and null pronouns in Spanish (a pro-drop language)?
2. If differently, how can we account for the difference?
3. When do speakers of both native languages begin to acquire the constraints on Spanish SPE?

Methods

Corpus

Data for this paper were drawn from the UC Davis Corpus of Written Spanish, L2/H (COWSL2/H; Yamada et al., 2020). The corpus consists of short essays collected from students enrolled in university-level Spanish courses in California. All essays, annotations, and corrections are available both as individual text files as well as comma-separated value (csv) files. Essays are divided based on the prompts used to collect the data, with topics including a famous person, the perfect vacation plan, a special person, and a terrible story. Each essay prompt is further divided by the academic quarter of data collection.

Participants

Participants ($N=131$) were either NSs of English or Mandarin Chinese who were studying Spanish as an L2 or L3 at a variety of levels, beginning with first year, first quarter of undergraduate study (labeled "Novice 1" in Table 1) and concluding with third year (labeled "Advanced"). The COWS Corpus collects metadata on age, gender, L1s, languages spoken at home, languages studied, if the participant had ever lived in a Spanish-speaking country, and self-reported ratings in listening and reading comprehension and speaking and writing abilities.

Because we were interested in exploring the role of language background in SPE, only participants who met specific criteria were selected from the corpus. For the L1 English group, participants were selected if they reported English as their only L1, did not speak any other languages at home, and had not lived in a Spanish-speaking country. For the L1 Chinese group, participants were selected if they reported Mandarin as their only L1, only spoke Mandarin at home, reported English as their only other L2, and had never lived in a Spanish-speaking country.

Many of the English L1 participants had begun studying Spanish prior to undergraduate study, but most of the Chinese L1 participants had only studied Spanish at the undergraduate level. Table 1 shows the number and distribution of participants by L1 and course level.

Table 1. Participants by language and course level

Course level	Mandarin L1	English L1
Novice 1	10	9
Novice 2	11	10
Novice 3	13	12
Intermediate 1	11	11
Intermediate 2	8	7
Intermediate 3	8	7
Advanced	7	7
Total	68	63

Coding

After extracting the essays from the corpus, a total of 2,892 SPE contexts were coded and analyzed according to several factors. The dependent variable was subject pronoun expression, with two possible variants: overt pronoun expression (1a) or null pronoun expression (1b).

(1) a. *ella es*   'she is'
    b. *Ø es*   '(she) is'

Contexts that typically demonstrate little to no variability were excluded from the study, including dative experiencer subjects (e.g., *me gusta* 'he/she likes', *le encanta* 'he/she loves', *nos interesa* 'we are interested in') and subject relative clauses (e.g., *las personas que viajaron* 'the people that traveled').

Following previous studies on SPE in Spanish, English, and Chinese, each token was coded for the following independent variables: switch reference, grammatical person/number, ambiguity of the verb, reflexivity, TMA, clause type, verb semantic type, L1 of the participant, and course level of Spanish. Each of these is further discussed below.

Switch reference

Switch reference is a binary category indicating whether the subject of the token in question is the same as the subject of the previous tensed verb (2a) or if it is different (2b). Tokens were coded as N/A if they appeared as the first verb in the essay.

(2) a. Switch: ...*estoy segura de que <u>nosotros vamos</u> a tener éxito.* '...I am sure that <u>we are going</u> to be successful.'
b. No switch: *Cuando era niña, me gustaba cocinar. <u>Cocinaba</u> cada domingo con mi familia.* 'When I was young, I liked to cook. <u>I cooked</u> every Sunday with my family.'

Based on previous research (Cameron, 1995; Otheguy & Zentella, 2012), we expected switch reference to be the strongest predictor of SPE, with change in subject from the preceding tensed verb favoring overt pronouns.

Grammatical person/number

Tokens were coded for verb person/number and resulted in four factor groups: first- and third-person singular and first- and third-person plural. Second-person pronouns are rare in essays, unless the writing is directly addressing the reader. In the essays coded for this study, there were too few second-person verb forms to include in the quantitative analysis without skewing the results (10 of 2sg. informal, 6 of 2sg. formal, 3 of 2pl.). Hence, second-person tokens were excluded from the quantitative analysis.

Because previous studies have found that singular subjects favor overt pronouns more than plural subjects (Geeslin & Gudmestad, 2008), we expected to see the same patterns in our data. We also hypothesized that first-person plural subjects, given how salient the *nosotros* 'we' pronoun and first-person plural inflection are in Spanish, would be the most likely to favor pronoun absence.

Ambiguity of the verb

In Spanish, there are some instances of TMA that result in ambiguity between first- and third-person singular verbs. That is, in the conditional, imperfect, pluperfect, and the subjunctive (past and present), first-person singular and third-person singular verbs are identical (for example, the first- and third-person singular imperfect forms of *estudiar* 'to study' are the same: *yo/ella estudiaba* 'I/she studied'). However, those same verbs in present indicative, preterite, future indicative, and present perfect do not demonstrate ambiguity between the first- and third-person singular forms (for example, in preterite, the conjugations differ: *yo estudié* 'I studied' and *ella estudió* 'she studied'). Whether morphological ambiguity leads to a higher rate of overt pronoun use, however, has been a subject of debate. Holmquist (2012) and Otheguy and Zentella (2012) found higher rates of overt use with ambiguous verbs, but others did not (e.g. Bentivoglio, 1987; Enríquez, 1984) while Bayley and Pease-Alvarez (1997) and Silva-Corvalán (2001) argued that the higher rates sometimes observed in tenses with ambiguous forms was a result of semantic factors. To test the possible effect of ambiguity, we coded both the factors of TMA and morphological ambiguity.

Tense/Mood/Aspect (TMA)

TMA is often included as an independent variable in SPE studies of Spanish, with the highest overt pronoun rate occurring with the imperfect and the lowest occurring with the imperative (Shin & Erker, 2015). However, it is unclear if the effect of TMA is conflated with ambiguity, as there are several TMA forms that are ambiguous (imperfect, subjunctive, conditional, pluperfect), and in some studies the SPE effect seems to be related to ambiguity rather than strictly TMA. We coded verbs for TMA, as in Examples 3a–3i. No other TMAs were present in the dataset.

(3) a. Present indicative   *hablo, estoy hablando* 'I speak, I am speaking'
    b. Imperfect indicative *hablaba, estaba hablando* 'I spoke, I was speaking'
    c. Preterite   *hablé* 'I spoke'
    d. Periphrastic future   *voy a hablar* 'I'm going to speak'
    e. Future indicative   *hablaré* 'I will speak'
    f. Conditional   *hablaría* 'I would speak'
    g. Present subjunctive *hable* 'I speak'
    h. Past subjunctive   *hablara* 'I spoke'
    i. Present perfect   *he hablado* 'I have spoken'

Semantic verb class

Following previous research (Abreu, 2009; Carvalho et al., 2015; Orozco & Guy, 2008; Travis, 2007), we also included semantic verb class as an independent variable. We divided verbs into five categories: psychological (e.g., *saber* 'to know', *pensar* 'to think', *suponer* 'to suppose'), speech acts (e.g., *decir* 'to say', *comunicar* 'to communicate', *anunciar* 'to announce', *pedir* 'to ask for'), motion (verbs that indicate actual movement such as *entrar* 'to enter', *llegar* 'to arrive', *ir* 'to go', *caminar* 'to walk'), copulas (e.g., *ser* and *estar* 'to be'), perception (e.g., *ver* 'to see', *oír* 'to hear', *escuchar* 'to listen to'), and other verbs that do not fall into one of the above categories (e.g., *tener* 'to have' and *querer* 'to want').

Reflexivity

Reflexive verbs in Spanish are obligatorily marked with a reflexive pronoun, which helps to disambiguate or reinforce the subject of the verb (see Examples 4a and 4b).

(4) a. Reflexive: *Me fui a casa.* 'I went home.'
    b. Non-reflexive: ... *hablé con mi padre....* '...I spoke with my father....'

Likely due to the additional referential information encoded in the reflexive pronoun, overt SPE is lower in reflexive verbs than non-reflexives (Abreu, 2009; Carvalho & Child, 2011; Michnowicz, 2015; Otheguy & Zentella, 2012).

Clause type

We considered clause type as an independent variable, as in examples 5a and 5b:

(5) a. Main clause: *El verano pasado, estaba a [sic] la casa de mis padres...* 'Last summer, I was at my parents' house.'
  b. Subordinate clause: *Mis padres viven con nuestro perro que hemos tenido por doce años.* 'My parents live with our dog that we have had for twelve years.'

Some studies have found that main clauses favor pronoun expression (Otheguy & Zentella, 2012; Shin & Montes-Alcalá, 2014); however, recent cross-linguistic work (Guy et al., forthcoming) has found that subordinate clauses favor overt pronouns in Spanish, Portuguese, Persian, and Swabian German. We therefore were agnostic about the possible effect of this constraint.

First language

The L1 of the participant — English or Mandarin — was also included as an independent variable. In English, overt pronoun use is nearly categorical, while overt pronoun use varies systematically in Mandarin and Spanish. Because SPE is variable in Mandarin, we expected our L1 Mandarin participants to be more adept at omitting overt pronouns in Spanish than their L1 English counterparts.

Course level

Finally, we considered the participants' experience studying Spanish. Participants were divided into seven groups according to the course in which they were enrolled: Novice 1, 2, and 3 (also referred to as first, second, and third quarter), Intermediate Spanish 1, 2, and 3 (also referred to as fourth, fifth, and sixth quarter), or Advanced Spanish (also referred to as seventh quarter or third year).[1] We anticipated that participants would decrease their use of Spanish overt pronouns as their experience in Spanish increased.

Analysis

Data were analyzed using a generalized linear mixed effects model (GLME) in R using the glmer() function in the lme4 package (Bates et al., 2015). Manual step-up analysis was used to determine the inclusion of variables and interactions. The inclusion of participant as a random intercept was also tested and found to

---

1. Like many universities in the western U.S., the university providing the data for this study was on the quarter system. Thus, a term refers to an academic quarter of 10 weeks.

improve model fit. We also used the drop1() function in R (Kuznetsova et al., 2017) to rank constraints.

Results

In this section, we present the results of multiple rounds of logistic regression. We tested five models: model 1 examined SPE by all students from all course levels, model 2 combined course levels as level 1 for first-year students and level 2 for students in their second year and beyond, and model 3 explored the interaction between clause type and L1. Because we observed the L1 effect in L2 and L3 SPE variation, we further examined the role of L1 by testing only L1 Mandarin speakers' SPE in model 4 and only L1 English speakers' SPE in model 5.

In both model 1 and model 2, significant linguistic constraints include course level, L1, coreference, reflexivity, person/number, and verb type. TMA and ambiguity did not reach significance in either model. Based on model comparison, model 3 fits our data better and provides more details about students' acquisition trajectory and interaction between constraints.[2] Thus, the following discussion focuses on the results reported in model 3, shown in Table 2.

As Table 2 shows, switch reference favored overt SPE ($\beta=0.787$, $p<.001$), while reflexives disfavored overt pronouns ($\beta=-1.36$, $p<.001$). For person/number, the dataset contained large numbers of first-person singular ($k=1334$) and third-person singular ($k=1168$) tokens, but relatively few first-person plural ($k=285$) and third person plural ($k=85$) tokens. As noted previously, there were too few second-person tokens to include in the analysis. The results show that third-person singular verbs strongly favored overt pronouns ($\beta=1.73$, $p<.001$). As for verb type, all verbs other than copulas disfavored pronouns, with speech act verbs ($\beta=-1.03$, $p<.001$), psychological verbs ($\beta=-0.66$, $p=.002$), and verbs other than motion or perception ($\beta=-0.55$, $p<.001$) reaching significance. TMA and ambiguity did not significantly contribute to this model.

Both course level and L1 were strong predictors of SPE variation. Specifically, students in third-quarter Spanish used significantly fewer pronouns than students in first and second quarter ($\beta=-1.31$, $p<.001$). Students in second year and beyond tended to use more null pronouns than first-year students. For L1 effects, Mandarin-speaking students tended to use fewer pronouns than their English-speaking peers ($\beta=-0.69$, $p=.020$). In addition, the interaction between clause type and L1 appeared to be a strong predictor of SPE variation ($\beta=-0.90$,

---

[2] For a detailed model comparison, please refer to supplemental materials available at https://osf.io/jrs4p/?view_only=b1f118a8177047f3927866b7bbf1b109

$p = .002$). As shown in Tables 3 and 4, clause type is significant for Mandarin speakers ($p < .001$) but not for English speakers.

Table 2. GLME analysis of L2 and L3 subject pronoun expression

Effect	Estimate	Std. Error	Odds Ratios	95% CI	Z value	Pr (>|z|)	N	Overt SPE%
(Intercept)	−0.17	0.38	0.84	[−0.91, 0.57]	−0.45	.650		
Switch_na	0.28	0.40	1.32	[−0.50, 1.06]	0.70	.482	50	28.00
Switch_s	0.79	0.11	2.20	[0.57, 1.00]	7.24	<.001	1038	40.94
Reflexive_r	−1.36	0.24	0.26	[−1.83, −0.88]	−5.60	<.001	197	14.21
Per/num_3	1.73	0.15	5.66	[1.45, 2.02]	11.82	<.001	1168	52.31
Per/num_ellos	0.46	0.32	1.58	[−0.17, 1.09]	1.41	.158	85	64.71
Per/num_nos	−0.26	0.23	0.77	[−0.71, 0.18]	−1.18	.240	285	19.30
Clause type_S	−0.14	0.21	0.87	[−0.54, 0.26]	−0.70	.486	504	25.60
Home lang_Man	−0.69	0.30	0.50	[−1.27, −0.11]	−2.34	.020	1431	34.03
Verb type_mot	−0.24	0.20	0.78	[−0.64, 0.15]	−1.20	.229	313	35.78
Verb type_oth	−0.55	0.13	0.58	[−0.81, −0.29]	−4.14	<.001	1463	35.20
Verb type_per	−0.44	0.33	0.64	[−1.08, 0.19]	−1.36	.173	87	31.03
Verb type_psy	−0.66	0.21	0.52	[−1.07, −0.24]	−3.12	.002	291	23.37
Verb type_spe	−1.03	0.27	0.36	[−1.56, −0.50]	−3.81	<.001	127	27.56
Novice 2 (2nd Quarter)	−0.29	0.37	0.75	[−1.03, 0.44]	−0.78	.435	374	45.99
Novice 3 (3rd Quarter)	−1.31	0.38	0.27	[−2.05, −0.58]	−3.50	<.001	588	28.91
Intermediate 1 (4th Quarter)	−1.19	0.41	0.30	[−1.99, −0.40]	−2.94	.003	571	32.92
Intermediate 2 (5th Quarter)	−1.41	0.46	0.24	[−2.32, −0.50]	−3.04	.002	292	28.77
Intermediate 3 (6th Quarter)	−1.52	0.38	0.22	[−2.26, −0.77]	−3.99	<.001	421	38.72
Advanced (7th Quarter)	−1.10	0.41	0.33	[−1.91, −0.29]	−2.68	.007	255	36.86
Clause_S x Home lang.Man	−0.90	0.30	0.41	[−1.48, −0.32]	−3.06	.002		

Note. Individual = 118, number of observations = 2866, σ^2 = 3.29, τ00ID = 2.17, ICC = 0.40, AIC = 2892.7, BIC = 3041.8, log likelihood = −1421.4, deviance = 2842.7, df. resid = 2841, Marginal R^2 = 0.261, Conditional R^2 = 0.555

While information about which constraints significantly condition learners' choices between a null and an overt pronoun is obviously useful, we are also interested in the relative strength of constraints and how constraint ranking compares with the ranking in native speech. To achieve this goal, we used the drop1 procedure in R (Kuznetsova et al., 2017), which shows the increase in the Akaike Information Criterion (AIC) if the factor is dropped from the model. According to this measure, the constraint ranking is Person/Number > Switch reference > Reflexivity > Verb type > Clause type > Course level > L1.[3] In the data analyzed here, neither TMA nor ambiguity contribute to the choice of an overt or null pronoun, and the inclusion of ambiguity actually worsens the model.

When considering the data by L1 and quarter of Spanish study, we found interesting results (see Tables 3 and 4 and Figure 1). In their first term of study, both L1 groups chose overt pronouns more than half of the time (54.25% for L1 English speakers and 53.41% for L1 Mandarin speakers). After the first quarter of study, Mandarin L1 students' use of the overt option decreased to 39.55%, although the decrease did not reach significance. However, by the third quarter of first-year Spanish, Mandarin L1 students were using overt pronouns at the very low rate of 17.27%, significantly lower than the rate at the first term ($\beta = -1.64$, $p < .050$). As shown in Table 3, the Mandarin L1 students continued to choose the overt option at significantly lower rates than in their first quarter of study throughout the second year and beyond. However, after they reached their lowest rate of pronoun usage in the third quarter, they steadily increased again each term, and by the advanced level, they had nearly returned to the rates seen in the first quarter of study (21.78% in fourth quarter, 35.33% in fifth quarter, 42.29% in sixth quarter, and 43.43% in seventh quarter). Nevertheless, as shown in Figure 1, there is considerable individual variation among the students in this group and there is ample fluctuation in rates after the first quarter of the second year of study.

As seen with the L1 Chinese speakers, the L1 English speakers also decrease in overt pronoun usage after the first quarter, although this drop does not reach significance until the fifth quarter (labeled intermediate 2, see Table 1): 51.03% in second quarter, 37.50% in third quarter, 46.92% in fourth quarter, 22.46% in fifth quarter, 35.48% in sixth quarter, and 21.79% in seventh quarter. Unlike the L1 Chinese speakers who reached their lowest pronoun usage at the end of their first year of study, the L1 English speakers did not reach their lowest pronoun usage until their third year of study. And while the Mandarin speakers tended to have the pronoun advantage early on, using less than half as many pronouns as their L1 Eng-

---

[3]. For further details, please see the supplemental material available at https://osf.io/jrs4p /?view_only=b1f118a8177047f3927866b7bbf1b109

lish counterparts at the end of the first year, by the third year, the two groups had reversed; Mandarin L1 students were using twice the overt pronouns compared to L1 English speakers.

Table 3. Subject pronoun expression by Mandarin-speaking students

Effect	Estimate	Std. Error	Odds Ratios	95% CI	Z value	Pr (>|z|)	N	Overt SPE%
(Intercept)	0.10	0.51	1.11	[0.41, 3.04]	0.20	.840		
Switch_na	0.43	0.57	1.54	[0.50, 4.70]	0.76	.449	27	25.93
Switch_s	0.64	0.16	1.90	[1.39, 2.60]	4.00	<.001	541	34.38
Reflexive_r	−1.48	0.35	0.23	[0.11, 0.45]	−4.19	<.001	105	11.43
Per/num_3	1.84	0.21	6.30	[4.17, 9.53]	8.73	<.001	561	49.55
Per/num_ellos	0.58	0.42	1.79	[0.79, 4.08]	1.39	.164	58	31.03
Per/num_nos	−0.06	0.34	0.95	[0.48, 1.85]	−0.16	.873	143	16.78
Clause type_S	−1.13	0.22	0.32	[0.21, 0.50]	−5.04	<.001	256	17.97
Verb type_mot	−0.07	0.34	0.93	[0.48, 1.80]	−0.21	.838	123	29.27
Verb type_oth	−0.49	0.20	0.61	[0.41, 0.91]	−2.45	.014	730	32.33
Verb type_per	−0.36	0.46	0.70	[0.28, 1.73]	−0.77	.442	47	27.66
Verb type_psy	−0.56	0.29	0.57	[0.32, 1.02]	−1.90	.058	177	21.47
Verb type_spe	−1.14	0.35	0.32	[0.16, 0.64]	−3.27	.001	87	26.44
Novice 2 (2nd Quarter)	−0.81	0.54	0.44	[0.15, 1.27]	−1.52	.129	177	39.55
Novice 3 (3rd Quarter)	−2.08	0.53	0.12	[0.04, 0.35]	−3.95	<.001	249	17.27
Intermediate 1 (4th Quarter)	−2.29	0.55	0.10	[0.03, 0.30]	−4.15	<.001	303	21.78
Intermediate 2 (5th Quarter)	−1.77	0.62	0.17	[0.05, 0.58]	−2.85	.004	150	35.33
Intermediate 3 (6th Quarter)	−2.00	0.53	0.14	[0.05, 0.38]	−3.79	<.001	201	42.29
Advanced (7th Quarter)	−1.31	0.56	0.27	[0.09, 0.81]	−2.35	.019	175	43.43

Note. Individual = 51, number of observations = 1431, σ^2 = 3.29, τ00ID = 2.50, ICC = 0.43, AIC = 1348.3, BIC = 1469.4, log likelihood = −651.2, deviance = 1302.3, df. resid = 1408, Marginal R^2 = 0.278, Conditional R^2 = 0.589.

Table 4. Subject pronoun expression by English-speaking students

	Estimate	Std. Error	Odds Ratios	95% CI	Z value	Pr (>|z|)	N	Overt SPE%
(Intercept)	−1.07	0.49	0.34	[0.13, 0.90]	−2.19	.029		
Switch_na	0.19	0.56	1.21	[0.41, 3.59]	0.34	.731	23	30.43
Switch_s	0.91	0.15	2.49	[1.86, 3.35]	6.08	<.001	497	48.09
Reflexive_r	−1.30	0.34	0.27	[0.14, 0.53]	−3.81	<.001	92	17.39
Per/num_3	1.61	0.21	5.00	[3.33, 7.51]	7.75	<.001	607	54.86
Per/num_ellos	0.18	0.53	1.20	[0.43, 3.39]	0.35	.728	27	37.04
Per/num_nos	−0.46	0.31	0.63	[0.35, 1.15]	−1.51	.131	142	21.83
Clause type_S	−0.03	0.21	0.97	[0.65, 1.47]	−0.14	.890	248	33.47
Verb type_mot	−0.39	0.26	0.68	[0.41, 1.13]	−1.51	.132	190	40.00
Verb type_oth	−0.60	0.18	0.55	[0.38, 0.78]	−3.30	.001	733	10.37
Verb type_per	−0.52	0.47	0.60	[0.24, 1.48]	−1.12	.264	40	35.00
Verb type_psy	−0.70	0.31	0.49	[0.27, 0.91]	−2.26	.024	114	26.32
Verb type_spe	−0.79	0.45	0.45	[0.19, 1.10]	−1.75	.079	40	30.00
Novice 2 (2nd Quarter)	−0.09	0.63	0.91	[0.27, 3.14]	−0.14	.885	194	51.03
Novice 3 (3rd Quarter)	−0.50	0.53	0.60	[0.21, 1.72]	−0.95	.344	336	37.50
Intermediate 1 (4th Quarter)	0.44	0.60	1.55	[0.48, 4.96]	0.73	.463	260	46.92
Intermediate 2 (5th Quarter)	−1.64	0.82	0.19	[0.04, 0.96]	−2.01	.045	138	22.46
Intermediate 3 (6th Quarter)	−0.69	0.59	0.50	[0.16, 1.58]	−1.18	.238	217	35.48
Advanced (7th Quarter)	−1.78	0.73	0.17	[0.04, 0.70]	−2.46	.014	78	21.79

Note. Individual = 68, number of observations = 1435, σ^2 = 3.29, τooID = 1.53, ICC = 0.32, AIC = 1545.9, BIC = 1667.1, log likelihood = −749.9, deviance = 1499.9, df. resid = 1412, Marginal R^2 = 0.249, Conditional R^2 = 0.488

In addition to differences in rates, Tables 3 and 4 show that the two groups differed in the effects of linguistic constraints. While co-reference, reflexivity, and person/number significantly constrained pronoun choice by both groups, clause type only reached significance for the Mandarin L1 group. In addition, the groups differed with respect to the effect of verb semantics. For Mandarin L1 students,

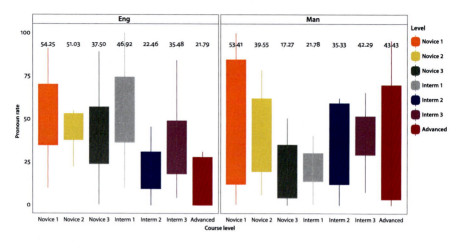

Figure 1. Subject pronoun expression by course level and L1

speech act verbs significantly disfavored overt pronouns; for English speakers, psychological verbs disfavored them.

Discussion and implications

Our results suggest that L1 speakers of English and Mandarin pattern both similarly and differently in their use of Spanish overt and null pronouns. In general, both L1 English and Mandarin speakers begin their Spanish studies using overt subject pronouns at a similarly high rate – over 50% of the time – but both groups' overt SPE decreases between their first and second years of study, reflecting what we see overall in the acquisition of sociolinguistic features: As learners' proficiency increases, they move toward NS norms, in this case toward greater use of null pronouns (Geeslin & Gudmestad, 2008; Geeslin et al., 2015).

As for when changes in SPE begin to occur, we observe different results for the English L1 and Mandarin L1 groups. The results indicate that the Mandarin group has an early advantage; for Chinese L1 speakers, it is quite soon – only after two quarters of study – that we begin to see significantly fewer subject pronouns used (by the third term of study, overt pronouns drop to just 17.27%), but for English L1 participants, we do not witness a significant drop in subject pronouns until the fifth quarter (22.46% overt). And while both groups decrease in overt SPE between the first and the seventh quarter of study, neither group drops in overt pronoun usage in a strictly linear fashion, although the English L1 group decreases more steadily over time than the Chinese group. After the end of the first year, when the Mandarin speakers have reached their lowest overt SPE rates, they begin to increase again in overt SPE in their second and third year, ending at a rate of 43.43% overt pronouns in the seventh quarter (still significantly lower than their first quarter average, but twice that of the English group's seventh quarter). The English speakers tended to demonstrate more of a linear pattern toward nativelike Spanish SPE over the three years, with their highest pronoun usage observed in the first quarter and their lowest in the seventh (21.79%), although not every quarter witnesses a drop.

While both groups move toward nativelike Spanish SPE rates, the Mandarin group demonstrates more of a U-shaped pattern, with the lowest rates occurring relatively early on and then increasing again with time but not reaching the initial level. This U-shaped pattern in pronoun usage is different from the one reported by Geeslin et al. (2015), which found that Spanish learners tended to start out using higher levels of null pronouns in first year, then decreased in years two to three, and then rose again in null pronoun use after four to five years of Spanish study, becoming similar to NSs in SPE at the graduate level. Here, our Mandarin speakers show nearly the opposite pattern, beginning with higher overt pronoun rates, then decreasing quickly and then increasing again; however, comparing patterns in the two studies requires caution, since not all of the same proficiency levels were tested.

The fact that Mandarin speakers' overt SPE decreased significantly by the end of the first year of Spanish study may be attributable to the fact that the Mandarin speakers already omit pronouns in their L1 and are thus able to notice this feature and/or implement it more quickly than the English group. However, the fact that the L1 Mandarin participants were quicker to acquire variation in SPE in Spanish may not be only due to the feature similarity in both languages; research has suggested that both linguistic transfer from previously learned languages and enhanced metalinguistic awareness garnered from prior language learning experiences affect L3 acquisition (Cenoz, 2003; Park & Starr, 2016). That is, the more experience a learner has with multiple languages, the more sensitive they are to novel linguistic features, facilitating their ability to recognize patterns and integrate them into a L3 (Bardel & Falk, 2012). It is unclear, however, why the overt SPE of the Mandarin group would increase during the second and third years of Spanish study; some of this variation could be explained by the low number of L1 Mandarin speakers in the corpus at the higher levels of Spanish, allowing for a couple of heavy overt pronoun users to skew the results, but further research is needed to verify this.

In addition to different trajectories in overt pronoun usage between the groups, we also see greater individual variability in Chinese-speaking as compared to English-speaking participants (see Figure 1). In both the first and seventh quarters of Spanish, for example, the Mandarin group's range of SPE is approximately twice that of the English group. This higher individual variation seen among Mandarin speakers may be attributable to the fact that with each additional language acquired, more variables are involved in crosslinguistic influence. As these speakers produce discourse in their L3, they may be drawing inference from structural, semantic, or conceptual representations of their L1 and/or L2 (see Jarvis, 2016), as well as being influenced by a wide range of learner variables. While the corpus from which the essays were drawn provides data regarding the participants' L1 and additional languages, other learner variables such as exposure, motivation, age of acquisition were not collected. Having a more nuanced understanding of the linguistic, affective, and educational experiences of the learners would help in understanding the varied trajectories of the Chinese group in particular.

In terms of constraint ranking, as shown in Tables 3 and 4, both English L1 and Chinese L1 speakers are sensitive to co-reference, reflexivity, and person/number. For both English and Mandarin speakers, person/number was the highest-ranking constraint. A small difference between the groups was that clause type significantly affected Mandarin speakers' choice of variant (subordinate clauses disfavored the overt form), while clause type failed to reach significance for English L1 speakers. We would expect constraints that are universal, such as switch reference, to be acquired first and rank most prominently in the constraint ranking, and then language-specific constraints, such as person/number or clause type, to be acquired later. In our data, person/number was the constraint that was acquired first and most strongly for all participants. Person/number has also been shown to be the highest-ranking constraint in other studies. For example, Guy et al. (forthcoming), in a crosslinguistic study that included more than 123,000 tokens collected in 10 Spanish-speaking communities, found that for Spanish, person/number was the strongest constraint. This contrasted with results for Persian, Mandarin, and Brazilian and European Portuguese, where switch reference was the first-order constraint. It appears, then, that learners are acquiring the strongest constraint in native speech first, before they acquire other constraints.

Our results indicate that for SPE development in Spanish as a L2 or L3, it is neither similarity in language typology in the L1 (as is the case for English) nor presence of the same feature in the L1 (as is the case in Mandarin) that fully predicts successful transfer into the L3. While language background plays a role in how pronouns develop over time, learners approach nativelike norms at different points in their Spanish study regardless of their L1. These results seem to support the Scalpel Model (Slabakova, 2017), which states that aspects of the L1 or L2 can be transferred selectively, as needed, according to the task at any time during L3 acquisition.

Conclusion

In this study, we compared the acquisition of SPE in Spanish written narratives by L1 speakers of English learning Spanish as a L2 and L1 speakers of Mandarin learning Spanish as a L3. We found higher overt SPE rates among all of our learners (37.5%), as compared to NSs of mainland Spanish in sociolinguistic interviews (15–37%; Guy et al., forthcoming), heritage speakers in narratives from the same corpus (20.1%; Bayley et al., 2023), and first-person SPE among heritage speakers in essays (8%; Fernández Flórez, 2023). But while the overall rates of our participants are higher, each group at their point of lowest overt pronoun usage, which is third quarter for Mandarin speakers (17.27%), and seventh quarter for English speakers (21.79%), is close to or lower than the overt SPE rate of the heritage speakers of Bayley et al. (2023) and well within the range of the large-scale NS Spanish data set of Guy et al. (forthcoming). Furthermore, our participants acquired many of the same constraints operating on NS SPE: person/number, reflexivity, and change of reference, underscoring their progress. In combination, our results suggest that over time, Spanish learners from different language backgrounds can acquire nativelike SPE.

While we find some similarities in our data to previous research on the acquisition of Spanish SPE among L2 learners (i.e., Geeslin & Gudmestad, 2008; Geeslin et al., 2015; Long, 2021, Zahler, 2018), especially in terms of the acquisition of the constraints on SPE, our learners do not always follow the same trajectory of pronoun use over time seen in those studies. Our English speakers demonstrate more of a linear trajectory from higher to lower pronoun use, but Chinese speakers demonstrate a U-shaped pattern, with quick drops in pronoun use early and then higher levels observed between years two and three. With the exception of Bayley et al.'s (2023) analysis of SPE in Spanish heritage speakers' essays, which is based on the same corpus as the current study, previous research on this topic is based primarily on oral data (mostly sociolinguistic interviews) and much less frequently on written data (from questionnaires and textbooks). The differences seen here suggest that sociolinguistic variations in interlanguage oral and written discourses are indeed very different, which underscores the importance of exploring different modalities. This paper contributes a first account of SPE in L2 and L3 narratives in Spanish, showing how SPE develops over time in L2 and L3 writing.

Despite its contributions, this study presents several questions regarding modality that future research should address. The essays analyzed here have substantially more referent continuity than a typical sociolinguistic interview, which is the basis for most previous SPE studies. Given the effect of modality across languages, we would expect fewer pronouns than in oral conversation where topics can change rapidly. However, the essay topics also call for singular pronouns, and we have ample evidence that Spanish speakers and learners use more pronouns with singular than plural verb forms. In addition, learners may tend to use more overt pronouns to avoid ambiguity and be safe in their references, which was also found in L2 oral discourse in previous studies (e.g., Li, 2010, 2014). Another possibility is that the learners in this study are still in the process of learning how to write in Spanish and need more time to develop their competence in composing more complex sentence structures with more integrated subordinate clauses. Thus, in order to more fully understand the acquisition of SPE in written narratives, future research should examine such data among both NSs and learners of a variety of proficiency levels from different linguistic backgrounds.

In conclusion, the findings of this study underscore the need to expand our theoretical assumptions and methodological procedures about the role of multilingualism in adult language acquisition. In the U.S., we often design our studies assuming that participants have English as their L1 or exclude from the study those who speak additional languages at home. Traditionally, we have thought about the role of English in the acquisition of a L2, but when students are increasingly from multilingual and mixed backgrounds, we need to consider a much more complex system of transfer. While all of the variables involved in language background make the empirical study of sociolinguistics challenging, we must continue to broaden our lens and consider the constraints from multiple language combinations as well as other L1s.

References

Abreu, L. (2009). Spanish subject personal pronoun use by monolinguals, bilinguals and second language learners [Unpublished doctoral dissertation. University of Florida.

Bardel, C., & Falk, Y. (2012). The L2 status factor and the declarative/procedural distinction. In J.A. Amaro, S. Flynn, & J. Rothman (Eds.), *Third language acquisition in adulthood* (pp. 165–194). John Benjamins.

Barrenechea, A. M., & Alonso, A. (1973). Los pronombres personales sujetos en el español de Buenos Aires. In K. Karl-Hermann & K. Rühl (Eds.), *Studia Iberica: Festschrift für Hans Flasche* (pp. 75–91). Francke.

Bates, D., Mächler, M., Bolker, B., & Walker, S. (2015). Fitting linear mixed-effects models using lme4. *Journal of Statistical Software, 67*(1), 1–48.

Bayley, R., Greer, K. A., & Holland, C. L. (2017). Lexical frequency and morphosyntactic variation: Evidence from U.S. Spanish. *Spanish in Context, 14*, 413–439.

Bayley, R., Holland, C., Rud, J. A., & Méndez Kline, T. (2023, October 12–14). *Variation in heritage Spanish writing: The case of subject personal pronouns* [Conference presentation]. Hispanic Linguistics Symposium, Provo, UT, United States.

Bayley, R., & Pease-Alvarez, L. (1997). Null pronoun variation in Mexican-descent children's narrative discourse. *Language Variation and Change, 9*, 349–371.

Beaman, K. (1982). Coordination and subordination revisited: Syntactic complexity in spoken and written discourse. In D. Tannen (Ed.), *Coherence in spoken and written discourse* (pp. 45–80). Ablex.

Bentivoglio, P. (1987). *Los sujetos pronominales de primera persona en el habla de Caracas.* Universidad Central de Venezuela, Consejo de Desarrollo Científico y Humanístico.

Biber, D., & Conrad, S. (2001). Quantitative corpus-based research: Much more than bean counting. *TESOL Quarterly, 35*, 331–336.

Cameron, R. (1992). Pronominal and null subject variation in Spanish: Constraints, dialects, and functional compensation [Unpublished doctoral dissertation]. University of Pennsylvania.

Cameron, R. (1995). The scope and limits of switch reference as a constraint on pronominal subject expression. *Hispanic Linguistics, 6*(7), 1–28.

Carvalho, A. M., & Child, M. (2011). Subject pronoun expression in a variety of Spanish in contact with Portuguese. In J. Michnowicz & R. Dodsworth (Eds.), *Selected proceedings of the 5th Workshop on Spanish Sociolinguistics* (pp. 14–25). Cascadilla Proceedings Project.

Carvalho, A., Orozco, R. & Shin, N. (2015). Introduction. In A. Carvalho, R. Orozco, & N. Shin (Eds.), *Subject pronoun expression in Spanish: A cross-dialectal perspective* (pp. xiii–xxvi). Georgetown University Press.

Cenoz, J. (2003). The additive effect of bilingualism on third language acquisition: A review. *International Journal of Bilingualism, 7*(1), 71–87.

Cerrón-Palomino, A., Loza, S., & Vana, R. (2023). A historical-variationist analysis of subject pronoun expression in 19th and early 20th century Arizonan Spanish. *Languages, 8*(1), 25.

Chafe, W. L. (1982). Integration and involvement in speaking, writing, and oral literature. In D. Tannen (Ed.), *Spoken and written language: Exploring orality and literacy* (pp. 35–53). Ablex.

Cherici, A. (2021). The role of L1 and L2 in the acquisition of null subjects by Chinese learners in L3 Italian. *International Journal of Multilingualism, 20*(3), 735–752.

Christensen, M. B. (2000). Anaphoric reference in spoken and written Chinese narrative discourse. *Journal of Chinese Linguistics, 28*(2), 303–336.

Clements, M., & Domínguez, L. (2018). Testing the predictions of the Scalpel Model in L3/Ln acquisition: The acquisition of null and overt subjects in L3 Chinese. In J. C. Cho, M. Iverson, T. Judy, T. Leal, & E. Shimanskaya (Eds.), *Meaning and structure in second language acquisition* (pp. 181–202). John Benjamins.

Dewaele, J.-M. (1998). Lexical inventions: French interlanguage as L2 versus L3. *Applied Linguistics, 19*, 471–490.

Dewaele, J.-M. (1999). Word order variation in interrogative structures of native and non-native French. *International Review of Applied Linguistics, 123–124*, 161–180.

Enríquez, E. V. (1984). *El pronombre personal sujeto en la lengua española hablada en Madrid.* Instituto Miguel de Cervantes.

Erker, D., & Guy, G. R. (2012). The role of lexical frequency in syntactic variability: Variable subject personal pronoun expression in Spanish. *Language, 88*(3), 526–557.

Fernández Flórez, C. (2023). Written subject pronoun expression among Spanish heritage language learners. *Estudios Humanísticos. Filología, 45*(2023), 165–190.

Flores-Ferrán, N. (2004). Spanish subject personal pronoun use in New York City Puerto Ricans: Can we rest the case of English contact? *Language Variation and Change, 16*, 49–73.

Flores-Ferrán, N. (2007). A bend in the road: Subject personal pronoun expression in Spanish after 30 years of sociolinguistic research. *Language and Linguistics Compass, 1*, 624–652.

Geeslin, K. L., Goebel-Mahrle, T., Guo, J., & Linford, B. (2023). Variable subject expression in second language acquisition: The role of perseveration. In P. Posio & P. Herbeck (Eds.), *Referring to discourse participants in Ibero-Romance languages* (pp. 69–104). Language Science Press.

Geeslin, K. L., & Gudmestad, A. (2008). Variable subject expression in second-language Spanish: A comparison of native and non-native speakers. In M. Bowles, R. Foote, & S. Perpiñán (Eds.), *Selected proceedings of the 2007 Second Language Research Forum* (pp. 69–85). Cascadilla Proceedings Project.

Geeslin, K. L., & Gudmestad, A. (2011). Using sociolinguistic analyses of discourse-level features to expand research on L2 variation: Native and non-native contrasts in forms of Spanish subject expression. In L. Plonsky & M. Schierloh (Eds.), *Selected proceedings of the Second Language Research Forum* (pp. 16-30). Cascadilla Proceedings Project.

Geeslin, K., & Linford, B. (2012, April). A cross-sectional study of the effects of discourse cohesiveness and perseveration on subject expression [Conference presentation]. 6th International Workshop on Spanish Sociolinguistics, Tucson, AZ, United States.

Geeslin, K. L., Linford, B., & Fafulas, S. (2015). Variable subject expression in second language Spanish: Uncovering the developmental sequence and predictive linguistic factors. In A. M. Carvalho, R. Orozco, & N. Lapidus Shin (Eds.), *Subject pronoun expression in Spanish: A cross dialectal perspective* (pp. 191–210). Georgetown University Press.

Gudmestad, A., & Geeslin, K. L. (2010). Exploring the roles of redundancy and ambiguity in variable subject expression: A comparison of native and non-native speakers. In C. Borgonovo, M. Español-Echevarría & P. Prévost (Eds.), *Selected proceedings of the 12th Hispanic Linguistics Symposium* (pp. 270-283). Cascadilla Proceedings Project.

Gudmestad, A., & Geeslin, K. L. (2011). Assessing the use of multiple forms in variable contexts: the relationship between linguistic factors and future-time reference. *Studies in Hispanic and Lusophone Linguistics, 4*(1), 3–33.

Guy, G. R., Adli, A., Bayley, R., Beaman, K., Erker, D., Orozco, R., & Zhang, X. (forthcoming). *Subject pronoun expression: A cross-linguistic variationist sociolinguistic study.* Cambridge.

Holmquist, J. (2012). Frequency rates and constraints on subject personal pronoun expression: Findings from the Puerto Rican highlands. *Language Variation and Change, 24*, 203–220.

Huang, T., Steinkrauss, R., & Verspoor, M. (2021). Variability as predictor in L2 writing proficiency. *Journal of Second Language Writing, 52*, Article 100787.

Jarvis, S. (2016). The scope of transfer research. In L. Yu & T. Odlin (Eds.), *New perspectives on transfer in second language learning* (pp. 17–47). Multilingual Matters.

Jia, L., & Bayley, R. (2002). Null pronoun variation in Mandarin Chinese. *University of Pennsylvania Working Papers in Linguistics, 8*, 103–116.

Kuznetsova, A., Brockhoff, P. B., & Christensen, R. H. B. (2017). lmerTest Package: Tests in Linear Mixed Effects Models. *Journal of Statistical Software, 82*(13), 1–26.

Li, W. (2004). Topic chains in Chinese discourse. *Discourse Processes, 37*, 25–45.

Li, X. (2010). Sociolinguistic variation in the speech of learners of Chinese as a second language. *Language Learning*, 60, 1–42.

Li, X. (2014). Variation of subject pronominal expression in L2 Chinese. *Studies in Second Language Acquisition*, 36(1), 39–68.

Li, X. (2017). Stylistic variation in L1 and L2 Chinese. *Chinese as a Second Language*, 52, 55–76.

Li, X., & Bayley, R. (2018). Lexical frequency and syntactic variation: Subject pronoun use in Mandarin Chinese. *Asia-Pacific Language Variation*, 4, 133–160.

Li, X., Chen, X., & Chen, W.-H. (2012). Variation of subject pronominal expression in Mandarin Chinese. *Sociolinguistic Studies*, 6, 91–119.

Linford, B., & Geeslin, K. L. (2022). The role of referent cohesiveness in variable subject expression in L2 Spanish. *Spanish in Context*, 19(3), 508–536.

Liu, H., & Van Dongen, E. (2013). The Chinese diaspora. Oxford Bibliographies. http://www.oxfordbibliographies.com/view/document/obo-9780199920082/obo-9780199920082-0070.xml

Long, A. Y. (2021). Korean learners' acquisition and use of variable first person subject forms in Spanish. *Languages*, 6(4), 208.

Maher, J. C. (2017). *Multilingualism: A very short introduction* (Vol. 525). Oxford University Press.

Marian, V., & Shook, A. (2012). The cognitive benefits of being bilingual. *Cerebrum: the Dana forum on brain science* (Vol. 2012). Dana Foundation.

McManus, K. (2022). *Crosslinguistic influence and second language learning*. Routledge.

Michnowicz, J. (2015). Subject pronoun expression in contact with Maya in Yucatan Spanish. In A. M. Carvalho, R. Orozco & N. Shin (Eds.), *Subject pronoun expression in Spanish: A cross-dialectal perspective* (pp. 103–122). Georgetown University Press.

Mougeon, R., Rehner, K., & Nadasdi, T. (2004). The learning of spoken French variation by immersion students from Toronto, Canada. *Journal of Sociolinguistics*, 8, 408–432.

Nagy, N. (2024). *Heritage languages: Extending variationist approaches*. Cambridge University Press.

Orozco, R., & Guy, G. (2008). El uso variable de los pronombres sujetos: ¿Qué pasa en la costa Caribe colombiana? In M. Westmoreland & J. A. Thomas (Eds.), *Selected proceedings of the 4th Workshop on Spanish Sociolinguistics* (pp. 70–80). Cascadilla Proceedings Project

Otheguy, R., & Zentella, A. C. (2012). *Spanish in New York: Language contact, dialectal leveling, and structural continuity*. Oxford University Press.

Park, M., & Starr, R. L. (2016). The role of formal L2 learning experience in L3 acquisition among early bilinguals. *International Journal of Multilingualism*, 13(3), 274–291.

Ramos, M. (2016). Continuity and change. First person singular subject pronoun expression in earlier Spanish. *Spanish in Context*, 13, 103–127.

Rothman, J. (2011). L3 syntactic transfer selectivity and typological determinacy: The typological primacy model. *Second Language Research*, 27(1), 107–127.

Rothman, J. (2015). Linguistic and cognitive motivations for the Typological Primacy Model (TPM) of third language (L3) transfer: Timing of acquisition and proficiency considered. *Bilingualism: Language and Cognition*, 18(2), 179–190.

Schwartz, B. D., & Sprouse, R. A. (1996). L2 cognitive states and the full transfer/full access model. *Second Language Research*, 12(1), 40–72.

Shin, N. L. & Erker, D. (2015). The emergence of structured variability in morphosyntax: Childhood acquisition of Spanish subject pronouns. In A. M. Carvalho, R. Orozco, & N. L. Shin (Eds.) *Subject expression in Spanish: A cross-dialectal perspective* (pp. 169–189). Georgetown University Press.

Shin, N. L. & Montes-Alcalá, C. (2014). El uso contextual del pronombre sujeto como factor predictivo de la influencia del inglés en el español en Nueva York. *Sociolinguistic Studies, 8*(1). 85–110.

Silva-Corvalán, C. (1994). *Language contact and change: Spanish in Los Angeles*. Clarendon Press.

Silva-Corvalán, C. (2001). *Sociolingüística y pragmática del español*. Georgetown University Press.

Simons, G. F., & Fennig, C. D. (2018). *Ethnologue: Languages of the world* (21st ed). SIL International.

Slabakova, R. (2017). The Scalpel Model of third language acquisition. *International Journal of Bilingualism, 21*(6), 651–665.

Travis, C. (2007). Genre effects on subject expression in Spanish: Priming in narrative and conversation. *Language Variation and Change, 19*, 101–36.

Trevise, A., & Noyau, C. (1984). Adult Spanish speakers and the acquisition of French negation forms: Individual variation and linguistic awareness. In R. Andersen (Ed.), *Second languages: A cross-linguistic perspective* (pp. 165–189). Newbury House.

Wagner, S. (2016). Never saw one – first person null subjects in spoken English. *English Language and Linguistics, 22*(1), 1–34.

Westergaard, M., Mitrofanova, N., Mykhaylyk, R., & Rodina, Y. (2017). Crosslinguistic influence in the acquisition of a third language: The linguistic proximity model. *International Journal of Bilingualism, 21*(6), 666–682.

Yamada, A., Davidson, S., Fernández-Mira, P., Carando, A., Sagae, K., & Sánchez-Gutiérrez, C. (2020). COWS-L2H: A corpus of Spanish learner writing. *Research in Corpus Linguistics, 8*, 17–32.

Zahler, S. (2018). *The relationship between working memory and sociolinguistic variation in first and second languages: The case of Spanish subject pronouns* [Unpublished doctoral dissertation]. Indiana University.

Zhang, X. (2021). Language variation in Mandarin as a heritage language: Subject personal pronouns. *Heritage Language Journal, 18*(1), 1–29.

SECTION 2

Breaking new ground

CHAPTER 6

University Spanish instructors' trill production within and outside of the language classroom

Sara L. Zahler, Danielle Daidone & Emily Kuder
North Carolina State University | University of North Carolina Wilmington | Connecticut College

In order to examine how a sociophonetic variable is realized in instructor input compared to speech outside the classroom, this study analyzed the production of the Spanish trill by instructors in both contexts. Different linguistic constraints conditioned the production of the multiple-occlusion variant across contexts. Additionally, participants adjusted their speech towards a more formal, standard pronunciation in the classroom, producing more canonical multiple-occlusion trills than in the conversations. However, each participant also produced a range of other variants: between one and eight distinct noncanonical variants in the classroom and between three and eight in the conversations. Thus, variation was still present in the classroom, indicating that students are exposed to trill variation in their classroom input.

Keywords: teacher talk, instructor input, Spanish trill, language variation, speech production, rhotics, naturalistic speech data, didactic speech, speech styles

Sociolinguistic research shows that the production of the Spanish trill /r/ is highly variable in native speech (e.g., Díaz-Campos, 2008; E. Willis, 2007; Zahler & Daidone, 2014). Separately, recent studies indicate that Spanish instructors' language in the classroom differs in several ways from Spanish used outside the classroom (e.g., Daidone, 2019; Dracos, 2018; Kuder, 2019, 2020). Additionally, research on variation in teacher talk in English, French, and Chinese finds that instructors frequently use formal speech in the classroom, sometimes even beyond that of speakers from the highest social class in the surrounding community (see Mougeon & Rehner, 2019). This suggests that teachers may be removing variation from their speech, despite increased calls for its inclusion in the classroom to help develop learners' sociolinguistic competence (e.g., Gutiérrez & Fairclough, 2006). However, as a field, we know relatively little about oral input in the Spanish language classroom, particularly for sociolinguistically variable forms. Thus, the current study examines trill variation in Spanish teacher talk compared to their speech outside the classroom to determine what phonetic variation, if any, instructors are including in their input to learners and how this input differs from the Spanish that learners hear outside the classroom.

Background

Connection between input and learner development

Usage-based theories of second language (L2) acquisition posit that characteristics of input shape learners' mental grammars (e.g., Bybee, 2008; Geeslin et al., 2023). According to these approaches, language users constantly track how often forms are used and in what contexts. Learners' grammars emerge from these properties and are continuously updated as more input is encountered. Thus, in order to understand L2 grammars, it is essential to understand the input that learners receive.

For many lower-level classroom language learners, much of their spoken input comes from teacher talk, and research suggests that learners are sensitive to this input. Hayes-Harb et al. (2022) had participants listen to both "students" and "teachers" while learning an artificial language. Afterwards, participants judged productions by another "student". The researchers found that the participants preferred the phonetic realizations that matched what they had heard in the "teacher" input instead of the "student" input, suggesting that learners privilege the input they receive from instructors over that of their peers. Additionally, studies typically find a clear relationship between instructor input and learner output. Hamayan and Tucker (1980) examined the production of French syntactic forms in teacher input and in learner output, finding that the frequency of nine structures in classroom input correlated with the rate of learners' target use of those forms. Rehner and Mougeon (2003) found in Ontario that French immersion learners' rates of use of different expressions of consequence (e.g., *alors* 'therefore') closely mirrored those of their instructors rather than rates of the expressions found in their textbooks and workbooks or produced by native Quebec French speakers. In a corpus of English as a Second Language teacher talk, Trofimovich et al. (2012) investigated the frequency of the phoneme /ð/ (as in *the*) in different phonetic contexts and compared it to the accuracy of this phoneme in the same contexts in learner speech. They reported that learners' accuracy changed over time only in the phonetic contexts with the highest frequency in their input, illustrating that phonological acquisition also mirrors patterns found in input. Furthermore, while learners typically receive explanations and targeted input for morphosyntactic structures as part of classroom instruction, the only source of information in the classroom about phonological categories may be the input heard during unrelated activities.

Pronunciation instruction in the classroom

In early approaches to language teaching before the 1960s (i.e., the Direct Method and Audiolingualism), acquiring native-sounding pronunciation was a high priority, and training was part of the curriculum. With the advent of Communicative Language Teaching and the Natural Approach in the 1980s, however, pronunciation training fell to the wayside (Jones, 2005). While there are renewed calls for its integration into the world language curriculum (e.g., Darcy, 2018; Levis & Echelberger, 2022) and efforts to incorporate it into Task-Based Language Teaching (see Mora & Levkina, 2017), pronunciation is still often absent from world language classrooms in general and from Spanish language classrooms in particular.

First, pronunciation is rarely mentioned in Spanish teaching materials. Arteaga (2000) reviewed 10 first-year Spanish textbooks and lab manuals published between 1996 and 1998, finding that only four had any pronunciation training in the textbook, and one had none at all in either the textbook or the lab manual. When present, pronunciation training appeared in less than half of the chapters, and all 10 textbooks contained inaccurate phonetic explanations. A recent study (Offerman, 2024) did a conceptual replication of Arteaga (2000), examining 10 additional first-year Spanish textbooks, finding that little has changed over the last 20 years. Popular Spanish textbook series still rarely include pronunciation instruction and were found to still contain some of the inaccuracies found in Arteaga's (2000) study.

Perhaps partially due to the lack of pronunciation instruction in written materials, pronunciation seldom forms part of a language curriculum, which is often focused solely on morphosyntactic structures and vocabulary, and it is rarely assessed. Furthermore, most language teachers are not trained to teach pronunciation and are not confident in their ability to do so. Subsequently, instructors tend to only address pronunciation in reaction to egregious errors (see Levis & Echelberger, 2022). This dearth of systematic pronunciation instruction in language courses makes documenting patterns in the input even more important for understanding the acquisition of phonology by classroom learners, particularly given the unique characteristics of teacher talk.

Features of instructor input

Speakers naturally accommodate their speech to their interlocutors in social, interactional environments (Gallois et al., 2005), and thus it is unsurprising that teacher talk often differs from language spoken outside the classroom (e.g., Daidone, 2019; Dracos, 2018; Kuder, 2020). In an investigation of past-tense forms, Daidone (2019) found that the spoken input provided by Spanish instructors was skewed toward the use of the preterit compared to those same verbs used in native speaker corpora, where the preterit and imperfect were more balanced. Concerning Spanish subject expression, Dracos (2018) discovered that teacher talk had a higher rate of overt subject pronoun use in the classroom compared to conversational data with the same instructors. In both studies, the authors suggested that the type of discourse used by instructors could partially account for these differences.

World language instructors are simultaneously using the target language for instructional and administrative purposes, resulting in a mixture of linguistic and paralinguistic cues in the input (Christie, 2002; J. Willis, 1992). Instructional speech typically features language grading, or modified speech that is similar to infant- and foreigner-directed speech styles. Like other presentational speech styles such as TED Talks, news broadcasts, and speeches, teacher talk often involves slower, louder, clearer, more deliberate speech with more pauses, more emphasis, limited verbal inflections, and restricted vocabulary (Crystal, 2005; Stanley & Stevenson, 2017; Thornbury & Watkins, 2007). Furthermore, research has reported that classroom input tends to contain more formal variants than speech outside the classroom. Li (2010) observed that the Chinese genitive, attributive, or nominalization marker *de* was deleted less often in instructor input than in sociolinguistic interviews with Mandarin native speakers. In a study examining a range of morphosyntactic and lexical variables, Mougeon and Rehner (2019) found that teachers in French-medium schools in Ontario tended to use variants matching the prescriptive norm at a higher rate than they were used in their wider speech community outside the classroom. As these researchers stated, "the formal setting of the classroom has been found to have a normalizing impact on teacher variant choice" (Mougeon & Rehner, 2019, p. 182).

Simplified and more formal characteristics of classroom speech have also been identified in studies on speech prosody. In read speech directed at language students, Spanish teachers used many traits of formal or emphatic speech styles such as increased pitch range, early F0 peak alignment, boundary tones to indicate important target forms, less F0 suppression, increased intensity, and a slower speech rate (Rao, 2011). Similarly, in Kuder's (2019) study of prosodic qualities of teacher talk using a portion of the data analyzed in the present study, the author found that teacher talk typically exhibited exaggerated articulation through increased intensity, slower speech rate, higher F0 mean, and wider F0 range, among other characteristics. She associated the modifications with those used during foreigner- and infant-directed speech for purposes of intelligibility and comprehensibility (see Stanley & Stevenson, 2017). A related study showed that the same L2 instructors produced rhythmic and emphatic rhetorical stress during classroom speech to gain the attention of the students and demonstrate authority (Kuder, 2020). Furthermore, evidence suggests that teachers manipulate the relative prosodic strength of constituents to indicate communicative importance. Gerard and Dahan (1995) discovered that readers mark the importance of a target word by reducing the speed of their speech leading up to it. Similarly, in a laboratory study of unscripted speech, Rao (2006) found that emotionally charged or important utterances are phonetically strengthened and exhibit early F0 peak alignment, strategies that mark prominence.

Given the research showing a higher rate of simpler and/or more formal morphosyntactic and lexical variants in the classroom and the documented prosodic modifications characteristic of didactic and emphatic speech styles, we hypothesize that teachers also tend to use the canonical realization of variable sounds. This remains an open question, however, because to our knowledge, studies have not examined instructors' production of sociophonetic variation in the classroom.

Native trill production in Spanish

The production of the Spanish trill /r/ is a good test case for examining sociophonetic variation in teacher talk because it is both highly variable — within and across speakers — and extensively documented in native speech outside the classroom. While the prescriptive variant is a voiced alveolar trill with multiple occlusions (Hualde, 2005, p. 181), numerous other variants have been attested such as approximants, fricatives, and taps or trills preceded or followed by another element (e.g., Bradley, 2006; Díaz-Campos, 2008; Diez Canseco, 1997; Henriksen, 2014; Lamy, 2015; Melero García, 2015; E. Willis, 2006, 2007; Zahler & Daidone, 2014). Indeed, some studies reported that the canonical voiced alveolar trill with multiple occlusions was not the most frequent variant in their data. For example, E. Willis (2007) classified 96% of tokens as other variants, mainly pre-breathy voiced taps or trills, in an investigation of Cibaeño Dominican Spanish. To a lesser degree, Melero García (2015) also reported a high rate of other variants, with 56% of tokens from Valencian Spanish speakers having less than two occlusions. Even in Henriksen's (2014) study of two conservative Peninsular varieties, 29% of the tokens were not produced as the canonical variant. Some of these studies also illustrate that variation is present within individual speakers. E. Willis (2006), for instance, reported that all 10 participants in his study produced at least three different variants.

This variation in /r/ realization is conditioned by linguistic and extralinguistic variables, including phonetic context, word frequency, dialect, task type, and speaker sex, age, and social class. Regarding phonetic context, some studies have reported no effect (e.g., Díaz-Campos, 2008; Zahler & Daidone, 2014), whereas others have found differing results for the effect of surrounding vowels. For example, while Lamy (2015) found that a preceding /o/ or /u/ favored the multiple-occlusion variant, Henriksen (2014) observed that a preceding /u/ was associated with fewer occlusions compared to a preceding /o/, but for only one of the two Peninsular dialects examined. Studies generally agree, however, that a preceding /s/ is less conducive to a canonical pronunciation compared to other segments (e.g., Bradley, 2006; Diez Canseco, 1997). More frequent words are less likely to be produced as the multiple-occlusion variant (Lamy, 2015; Zahler & Daidone, 2014), although Melero García (2015) reported the opposite effect. In terms of social variables, women tend to produce more normative variants (e.g., Díaz-Campos, 2008; Henriksen, 2014), but not always (e.g., Diez Canseco, 1997; Lamy 2015). Task type also affects trill production, with more controlled tasks resulting in more canonical realizations than interviews or conversations (Diez Canseco, 1997).

This review shows that /r/ can be realized in various ways and influenced by numerous factors. Additionally, not all noncanonical variants are stigmatized or limited to individuals unlikely to become language instructors. For example, Willis (2007) found the canonical trill to be the least common variant among college students, and Díaz-Campos (2008) observed that the upper class in Caracas, Venezuela disfavored the canonical variant. Thus, while we may predict that Spanish instructors use the more formal, prescriptive multiple-occlusion variant in the classroom, other variants may also be represented.

Second language trill production

Research on the acquisition of the Spanish trill by English-speaking learners shows that the use of the canonical variant tends to rise as proficiency increases (e.g., Face, 2006; Olsen, 2012; Reeder, 1998; Rose, 2010). For instance, Reeder (1998) found that first-semester Spanish students produced the normative trill in 7% of tokens, third-semester students in 13%, and upper-level undergraduate and graduate students in 37%. Besides the canonical variant, learners may produce an approximant with or without a lowered third formant, a tap, a tap followed by assibilation or r-coloring, or a fricative, among other realizations (e.g., Daidone & Zahler, 2021; Face, 2006; Rose, 2010; Zahler & Daidone, 2023). While this variation partly reflects developmental steps towards producing the articulatorily difficult canonical trill (see Daidone & Zahler, 2021), learners might also encounter some of these variants in their input from instructors. Investigating teacher talk can help us understand the likelihood of different variants serving as target realizations for L2 learners.

The current study

According to Face (2006), the canonical voiced alveolar trill with multiple occlusions is "uniformly the sound taught to students studying Spanish as a L2 in the United States" (p. 48). Similarly, Olsen (2012) cited Face (2006) and stated that although variation exists, "rhotics that L2 learners are taught in classroom settings in the United States can be described simply as alveolar taps and alveolar trills" (p. 68). However, research suggests that students are unlikely to encounter more than a brief, unplanned explanation of this sound outside of a Spanish phonetics class. Given the centrality of input in the development of an L2 and the likelihood of little to no explicit pronunciation instruction, we believe it is particularly important to investigate phonological characteristics of teacher talk. While sociolinguistic studies have extensively documented variation in native speech, we have yet to learn how patterns of sociophonetic variation translate to the classroom in terms of both frequency of variants and factors affecting their use. With the Spanish trill as a first step in this line of research, the present study aims to answer the following research questions:

1. What trill variants do instructors use in and outside the classroom and at what rate?
2. What factors condition the use of the canonical multiple-occlusion variant in and outside the classroom? Do the conditioning factors differ between contexts?

Method

Participants

The participants in this study were six female instructors of Spanish who identified as native Spanish speakers and who were all also either advanced speakers of English (*n* = 4) or who had English as their co-primary language (*n* = 2).[1] Marta, Carmen, and María were born in Spain and Elena in Puerto Rico, all with Spanish-speaking caregivers, and all of whom moved to the continental U.S. as

---

1. Participants are subsequently described using pseudonyms.

adults. Sofía was born in Madrid, Spain to a Spanish-speaking father and English-speaking mother from the U.S. She grew up bilingual in both languages and moved to the U.S. at age 23, although she traveled there frequently as a child to visit extended family. Juana was born in the U.S. to two Spanish-speaking parents, one from the Dominican Republic and one from Argentina. She was exposed primarily to Spanish in the home until age 3 when she began to attend an English-language preschool. A summary of instructor demographic information is found in Table 1.

Table 1. Participant demographic and educational profiles

Instructor	Spanish dialect exposure from birth	Age	Age of first exposure to English	Length of time living in U.S.	# years teaching Spanish at time of study	Level of study and subfield of graduate study
Marta	Valladolid, Spain	24	7	5 months	< 1	MA student, Spanish literature and linguistics
Carmen	Canary Islands, Spain	29	8	5 months	2.5	MA student, Spanish literature and linguistics
Juana	Dominican Republic, Argentina	23	3	22.5 years	< 1	MA student, Spanish literature
Elena	Mayaguez, Puerto Rico	26	5	6.5 years	3.5	PhD student, Spanish literature
María	Málaga, Spain	33	6	4.5 years	6.5	PhD student, Spanish linguistics
Sofía	Madrid, Spain	45	0	25 years	19	PhD student, Spanish linguistics

Recordings

For the classroom data, this study analyzed 18 recorded class sessions, with three recordings from each of the six participants. Two of the participants (Marta and Carmen) were recorded during Spring 2015 at a large public U.S. university, each providing three 50-minute in-person recordings from their third-semester Spanish courses taught in person. The instructors wore discreet clip-on Olympus digital audio recorders attached to their clothing while teaching. The remaining four instructors (Juana, Elena, María, and Sofía) taught hybrid or fully online courses during Spring 2021 at a different large public U.S. university. Classes were recorded via Zoom, using either the microphone on the instructors' laptops or on AirPods. Participants were instructed to find a spot with minimal background noise and in which they were alone. Given that the participants' microphone quality varied based on their selection, and they were recorded in environments that differed in degree of background noise (i.e., fans, pets, etc.), the recordings varied in their level of interference. Juana taught a fully online second-semester course that took place for 75 minutes, three days a week. María taught a hybrid first-semester course with one day online and two days in person for 75 minutes each week. Elena taught a hybrid third-semester course that took place two days a week for 80 minutes, with one day online and one day in person. Lastly, Sofía taught a fully online third-semester course that held two 80-minute classes a week. Thus, the total number of minutes analyzed per instructor varied, as indicated in Table 2.

Table 2. Number of minutes of classroom audio analyzed per instructor

Instructor	Number of minutes analyzed	Class type	Level
Marta	150	In-person	3rd semester
Carmen	150	In-person	3rd semester
Juana	225	Online	2nd semester
Elena	240	Online	3rd semester
María	225	Online	1st semester
Sofía	240	Online	3rd semester
Total	1,230		

The conversational data for this study originated from two informal oral tasks completed by the instructors outside the classroom. The data were drawn from two distinct datasets collected for separate projects but combined here to increase the size of the dataset for the current study. Participants Juana, Elena, María, and Sofía completed a sociolinguistic interview with the first author after the course ended, conducted via Zoom and totaling three hours of audio data. The interviewer (the first author) was a colleague of the participants, and a former instructor of three of them. She had known each participant for at least two years at the time of data collection and had spent time with them in work and more casual settings. The interviewer and three of the participants who completed the sociolinguistic interview regularly interacted (two or more times per week) at the time of data collection. The interviewer interacted approximately twice per month with Elena. The interviewer ordered questions from more general, impersonal, or non-specific topics to more specific, personal ones following norms in the field of sociolinguistics (Labov, 1972). These questions were designed to elicit narratives about participants' personal experiences to encourage the use of more vernacular forms used in conversational speech styles. The interviews were recorded via Zoom, and participants used either their computer microphone or AirPods.

Participants Marta and Carmen completed a 45-minute in-person focus group interview to elicit conversational speech. This activity involved an interaction between two members of the same social group, in this case the two instructors, in which the participants were asked to engage in regular conversation about any topic of interest. Participants had a list of suggested discussion questions on a variety of topics, and a third individual (another native speaker of Spanish not associated with the study) was present to facilitate the discussion. Participants Marta and Carmen were friends and colleagues in the same academic program and regularly interacted. This familiarity between the instructors increased the likelihood that they would produce speech resembling a natural conversation even with the presence of individual voice-recorders. Despite the different data elicitation methods used for the conversational speech data, the datasets are combined in this study to serve the purpose of providing a baseline for conversational speech style as it contrasts with didactic speech used in the classroom.

Coding of dependent variable

The dependent variable for this study was the phonetic realization of all tokens found in the phonological trill context, specifically word-initial <r> (e.g., *rana* 'frog'), intervocalic <rr> (e.g., *carro* 'car'), and syllable-initial <r> after a homorganic consonant (e.g., *alrededor* 'around'; Hualde, 2005, p.183). Each token of phonemic /r/ was identified (classroom, $k=515$, conversation, $k=334$) and classified as one of 13 variants, excepting any instances where background noise or overlapping speech made a token unanalyzable. These categories came from previous literature on the trill (e.g., Rose, 2010; E. Willis, 2007; Zahler & Daidone, 2023), as well as variants observed in the current dataset. We used Praat (Boersma & Weenink, 2019) to examine each token and classify it based on the acoustic properties outlined below.

1. A voiced alveolar trill with two to three and a half occlusions (canonical multiple-occlusion variant <4; Figure 1)
2. A voiced alveolar trill with four or more occlusions (canonical multiple-occlusion variant ≥4; Figure 2)
3. An alveolar tap (one occlusion; Figure 3)
4. A tap followed by a partial occlusion or a nativelike approximant (Figure 4)
5. A tap followed by frication (Figure 5)
6. An approximant with a flat F3 and formant structure visible throughout (Figure 6)
7. An assibilated variant (Figure 7)
8. A pre-aspirated or pre-breathy voiced multiple-occlusion variant (Figure 8)
9. An epenthetic vowel before a tap or tap plus partial occlusion (Figure 9)
10. An epenthetic vowel before a multiple-occlusion variant (Figure 10)
11. Deletion (elision; Figure 11)
12. An approximant with a lowered F3 and audible r-coloring (Figure 12)
13. A trill that was a combination of more than one of the previous categories or did not fit into one of the categories (Figure 13)

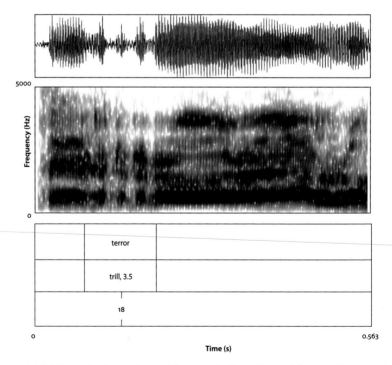

Figure 1. Multiple-occlusion variant with 3.5 occlusions. *Terror.* Elena – Conversation

Chapter 6. Trill production in instructor input **155**

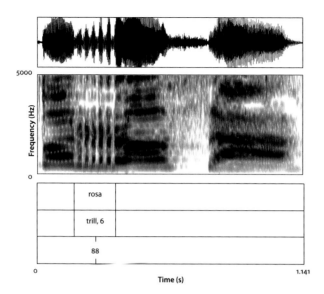

Figure 2. Multiple-occlusion variant with 6 occlusions. *(Equi)po rosa.* Carmen — Class 1

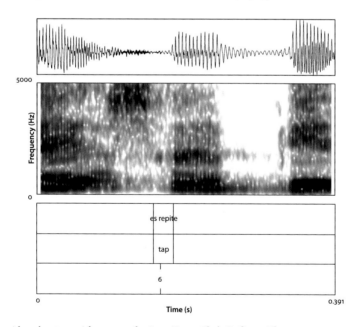

Figure 3. Alveolar tap with one occlusion. *Es repi(te).* Sofia — Class 2

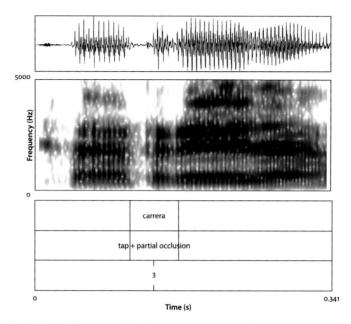

Figure 4. Tap followed by a partial occlusion. *Carrera*. María — Conversation

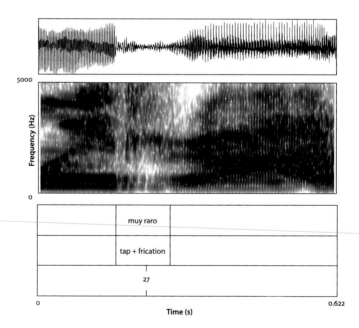

Figure 5. Tap followed by frication. *(M)uy ra(ro)*. Elena — Conversation

Chapter 6. Trill production in instructor input 157

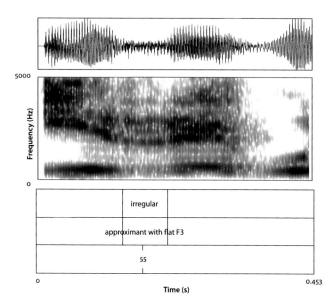

Figure 6. Approximant with flat F3. *Irregu(lar)*. Elena — Class 2

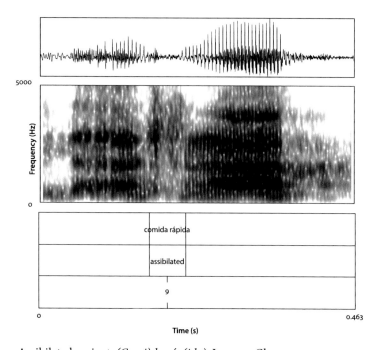

Figure 7. Assibilated variant. *(Comi)da ráp(ida)*. Juana — Class 2

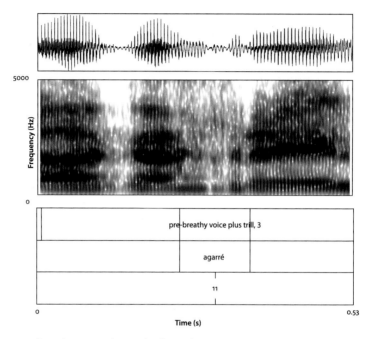

Figure 8. Pre-breathy voice plus multiple-occlusion variant. *Agarré*. Juana — Class 1

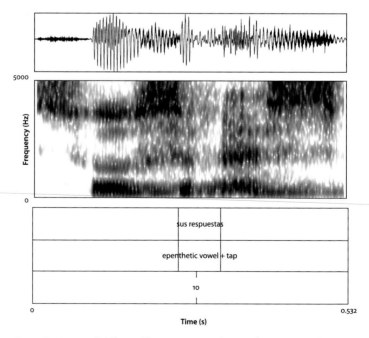

Figure 9. Epenthetic vowel followed by tap. *Sus res(puestas)*. Juana — Class 3

Chapter 6. Trill production in instructor input 159

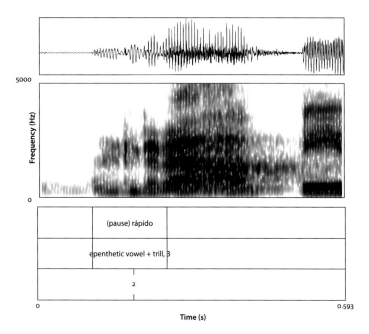

Figure 10. Epenthetic vowel followed by 3 occlusions. *Rápi(do)*. Juana — Class 3

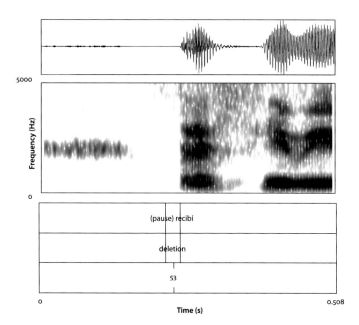

Figure 11. Deletion. *Recibí*. María — Conversation

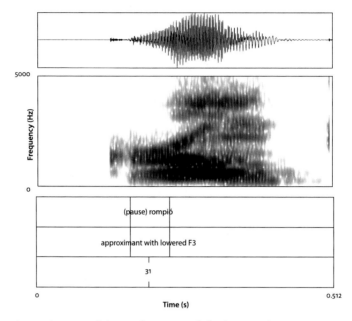

Figure 12. Approximant with lowered F3. *Romp(ió)*. Elena – Class 3

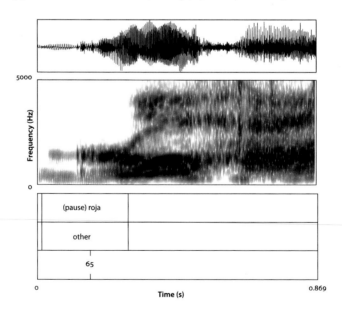

Figure 13. Other: Pre-voicing + 2.5 occlusions + approximant with lowered F3. *Roja*. Elena – Class 1

Coding of independent variables

The data were coded for several linguistic features. The first variable considered was the manner of articulation of the preceding segment, categorized as /a/, /e/, /i/, /o/, /u/, sonorant, obstruent, or pause. High vowels were grouped together in both analyses due to patterning similarly and low token count for /u/; however, /e/ and /o/ were only combined into a mid-vowel category in the classroom analysis because their behavior patterned differently in the conversational data. The second constraint was following vowel, in which each of the five Spanish monophthong vowels were coded into separate categories. High vowels were again combined in both analyses due to patterning similarly. We also included a measure of broad lexical frequency by using the EsPal log-frequency score from the Castilian Spanish subtitle subcorpus (Duchon et al., 2013) for the word containing the trill token. This variable was included since more frequent words in a language user's repertoire are expected to be phonetically reduced more often (e.g., Bybee, 2002) and since lexical frequency has been shown to impact trill variation in prior studies (Lamy, 2015; Zahler & Daidone, 2014). The coding for the aforementioned variables was based on Zahler and Daidone (2023).

We included several factors specific to our dataset. First, we coded for the frequency of the lexical item within the recording. We expected that classroom lexical frequency may differ from overall lexical frequency in Spanish, although the same could be the case with the conversational data. We wanted to capture these potential differences to determine if and how the two measures of frequency affected variation. EsPal frequency measures were not correlated with word frequency in the classroom data or conversational data (both $r < 0.50$), and thus the two types of frequency measures could be included together in the models.

Lastly, for the classroom data, we coded for two discursive variables in order to account for the potentially differentiated use of trill variants related to focus and discourse function. Because reduced speech rate has been associated with marking communicative salience (Gerard & Dahan, 1995), it is possible that instructors also strengthen segmental variants when introducing target words for the first time, especially during grammar or vocabulary instruction. Consequently, we coded the data to account for whether it was the first use of the word or not within each class session. We also coded all tokens to account for the pluralistic communicative, pragmatic, and didactic functions at play during instructional speech due to their documented correlation with acoustic prominence (Christie, 2002; Rao, 2006, 2011; J. Willis, 1992). This variable included three categories modeled after those used in Kuder (2019), each containing several related discursive and pragmatic functions that occurred in the classroom. The first category was administrative acts, which included dictation of written instructions, prompts for oral or written production, and leading questions for discussion or comprehension. The second set contained descriptive acts, which included oral instructions for activities, grammar explanations, discussion of vocabulary or neutral functions, such as greeting students, salutations, jokes, and asides. Lastly, we included a category for interpersonal, response-seeking acts that contained behaviors such as correcting a student using repair or recast, modeling the language to elicit a response, and tags and praises. We posited that instructors would use more emphatic trill variants such as the multiple-occlusion variant during administrative acts when presenting new, important information and holding students' attention.

Analysis

Before data analysis, we completed a reliability check of the coding for the dependent and independent variables of preceding segment, following vowel, and discourse type because each author individually coded approximately one third of the tokens. The coding of these variables for 174 of the conversational speech tokens and 209 of the classroom speech tokens were verified by another author. We then met to discuss any discrepancies between coding or items for which we were unsure ($k=70$) and came to a consensus. Each author subsequently recoded their remaining tokens accordingly. Most discrepancies were due to three recurrent issues. First, one author coded all trills with 3.5 occlusions as the ≥ 4 occlusion variant. This was changed so that all tokens with 3.5 occlusions were coded as the <4 occlusion variant. Second, some trills that were coded as a tap were recoded to include a partial occlusion that was originally missed. Third, one author coded the preceding segment as an obstruent if it was a deleted syllable-final /s/, while the other two authors coded it for the vowel preceding the /s/. After consultation, we agreed to code it for the vowel since the /s/ was not phonetically realized. In cases where the /s/ was phonetically realized as [s] or [h], we coded the preceding context as an obstruent. These changes were implemented, and any difficult cases were subsequently discussed between the authors.

After calculating descriptive statistics for the data, we conducted two generalized linear mixed-effects regression analyses in SPSS, one for the classroom speech data and one for the conversational speech data. For each analysis, the dependent variable was binary: the production was categorized as either the canonical multiple-occlusion variant (with two or more occlusions; categories 1 and 2) or as another variant (categories 3 through 13). We chose to use a binary dependent variable since our research objective is to determine the factors that condition the use of the canonical multiple-occlusion variant in each context, given that this variant is the prescriptive norm and highly salient. Thus, we expect the canonical multiple-occlusion trill to occur more in didactic or emphatic speech, which we expect to be more prevalent in the classroom. However, we must acknowledge that in collapsing the dependent variable categories into a binary distinction between the canonical variant and all other variants, we are unable to analyze whether the other variants occur in distinct contexts from each other. We do not assert that all noncanonical variants are used in the same way by participants or that they occur in the same linguistic and social contexts.

The independent variables for the classroom data were the following: (1) manner of articulation of the preceding segment; (2) following vowel; (3) whether it was the first use of the word in the recording or not; (4) discourse type; (5) EsPal log frequency; (6) lexical frequency in the class recording. The independent variables for the conversational data were the following: (1) manner of articulation of the preceding segment; (2) following vowel; (3) EsPal log frequency; (4) lexical frequency in the conversational data. For both analyses, participant was included as a random effect. We did not include individual lexical item as a random effect because that would require us to only use those tokens for which the lexical item occurred more than once in our dataset. This would exclude 88 tokens from the classroom data ($k=515$) and 117 tokens from the conversational data ($k=334$). This degree of data reduction was not, ultimately, feasible.

Results

Table 3 displays the overall token counts and percentages for each variant by context. As can be seen in this table, canonical trills with two or more occlusions (the first two variants) were the most frequent type of realization in both contexts, and these variants constituted a greater percentage of the classroom speech (69%) compared to the conversational speech (49.7%).

Figures 14 and 15 visually present the number of tokens of each variant produced by individual speakers for each of the classroom and conversation contexts, respectively. Note that the y-axis differs between these figures due to the smaller number of tokens in the conversational data. Figure 16 displays a comparison between the two contexts in percentages. Detailed tables for each context that contain the token counts and percentages for each variant by participant can be found in the Appendix. Findings demonstrate that each speaker produced between three and ten variants in each speech context. The speaker that showed the least amount of variability in any context is María, who produced three different types of variants in her classroom data. The remaining instructors demonstrated more variation in their classroom speech, and all instructors produced four or more distinct variants when speaking conversationally. Furthermore, all participants used more trills with four or more occlusions in classroom speech

Table 3. Summary of variants produced in classroom speech and conversational speech

Variant	Classroom speech k	%	Conversational speech k	%
Trill (2–3 occ.)	295	57.3	161	48.2
Trill (4+ occ.)	60	11.7	5	1.5
Pre-aspirated/Pre-breathy	2	0.4	1	0.3
Tap + frication	10	1.9	12	3.6
Tap + approx.	48	9.3	51	15.3
Tap	16	3.1	23	6.9
Approx. (flat F3)	36	7.0	44	13.2
Approx. (lowered F3)	13	2.5	1	0.3
Assibilated	20	3.9	29	8.7
Epenthetic vowel + tap	5	1.0	5	1.5
Epenthetic vowel + trill	5	1.0	1	0.3
Other	5	1.0	1	0.3
Total	**515**	**100%**	**334**	**100%**

compared to conversational speech, while five of the six participants also used a greater percentage of trills with two to three occlusions in the classroom. However, Sofía used the variant with two to three occlusions more than 75% of the time during conversational speech but only about 40% during classroom speech. Instead, this speaker uttered several variants not observed in her conversational speech data such as approximants and taps.

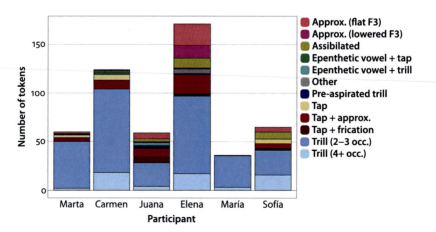

Figure 14. Number of tokens of each variant by participant in classroom speech

Chapter 6. Trill production in instructor input   165

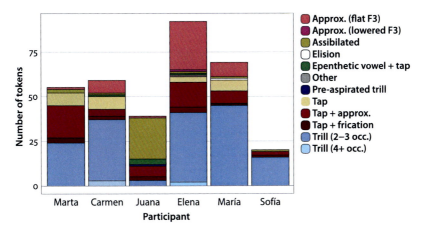

Figure 15. Number of tokens of each variant by participant in conversational speech

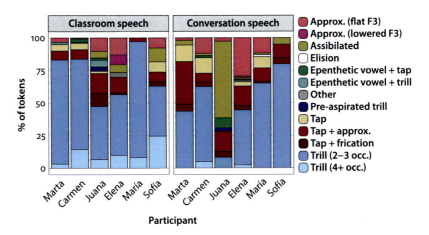

Figure 16. Comparison of trill production in classroom and conversational speech

Table 4 presents the number of all canonical variants with two or more occlusions produced by each speaker in each context, as well as their average number of occlusions.

The average number of occlusions for the canonical variant was higher in the classroom than in the conversations for all participants except Juana, for whom it was approximately equal across contexts (average of 2.68 versus 2.67 occlusions, respectively). Comparing the classroom and conversational data overall, this difference was statistically significant with a medium effect size according to an unpaired *t* test and Cohen's *d* effect size measure, $t(519) = 7.14$, $p < .001$, $d = 0.68$, 95% CI [0.49, 0.86]. By individual participant, this difference was significant for María with a large effect size, $t(78) = 4.09$, $p < .001$, $d = 0.91$, [0.44, 1.37]; for Elena with a medium effect size, $t(136) = 3.68$, $p < .001$, $d = 0.68$, [0.31, 1.05]; for Sofía with a large effect size, $t(55) = 4.21$, $p < .001$, $d = 1.18$, [0.55, 1.78]; and for Marta with a

Table 4. Average number of occlusions for multiple-occlusion variants by participant and context

Participants	Classroom speech M # of occlusions	k	Conversational speech M # of occlusions	k
Marta	2.53 (SD=0.56)	50	2.23 (SD=0.39)	24
Carmen	2.90 (SD=0.91)	104	2.58 (SD=0.77)	37
Juana	2.68 (SD=0.77)	28	2.67 (SD=0.58)	3
Elena	3.04 (SD=0.77)	97	2.55 (SD=0.57)	41
María	2.71 (SD=0.72)	35	2.20 (SD=0.39)	45
Sofia	3.45 (SD=1.02)	41	2.39 (SD=0.40)	16
Average/Total	2.92 (SD=0.85)	355	2.40 (SD=0.56)	166

medium effect size, $t(72)=2.38$, $p=.020$, $d=0.59$, [0.08, 1.08]. This difference was not significant for Juana, $t(29)=0.03$, $p=0.98$, $d=0.01$, [–1.18, 1.20], or for Carmen, $t(139)=1.92$, $p=.056$, $d=0.38$, [–0.01, .074].

Table 5 presents the results of the mixed-effects binomial regression analysis for the classroom context. The analysis determined the independent variables that significantly predicted the use of the canonical multiple-occlusion variant with two or more closures versus all other variants. For each nominal variable (preceding segment, following segment, first use, and type of discourse), one of the categories of that variable was set as the reference category. For example, for preceding segment, the category of pause/obstruent was set as the reference. The rate of the canonical multiple-occlusion variant in each other category within that nominal variable was compared to the reference category. A positive estimate indicates that more canonical trill occurs in the nonreference category compared to the reference category. For continuous variables (the frequency measures), a positive estimate indicates that for a one step increase in the variable of interest, there is a higher rate of multiple-occlusion trill, while a negative estimate indicates the opposite effect. The exponentiation of the B coefficient ("Exp(B)") is an odds ratio that compares the relative odds of the occurrence of the canonical trill, given the variable of interest (e.g., EsPal frequency) and can be used as a proxy for effect size.

Only preceding segment and following vowel significantly constrained instructors' production of the trill in the classroom. Compared to a preceding obstruent/pause, the canonical multiple-occlusion variant occurred significantly more when preceded by all remaining categories of this variable (i.e., low vowels, sonorants, mid vowels, and high vowels). For following vowel, compared to when followed by a high vowel, the canonical multiple-occlusion variant was used significantly less with a following /e/. No other comparisons were significant for following high vowel. Whether the token was the first use of the word and discourse type did not constrain variation, nor did either frequency measure.

Table 5. Factors affecting production of the multiple-occlusion variant in the classroom

Factor groups	Estimate	95% CI Lower	95% CI Upper	SE	t	Exp (B)	p	k	% MOV*
Intercept	1.08	−.37	2.52	.73	1.47	2.93	.143	515	68.9
Preceding segment manner (p<.001)									
Low vowel	2.18	1.45	2.91	.37	5.87	8.86	<.001	132	84.1
Sonorant	1.40	.50	2.29	.46	3.07	4.04	.002	40	67.5
Mid vowel	1.19	.56	1.81	.32	3.71	3.28	<.001	156	72.4
High vowel	.81	.02	1.59	.40	2.02	2.25	.044	88	63.6
Pause/ obstruent†	0	–	–	–	–	–	–	99	48.5
Following vowel (p=.005)									
/o/	−.57	−1.49	.36	.47	−1.20	.57	.230	139	74.1
/a/	−.96	−1.96	.04	.51	−1.88	.38	.061	64	71.9
/e/	−1.31	−2.11	−.52	.41	−3.23	.27	.001	234	59.8
High vowel†	0	–	–	–	–	–	–	78	84.6
First use of word (p=.398)									
No	−.21	−.70	.28	.25	−.85	.81	.40	250	65.2
Yes†	0	–	–	–	–	–	–	265	72.5
Type of discourse (p=.629)									
Administrative acts	.30	−.37	.97	.34	.88	1.35	.382	94	78.7
Descriptive acts	.01	−.50	.51	.26	.02	1.01	.982	249	63.5
Interpersonal acts†	0	–	–	–	–	–	–	172	71.5
EsPal log frequency (p=.767)									
	−.06	−.44	.33	.20	−.297	.94	.767	–	–
Class frequency (p=.975)									
	−.002	−.10	.09	.05	−.032	.10	.975	–	–

Random effect	Estimate	95% CI Lower	95% CI Upper	SE	z	p
Var(Intercept)	1.28	.29	5.65	.97	1.32	.187

* MOV = multiple-occlusion variant
† indicates reference level

Table 6 presents the results of the mixed-effects binomial regression analysis for the conversational context. Only following vowel was a significant predictor in this analysis. The canonical multiple-occlusion variant was used significantly more when the /r/ token was followed by an /o/ compared to the reference level of high vowels. There was no significant difference between following /a/ or /e/ and high vowels. None of the remaining factors were significant.

Table 6. Factors affecting production of the multiple-occlusion variant in the conversations

Factor groups	Estimate	95% CI Lower	95% CI Upper	SE	t	Exp (B)	p	k	% MOV*
Intercept	−.41	−1.91	1.10	.77	−.53	.67	.597	334	49.7%
Following vowel (p=.033)									
/o/	1.10	.13	2.07	.49	2.22	3.00	.027	48	56.2%
/a/	.75	−.16	1.66	.46	1.62	2.11	.105	52	59.6%
/e/	.06	−.63	.76	.35	.18	1.06	.860	53	47.2%
High vowel†	0	–	–	–	–	–	–	181	45.9%
Preceding segment manner (p=.475)									
High vowel	1.00	−.34	2.34	.68	1.474	2.72	.141	22	68.2%
/o/	.49	−.57	1.55	.54	.910	1.63	.364	73	50.7%
/a/	.41	−.61	1.42	.52	.786	1.50	.432	82	56.1%
Sonorant	.08	−1.07	1.23	.59	.138	1.08	.890	35	45.7%
/e/	.02	−1.00	1.04	.52	.033	1.017	.974	98	41.8%
Pause/ obstruent†	0	–	–	–	–	–	–	24	45.8%
EsPal log frequency (p=.334)									
	−.18	−.55	.19	.19	−.968	.835	.334	–	–
Conversation frequency (p=.968)									
	.002	−.12	.12	.06	.04	1.00	.968	–	–

Random effect	Estimate	95% CI Lower	95% CI Upper	SE	z	p
Var(Intercept)	1.60	.37	6.92	1.20	1.34	.181

* MOV = multiple-occlusion variant
† indicates reference level

Discussion

Addressing our first research question, the data show distinct patterning of trill /r/ realizations across the two speech contexts with more formal or standard pronunciation of trill /r/ in the classroom overall. While all coded variants of the trill appeared throughout the classroom speech data except for elision, which was used only once in the conversations, canonical trill variants with two or more occlusions constituted 69% of tokens produced during classroom speech but only 50% of the conversational speech data. Similarly, five of the six instructors produced canonical trill variants with a higher number of occlusions on average in the classroom compared to in the conversations. All participants in this study produced cases of the trill /r/ with four or more occlusions in the classroom whereas this type of production was rare in the conversations for two speakers and entirely absent for the remaining four. These findings are consistent with previous research characterizing classroom speech as a formal, emphatic speech style (e.g., Kuder, 2019; Li, 2010; Mougeon & Rehner, 2019; Rao, 2011).

An explanation for the discrepancy in trill usage between contexts could be related to the communicative and pragmatic functions of classroom speech. Research shows that student-directed speech is used to engage students, direct attention, communicate value of target items, guide classroom activities, and facilitate comprehension (Christie, 2002; Kuder, 2020; J. Willis, 1992). Thus, it is plausible that the instructors in our study favored canonical variants and avoided nonstandard variants while teaching to accommodate their speech to the learners and use more recognizable sounds that match the prescriptive norm (Kuder, 2019; Rao, 2011; Stanley & Stevenson, 2017). Juana produced less assibilated /r/ when speaking to her students in the classroom compared to in her conversation. This same trend is seen in Elena and Carmen's lesser use of the approximant realization and Marta's lower frequency of the tap plus approximant realization in the classroom context compared to their conversations. Our data show that María used noncanonical variants such as the approximant, the tap, and the tap plus approximant over 25% of the time in conversation but produced almost exclusively canonical trills in the classroom. These trends support the finding that, in the classroom, teachers tend to opt for more canonical realizations of a sound that, in more conversational contexts, is highly variable. However, they are not completely removing variation while addressing students in the classroom, since participants' use of noncanonical variants ranged from 3% to 52%.

Additionally, it merits mention that one of the six instructors (Sofía) did, in fact, produce more noncanonical variants in the classroom compared to conversation. However, the canonical trills that she produced in the classroom had a higher average number of occlusions, suggesting that she was also opting for more emphatic variants in instructor input than in conversation, but how she enacted a teacher talk style was realized differently compared to her peers. Thus, the data reveal stylistic variation in the form of individual differences in the ways teachers instantiate teacher talk style. Nevertheless, broadly speaking, in the classroom, instructors opted for either more canonical multiple-occlusion trills, longer canonical trills (more occlusions), or both strategies when adopting a teacher talk style, but did not exclusively use the prescriptive or canonical variant. This finding is unsurprising considering the perspective of third wave sociolinguistics (Eckert, 2018; Schilling, 2013). In third wave sociolinguistics, language may be viewed as a dynamic practice, variation is performative, and identity is seen as being constructed through sociolinguistic variants that may be selected either consciously or unconsciously by speakers to achieve specific effects or goals. Language instructors, in addition to accommodating learners' needs by producing more recognizable and prescriptive sounds, may also be employing this variant to construct their identity as an instructor, to convey linguistic authority in the classroom, or to highlight particular forms or content by making them more salient, among other goals. Nevertheless, they do not exclusively produce the canonical multiple-occlusion variant, and this may be because the instructors often embody various roles or convey different meanings or emotions in the classroom (e.g., educator, authority, empathy, encouragement, humor, etc.). Future research should consider employing discursive analysis techniques to understand how the canonical multiple-occlusion variant is used in the classroom context to establish student and teacher roles and relationships, shape identity, create meaning, and make content more salient.

Regarding our second research question, in addition to differing distributions of variants across speech contexts, results suggest that there may be differences in the constraints that influence trill variation within and outside the classroom. However, because two separate analyses were performed, this is not a statistical certainty. Preceding segment manner and following vowel significantly constrained instructors' production of the trill /r/ in the classroom data, while in the conversational data the only factor that predicted trill variation was following vowel. Moreover, following vowel conditioned variation differently in the two speech contexts. Whereas the multiple-occlusion trill was produced more frequently when followed by high vowels in the classroom, it was more likely with following /o/ during conversational speech. Upon further exploration, this difference in the patterning for following vowel between the two contexts may be due to the specific words produced in the classroom environment and their distribution across speakers. Outside of the classroom, 51.8% of words uttered were distinct to the dataset, while only 38% of tokens occurring during classroom speech were unique. Thus, many words in classroom speech were repeated, often as target vocabulary items or verbs conjugated during instruction, or they were related to class management and administration. We observed that some specific words were found in a sequence of repetitions that we perceived as displaying a large amount of emphasis on the speaker's part and often produced with the multiple-occlusion variant. It is possible that a handful of words with following high vowels were produced in emphatic contexts by one or two speakers who were also high producers of the multiple-occlusion variant, while a handful of words with following non-high vowels were produced in low emphasis contexts or by speakers who less frequently produced the canonical variant. Thus, this distribution of words by speaker could lead to a skewed result for phonetic context. One such example is below in (1), in which María produced the word *rubio/rubia* four times during a vocabulary explanation using the canonical multiple-occlusion trill for all four productions (translations in brackets []).

(1) Yeah, you can say *yo soy rubia* [I am blonde]. Usually when you say *yo soy rubia* [I am blonde] or *yo soy morena* [I am dark-haired], it's usually related to the hair. You can say *yo tengo pelo rubio* [I have blonde hair], but if you say *yo soy rubia* [I am blonde], it's easier and faster.

María was a high producer of the canonical variant overall. Given the level of her class, first-semester Spanish, and the topic of discussion during two of the recordings (self-descriptions), the word *rubio/rubia* 'blonde' appeared 10 times in her 36 tokens in the classroom, mostly in explanations of how to use the word. Other frequently repeated words in her dataset were *rizado* 'curly' and *rico/rica* 'rich'. These words all have following high vowels after the trill token. While this is only one example, it may be contexts such as these that are driving the patterns that we see for the classroom data, namely that following high vowels favored the canonical variant. While we could not include lexical item as a random effect in our analyses due to the number of unique words, a detailed item-by-speaker analysis in a larger sample would help clarify how individual patterns of variation influence group trends. A more individualized analysis could also shed light on whether frequency plays any role in enhancing or diminishing the effects of other factors, since frequency measures alone were not significant predictors of canonical trill use in either speech context in our study.

Our coding for first use and discourse type attempted to capture the difference between contexts where the instructor may have adopted a more emphatic or didactic speaking style and those that were more conversational or less didactic. Words uttered for the first time during a class period were generally produced with more occlusions than those uttered for a second or subsequent time. Additionally, multiple-occlusion variants were relatively more common during administrative acts involving dictation of written instructions, prompts for oral or written production, and leading questions for discussion or comprehension when compared to discourse related to descriptive and interpersonal acts. However, these discursive factors were not statistically significant in our results. It may be that the instructors are indeed using the multiple-occlusion variant in more emphatic or didactic speech styles, but that our coding did not adequately capture these nuances. Future research should consider whether trill production correlates with other features of emphatic speech, such as slower speech rate, early F0 peak alignment, less F0 suppression, and increased intensity.

It also merits mention that four of our instructors' recordings were from online classes while two provided in-person recordings. It is possible that modality influenced our participants' productions. We could not include this variable in the analysis given its overlap with our participant variable. However, a glance at our findings do not suggest a clear trend or difference between in-person instructors (Marta, Carmen) and online instructors (Juana, Elena, María, and Sofía). All six participants produced a range of variants, and the in-person instructors produced rates of multiple-occlusion variant production that fell within the range of the online instructors.

Regarding the connection between input and L2 development, although the canonical trill is the prescriptive norm taught in the classroom (Face, 2006; Olsen, 2012), our results show that learners are also exposed to numerous other variants. Along with developmental factors, this exposure may explain why learners produce a range of nativelike and nonnative variants (Daidone & Zahler, 2021; Rose, 2010). For example, in Rose (2010), classroom learners produced taps and taps plus frication, similar to those produced by our instructors in the classroom. Daidone and Zahler (2021) found that advanced learners of Spanish (895 hours of classroom instruction plus a year in Spain) produced eight distinct trill variants, all also found in the current study. Zahler and Daidone (2023) found that U.S. graduate learners of Spanish produced 10 distinct trill variants. Additionally, Daidone and Zahler (2021) found that neither preceding nor following segment conditioned learners' production of the multiple-occlusion variant. This lack of effect of phonetic context for learners, a significant constraint for the native speakers in our study and theirs, may result from conflicting patterns for the effect of preceding and/or following context in native speaker classroom and conversational speech. It is possible that exposure to distinct patterns of trill variation according to phonetic context within and outside the classroom poses additional challenges for learners in terms of acquiring these patterns of variation.

Conclusion

Overall, our study indicates that classroom speech compared to conversational speech exhibits more standard pronunciation of the trill, in both a higher rate of the canonical variant and a higher average number of occlusions for this variant. Our findings also indicate that distinct linguistic constraints impacted instructors' trill variation in the classroom versus in the conversations. Although the canonical multiple-occlusion trill was dominant in the classroom data, all instructors produced an array of noncanonical trill variants in this context, suggesting that L2 teachers are not completely removing phonetic variation during instruction. Additionally, the individual instructors in this study varied substantially from one another in their production of the trill phoneme while teaching, revealing that learners are exposed to different variants of /r/ at different rates during classroom input depending on their instructor. Given this individual variation among speakers, an expansion of the current study to include a wider range of participants could potentially reveal how instructors adapt their speech in the classroom according to additional instructor characteristics such as linguistic background, amount of teacher training, and years teaching.

The differences we found in trill production among speakers and between speech contexts also suggest the importance of having a diversity of auditory class materials that represent distinct dialects, social contexts, speech styles, and registers to provide a more representative picture of everyday speech in Spanish. Curricula can incorporate these diverse sources of input by building courses that include multimedia assignments using movies and music, YouTube videos, field trips and excursions, presentations and visits from different speakers, and local or global conversation partners. These curricular choices are especially important as explicit pronunciation instruction is relatively rare in Spanish courses, and the sounds heard in the classroom may be the main source of L2 learners' phonological input, particularly for lower-level learners.

References

Arteaga, D. L. (2000). Articulatory phonetics in the first-year Spanish classroom. *The Modern Language Journal, 84*(3), 339–354.

Boersma, P., & Weenink, D. (2019). Praat: Doing phonetics by computer [version 6.0.52]. Retrieved from: http://www.praat.org

Bradley, T. (2006). Phonetic realizations of /sr/ clusters in Latin American Spanish. In M. Díaz-Campos (Ed.), *Selected proceedings of the 2nd Conference on Laboratory Approaches to Spanish Phonetics and Phonology* (pp. 1–13). Cascadilla Proceedings Project.

Bybee, J. (2002). Word frequency and context of use in the lexical diffusion of phonetically conditioned sound change. *Language Variation and Change, 14*(3), 261–290.

Bybee, J. (2008). Usage-based grammar and second language acquisition. In P. Robinson & N.C. Ellis (Eds.), *Handbook of cognitive linguistics and second language acquisition* (pp. 216–236). Rodopi.

Christie, F. (2002). *Classroom discourse analysis: A functional perspective*. Bloomsbury Publishing.

Crystal, D. (2005). *How language works: How babies babble, words change meaning, and languages live or die*. Avery.

Daidone, D. (2019). Preterite and imperfect in Spanish instructor oral input and Spanish language corpora. *Hispania, 102*(1), 45–58.

Daidone, D., & Zahler, S.L. (2021). A variationist analysis of second language Spanish trill production. *Studies in Hispanic and Lusophone Linguistics, 14*(1), 1–37.

Darcy, I. (2018). Powerful and effective pronunciation instruction: How can we achieve it? *CATESOL Journal, 30*(1), 13–45.

Díaz-Campos, M. (2008). Variable production of the trill in spontaneous speech: Sociolinguistic implications. In L. Colantoni & J. Steele (Eds.), *Selected proceedings of the 3rd Conference on Laboratory Approaches to Spanish Phonology* (pp. 47–58). Cascadilla Press.

Diez Canseco, S. (1997). Language variation: The influence of speakers' attitudes and gender on sociolinguistic variables in the Spanish of Cusco, Perú [Unpublished doctoral dissertation]. University of Pittsburgh.

Dracos, M. (2018). Teacher talk and Spanish subject personal pronouns. *Journal of Spanish Language Teaching, 5*(1), 1–15.

Duchon, A., Perea, M., Sebastián-Gallés, N., Martí, A. & Carreiras, M. (2013). EsPal: One-stop shopping for Spanish word properties. *Behavior Research Methods, 45*(4), 1246–1258.

Eckert, P. (2018). *Meaning and linguistic variation: The third wave in sociolinguistics*. Cambridge University Press.

Face, T. (2006). Intervocalic rhotic pronunciation by adult learners of Spanish as a second language. In C.A. Klee & T.L. Face (Eds.), *Selected proceedings of the 7th Conference on the Acquisition of Spanish and Portuguese as First and Second Languages* (pp. 47–58). Cascadilla Proceedings Project.

Gallois, C., Ogay, T., & Giles, H. (2005). Communication accommodation theory: A look back and a look ahead. In W. Gudykunst (Ed.), *Theorizing about intercultural communication* (pp. 121–148). Sage.

Geeslin, K., Daidone, D., Long, A.Y., & Solon, M. (2023). Usage-based models of second language acquisition: Language use in context and additional language learning. In M. Díaz-Campos & S. Balasch (Eds.), *The handbook of usage-based linguistics* (pp. 345–361). Wiley-Blackwell.

Gerard, C., & Dahan, D. (1995). Durational variations in speech and didactic accent during reading. *Speech Communication, 16*(3), 293–311.

Gutiérrez, M.J., & Fairclough, M. (2006). Incorporating linguistic variation into the classroom. In R. Salaberry & B.A. Lafford (Eds.), *The art of teaching Spanish* (pp. 173–191). Georgetown University Press.

Hamayan, E. V., & Tucker, G. R. (1980). Language input in the bilingual classroom and its relationship to second language achievement. *TESOL Quarterly, 14*(4), 453–468.

Hayes-Harb, R., Barrios, S. L., & Tripp, A. (2022). Whose input matters? The influence of socially-differentiated input sources in adult Lx phonetic learning. *Journal of Second Language Pronunciation, 8*(3), 363–388.

Henriksen, N. (2014). Sociophonetic analysis of phonemic trill variation in two sub-varieties of Peninsular Spanish. *Journal of Linguistic Geography, 2*(1), 2–24.

Hualde, J. I. (2005). *The sounds of Spanish*. Cambridge University Press.

Jones, R. H. (2005). Beyond "listen and repeat": Pronunciation teaching materials and the theories of second language acquisition. In J. C. Richards & W. A. Renandya (Eds.), *Methodology in language teaching: An anthology of current practice* (pp. 178–187). Cambridge University Press.

Kuder, E. (2019). *Second language teacher prosody*. Routledge.

Kuder, E. (2020). Rhetorical stress in Spanish second language classroom instruction. *Hispania, 103*(2), 225–244.

Labov, W. (1972). Some principles of linguistic methodology. *Language in Society, 1*(1), 97–120.

Lamy, D. (2015). A sociophonetic analysis of trill production in Panamanian Spanish. In R. Klassen, J. M. Liceras, & E. Valenzuela (Eds.), *Hispanic linguistics at the crossroads: Theoretical linguistics, language acquisition and language contact* (pp. 313–336). John Benjamins.

Levis, J. M., & Echelberger, A. (2022). Integrating pronunciation into language instruction. In J. M. Levis, T. M. Derwing, & S. Sonsaat-Hegelheimer (Eds.), *Second language pronunciation: Bridging the gap between research and teaching* (pp. 19–41). Wiley Blackwell.

Li, X. (2010). Sociolinguistic variation in the speech of learners of Chinese as a second language. *Language Learning, 60*(2), 366–408.

Melero García, F. (2015). Análisis acústico de la vibrante múltiple en el español de Valencia (España). *Studies in Hispanic and Lusophone Linguistics, 8*(1), 183–206.

Mora, J. C., & Levkina, M. (2017). Task-based pronunciation teaching and research: Key issues and future directions. *Studies in Second Language Acquisition, 39*(2), 381–399.

Mougeon, R., & Rehner, K. (2019). Patterns of sociolinguistic variation in teacher classroom speech. *Journal of Sociolinguistics, 23*(2), 163–185.

Offerman, H. (2024). The current state of pronunciation in Spanish textbooks. In D. Olson, J. Sturm, O. Dmitrieva, & J. Levis (Eds.), *Proceedings of 14th Pronunciation in Second Language Learning and Teaching Conference* (pp. 1–11). Iowa State University Digital Press.

Olsen, M. K. (2012). The L2 acquisition of Spanish rhotics by L2 English speakers: The effect of L1 articulatory routines and phonetic context for allophonic variation. *Hispania, 95*(1), 65–82.

Rao, R. (2006). On intonation's relationship with pragmatic meaning in Spanish. In T. L. Face & C. A. Klee (Eds.), *Selected proceedings of the 8th Hispanic Linguistics Symposium* (pp. 103–115). Cascadilla Proceedings Project.

Rao, R. (2011). Intonation in Spanish classroom-style didactic speech. *Journal of Language Teaching & Research, 2*(3), 31–75.

Reeder, J. T. (1998). English speakers' acquisition of voiceless stops and trills in L2 Spanish. *Texas Papers in Foreign Language Education*, *3*(3), 101–108.

Rehner, R., & Mougeon, K. (2003). The effect of education input on the development of sociolinguistic competence by French immersion students: The case of expressions of consequence in spoken French. *The Journal of Educational Thought (JET)*, *37*(3), 259–281.

Rose, M. (2010). Intervocalic tap and trill production in the acquisition of Spanish as a second language. *Studies in Hispanic and Lusophone Linguistics*, *3*(2), 379–419.

Schilling, N. (2013). Investigating stylistic variation. In J. K. Chambers, & N. Schilling (Eds.), *The handbook of language variation and change* (2nd ed., pp. 325–349). Wiley-Blackwell.

Stanley, P., & Stevenson, M. (2017). Making sense of not making sense: Novice English language teacher talk. *Linguistics and Education*, *38*, 1–10.

Thornbury, S., & Watkins, P. (2007). *The CELTA course: Trainee book*. Cambridge University Press.

Trofimovich, P., Collins, L., Cardoso, W., White, J., & Horst, M. (2012). A frequency-based approach to L2 phonological learning: Teacher input and student output in an intensive ESL context. *TESOL Quarterly*, *46*(1), 176–187.

Willis, E. (2006). Trill variation in Dominican Spanish: An acoustic examination and comparative analysis. In N. Sagarra & A. J. Toribio (Eds.), *Selected proceedings of the 9th Hispanic Linguistics Symposium* (pp. 121–131). Cascadilla Proceedings Project.

Willis, E. (2007). An acoustic study of the "pre-aspirated trill" in narrative Cibaeño Dominican Spanish. *Journal of the International Phonetic Association*, *37*(1), 33–49.

Willis, J. (1992). Inner and outer: Spoken discourse in the language classroom. In M. Coulthard (Ed.), *Advances in spoken discourse analysis* (pp. 162–182). Routledge.

Zahler, S. L. & Daidone, D. (2014). A variationist account of trill /r/ usage in the Spanish of Málaga. *IULC Working Papers*, *14*(2), 17–42.

Zahler, S. L. & Daidone, D. (2023). Individual differences do not affect trill variation by advanced learners of Spanish. In S. Fernández Cuenca, T. Judy, & L. Miller (Eds.), *Innovative approaches to research in Hispanic linguistics: Regional, diachronic, and learner profile variation* (pp. 196–224). John Benjamins.

Appendix

Table A. Trill variants produced in the classroom context by participant

Variant	Marta n	Marta %	Carmen n	Carmen %	Juana n	Juana %	María n	María %	Elena n	Elena %	Sofía n	Sofía %	Total n	Total %
Trill (2–3 occ.)	48	80	86	69	24	41	32	89	80	47	25	38	295	57
Trill (4+ occ.)	2	3	18	15	4	7	3	8	17	10	16	25	60	12
Pre-aspirated trill	0	0	0	0	2	3	0	0	0	0	0	0	2	<1
Tap + frication	0	0	0	0	6	10	0	0	2	1	2	3	10	2
Tap + approx.	4	7	9	7	9	15	1	3	20	12	5	8	48	9
Tap	3	5	6	5	1	2	0	0	1	1	5	8	16	3
Approx. (flat F3)	2	3	1	1	6	10	0	0	22	13	5	8	36	7
Approx. (lowered F3)	0	0	0	0	0	0	0	0	13	8	0	0	13	3
Assibilated	0	0	0	0	3	5	0	0	10	6	7	11	20	4
Epenthetic vowel + tap	0	0	3	2	1	2	0	0	1	1	0	0	5	1
Epenthetic vowel + trill	1	2	1	1	3	5	0	0	0	0	0	0	5	1
Other	0	0	0	0	0	0	0	0	5	3	0	0	5	1
Total	60	12	124	24	59	11	36	7	171	33	65	13	515	100

Note. Percentages in last row show the percentage of the total data represented by each participant.

Table B. Trill variants produced in the conversational context by participant

Variant	Marta n	Marta %	Carmen n	Carmen %	Juana n	Juana %	María n	María %	Elena n	Elena %	Sofía n	Sofía %	Total n	Total %
Trill (2–3 occ.)	24	44	34	58	3	8	45	65	39	42	16	80	161	48
Trill (4+ occ.)	0	0	3	5	0	0	0	0	2	2	0	0	5	1
Pre-aspirated trill	0	0	0	0	1	3	0	0	0	0	0	0	1	<1
Tap + frication	3	5	2	3	2	5	1	1	3	3	1	5	12	4
Tap + approx.	18	33	4	7	6	15	7	10	14	15	2	10	51	15
Tap	7	13	7	12	0	0	6	9	3	3	0	0	23	7
Approx. (flat F3)	1	2	7	12	1	3	8	12	27	29	0	0	44	13
Approx. (lowered F3)	0	0	0	0	0	0	0	0	1	1	0	0	1	<1
Assibilated	2	4	1	2	23	59	1	1	1	1	1	5	29	9
Epenthetic vowel + tap	0	0	1	2	3	8	0	0	1	1	0	0	5	1
Elision	0	0	0	0	0	0	1	1	0	0	0	0	1	<1
Other	0	0	0	0	0	0	0	0	1	1	0	0	1	<1
Total	55	16	59	18	39	12	69	21	92	28	20	6	334	100

Note. Percentages in last row show the percentage of the total data represented by each participant.

CHAPTER 7

Interlocutor perceptions of regional phone use in L2 Spanish
The Castilian Spanish /θ/

Stacey Hanson & Elena Schoonmaker-Gates
Indiana University | Elon University

This study examines native and second-language (L2) learner perceptions of the regionally indexed Castilian Spanish /θ/ in learner speech. Native and L2 listeners evaluated how intelligent, kind, and nativelike L2 learners sounded in Spanish when they produced read speech with /θ/ and /s/. Significantly higher intelligence ratings were given to speech with /θ/, but only by native listeners from outside of North-Central Spain. In contrast, L2 listeners rated speech with /s/ as more intelligent and, in some cases, more nativelike than speech with /θ/, with some individual speaker variability occurring, especially when overall pronunciation scores were lower. These findings suggest that L2 learners may be perceived differently by native speaker and peer interlocutors when they adopt regional variants.

Keywords: regional variation, second language acquisition, matched guise, Castilian Spanish, attitudes

López García (1998, p. 14, authors' translation from Spanish) writes "The consideration of an individual as a good or bad speaker of a language — especially if they are a foreigner — is based on their proximity or similarity to the prototype." But what prototype are second-language (L2) learners expected to learn, and how does this concept vary among native and L2 interlocutors or across regional varieties? Are specific regional cues included in that prototypical target? Furthermore, the view that it is especially important for nonnative speakers (or "foreigners") to adhere to a particular prototype raises the question of how L2 learners are viewed when they adopt specific regional cues that carry sociolinguistic meaning. If they are viewed more favorably, it could impact the feedback they receive about their L2 use, their relationships with and access to native speakers, and ultimately their language learning.

This is an exploratory study that aims to examine how native and L2 listeners perceive the adoption of the interdental fricative 'theta' /θ/, a regional phone that occurs in Spain, by L2 learners. In this chapter, we will examine perceptions of /θ/ production as it relates to L2 learners' prestige (intelligence), solidarity (kindness), and nativeness (nativelike pronunciation). Because it examines interlocutor perceptions of a phone used almost exclusively in Spain, this study is well-positioned to test whether the prestige and correctness associated with Castilian Spanish (e.g., Chiquito & Quesada Pacheco, 2014; George & Hoffman-González, 2023; Regan, 2022) also applies to L2 speech that incorporates characteristics of that variety and to explore the possible communicative implications this incorporation has on future language learning.

Background

Beliefs and perceptions of "correct" Spanish in and outside of the classroom

In language standardization, what is considered accurate and canonical is prescriptively defined and usually taken by speakers to be a universal truth that needs no explanation or rationalization (Milroy, 2001). This is in contrast with the constantly changing and variable nature of human language, a duality especially marked in the case of L2 learners whose first exposure to language is often in a highly controlled, classroom environment with high value placed on what is correct or academic, and less emphasis on learning popular or variable structures. Yule (2006) notes that the language taught to L2 learners also typically has its roots in a socially prestigious dialect associated, at least initially, with a cultural or political hub, like Paris for French and London for British English. Although educated standards exist throughout the Spanish-speaking world (Lope Blanch, 2002), the variety of Spanish used in North-Central Spain has been cited as being a highly prototypical variety due to the historical, political, and cultural prestige of the region (López García, 1998; Moreno Fernández, 2000). Empirical studies examining perceptions both inside and outside of Spain have confirmed this perspective among native speakers of Spanish (Alfaraz, 2014; Callesano & Carter, 2019; Chiquito & Quesada Pacheco, 2014; Sobrino Triana, 2018). For instance, Chappell and Barnes (2023) found that Spaniards rated the speech of a man from Spain significantly higher for status than the speech of men from Colombia and Argentina. In Callesano and Carter (2019), Latinx Spanish speakers in the United States rated a speaker from Spain as more competent than speakers from Colombia or Cuba.

Learners have also been found to hold attitudes regarding what sounds prestigious in their L2. For example, Geeslin and Schmidt (2018) studied L2 Spanish speakers' attitudes towards various regional varieties of Spanish and found that learners who had studied abroad in Spain rated Castilian Spanish as more prestigious than other varieties. Similarly, Schmidt and Geeslin (2022) examined the attitudes of L2 Spanish speakers towards native speakers from Argentina, Mexico, Puerto Rico, and Spain, finding that advanced learners rated Castilian Spanish as significantly more prestigious than Mexican Spanish. Likewise, Chappell and Kanwit (2022) observed effects of study abroad and L2 proficiency on learners' perception of status related to regional variation in Spanish. Their study used a matched guise task in which speakers from Mexico and Puerto Rico were recorded multiple times producing the same content with coda [s] and coda [h] (aspirated /s/). L2 learners of Spanish across various proficiency levels rated each stimulus on a 6-point scale according to measures of solidarity, status, and confidence. The results revealed that more advanced learners showed greater sensitivity to sociophonetic information and those with prior study abroad experience in /s/-aspirating regions were more likely to associate coda [s] with higher status.

Not only do language learners and native speakers hold beliefs and attitudes about what regional varieties sound more prestigious in the L2, but they also hold opinions about what constitutes more nativelike L2 speech. McBride (2015) found that native listeners cited suprasegmental cues like fluency and voice quality more than segmentals when asked to identify the positive and negative features of L2 pronunciation. In George (2017), native listeners cited primarily nonnative speech cues when justifying their assessments of speech with higher foreign accent ratings, but primarily regional cues when justifying assessments of speech with lower foreign accent ratings. Research on L2 listeners suggests they are harsher critics of the pronunciation of their peers than native listeners or language instructors (Fayer & Krasinski, 1987) and that they use their L2 phonological competence rather than their first-language (L1) knowledge in assessing degree of foreign accent in the L2 (Munro et al., 2006), but additional study is needed to determine whether native and L2 listeners perceive learner pronunciation as more nativelike when it includes regional phonetic cues like /θ/.

The discussion of what constitutes nativelike L2 pronunciation raises the question of what variety of Spanish should be taught in the L2 language classroom. George and Hoffman-González (2023) reported that Castilian Spanish was one of the most preferred varieties by instructors and their students, and other studies have found that Spanish teachers in Australia, the United States, and Spain rated Castilian Spanish as more prestigious than other varieties (Martinez Franco, 2019; Ortiz-Jiménez, 2019). However, the same studies also confirmed that instructional preferences are far from ubiquitous, as George and Hoffman-

González (2023) reported an equal preference for Central American Spanish among US Spanish instructors, and Ortiz-Jiménez (2019) found generally positive solidarity ratings towards all regional Spanish varieties among native and nonnative teachers of L2 Spanish in Australia and Spain. Instructors' views also differ on whether students should learn only one or various regional varieties of Spanish (Bárkányi & Fuertes Gutiérrez, 2019; Grammon, 2021; Korell, 2022). Overall, native speakers, L2 learners, and instructors exhibit often clear attitudes towards what regional varieties of Spanish are the most standard, correct, and prestigious, but more research is needed to explore how L2 learners' use of regional variants impacts listener attitudes towards speech.

Occurrence of /θ/ and L2 learner adoption rates

The voiceless interdental fricative /θ/ occurs in Castilian Spanish in North-Central Spain and is produced categorically in cases of orthographic <ce, ci, z>, while the voiceless alveolar (apico-alveolar) fricative /s/ is produced for orthographic <s>, a phenomenon known as *distinción* 'distinction'. Virtually all other regional varieties of Spanish across Latin America, the Caribbean, and parts of Andalusia are characterized by *seseo*, the production of /s/ in all instances of orthographic <ce, ci, z, s> (Hualde, 2014), and in these varieties /θ/ does not occur. In Southern Spain, Andalusian Spanish is also characterized by the production of /θ/ and /s/ occurring in free variation with orthographic <ce, ci, s, z>, a phenomenon known as *ceceo*. Although *distinción* and *seseo* also occur in Andalusian Spanish, *distinción* has become more common in recent years and is primarily used by younger, educated individuals living in urban areas in Southern Spain (Regan, 2017, 2020; Santana Marrero, 2016; Villena Ponsoda & Vida Castro, 2017). Table 1 provides examples of how the Spanish words *casa* 'house' and *caza* 'he/she hunts' are produced following norms of *distinción, seseo,* and *ceceo*.

Table 1. Production norms of 'distinción', 'seseo', and 'ceceo'

Phenomenon	*Casa* 'house'	*Caza* 'he/she hunts'
Distinción	['ka.sa]	['ka.θa]
Seseo	['ka.sa]	['ka.sa]
Ceceo	['ka.θa]/['ka.sa]	['ka.θa]/['ka.sa]

Although the present study does not examine production rates of /θ/ by L2 learners, research examining this phenomenon has generally shown low rates of use among learners even after exposure to the variant through study abroad (e.g., Geeslin & Gudmestad, 2008a; George, 2014; Knouse, 2013; Ringer-Hilfinger,

2012). Although Knouse (2013) found significant L2 proficiency level differences in /θ/ production, the variant was produced in only 1.7% of possible contexts by learners following a 6-week study abroad experience in Salamanca, Spain. Similarly, Ringer-Hilfinger (2012) found that L2 learners produced /θ/ only six times out of a total of 209 possible contexts after spending 13 weeks in Madrid, Spain. These findings are in stark contrast with research on the adoption by L2 learners of other salient regional cues, like *zheísmo/sheísmo* in Argentina, which recent studies have shown is often adopted by intermediate and advanced learners even after short periods abroad (Pozzi & Bayley, 2021; Schmidt, 2020). High but variable rates of adoption have also been observed for certain regional cues in other second languages like Arabic (Raish, 2015; Trentman, 2013) and French (e.g., Howard et al., 2006). Further investigation into learners' attitudes toward use of /θ/ among their L2 peers may provide additional insight as to why rates of adoption remain relatively low among L2 speakers.

Comparing perceptions by regional varieties

Regional variation has been shown to exist, both across the Spanish-speaking world and within specific countries, in the perceptions held by native speakers towards Castilian Spanish (Chiquito & Quesada Pacheco, 2014). That said, there is also an interesting uniformity in perceptions within Latin America, as Chiquito and Quesada Pacheco (2014) found that Spanish from Spain was cited as the most or second most correct, prestigious variety by the majority of participants in every Spanish-speaking country studied but one, with the percentage of respondents citing Castilian Spanish ranging from 13% to 66%. Cestero and Paredes (2018) performed a large study that examined the cognitive and affective attitudes of young university students towards speech from Spain (central, southern, and Canary Islands), Mexico, the Caribbean, Chile, Argentina, and the Andes. Participants were mostly from Spain but also from Chile, Colombia, and Argentina. Their study points to differences in perceptions between North-Central Spain and other locations, as 90% of respondents from Madrid believed that their Spanish was the most correct, a percentage well above those held in other regions in Chiquito and Quesada Pacheco (2014). Cestero and Paredes (2018) and other studies have shown that Spanish from southern Spain is not ideologically linked to prestige the way North-Central Spanish is (Moreno Fernández & Moreno Fernández, 2002; Santana Marrero, 2018). Furthermore, Ardila (2020) and Moreno Fernández and Moreno Fernández (2002) provide interesting perspectives that suggest greater cultural and linguistic similarities between Andalusian Spanish and Latin American varieties than between the Spanish spoken in North-Central and Southern Spain. Thus, it might be argued that combining perceptions held by Andalusian and Latin American speakers is plausible and could perhaps result in data that are a better representation of perceptions of regional varieties than combining perceptions held by speakers from North-Central and Southern Spain.

Theoretical framework and research questions

Understanding how learners who adopt regional variants are perceived by their L2 peers and native interlocutors is also relevant to the field's exploration of the relationship between learner characteristics and their access to input. Geeslin (2020, 2023) proposed a variationist model that aims to address the complexity of factors that can impact learner interaction with their interlocutors, building on the work of Preston (2000) and incorporating the effect that learner characteristics like age or ethnicity (or regional phone use) can have on L2 production and, therefore, on opportunities for future interaction with an interlocutor. Importantly, the model conceptualizes the effect that context (the perception of and response to a conversation partner) may have on a learner's opportunities for input. For instance, if a learner is perceived as having a very low proficiency level in the L2, native speaker interlocutors may provide different or modified input (i.e., slower speech, fewer words) or be less willing to engage with the learner based on this perception. In light of this potential connection between how a learner is perceived and their access to future input or interaction, a fundamental question that arises is how native and L2 interlocutors perceive learners' use of regional variants, and how that perception might impact the quantity and quality of the input available to the learner. This framework and the previous literature on this topic have led to the following research questions that guide the present investigation:

1. To what extent do native listeners' social perceptions (prestige, solidarity, nativelike pronunciation) of L2 speech vary according to the presence of [θ] or [s]?
2. To what extent do intermediate-level L2 listeners' social perceptions (prestige, solidarity, nativelike pronunciation) of L2 speech vary according to the presence of [θ] or [s]?

Method

Participants

Native listeners in the present study were grouped into two categories of origin, those from North-Central Spain ($n=8$) and those from other areas where Spanish is spoken (*n* = 8), including one participant from Honduras, one from Mexico, one from Venezuela, two from Colombia, and three from Western Andalusia in Southern Spain. We recognize that the listeners from Andalusia, because of the presence of *ceceo* in the region, may hold different perspectives on /θ/ use than listeners from Latin America. However, the participants from Andalusia were grouped with listeners from Latin America rather than excluded because this is an exploratory study and their perceptions add value to the current investigation (see section *Combining Regional Varieties* for a detailed review). However, future work is needed that parses out the perceptions of /θ/ use by L2 speakers for native listeners from southern Spain and listeners from other specific varieties within Latin America. In creating a listener group made up of native speakers from Honduras, Mexico, Venezuela, Colombia, and Andalusia, we are not suggesting that these individuals all speak the same variety, and we recognize that considerable variability in their perceptions may exist, which could make drawing uniform conclusions difficult.

Table 2 provides demographic information about the native listeners in each group, whose ages ranged from 20 to over 50 years old, who were equally distributed for gender in the North-Central (NC) Spain group, and who were five women and three men in the group from other regions. Participants checked a listed option for age where the oldest age provided was '50+'. Therefore, we report the minimum and maximum ages of the native listener participants.

Table 2. Native listener participant demographics

Origin	*n*	Min. age	Max. age	Gender Woman	Man
NC Spain	8	24	50+	4	4
Other regions	8	20	50+	5	3

Note. NC = North-Central

L2 listener participants were 36 L1 English-L2 Spanish speakers enrolled in intermediate-level Spanish classes (third and fourth semester college classes) who did not report any prior exposure to native speakers from North-Central Spain through their past or present instructors, friends, family, or acquaintances. The L2 learners were 15 women, 18 men, 2 non-binary identifying individuals, and one individual who preferred not to identify their gender, whose ages ranged from 18–21 years with a mean age of 19.77 years ($SD = 1.10$).

Instruments and stimuli

Three tasks were employed: a matched guise task (Lambert et al., 1960), a Spanish grammar test (Geeslin & Gudmestad, 2008b), and a background questionnaire. Matched guise is a sociolinguistic technique meant to elicit indirect attitudes towards regional varieties or variants. Speakers, in this case four individuals observed to use both *distinción* and *seseo* in different settings, are recorded twice, once in each variety they speak. The stimuli are then presented to participants who rate the speech according to different attributes. In the present study, the stimuli used in the matched guise were elicited through a reading task completed by two men and two women who were L2 learners with extensive experience speaking and studying Spanish at the graduate level, and all four were college-level instructors of Spanish at the time of recording. The speakers' ages ranged from 30–50 years, and all reported English as their first language. One speaker, Nash, also reported being a near-native Catalan speaker. All speakers but Sarah reported living or studying abroad in North-Central Spain for between 1.5 and 33 months, and Emma and Sarah also reported spending approximately one year in various locations in Latin America (see Table 3). Sarah reported using /θ/ in class to expose her students to the North-Central Spanish dialect, having learned it from previous instructors and media consumption. Speaker was included as an independent variable in all statistical analyses performed in order to account for any variability resulting from speaker differences.

The purpose of the matched guise task in the present study was to examine listener attitudes towards the use of /θ/ (*distinción*) or /s/ (*seseo*), so three target sentences were created that each contained one instance where /θ/ or /s/ would be produced depending on the variety that the speaker employed (e.g., *Catalina prepara el pan en la cocina* 'Catalina makes bread in the kitchen'). Each target sentence was recorded by each speaker twice, once with /θ/ and once with /s/. Three additional distractor sentences were read for a total of nine sentences per speaker and 36 stimuli heard by each participant. The stimuli were pseudo-randomized in a Qualtrics survey so that the same speaker and/or sentence did not appear consecutively. Three different versions were used to ensure that there was no effect of order, and each stimulus was presented once, after which participants used a 6-point scale to rate intelligence (prestige), kindness (solidarity), how nativelike the pronunciation sounded, and how natural or fake the pronunciation sounded (see Figure 1).

L2 participants also completed a background questionnaire that included extensive information about the specific regions of the Spanish they had been exposed to, their past instructors' origins, details about any study abroad experience, and origin of any native Spanish-speaking friends, family, or acquaintances.

Table 3. Speaker demographics

Speaker	Age	Gender	Abroad experience NC Spain	Abroad experience LA	Average time in NC Spain (months)	Average time in LA (months)
Emma	44	W	Burgos	Quito, Ecuador; Arequipa, Peru; Heredia, Costa Rica; Guatemala	1.5	13
Sarah	50	W		Morelia, Mexico; Cuernavaca, Mexico; San Jose, Costa Rica	0	12
Noah	32	M	Salamanca, Leon, Zaragoza, Segovia, Barcelona		33	0
Nash	30	M	Alcalá de Henares, Barcelona		15.25	0

Note. LA = Latin America

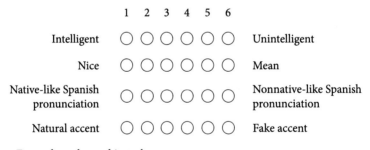

Figure 1. Example scale used in task

On their background questionnaire, native speaker participants were asked about their knowledge of English and other languages and their residential history. After a short training session to ensure their volume was adjusted properly and that they understood how to participate in the task, participants completed the matched guise activity in a quiet location using headphones, after which L2 listeners completed the grammar test. All listeners then completed the background questionnaire. Learners completed the tasks on individual computers as an in-class activity, and native listeners completed the tasks individually.

Independent and dependent variables and statistical analysis

Data were coded for the independent variables variant produced (/s/ or /θ/), participant (i.e., listener), and speaker. The native listener data were also coded for the independent variable listener origin (North-Central Spain or Other Regions). Three separate continuous dependent variables were examined, each in a separate mixed-model ANOVA in SPSS, measured by listeners' responses on the 6-point scale for intelligence (prestige), kindness (solidarity), and nativelike pronunciation. Mixed-model ANOVAs were employed for the native listener data because they are appropriate for a statistical analysis with a continuous dependent variable (ratings from 1–6) and at least two independent categorical variables, at least one being between-subjects (origin) and one being within-subjects variables (variant and speaker). Two-way repeated measures ANOVAs were used to analyze the L2 listener rating data because these analyses only involved within-subjects measures (variant and speaker). ANOVAs were chosen for the statistical analysis over other analyses because this study is examining mean differences of specific attributes between L2 speakers' use of /θ/ and /s/ and not the association of a specific attribute with /θ/ and /s/ or how individual factors (e.g., exposure or instruction) predict accurate identification of a dialect. Ratings of how natural the pronunciation sounded were also collected for quality control of the speakers' guises, to ensure that their use of /s/ or /θ/ did not sound forced or fake. The scale ranged from 1 (positive attribute) to 6 (negative attribute), as exemplified in 1 = intelligent and 6 = not intelligent. Consequently, ratings were inverted such that 1 became 6, 2 became 5, 3 became 4, 4 became 3, 5 became 2, and 6 became 1. This was done for reporting purposes, so that a higher score reflected more positive attributes.

Results

Native listener ratings

The mean ratings given by native listeners according to native speaker origin (those from North-Central Spain and those from other regions) and whether the speech contained /s/ or /θ/ are shown in Figure 2 separated out for each dependent variable: intelligence, kindness, and nativelike pronunciation. Although listeners from other regions rated the L2 speech about half a point higher for both intelligence and kindness than those from North-Central Spain did, ratings of nativeness did not show this trend. Of special interest in this study is whether each native listener group rated L2 speech differently based on the presence of /θ/ or /s/, and the largest differences are present in the other regions group, with higher intelligence ratings for /θ/ than /s/ by 0.18 points and higher nativeness ratings for /s/ than /θ/ by 0.27 points. Whether or not these differences were significant was examined via a mixed-model ANOVA.

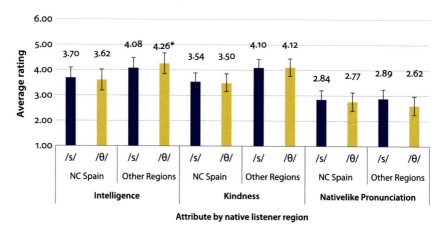

Figure 2. Native listener attributes by variant
*=p<0.05

A mixed-model ANOVA was run for each of the three continuous dependent variables (intelligence ratings, kindness ratings, and nativelike pronunciation ratings) with variant (/s/ or /θ/), listener origin (from North-Central Spain, from other regions), and speaker (Emma, Sarah, Nash, Noah) as categorical, fixed independent variables, and participant as a random factor. The ANOVA that examined the intelligence ratings of native listeners found a significant interaction effect between variant and listener origin $F(1, 360) = 5.29$, $p = .022$, but no main effect was present for variant or listener origin, indicating that native listener intelligence ratings did not vary significantly according to whether they heard /θ/ or /s/, and overall ratings did not differ between the two groups of native listeners according to their origin. Posthoc analysis with LSD corrections revealed that listeners from other regions rated L2 speech with /θ/ as significantly more intelligent ($M = 4.26$, $SD = .89$) than speech with /s/ ($M = 4.08$, $SD = .94$, $p = .028$), but listeners from North-Central Spain showed no difference in their intelligence ratings based on the presence of /θ/ ($M = 3.61$, $SD = 1.48$) or /s/ ($M = 3.7$, $SD = 1.41$, $p = .298$). Table 4 shows the differences of estimated marginal means for native listeners' intelligence ratings in terms of listener origin and variant.

The mixed-model ANOVA with kindness ratings as the continuous dependent variable found no significant main effects or interaction effects, although speaker approached significance $F(3, 360) = 2.54$, $p = .056$, and posthoc analysis with LSD adjustments revealed that one of the male speakers, Nash, received lower kindness

Table 4. Summary of differences in estimated marginal means (EMMs) of native listeners' intelligence ratings according to Variant*Listener Origin

Listener origin	Variant	Comparison variant	EMM	SE	95% CI	p
NC Spain	/θ/	/s/	−0.08	0.08	[−0.24, 0.07]	.298
LA/Andalusia	/θ/	/s/	0.18	0.08	[0.02, 0.33]	.028*

* $p < 0.05$

ratings ($M = 3.7$, $SD = 1.2$) than Emma ($M = 3.9$, $SD = 1.11$, $p = .045$), Sarah ($M = 3.9$, $SD = 1.16$, $p = .027$), and Noah ($M = 3.9$, $SD = 1.16$, $p = .015$). No significant main effects were observed for variant ($p = .822$) or listener origin ($p = .214$) as predictors of kindness ratings, and the interaction between variant and listener origin was also not significant $F(1, 360) = .68$, $p = .41$. These results suggest that both groups of native listeners, those from North-Central Spain and those from other regions, rated the kindness of the L2 speech similarly, and that those kindness ratings did not vary based on whether the speech contained /θ/ or /s/.

The mixed-model ANOVA that examined native listener nativelike pronunciation ratings as the dependent variable found a significant main effect of speaker $F(1, 360) = 5.37$, $p = .001$, but variant ($p = .253$) and listener origin ($p = .907$) were not significant and neither was the interaction between them $F(1, 360) = .435$, $p = .510$. Posthoc analysis with LSD corrections revealed that one of the men speakers, Noah, was rated as significantly less nativelike ($M = 2.28$, $SD = 1.64$) than Sarah ($M = 2.8$, $SD = 1.76$, $p = .015$), Emma ($M = 2.98$, $SD = 1.78$, $p = .001$), and Nash ($M = 3.05$, $SD = 1.61$, $p < .001$), but use of /θ/ and /s/ did not predict native listeners' nativelike pronunciation ratings in either listener origin group.

L2 listener ratings

The motivation behind collecting L2 listener ratings was not for comparison with the native listener ratings, as we would not expect language learners to respond to their peers' adoption of dialectal cues the same as native listeners would. However, understanding the perceptions and responses of both native listeners *and* L2 listeners towards L2 speech that contains regional variants is important, as these perceptions can impact learners' access to and relationship with their native and peer interlocutors and their desire to continue developing regional speech patterns or not. Figure 3 presents the mean ratings of L2 listener participants. L2 listeners' mean ratings for all three measures were higher with /s/ than with /θ/, although the differences were small for measures of kindness (.02) and nativelike pronunciation (.08).

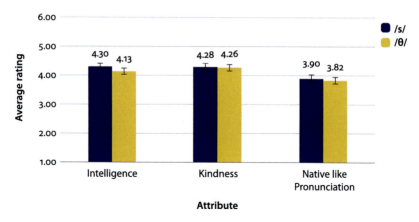

Figure 3. L2 listener ratings by variant

Because the L2 listeners represented a homogenous group, this analysis did not include a between-subjects variable and so two-way repeated measures ANOVAs were used to explore the effect of the independent within-subjects variables speaker and variant on each continuous dependent variable: intelligence ratings, kindness ratings, and nativeness ratings. The two-way repeated measures ANOVA that examined intelligence ratings revealed a significant main effect of speaker $F(3, 33) = 9.87$, $p < .001$ on L2 listener perceptions of intelligence, as well as a significant interaction effect between variant and speaker $F(3, 33) = 3.55$, $p = .017$. L2 listeners rated items with /s/ as sounding more intelligent ($M = 4.26$, $SD = 1.23$) than those with /θ/ ($M = 4.13$, $SD = 1.17$), a difference that approached but did not reach significance $F(1, 35) = 4.12$, $p = .05$. Posthoc analysis on the speaker data revealed that in general Noah was rated as significantly less intelligent ($M = 3.67$, $SD = 1.34$) than Sarah ($M = 4.19$, $SD = 1.13$, $p = .002$), who was rated as significantly less intelligent than Emma ($M = 4.45$, $SD = 1.06$, $p = .022$) and Nash ($M = 4.47$, $SD = 1.06$, $p = .015$). Figure 4 illustrates the mean intelligence ratings given by L2 listeners for each speaker based on whether they were producing /θ/ or /s/, with higher ratings observed with /s/ than with /θ/ for all speakers except Noah, whose utterances with /θ/ were rated higher than utterances with /s/.

Posthoc analysis with LSD corrections showed that Sarah was rated as significantly more intelligent when she produced utterances with /s/ ($M = 4.34$, $SD = 1.1$) than when she produced utterances with /θ/ ($M = 4.03$, $SD = 1.14$, $p = .002$). Emma's intelligence ratings showed a similar trend that approached significance ($p = .063$). Because the intelligence ratings for Noah and Nash did not show significant differences between /θ/ and /s/ ($p = .197$ and $p = .134$, respectively), an additional two-way repeated measures ANOVA was run with intelligence as the dependent variable and speaker gender and variant as the independent variables.

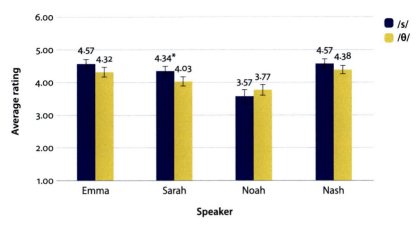

Figure 4. L2 listener intelligence rating by speaker
*$p<.05$

This analysis revealed a significant main effect for speaker gender $F(1, 35) = 9.03$, $p = .005$ and a significant interaction effect between variant and speaker gender $F(1, 35) = 5.84$, $p = .021$. The main effect of variant again approached significance $F(1, 35) = 4.12$, $p = .05$. Overall, the women speakers ($M = 4.32$, $SD = 1.1$) were rated significantly higher for intelligence than the men speakers ($M = 4.07$, $SD = 1.27$), and posthoc analysis with LSD corrections revealed that women were rated significantly higher for intelligence with /s/ ($M = 4.46$, $SD = 1.04$) than with /θ/ ($M = 4.18$, $SD = 1.15$, $p = .002$), a difference not present in the intelligence ratings given to the men speakers for speech with /s/ ($M = 4.06$, $SD = 1.36$) and /θ/ ($M = 4.07$, $SD = 1.18$, $p = .257$) (see Figure 5). Table 5 summarizes the estimated marginal mean differences involving variant that reached significance in the analyses of L2 listeners' intelligence ratings.

The two-way repeated measures ANOVA that examined the dependent variable kindness showed a significant main effect of speaker $F(3, 33) = 3.92$, $p = .017$ but no significant main effect for variant ($p = .827$) and no interaction effect between variant and speaker ($p = .176$). This indicates that L2 listeners' kindness ratings did not vary according to whether /θ/ or /s/ was present. Posthoc analysis with LSD corrections revealed that one of the women speakers, Emma, was rated significantly lower on the kindness scale ($M = 3.98$, $SD = 1.3$) than Noah, Sarah, or Nash ($M = 4.29$, $SD = 1.1$; $M = 4.35$, $SD = 1.11$; $M = 4.46$, $SD = .94$, respectively).

The two-way repeated measures ANOVA that explored the dependent variable nativelike pronunciation and the independent variables variant and speaker revealed a significant main effect of speaker $F(3, 33) = 59.84$, $p < .001$ but not variant ($p = .465$). The posthoc analysis with LSD adjustments revealed that, just as native listeners did, L2 listeners rated Noah as significantly less nativelike

Table 5. Summary of differences in estimated marginal means (EMMs) of L2 listeners' intelligence ratings of /θ/ compared to /s/ by speaker and speaker gender

	Variant	Comparison variant	EMM	SE	95% CI	p
	/θ/	/s/	−0.13	0.07	−0.27, 0.00	.050
Speaker*variant		**Comparison variant**	**EMM**	**SE**	**95% CI**	**p**
Emma	/θ/	/s/	−0.25	0.13	[−0.52, 0.02]	.063
Sarah	/θ/	/s/	−0.32	0.10	[−0.51, −0.12]	.002**
Noah	/θ/	/s/	0.20	0.16	[−0.11, 0.52]	.197
Nash	/θ/	/s/	−0.18	0.16	[−0.41, 0.06]	.134
Speaker gender*variant		**Comparison variant**	**EMM**	**SE**	**95% CI**	**p**
Women	/θ/	/s/	−0.40	0.17	[−0.63, −0.16]	.002**
Men	/θ/	/s/	−0.10	0.09	[−0.28, 0.08]	.257

* $p<.05$ ** $p<.01$
*** $p<.001$

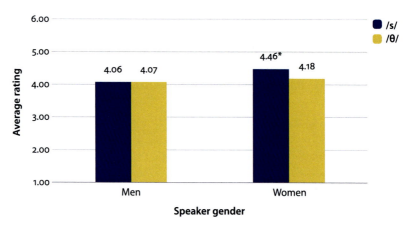

Figure 5. L2 listener intelligence rating by speaker gender and variant
*$p<.05$

($M=2.35$, $SD=1.49$) than Sarah, Nash, and Emma ($M=4.24$, $SD=1.38$; $M=4.39$, $SD=1.3$; and $M=4.44$, $SD=1.29$, respectively). The ANOVA also revealed a significant interaction effect between speaker and variant $F(3, 33)=9.88$, $p<.001$. Figure 6 presents the L2 listener mean ratings of nativelike pronunciation for each speaker depending on whether they produced /θ/ or /s/, and as was observed in the ratings of intelligence, higher scores were given to speech with /s/ than with /θ/ for all speakers but Noah.

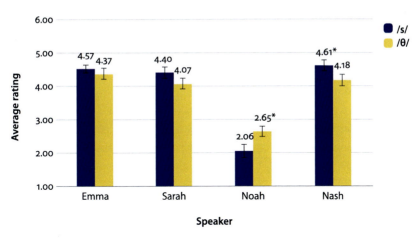

Figure 6. L2 Listener nativelike pronunciation rating by speaker
*p<.05

Posthoc analysis revealed that Noah's utterances with /θ/ were deemed to be significantly more nativelike ($M=2.65$, $SD=1.57$) than his utterances with /s/ ($M=2.06$, $SD=1.36$, $p=.003$), and the opposite was true of the other male speaker, Nash, whose utterances with /s/ were rated significantly higher for nativeness ($M=4.61$, $SD=1.3$) than his utterances with /θ/ ($M=4.17$, $SD=1.27$, $p=.005$). Neither Emma nor Sarah was rated differently for nativelike pronunciation according to whether they spoke with /θ/ or /s/. Table 6 summarizes the estimated marginal mean differences in the nativelike pronunciation ratings given to each speaker with /θ/ and /s/.

Table 6. Summary of differences in estimated marginal means (EMMs) of nonnative listeners' nativelike pronunciation ratings of /θ/ compared to /s/ by speaker

Speaker*variant		Comparison variant	EMM	SE	95% CI	p
Emma	/θ/	/s/	−0.15	0.15	[−0.45; 0.16]	.332
Sarah	/θ/	/s/	0.32	0.19	[−0.71; 0.06]	.094
Noah	/θ/	/s/	0.59	0.18	[−0.22; 0.97]	.003**
Nash	/θ/	/s/	−0.44	0.15	[0.74; −0.15]	.005**

* $p<.05$ ** $p<.01$
*** $p<.001$

Discussion

Intelligence ratings

Intelligence ratings were found to vary among native listeners based on variant but only in the case of participants from outside of North-Central Spain. Specifically, native listeners in the "other regions" category, speakers of varieties in which /θ/ is not used categorically or at all, rated L2 speech with /θ/ as more intelligent than L2 speech with /s/, a novel, though not surprising, finding. Previous research has established that native speakers across the Spanish-speaking world perceive the variety spoken in North-Central Spain as highly prestigious and correct (Callesano & Carter, 2019; Chappell & Barnes, 2023; Sobrino Triana, 2018). The present findings suggest that this prestige may also extend to learner speech that contains regional variants, at least among native speakers of varieties where the variant in question is not used (Latin America) nor holds significant social value (Andalusia). Interestingly, unlike speakers from other regions, native listeners from North-Central Spain did not rate the learner speech as more intelligent with /θ/ than with /s/. It could be that beliefs about the prestige or correctness of Castilian Spanish are stronger outside of the regions where it is spoken. Another possible explanation is that the adoption of regional variants may impact native perceptions of learner speech differently based on whether the regional cues occur in one's own dialect or in a different dialect.

In terms of the L2 learner perceptions, previous research has shown that both L2 classroom learners and those who have studied abroad perceive native Castilian Spanish as significantly more prestigious than other regional varieties (Schmidt & Geeslin, 2022). Breaking from previous results, the L2 listener participants in the present study rated the speech of certain learners as significantly less prestigious when it contained /θ/ than when it contained /s/. Of course, it is possible that L2 learners hold their peers and native speakers to different standards and expectations, and had they been presented with native speech, would have rated utterances with /θ/ higher for prestige than utterances with /s/. That said, one thing that is unclear in the present study is whether the L2 listener participants were even aware of or had ever been exposed to the sociolinguistic ideologies often associated with Castilian Spanish. As intermediate-level classroom learners who reported no prior exposure to Castilian Spanish through their instructors and acquaintances, it is likely that this particular group of learners held as their target or prestige variety some version of educated Latin American or Mexican Spanish, a phenomenon discussed by Grammon (2021). It seems therefore probable that the classroom learners studied here were either unaware of or indifferent to the ideologies normally linked to Castilian Spanish in the Spanish-speaking world.

The learners' L1 English background is an additional perspective from which to consider why the use of /s/ sounded significantly more prestigious than the use of /θ/ to the L2 listeners. In English, the use of /θ/ in place of /s/ tends to be viewed negatively, as an instance of the stigmatized phenomenon commonly referred to as lisping, which research has shown to be associated with perceived lower intelligence ratings (Allard & Williams, 2008; Lockenvitz et al., 2020). This topic has been applied to the realm of Spanish language instruction by Aronson (1973), who reported observations that L1 English speakers learning Spanish seem "embarrassed" to adopt the /θ/ because of its association with lisping in English. This interpretation aligns with the low adoption rates of /θ/ observed in numerous studies of the L2 acquisition of sociolinguistic variation (e.g., Geeslin & Gudmestad, 2008a; Knouse, 2013; Ringer-Hilfinger, 2012), and seems especially likely to be due to the participants' lack of experience with Castilian Spanish, which could explain why L2 speech with /θ/ sounded less intelligent to L2 listeners than L2 speech with /s/. More experience with regional variation in the L2 could curb or even inhibit the impact of L1 sociolinguistic attitudes like the stigmatization of lisping in English on L2 perception, but further analysis beyond the reach of the present study is needed to explore this.

An additional finding of the present study was that /s/ was perceived as more intelligent than /θ/ by L2 learners specifically in their perception of the two L2 women's voices. In the case of the two L2 men's voices, the variant used did not significantly predict their degree of perceived intelligence. It is possible that the null finding for the men's voices was simply due to the fact that one of the men speakers, Noah, was rated as significantly less intelligent and less nativelike than all other speakers, and also exhibited trends in ratings that diverged from the other speakers, sounding more intelligent and more nativelike with /θ/ than with /s/ (although not always to a significant degree). The fact that Noah was such an outlier could have meant there was less uniformity in the ratings given to the men's voices than to the women's voices. However, an alternative interpretation is that the L2 women's voices truly sounded more intelligent with /s/ than with /θ/ while the men's voices did not. It could be that because men generally hold more privilege than women in society (Coates, 2016; Lakoff, 1973), the prestige male speakers are attributed may be less dependent on their linguistic behavior than the prestige attributed to women. This seems likely in light of the existence of sociolinguistic phenomena like covert prestige, in which speakers identifying as men tend to use more nonstandard and lower-status language forms to enhance their solidarity while women tend to use more standard, high-prestige forms to enhance their status (Trudgill, 1972). The greater prestige attributed to /s/ in the speech of the women also aligns with the ideas that the L2 listeners may have been taking Latin American varieties with *seseo* to be their target as a result of their previous experience, or that they were hearing the /θ/ variant as a stigmatized lisp rather than a regional phone.

Kindness ratings

The fact that kindness ratings did not vary significantly according to whether /θ/ or /s/ was present, for either native or L2 listeners, suggests that when L2 learners choose to adopt regional variants, it does not enhance or diminish the degree of solidarity that their native or peer interlocutors feel towards them. Past research did not find higher solidarity ratings of Castilian Spanish when native listeners rated native speech (Callesano & Carter, 2019; Chappell & Barnes, 2023), and the present results suggest that this is true of L2 speech produced with Castilian /θ/ as well. This finding has implications for language learners because many L2 learners who choose to adopt the /θ/ and other regional variants do so in order to assimilate culturally and enhance their connection to native speakers (Kinginger, 2004; Lybeck, 2002; Pope, 2016). The present findings suggest that although it may enhance perceptions of learner intelligence among native interlocutors, the use of /θ/ will likely not lead to greater perceived kindness. That said, the effects reported here are likely cue- and region-specific, so if learners adopt the cues of regional varieties associated with lower status or higher kindness according to previous literature, they might be perceived as native speakers are. Additional research is needed to determine this.

Nativelike pronunciation ratings

Just as was observed for kindness ratings, native interlocutors were not found to perceive L2 speech with the regional phone /θ/ as more nativelike than /s/. Studies on the perception of foreign accent have reported that language that incorporates nativelike speech cues sounds less foreign accented to native listeners (Schoonmaker-Gates, 2015; Solon, 2015). The present findings suggest that this effect does not extend to the use of regional variants, at least not the use of /θ/, and that if L2 learners choose to speak with this variant, their speech will not necessarily sound more nativelike to native interlocutors. However, additional work is needed to establish whether this is true of other variants. The finding that native listeners do not perceive L2 speech as more nativelike when /θ/ is used could potentially explain why such low levels of /θ/ adoption have been observed among learners as compared to other regional variants like Argentine *sheísmo/zheísmo* (e.g., Pozzi & Bayley, 2021; Ringer-Hilfinger, 2012).

The findings from the L2 listener ratings for nativelike pronunciation suggest that the effects of /θ/ on perception could be tempered by how nativelike a learner's speech sounds in general. L2 listeners rated the speech of one individual, Noah, as significantly more nativelike when he used /θ/ than when he used /s/, but all other voices were rated as more nativelike with /s/ than with /θ/ (a trend that only reached significance for Nash). This could mean that learners rate pronunciation more positively when regional variants like /θ/ are present, but only at certain, low levels of nativeness (as Noah's ratings in this category were substantially lower than the other three speakers'). George (2017) found evidence of a potential correlation between regional variant use and more nativelike pronunciation, and in the present study, use of /θ/ also correlated with higher pronunciation ratings given by L2 listeners, but only when the speaker's pronunciation was rated significantly worse than the other voices. Both findings suggest a positive relationship between the adoption of regional variants and perceived pronunciation for native and L2 listeners. However, the effect in the present study appears to be limited to L2 speakers with less nativelike pronunciations, whereas in George (2017), regional variation had a greater effect on those with more nativelike pronunciation. In the present study, because the speech of only one individual showed this benefit, additional work that includes speech representing a wider range of nativelike and nonnativelike pronunciations is needed to confirm whether this effect can be generalized. For example, it is possible that Noah's speech sounded more nativelike with /θ/ than with /s/ simply because he had spent more time in Spain and less time in Latin American than two of the other speakers (Sarah and Emma), which could have made his Castilian (*distinción*) guise sound more nativelike and his Latin American (*seseo*) guise sound less nativelike than the other speakers' speech. That said, the fourth speaker, Nash, also reported having spent more time in Spain and less in Latin America but was rated as sounding more nativelike when his speech included /s/, so it is possible that other factors not examined in this study could be responsible for this finding. In general, additional research is needed to explore this and the potential relationship between regional variants and the perception of nativelike pronunciation.

These findings show that while L2 listener attitudes towards the pronunciation of certain learners vary with the presence and absence of /θ/, native listener attitudes do not seem to vary in this way. This may suggest that native listeners do not include the use of /θ/ (or possibly any) regional variants in their idea of what constitutes accurate or correct L2 speech, while L2 listeners' perceptions are impacted by the presence or absence of regional variants. For learners this could be due to attitudes about Castilian Spanish influenced by L1 English sociolinguistic knowledge when perceiving /θ/ use among their peers. That said, in light of previous research that has shown L2 sociophonetic development even among less experienced learners (Chappell & Kanwit, 2022; Schmidt & Geeslin, 2022), it is interesting that L2 listeners in the present study did not exhibit the association observed in previous studies between /θ/ and higher prestige (intelligence). Because the findings suggest that for some listeners L1 attitudes from English may have influenced their perception, the present findings may indicate that L2 sociolinguistic learning does not follow the same path for all sociophonetic cues.

Implications

These finding have important implications for the developing field of L2 sociolinguistics, as they suggest that certain social meanings associated with status and nativelike pronunciation may transfer to L2 speakers' use of Spanish and could even lead L2 speech to be rated more highly in these measures than native speech from certain regional varieties. These findings also have important implications for L2 learners and their instructors, since they suggest that use of regional variants by L2 learners could impact how they are perceived by their interlocutors. As mentioned at the beginning of this chapter, Geeslin (2020, 2023) presents a theoretical model that postulates the importance of interlocutor perceptions for L2 learners. In light of this model, the present findings that some learners who adopt /θ/ may sound more intelligent or more nativelike to certain interlocutors could mean that learners who adopt regional variants enjoy certain benefits that their peers do not. For instance, their use of regional variants may increase access to native interlocutors, who may provide learners with higher quality interactions in Spanish, exposing them to more present and future input than their peers who do not adopt the regional variant. It is important to note that the adoption of regional variants is a personal decision, dependent on myriad factors including social ties, personal preference, and the concepts of self and identity. That said, the present findings suggest that there may be important communicative outcomes for learners who choose to speak with regional variants that future studies should address.

Conclusion

In sum, the findings from the current study show significant differences in intelligence and nativelike pronunciation ratings given to L2 speech by native and L2 listeners based on the presence of /θ/ or /s/. Specifically, native listeners from other regions rated L2 speech with /θ/ as significantly more intelligent than L2 speech using /s/, while North-Central Spain listeners showed no significant differences in ratings for intelligence. Additionally, L2 listeners rated the speech of L2 women speakers as more intelligent with /s/ than with /θ/, but the degree to which /θ/ sounded more nativelike to the L2 listeners varied depending on the speaker, with the least nativelike speaker benefitting from /θ/ use and other more nativelike speakers not showing this trend.

The present study expands previous research exploring attitudes towards language variation by examining native and L2 listeners' perceptions of the regionally indexed interdental fricative /θ/ in L2 speech. The results suggest that L2 learners who adopt this phone may be perceived as more intelligent by native listeners who speak varieties in which /θ/ does not occur or does not occur categorically, but less intelligent by inexperienced, intermediate-level L2 listeners. Additionally, the findings suggest that L2 learners may be perceived by their peers as sounding more nativelike when they employ /θ/, at least when their pronunciation is generally nonnativelike, as might be the case of lower-level learners or those with heavy foreign accents in the L2. If interlocutor perceptions determine learner access to input, as Geeslin (2020, 2023) suggests, then these differences in perceptions could result in more opportunities for engagement with interlocutors and ultimately greater L2 gains for learners who choose to adopt regional variants. Because the scope of the present findings is limited to /θ/ and to L2 listeners who reported no experience with Castilian Spanish where the variety is used, additional work is needed to determine if these results apply to other regional variants and to more experienced L2 listeners.

References

Alfaraz, G. G. (2014). Dialect perceptions in real time: A restudy of Miami-Cuban perceptions. *Journal of Linguistic Geography*, 2(2), 74–86.

Allard, E. R., & Williams, D. F. (2008). Listeners' perceptions of speech and language disorders. *Journal of Communication Disorders*, 41(2), 108–123.

Ardila, A. (2020). Who are the Spanish speakers? An examination of their linguistics, cultural, and societal commonalities and differences. *Hispanic Journal of Behavioral Sciences*, 42(1), 41–61.

Aronson, H. I. (1973). The role of attitudes about languages in the learning of foreign languages. *The Modern Language Journal*, 57(7), 323–329.

Bárkányi, Z., & Fuertes Gutiérrez, M. (2019). Dialectal variation and Spanish language teaching (SLT): Perspectives from the United Kingdom. *Journal of Spanish Language Teaching*, 6(2), 199–216.

Callesano, S., & Carter, P. M. (2019). Latinx perceptions of Spanish in Miami: Dialect variation, personality attributes and language use. *Language & Communication*, 67, 84–98.

Cestero, A. M., & Paredes, F. (2018). Creencias y actitudes hacia las variedades cultas del español actual: el proyecto PRECAVES XXI. *Boletín de filología*, 53(2), 11–43.

Chappell, W., & Barnes, S. (2023). Stereotypes, language, and race: Spaniards' perception of Latin American immigrants. *Journal of Linguistic Geography*, 11(2), 104–118.

Chappell, W., & Kanwit, M. (2022). Do learners connect sociophonetic variation with regional and social characteristics?: The case of L2 perception of Spanish aspiration. *Studies in Second Language Acquisition*, *44*(1), 185–209.

Chiquito, A. B., & Quesada Pacheco, M. Á. (Eds.). (2014). *Actitudes lingüísticas de los hispanohablantes hacia el idioma español y sus variantes*. *Bergen Language and Linguistic Studies*, *5*. University of Bergen.

Coates, J. (2016). *Women, men and language: A sociolinguistic account of gender differences in language* (3rd ed.). Routledge.

Fayer, J. M., & Krasinski, E. (1987). Native and nonnative judgments of intelligibility and irritation. *Language Learning*, *37*(3), 313–326.

Geeslin, K. (2020). Variationist perspective (s) on interlocutor individual differences. In L. Gurzynski-Weiss (Ed.), *Cross-theoretical explorations of interlocutors and their individual differences* (pp. 127–158). John Benjamins.

Geeslin, K. L. (2023). Epilogue. In S. L. Zahler, A. Y. Long, & B. Linford (Eds.), *Study abroad and the second language acquisition of sociolinguistic variation in Spanish* (pp. 351–368). John Benjamins.

Geeslin, K. L., & Gudmestad, A. (2008a). The acquisition of variation in second-language Spanish: An agenda for integrating studies of the L2 sound system. *Journal of Applied Linguistics*, *5*(2), 137–157.

Geeslin, K. L., & Gudmestad, A. (2008b). Variable subject expression in second-language Spanish: A comparison of native and non-native speakers. In M. Bowles, R. Foote, S. Perpiñán, & R. Bhatt (Eds.), *Selected proceedings of the 2007 Second Language Research Forum* (pp. 69–85). Cascadilla Proceedings Project.

Geeslin, K. L., & Schmidt, L. B. (2018). Study abroad and L2 learner attitudes. In C. Sanz & A. Morales-Front (Eds.), *The Routledge handbook of study abroad research and practice* (pp. 385–405). Routledge.

George, A. (2014). Study abroad in central Spain: The development of regional phonological features. *Foreign Language Annals*, *47*(1), 97–114.

George, A. (2017). Effects of listener and speaker characteristics on foreign accent in L2 Spanish. *Journal of Second and Multilingual Language Acquisition*, *5*(4), 127–148.

George, A., & Hoffman-González, A. (2023). Regional variety preferences by teachers in USA: The case of pluricentric Spanish. *Revista de Lingüística y Lenguas Aplicadas*, *18*, 89–101.

Grammon, D. (2021). Consequential choices: A language ideological perspective on learners' (non-)adoption of a dialectal variant. *Foreign Language Annals*, *54*(3), 607–625.

Howard, M., Lemée, I., & Regan, V. (2006). The L2 acquisition of a phonological variable: The case of /l/ deletion in French. *Journal of French Language Studies*, *16*(1), 1–24.

Hualde, J. I. (2014). *Los sonidos del español*. Cambridge University Press.

Kinginger, C. (2004). Alice doesn't live here anymore: Foreign language learning and identity reconstruction. In A. Pavlenko & A. Blackledge (Eds.), *Negotiation of identities in multilingual contexts* (pp. 219–242). Multilingual Matters.

Knouse, S. M. (2013). The acquisition of dialectal phonemes in a study abroad context: The case of the Castilian theta. *Foreign Language Annals*, *45*(4), 512–542.

Korell, J. L. (2022). Exploring teachers' beliefs and practices of dialectal variation in the Spanish foreign language classroom in secondary schools: An empirical study in Germany. *European Journal of Foreign Language Teaching*, *6*(2), 94–113.

Lakoff, R. (1973). Language and woman's place. *Language in Society*, 2(1), 45–80.

Lambert, W. E., Hodgson, R. C., Gardner, R. C., & Fillenbaum, S. (1960). Evaluational reactions to spoken languages. *The Journal of Abnormal and Social Psychology*, 60(1), 44–51.

Lockenvitz, S., Tetnowski, J. A., & Oxley, J. (2020). The sociolinguistics of lisping: A review. *Clinical Linguistics & Phonetics*, 34(12), 1169–1184.

Lope Blanch, J. M. (2002). La norma lingüística hispánica. *Anuario de Letras. Lingüística y Filología*, 40, 23–41.

López García, Á. (1998). Los conceptos de lengua y dialecto a la luz de la teoría de prototipos. *La Torre: Revista de la Universidad de Puerto Rico*, 3(7–8), 7–19.

Lybeck, K. (2002). Cultural identification and second language pronunciation of Americans in Norway. *The Modern Language Journal*, 86(2), 174–191.

Martinez Franco, S. P. (2019). Navigating a pluricentric language in the classroom: attitudes towards regional varieties of Spanish [Unpublished doctoral dissertation]. University of Alabama.

McBride, K. (2015). Which features of Spanish learners' pronunciation most impact listener evaluations? *Hispania*, 98(1), 14–30.

Milroy, J. (2001). Language ideologies and the consequences of standardization. *Journal of Sociolinguistics*, 5(4), 530–555.

Moreno Fernández, F. (2000). *¿Qué español enseñar?* Arcos Libros.

Moreno Fernández, J., & Moreno Fernández, F. (2002). Madrid perceptions of regional varieties in Spain. In D. Long, & D. R. Preston (Eds.), *Handbook of perceptual dialectology* (Vol. 2, pp. 295–320). John Benjamins Publishing Company.

Munro, M. J., Derwing, T. M., & Morton, S. L. (2006). The mutual intelligibility of L2 speech. *Studies in Second Language Acquisition*, 28(1), 111–131.

Ortiz-Jiménez, M. (2019). Actitudes lingüísticas de los profesores de español en España y Australia hacia las variedades dialectales. *Journal of Spanish Language Teaching*, 6(2), 182–198.

Pope, J. (2016). The role of social networks in the acquisition of a dialectal features during study abroad. In S. Sessarego, & F. Tejedo-Herrero (Eds.), *Spanish language and sociolinguistic analysis* (pp. 177–196). John Benjamins.

Pozzi, R., & Bayley, R. (2021). The development of a regional phonological feature during a semester abroad in Argentina. *Studies in Second Language Acquisition*, 43(1), 109–132.

Preston, D. (2000). Three kinds of sociolinguistics and SLA: A psycholinguistic perspective. In F. M. B. Swierzbin, M. Anderson, C. Klee, & E. Tarone (Eds.), *Social and cognitive factors in second language acquisition: Selected proceedings of the 1999 Second Language Research Forum* (pp. 3–30). Cascadilla Proceedings Project.

Raish, M. (2015). The acquisition of an Egyptian phonological variant by U.S. students in Cairo. *Foreign Language Annals*, 48(2), 267–283.

Regan, B. (2017). The effect of dialect contact and social identity on fricative demerger [Unpublished doctoral dissertation]. The University of Texas at Austin.

Regan, B. (2020). The split of a fricative merger due to dialect contact and societal changes: A sociophonetic study on Andalusian read-speech. *Language Variation and Change*, 32(2), 159–190.

Regan, B. (2022). Analyzing Andalusian coronal fricative norms (ceceo, seseo, and distinción) using a sociophonetic demerger index. In M. Díaz-Campos (Ed.), *The Routledge handbook of variationist approaches to Spanish* (pp. 137–158). Routledge.

Ringer-Hilfinger, K. (2012). Learner acquisition of dialectal variation in a study abroad context: The case of the Spanish [θ]. *Foreign Language Annals*, 45(3), 430–446.

Santana Marrero, J. (2016). Seseo, ceceo y distinción en el sociolecto alto de la ciudad de Sevilla: Nuevos datos a partir de los materiales de PRESEEA. *Boletín de Filología de la Universidad de Chile*, 51(2), 255–280.

Santana Marrero, J. (2018). Creencias y actitudes jóvenes universitarios sevillanos hacia las variedades normativas del español de España: Andaluza, Canaria, Castellana. *Pragmática sociocultural*, 6(1), 71–97.

Schmidt, L. B. (2020). Role of developing language attitudes in a study abroad context on adoption of dialectal pronunciations. *Foreign Language Annals*, 53(4), 785–806.

Schmidt, L. B., & Geeslin, K. L. (2022). Developing language attitudes in a second language: Learner perceptions of regional varieties of Spanish. *Revista Española de Lingüística Aplicada/Spanish Journal of Applied Linguistics*, 35(1), 206–235.

Schoonmaker-Gates, E. (2015). On voice-onset time as a cue to foreign accent in Spanish: Native and nonnative perceptions. *Hispania*, 98(4), 779–791.

Sobrino Triana, R. (2018). Las variedades de español según los hispanohablantes: Corrección, incorrección y agrado lingüísticos. *Cuadernos de lingüística de El Colegio de México*, 5(2), 79–119.

Solon, M. (2015). L2 Spanish /l/: The roles of F2 and segmental duration in foreign accent perception. In E. W. Willis, P. M. Butragueño, & E. Herrera (Eds.), *Selected proceedings of the 6th Conference Laboratory Approaches to Romance Phonology* (pp. 83–94). Cascadilla Proceedings Project.

Trentman, E. (2013). Imagined communities and language learning during study abroad: Arabic learners in Egypt. *Foreign Language Annals*, 46(4), 545–564.

Trudgill, P. (1972). Sex, covert prestige, and linguistic change in the urban British English of Norwich. *Language in Society*, 1(2), 179–195.

Villena Ponsoda, J. A., & Vida Castro, M. (2017). Variación, identidad y coherencia en el español meridional. *Lingüística en la Red*, Monográfico, XV, 1–32.

Yule, G. (2006). *The study of language* (3rd edition). Cambridge University Press.

CHAPTER 8

Sociopragmatic variation and identity construction in L2 Spanish
An analysis of context and group membership

Shana Scucchi & Paul A. Malovrh
University of South Carolina

To better understand how L2 learners navigate multilingual and/or multicultural contexts, this chapter examines the (co)construction of identity among L2 speakers when interacting among each other, in the target language, as members of the same L2 group, versus when interacting with native speakers of the target language. Using the variationist framework, we demonstrate how group membership with interlocutors, native-language speaking status, and situational context affect varying patterns of language play and how L2 learners construct a unique speaker identity that is autonomous from the norms of their own native language and from those of the target-language culture. We find that L2 identity construction is fluid, varying according to the situational and sociopragmatic context in which an L2 learner interacts.

Keywords: L2 identity, study abroad, variationist SLA, language play, sociopragmatic variation

In the era of increased globalization, the need for multicultural and multilingual competence as essential characteristics among speakers who engage in intercultural exchanges continues to grow (Brecht et al., 2017; Malovrh & Moreno, 2018). In the fields of second language acquisition (SLA) and pedagogy, we see ample evidence of how academe has responded to such global phenomena and formal calls for action as research increasingly explores advanced language use, sophisticated language use, and identity construction (Czerwionka et al., 2022; Malovrh & Moreno, 2023; Menke & Malovrh, 2021). In terms of identity construction, recent research emphasizes the need to gain a better understanding of the identity of second-language (L2) learners (in intercultural contexts), how it is co-constructed, and how it relates to language use and the construction of shared meaning (Czerwionka et al., 2022; Malovrh & Moreno, 2023). The timeliness and

https://doi.org/10.1075/ihll.43.08scu
© 2025 John Benjamins Publishing Company

importance of the present volume cannot be underscored as our increasingly dynamic sociocultural and geopolitical landscapes, and their relationship with higher education, engender a complex and fruitful research agenda.

The present chapter distinguishes itself from others in this volume by focusing on sociopragmatic aspects of L2 Spanish use that are typically not analyzed through a variationist lens. As more research examines L2 advancedness and sophisticated language use, their relationship with global citizenship and the ability to affect positive social change becomes more pronounced. That is, sophistication — one of the hallmarks of advanced language use — relies to a large extent on a speaker's pragmatic competence and awareness of situational and contextual phenomena in real time, and on how they exercise their own agency as they interact with such phenomena. In that sense, we distinguish between a member of a global community and an actor in one; the former status can be achieved in intercultural contexts simply by being present as a passive observer, whereas the latter requires an individual's awareness of self and others and action. To better understand how L2 learners navigate multilingual and/or multicultural contexts, we examine the (co)construction of identity among L2 speakers when interacting among each other, in the target language, as members of the same L2 group, versus when interacting with native speakers of the target language. The variationist framework allows us to demonstrate how group membership with interlocutors, native-language speaking status, and situational context affect varying patterns of language use, and how L2 learners construct a unique speaker identity that is autonomous from the norms of their own native language and from those of the target-language culture.

The purpose of the present study is twofold. First, using a variationist approach, we aim to identify patterns of interactive behavior as a L2 learner establishes her group identity among other L2 learners, compared to when she interacts with only native speakers. Second, we aim to explore the extent to which linguistic proficiency is a correlate of L2 speaker identity, in terms of (non)expertise, across varying contexts characterized by group membership and levels of previous experience with specific contextual interactions as relative to microsocial pragmatic variations (Barron & Schneider, 2009) in power and social distance, respectively.

Background

L2 sociopragmatic variation and group identity

Sociolinguistic competence, an aspect of pragmatic competence according to Bachman (1990), refers to "appropriate" language use — that is, the ability to vary one's speech and comprehension according to dialect, register, naturalness, and culturally bound references based not only on the grammatical aspects of the L2 but also the situational context of the communicative act within the target language. When there is a lack of sociolinguistic competence, the consequences of this type of failure can be just as great as those of grammatical failure. A lack of sociolinguistic competence can lead to failure to convey formality, politeness, solidarity, friendship, or group membership, any of which could negatively affect the communicative outcome (Geeslin, 2020; Geeslin et al., 2018). From an intercultural communication perspective, it could result in one's inability to show an awareness of self as well as of other interlocutors within a given context, and thus an inability to act in a way that fosters positive (and harmonious) change within a group. That is, appropriateness of language use is not exclusively governed by one's awareness of sociopragmatic rules and phenomena. It is also determined by one's level of intercultural competence. Using Bennett's (1986, 1993) Developmental Intercultural Competence Model (DICM) as an analytic framework, we operationalize intercultural competence in terms of one's ability to act on their awareness of self and of other through critical analysis of similarities and differences across cultural groups, in real time, as interlocutors co-index identity and shared meaning harmoniously.

Sociolinguistic rules, often accessed unconsciously by first-language (L1) speakers of a given language, must be learned by any L2 speaker of the language, because there is inherent variability in patterns of language use; they are systematic and are conditioned by varying linguistic, social, and situational factors (Geeslin, 2020). A host of social factors influence language performance; age, gender, social class, ethnicity, and education of the interlocutors are characteristics that are reflected within communicative acts (Geeslin, 2020; Geeslin & Hanson, 2022; Hymes, 1972; Trudgill, 1972) and show up in patterns of language use that may vary as the speakers (co)construct not only their identities but also their perceptions of their communicative partners (Geeslin & Hanson, 2022; Trudgill, 1972).

The variationist approach has been well represented in the assessment of sociolinguistic variation and sociolinguistic competence over the last decade (Geeslin, 2020, 2021; Geeslin et al, 2018; Geeslin & Hanson, 2022; Geeslin & Long, 2014); however there remains a dearth of research working within the approach examining variables relating to sociopragmatic variation. Meanwhile, the field of variational pragmatics takes a similar approach (i.e., the investigation of systemic variability in pragmatic variation as a function of typical Labovian macro-categories such as age, gender, region, etc.; Barron, 2005; Barron & Schneider, 2009; Schneider & Barron, 2008). The present chapter seeks to bring the two approaches together to determine whether a L2 learner of Spanish is susceptible to acquiring sociopragmatic phenomena of a specific group of the Spanish-speaking world, and to examine the influence of such phenomena on their use of the L2 while (co)constructing an L2 identity by investigating the learner's pragmatic variation as correlated to microsocial categories such as power (L2 proficiency) and social distance (group membership) (Barron & Schneider, 2009). In this regard, we consider 'L2 speaker' and 'Native Speaker' to be the two prototypical groups under analysis. Previous research reveals specific behavior patterns among L2 learners that suggest they comprise a specific social group with a unique identity (Colcher, 2022; Malovrh & Moreno, 2023) and that how they co-index shared meaning and identity varies according to the group membership of their interlocutor(s).

Geeslin et al. (2018) highlights areas such as the frequency of use of a given form or variant in a particular context, the linguistic and extralinguistic factors that constrain such use, the direction of the effect of those factors, and their relative importance to one another, as staples of the variationist approach to sociolinguistic competence. However, these metrics can also be applied to the intersection of sociolinguistic variation and sociopragmatic variation, where factors of age, gender, education, class, and language (non)expertise are analyzed alongside factors of social power and social distance and their influences on each other in the variation of L2 sophisticated language use. In the present study, we focus on the construct of expertise as a correlate of power and solidarity. Recent research has shown that linguistic superiority, based on perceptions of self and of other in interactional contexts involving combinations of L2 speakers, heritage learners, and native speakers, affect conversational behavior and identity co-construction in terms of varying levels of deference, claimed expertise, or claimed non-expertise (Czerwionka et al., 2022). It is unclear, however, how notions of expertise may vary when it is not merely a correlate of linguistic proficiency but also a reflection of contextual knowledge. For example, how might the interaction around solving a math problem between a L2 speaker and a native speaker vary when both interlocutors have the same level of math skills compared to when the L2 learner is at the level of calculus and the native speaker is at the level of algebra? Would we see similar patterns of deference and/or claimed expertise, or would the expertise in math overshadow the linguistic imbalance and thus establish a different power dynamic?

Scollon et al. (2012) exemplifies how sociopragmatic factors may vary in ranking through their model of hierarchical face systems, which considers rankings of +/− power (P), +/− distance (D), and the weight of imposition (I) when necessary. +P reflects a hierarchical relationship while −P reflects egalitarian relationships. −D indicates strong familiarity between the interlocutors whereas +D indicates a lack of familiarity. As power and distance interact, three face systems are possible: −P, +D (deference), −P, −D (solidarity), and +P, +/− D (hierarchical). In the deference system, participants within the interaction may consider themselves equal (−Power) but treat each other distantly (+Distance). In the solidarity system, participants consider themselves equal in power (−P) and having close familiarity (−D). Lastly, in the hierarchical system, one participant clearly has social power over the others (+P), whether the participants are socially distant (+D) or share familiarity with one other (−D). Scollon et al. proposes that strategies of involvement and independence are observable within these three social systems, though these notions are culturally bound and may vary depending on the sociocultural context of the communicative act.

In a recent study, Malovrh and Moreno (2023) asserted that L2 speakers inherently presume an identity of 'learner' (i.e., non-expert), and therefore, default to deference (−P, +D) as a strategy of facework in intercultural interactions. However, they did not have sufficient data or analyses to substantiate their claim. At the same time, they hypothesized that L2 learnerhood consists of the development of an autonomous L2 identity, one that distinguishes itself from the speaker's native language and from the culture of the target language. The present study challenges that hypothesis by exploring the possibility that L2 identity is more fluid than that; perhaps it varies according to the situational context in which a L2 learner interacts.

L2 language play: Humor, smiling, and self-deprecation

The study of humor as a vehicle and context for social interaction has enjoyed a long history (Shively, 2018). Unlike canned humor (i.e., joke telling), conversational humor refers to spontaneous and playful verbal acts that are contextually and situationally dependent (Boxer & Cortés-Conde, 1997). Speakers frame their actions as being either serious or playful (Bateson, 1953), and they signal humorous intent to facilitate the hearer's inferencing of it through cues such as facial expressions and/or laughter. Humor, therefore, requires collaboration between the speaker and hearer (Gumperz, 1992). As a conversational phenomenon, it can be used to a speaker's benefit, or, if misused, can become a threat to the speaker's face (Bell, 2015), thus making it a risky strategy to employ. Why would a speaker jeopardize a conversation with such a gamble? There are multiple reasons: to entertain an interlocutor (Bell & Attardo 2010), to emphasize differences in power, to protect oneself or deflect another's bad intention, to establish and maintain solidarity with an interlocutor (Hay, 1995), or to manage rapport (Spencer-Oatey, 2005). Humor can create social distance by being aggressive or antagonistic or by teasing, or it can mitigate social distance by being self-deprecating or through (playful) teasing and ultimately laughing together, which, in its essence, creates intersubjectivity. Conversational humor, thus, is a defining characteristic of who we are relative to another.

Relevant to the present study, Shively (2018) analyzed the use of conversational humor among six study-abroad participants residing in Spain with the aim of exploring their use and development of humor to better understand L2 humor in general and to examine more specific constructs of L2 pragmatics. To that end, she audio-recorded conversations between individual L2 learners and their respective native-speaking host families as well as their respective native-speaking peer groups. She then transcribed the conversations and analyzed them using a conversational analytic framework. Among her findings were that L2 learners used humor to amuse their interlocutor, to show a desire to affiliate, to soften their own negative stance or criticism toward a particular issue, to show modesty by downgrading a compliment, to influence their interlocutor, and to construct individual and/or group identities. Addressing the variable use of humor, Shively noted that not one single L2 learner used all strategies and that every single L2 learner used multiple strategies. Most importantly, she found that L2 learners most used humor as a tool to affiliate with their interlocutor. One learner used it to mock their interlocutor but in a way that established trust and closeness. When speaking to each other, several L2 learners used humor in a self-deprecating manner to identify as fellow language learners, usually by making fun of their own use of Spanish, and all L2 learners used it to reinforce their sense of national identity, either relating to their own national identity or to that of their Spanish counterparts.

Recent research examining figurative language and humor also focuses on the negotiation of face and of meaning through *non-linguistic* communication. Sampietro (2019), for example, found that when using social media, native Spanish speakers use emojis for various pragmatic functions, such as upgrading or downgrading a previous utterance, framing and initiating humorous exchanges, and negotiating illocutionary acts. Priego-Valverde et al. (2018), as another example, analyzed the act of smiling as a marker to frame humorous events and found patterns of smiling that correlated with interlocutors' attempts to negotiate meaning. In the present study, we consider non-linguistic forms of communication — namely, smiling and laughter — as being intrinsically embedded in a larger definition of language play. As previous research has shown, L2 learners often use such play as strategies to compensate for a limited ability to be playful with language when using their L2, depending on their own level of sociopragmatic competence, and as the most accessible tool for them to establish a sense of affiliation with a group (Shively, 2018).

The present study is unique from most other studies working within a variationist framework. We are not aiming to determine how exposure to native Spanish speakers of a similar Peninsular demographic affects the linguistic behavior of L2 learners. Rather, we analyze how (non)native-speaking status of interlocutors affects the behavior of L2 speakers, as measured according to language play. It is a study of the effects of group membership on identity co-construction in L2 intercultural contexts.

The current study

The aim of the present study is to better understand the variable use of language play from strictly L2 groups to groups that combine L2 speakers with native speakers of a specific region of the Spanish-speaking world. We aim to identify a relationship between L2 sociopragmatic variation and identity construction when communicating with members versus non-members of a L2 language group. To that end, over the course of three months, we video recorded collaborative boardgame sessions, first in a non-study-abroad context consisting of only L2 learners and then in a study-abroad context involving a combination of L2 and native speakers. We then tracked the sociopragmatic behavior (operationalized in terms of language play, in the form of smiling and laughter) of one specific individual, as they established their identity among specific groups of Spanish speakers. Do L2 learners exhibit the sociopragmatic (and intercultural) competence to co-construct specific identities depending on the situation in which they are communicating? The ability to do so would be indicative of a more advanced, sophisticated level of language use. As Czerwionka (2021) found, the development of intercultural competence is autonomous from the development of language proficiency. Given such autonomy, how might strategies to realize such competence vary according to different situations? To gain a better understanding of such phenomena, the present study is guided by the following research questions:

1. Over the course of playing a collaborative board game, how does a L2 learner use aspects of language play (smiling and laughter) as a strategy to foster involvement with or independence from their interlocutors?
2. How does a L2 learner co-construct self and group identity with interlocutors according to varying interactions of power and distance within the group?
3. How does a L2 learner exhibit variation in their sociopragmatic behavior to co-construct identity when comparing their interaction with other L2 learners to when they interact with a native-speaking group?

Method

We analyzed the video recordings and transcripts of six different hour-long boardgame sessions in which four participants collaborated to complete the game. The same board game (*Pandemic*) was used for all six sessions and was chosen due to its collaborative nature. One does not compete with other people to win the game. Rather, the game can only be won through collaboration among the players involved; either everyone wins, or everyone loses. Throughout the recordings, we identified all 'turns' of a specific player as the game was played among different partners, and we recorded their (extra)linguistic behavior each time it was their turn to advance the game. Specifically, we analyzed their use of language as well as their initiation of language play, its effect on other members, and its outcome as the game progressed. In addition, we evaluated their behavior as being reflective of sociopragmatic variation based on factors such as power and social distance, and we examined how the individual behaves when interacting only with other L2 learners compared to when interacting with only native speakers.

Participants

Ten people participated in the present study. Six of them were L2 learners of Spanish, and four were native speakers of Andalusian Spanish residing in Cádiz, Spain during the summer of 2023. Table 1 provides biographical data.

The present case study focuses on Eva, whose biographical data is shaded in Table 1, because she was present for all data-collection sessions (in at-home and in-Spain contexts) throughout the duration of the project. When the study began, Eva was preparing to embark on a study-abroad trip to Cádiz, Spain, during the summer of 2023. Before her study abroad program began, she attended three different game-playing sessions at her home university in the United States during the month of April 2023. During that month, she played the board game with Kylie, Riley, and Annie, all of whom were also L2 learners of Spanish. Among the at-home L2 learners, Eva is distinct in the following ways: She is the youngest in age, she had completed fewer years of university, and her oral proficiency in Spanish was rated lower than the other L2 learners. Eva was rated as Intermediate-High as determined by the STAMP test (Avant Assessment), the guidelines of which conform to the ACTFL OPI rating scale, whereas the others were rated at the advanced level.

With regard to the 'In-Spain' L2 participants, Eva had more in common with her counterparts. Betty and Gail were 20 and 21 years old, respectively, they had spent one month living in a Spanish-speaking country prior to data collection, and they were at the same level of proficiency and of university instruction as Eva.

Table 1. Biographical data of participants

Name	Native language	Age	Age of onset of L2 Spanish	Time spent in Spain	Prof. level	Education level	Context
Eva	English	19	13	1 month*	Int. high	3rd-year university	At home & in Spain
Annie	English	21	7	1 month	Adv. low	4th-year university	At home
Kylie	English	22	7	N/A	Adv. low	4th-year university	At home
Riley	English	22	19	6 months	Adv. low	4th-year university	At home
Betty	English	20	13	1 month**	Int. high	3rd-year university	In Spain
Gail	English	21	6	1 month**	Int. high	3rd-year university	In Spain
Angela	Spanish	23	N/A	N/A	N/A	Masters	In Spain
Paula	Spanish	22	N/A	N/A	N/A	Masters	In Spain
Barbara	Spanish	25	N/A	N/A	N/A	PhD	In Spain
Felipe	Spanish	22	N/A	N/A	N/A	Masters	In Spain

* Before the at-home data collection began, Eva had spent one week in a Spanish-speaking country.
** Betty and Gail had not spent time living among the target culture in a Spanish-speaking country at the beginning of the data collection in Spain, but they would accrue one month throughout the data collection.

Furthermore, Eva, Betty, and Gail all accumulated their amount of time living in a Spanish-speaking country together, as roommates, while they completed their study-abroad program in Cádiz.

For all L2 participants, we made no *a priori* judgements regarding their individual communication strategies or whether they favored involvement- versus independence-driven discourse. Our aim was to analyze their communication strategies from the perspective of autonomous L2 learners who may behave according to a specific L2 identity, in a way that may not be characterized by their native language and culture or by the target language and culture.

The four native Spanish speakers were all born and raised in Andalucía, Spain, and they resided in Cádiz at the time of data collection. They all had completed graduate-level education; Angela, Paula, and Felipe had just finished their master's degrees and were searching for professional employment; Barbara had a doctorate and worked as an instructor at the Universidad de Cádiz.

With regard to sociopragmatic variation in terms of playful language use in Peninsular Spanish, we acknowledge that the behavior of four individuals does not provide a generalizable reflection of cultural behavior. We also note the findings of studies that have yielded specific assertions. Research indicates that some forms of language play and self-deprecating language use are ill-preferred forms of communication in Spain; speakers aim to avoid misunderstandings or behavior that could indicate a lack of seriousness (Cantos-Delgado & Maíz Arévalo, 2023). And Bravo (1996), comparing Mexican, Spanish, and Swedish business people, found that Spaniards used irony in contexts of business negotiation less than Mexican business people did, explaining that the former opted for more autonomy-driven strategies to respect the seriousness of business situations from the perspective of their counterparts. Spaniards opted for a more serious discourse that would avoid misunderstandings, whereas the Mexican business people opted for more affiliative strategies, to alleviate tension and foster an affiliative group identity. In the present study, we view the behavior of our four Spanish participants as a baseline from which to compare our L2 speakers; given the small participant pool, it would be unrealistic to categorize four individuals as prototypical representatives of a specific geographical region. We know, through previous research, that L2 speakers, as well as native Spanish speakers, recognize the sociopragmatic significance of language play and that their sociopragmatic competence governs its (non)use. Of specific interest in the present study is how (or if) L2 speakers choose to use language play differently according to the group-membership of their interlocutors.

Materials

STAMP test

To determine the proficiency levels of our L2 speakers, we used an independent proficiency test known as the STAMP test (Avant Assessment), which adopts the criteria of the ACTFL (2012) proficiency guidelines. L2 participants completed the assessment virtually and were rated by three blind reviewers.

Background questionnaire

Each participant completed a linguistic background questionnaire for us to determine specific biodata. The questionnaire allowed us to determine their native and second languages, their previous experience of living in a Spanish-speaking country outside of the United States, and their level of education.

Board game: Pandemic

We chose to use a collaborative board game as our medium of data collection for a number of reasons. First, a board game allows us to establish a uniform set of rules that all participants need to understand and follow in order to play the game. In that regard, we consider the game rules to be analogous to social rules that govern behavior. They are neither 'nativelike' nor 'targetlike' but rather are specific to the culture and situation of the game itself. Second, the game allows us to control for the variable of expertise; our participants either had experience playing the game or they did not. As previously noted, expertise relates to (non)deferential behavior among interlocutors, which in turn affects the co-indexing of identity (Colcher, 2022). Third, the game requires communication among the participants in order for it to be played. Since the game is collaborative (i.e., not competitive), it invites interaction.

Pandemic, the game we chose for the present study, requires that four players work together to rid the world of viruses. Each player is assigned a role (e.g., engineer, medic, logistics manager) as well as specific actions they are able to perform. As employees of the Center for Disease Control, their task is to strategize on how they should fight the spread of viruses in different parts of the globe. We used an English version of the game for our at-home phase, but then switched to a Spanish version of the game for our data collections in Spain. Regardless of the native language of the board game, the game's rules remained the same.

Procedure

All participants in the present study were recruited by the authors based on either their L2 status and their participation in an upcoming study-abroad program or their native-speaking status and residence in Cádiz, Spain. Participants were recruited from a pool of undergraduate students preparing to study abroad in Cádiz, Spain during the summer of 2023 and from a group of graduate students studying at the Universidad de Cádiz. The one participant, Eva, was chosen as a focus of our case study because she participated in all three of our pre-departure game-playing sessions and then went on to Spain for her study abroad program and proceeded to play the same game with native Spanish speakers as well as with L2 learners while living in Spain.

All participants filled out a consent form, as well as a background questionnaire. Volunteers who met our selection criteria and signed the consent form were chosen to participate. Each participant was paid $ 20 for each boardgame session they attended. And for all game sessions, the participants were given only two main pieces of instruction: to use only Spanish and to enjoy the game. The entire data collection consisted of three distinct phases, which occurred in chronological order.

Phase I

Phase I refers to the pre-departure sessions where only L2 learners, including Eva, came together to play the board game on three different occasions. Each occasion lasted one hour, so Eva played the same board game for three hours over the course of one month. The same four participants (Eva and three other L2 learners) met in a university office for each session, where a table was set up with the board game, the rule sheet, and snacks. They were told ahead of time that they would be video recorded while playing the game. The researchers set up all audiovisual equipment before their arrival and greeted them as they arrived. Once they were all present, the researchers turned on the camera and left the room, where only the four participants remained to play the game.

Phase II

Phase II took place in Cádiz, Spain, during the summer of 2023, approximately one month after the end of the Phase I. During Phase II, Eva (our L2 speaker) met with three native speakers of Spanish to play the same game. Unlike the previous phase, in Phase II, Eva was the only nonnative speaker of Spanish playing the game. In addition, unlike in Phase I, where all L2 learners learned the rules of the game together, in Phase II, only Eva had previous experience playing the game. In this regard, Eva had expertise with the game, whereas the native speakers did not. During Phase II, Eva played the game with the same native speakers over the course of two different sessions, with each session lasting approximately one hour.

Phase III

To compare the performance of our L2 speakers and native speakers, we also recorded two other sessions of the board game. One consisted of just native Andalusian speakers of Spanish playing among each other. The other consisted of Eva and two other L2 learners of Spanish (native English speakers), all of whom were study-abroad participants in the same program, playing the game with each other, while residing in Spain. Phase III provides us with a control group, in the form of the native-speaking group, as well as the opportunity to compare L2 phenomena when learners interact with each other in an 'at-home' context versus in a study-abroad context.

Data analysis

To track Eva's progress throughout the three phases of the data collection, we chose to isolate all instances of her turns while playing the board game. Because the board game establishes the context/situation of each meeting, it also establishes a structure to the discourse that ensues while playing the game. We view the turn-taking component of the game as an opportunity to evaluate how each player takes advantage of their turn to co-construct identity with their collaborators. Each turn is an opportunity to assert oneself in the game or to defer to another player's interpretation of the rules, and each turn presents the respective player with a choice they need to make in terms of how they wish to contribute to the game. Therefore, we tracked all of Eva's turns during all phases of the study and recorded how she initiated her turn, whether her initiation was communicated in linguistic or extralinguistic terms, and how the communication was received and interpreted by her interlocutors. Finally, using Scollon et al.'s (2012) Model of Hierarchical Systems, we coded Eva's relationship with the other game players during each session in terms of +/– power and +/– distance, which we used to establish different types of individual and group identities (i.e., deferential, hierarchical, and/or solidarity), and we examined Eva's communication strategies as being either involvement- or independence-driven.

Results

Phase I: At-home; all L2 learners (before Eva's study abroad program)

Phase I consisted of three different sessions, spread over the course of three weeks, each being one week apart from the next. While the independent variables of [+/–native language of interlocutors] and context (i.e., at-home or study abroad) remained constant within each phase, those pertaining to [+/– power] and [+/– distance] may have developed from one session to the next within a specific phase. We noted a development in how Eva realized her turns over the course of Phase I, and we break them down (below) according to each meeting session. It is evident that as distinctions in L2 proficiency level became more pronounced, a hierarchy (in terms of authority) would become more pronounced.

Session I: −Power, +Distance (Deference)

After examining each of Eva's turns, we characterize the face system of the first session of Phase I in terms of deference. That is, we considered all four players to be symmetrical in terms of power, insofar as they were all L2 learners, unaware of each other's proficiency level, and they were all novel learners of the game's rules. Because none of the players knew each other prior to the first session, we considered Eva's relationship with the other players as +Distance. Table 2 provides a breakdown of her moves.

As Table 2 shows, she had her first turn at about the 11-minute mark, which consisted of her asking the other players if she understood the directions correctly.

Table 2. Summary of Eva's turns during Phase I, Session I

Turn #	Time in video	Action	Effect	ID co-construction
1	11:11	Requests approval, while smiling (*Yo puedo...?* 'I can...?')	Receives approval	Deferential
2	13:00	Eva clarifies for Annie	Annie corrects Eva	Deferential
3	22:00	Eva starts to speak; stalls	Annie moves pieces for Eva	Deferential
4	34:30	Eva shows others her card	Annie and Kylie show her what to do	Deferential
5	35:26	Justifies her move	Others still move for her	Deferential
6	40:26	Asks if she's correct	Annie explains for her	Deferential
7	43:31	Kylie tells Eva that it's her turn	Eva shows Kylie her card; Kylie helps her	Deferential
8	48:54	Shows others her card	Annie moves for her	Deferential

She stayed completely in the target language (as did the other L2 members), though showed signs of being linguistically disadvantaged. It was normal for Eva to begin articulating her action, typically narrating her move in the first-person singular (*yo...* 'I...'), before stalling linguistically, then smiling and/or laughing self-deprecatingly due to her inability to access the language she needed, and then allowing another player to finish her sentence for her. An example of such an exchange is Turn #1, provided in Excerpt 1.

Excerpt 1.

Eva: *Yo puedo..um..[smiling while pausing]..muvar..todos los cosas [pointing at pieces and looking at Annie]* –
'I can...um..[smiling while pausing]..move..all of the things [pointing at pieces and looking at Annie]'

Annie: – *Sí.*
– 'Yes.'

Eva: – *En un ciudad cuando yo no..um..tratar-*
– 'In a city when I don't..um..try-'

Annie: – *No necesito solo uno..es todo [interrupts Eva and finishes her thought].*
– 'No, I only need one..that's all.'

In the first session, Eva had a total of eight turns, and six of them were characterized by her extralinguistic behavior to compensate for her lack of linguistic knowledge by requesting help. Such moves consisted of smiling accompanied by laughter while furrowing her brow to appear confused or showing the other players her card so that they could read it, or by using silence to indicate the need for help. She was successful in learning the rules of the game along with the other participants, and she provides evidence that she is indeed following the progress of the game correctly; yet in six of her eight turns (75%), she deferred to Annie for linguistic support or solutions to the game. By the end of the session, a group hierarchy began to develop, constructed based on players' L2 proficiency.

Session II: +Power, +Distance (Hierarchical)

Because a group hierarchy had developed throughout the first session, we consider the power dynamic among the four individuals to have shifted by the second session. That is, Eva assumed a deferential role as the least proficient speaker, despite sharing the same level of expertise regarding the game. In the second session Eva took six turns, described in Table 3.

Table 3. Summary of Eva's turns during Phase I, Session II

Turn #	Time in video	Action	Effect	ID co-construction (strategy type)
1	3:30	Begins move by narrating, *Yo puedo dar 3 0 4...* 'I can give 3 or 4...' Then stops and looks to Annie for approval.	Receives approval	Eva = novice; Annie = expert
2	13:00	Eva smiles and looks to Annie for help	Annie helps; Eva laughs and agrees.	Eva = novice; Annie = expert; (Involvement)
3	14:52	Eva asks Annie for help.	Annie helps Eva.	Eva = novice; Annie = expert; (Involvement)
4	18:00	Starts laughing while saying, *No sé* 'I don't know'	Self-deprecating; Silence from others	Eva = novice
5	20:05	Eva claps and cheers.	Others smile and laugh	Eva = supporter (Involvement)
6	23:06	Eva speaks and clarifies rules	Others agree	Eva = group participant; (Involvement)

As Table 3 reveals, Eva confirmed her role as a novice to the game throughout the session by either asking for help, laughing self-deprecatingly, or by using silence to signal that she needed help. Annie most often provided Eva whatever help she needed. Therefore, we see the simultaneous development of Annie's role as expert. We also see a continuation of Eva's affiliative language play strategies.

By assuming her role as novice and accepting Annie's role as expert, she played an active part in the group hierarchy. We also note continued use of clapping and cheering for each other during the session as another strategy to foster group involvement among the L2 speakers.

Session III: +Power, −Distance (Hierarchical)

By the final session of Phase I, the L2 group had established itself as being hierarchical; expertise toward the game appears to have been established alongside L2 proficiency level, insofar as Eva continues to co-index her non-expert identity, most often with Annie. This session consisted of a total of five turns for Eva, described in Table 4.

Table 4. Summary of Eva's turns during Phase I, Session III

Turn #	Time in video	Action	Effect	ID co-construction
1	7:45	Negotiates rules with others	She appears more assertive.	Eva = contributor
2	18:30	Eva picks her cards, shows them to others while smiling and laughing	Self-deprecating; others help her	Eva = non-expert
3	19:05	Eva claps and cheers for previous move	Supportive of group	Eva = group member
4	42:05	Eva asks for rule clarification	Annie explains rule	Eva = non-expert; Annie = expert; Both group members
5	47:19	Eva asks Annie if it's her turn (it is), while laughing apologetically	Self-deprecating	Eva = non-expert

Given that most of the turns Eva took throughout the three sessions of Phase I appeared as strategies to index affiliation, we conclude that the L2 (at-home) group developed a hierarchical group identity that fostered involvement with one another. In practically every case, Eva received help when she signaled for it, and most of her turns within gameplay were collaborative in nature.

Phase II: In Spain, Eva playing with native speakers

Phase II of the data collection consisted of two different sessions. During the two sessions, in addition to the obvious distinction of L2 versus native-speaking status, the group dynamic was also different in that not all players had the same level of expertise regarding the game; Eva was the only player who knew the rules, the native speakers did not.

Session I: +Power, +Distance (Hierarchical)

Given the obvious linguistic inferiority of Eva compared to the native speakers, and because they had never met before, we coded the first session such that there was a differential of power and distance — a hierarchical group structure. During the first session, Eva had a total of seven turns, which we describe in Table 5.

Table 5. Summary of Eva's turns during Phase II, Session I

Turn #	Time in video	Action	Effect	ID co-construction / strategy
1	4:25	Eva silently takes her turn; Ángela challenges her.	Eva starts to defer, but then defends her move, and holds ground	Eva = authoritative / independent
2	5:47	Eva starts to take turn; stops to consult with Paula	Paula nods; says nothing.	Eva = nonexpert / involvement
3	13:00	Eva smiles at Paula, seeking approval of her turn.	Paula doesn't respond. Eva continues to make move.	Eva = nonexpert / seeking involvement
4	19:04	Eva uses body language to show uncertainty, smiles.	Paula and Ángela don't engage and wait for her to complete her turn, which she does.	Eva = nonexpert / seeking involvement
5	21:04	Eva takes turn with no help or communication.	Table is silent. Game proceeds.	Eva = active participant / independence
6	29:04	Eva makes playful, dancelike gesture, while smiling with uncertainty, and not sure what to do.	Nobody laughs. Then Eva explains her move.	Eva = playful, active participant / seeking involvement
7	35:41	Ángela corrects Eva's move, but Eva defends it.	Ángela ends up agreeing with Eva and smiles.	Eva = expert / independence

As we see in Table 5, the group identity evolves differently than we expected. While Eva is clearly inferior from a linguistic perspective, she is not powerless; her expertise regarding the game's rules, and the lack thereof among the native speakers, ultimately leads to a group identity in which the defining characteristic of each member is to independently understand the game, to play it according to the rules, and ultimately win. Eva begins the session by exhibiting some of the same strategies that she exhibited in Phase I of the study. She attempts to communicate extralinguistically with other members through smiling and/or laughing, but the other members do not reciprocate (at least not when it involves Eva taking her turn). In these contexts, they avoided eye contact and remained focused on the gameboard. The tone of the group during the turn-taking moments is much more serious, and each turn-taker is expected to take their turn independently, then discuss with the group afterwards. The serious tone forces Eva out of her shell; she must participate and communicate with language, and she does. As a result, Eva's identity evolves during the session as one that is not defined by her L2-speaking status but rather by her knowledge of the game. She becomes more independent, while the group identity shifts toward one of deference in which each member defers to the others' ability to play the game. Excerpt 2 provides an example of such an exchange.

Excerpt 2.
Eva: [*As she begins her move*] Necesito una carta más de –
'I need one more card to'-
Ángela: [*Interrupting Eva and finishing for her*] Puedo moverle a ella a Nueva York, eh -
'I can move her to New York, and'-
Eva: No..pero sí puedo moverme allí también con uno, dos, tres [moving piece]-
'No..but I can move THERE too with one, two, three... [moving piece]'
Ángela: Ahh..sí sí sí.
'Ahh, yes yes yes.'

Session II: −Power, +Distance (Deferential)

We characterize Session II differently than Session I, since Eva cultivated an identity for herself as an expert of the game's rules, which makes her more powerful. It appeared that the native speakers treated her as an equally important member of the group (−P), in that they followed her advice and even requested it. Table 6 provides a breakdown of Eva's turns.

Eva took six turns during this session, and each turn was used as an opportunity to co-index an identity of expertise within the context of the game. As Excerpt 3 demonstrates, Eva, as a player of the game *Pandemic*, transformed from being a nonexpert L2 learner who seeks the approval and help of her fellow players through predominantly extralinguistic strategies such as smiling, laughing, cheering, clapping, and being self-deprecating, to a nonnative-speaking expert of the game's rules and an independent and important stakeholder in the outcome of the game.

Table 6. Summary of Eva's turns during Phase II, Session II

Turn #	Time in video	Action	Effect	ID co-construction / strategy
1	2:23	Eva asks Ángela for her name, laughing. Then the table gets quiet and the others wait for her to take her turn.	Ángela smiles back, reminded her of her name, and then waited for her to make her move.	Eva = group member / involvement
2	7:00	As she takes her turn, Eva explains to Bárbara what she should plan to do.	Bárbara listens	Eva = expert / independence
3	20:10	Eva makes her move silently, but smiling.	Everyone else remains silent while she makes her move.	
4	21:20	Eva makes move quietly, and then begins to explain to Ángela how she should make her own subsequent move	Ángela follows Eva's advice	Eva = expertise / independence
5	26:01	Eva narrates her move while she's making it.	Silence.	Eva = expertise / independence
6	30:31	Eva narrates her move while she's making it. Then she asks another player to hand her some game pieces.	The other player hands her the game pieces.	Eva = expertise / independence

Excerpt 3.

Eva: *Tengo tres ...* [then makes her move silently]
'I have three ...'

Ángela: *Entonces lo azul... me moy a Chicago...* [begins making move]
'Then the blue one ... I'm going to Chicago...'

Eva: *No no...tú puedes ir allí porque es más fácil..* [pointing to other place on board]
'No no you can go there because it's easier.'

Ángela: *Ah ok ok.*

The Eva we see playing the game among the native-speaking group reveals a pattern of stance-taking moves that distinguishes her from the other members of the group not only in terms of native-speaking status but also in terms of her ability to play the game correctly and to help others do so as well.

Phase III: In Spain (L2-only group and native-speaker-only group)
Phase III consisted of two simultaneous game-playing sessions (occurring in different rooms) one week after the previous session. One of the sessions consisted of Eva and two other L2 Spanish speakers who were members of the same study abroad program and were Eva's roommates for the previous month in Spain. The other session consisted of only native speakers, three of whom had been playing the game with Eva the previous two weeks and one who was new to the group but who had been playing the game previously with the other L2 learners. At this phase, everyone participating in both sessions had a full understanding of the rules of the game. And, because the Spaniards reported being acquainted with each other before the time of the study, both groups were characterized by lack of social distance. Results from the native-speaking group are excluded here but available within the larger study's findings.

L2 Session: −Power, −Distance (Solidarity)
The L2 study-abroad group identity was much different than the L2 at-home group identity. All members of the study-abroad group had the same level of oral proficiency, they were first-time study abroad participants, they all had experience playing the board game (completely in Spanish), and they all understood the rules. Whereas the at-home L2 group started off as being characterized by deference and then developed toward being hierarchical, the study-abroad L2 group showed immediate signs of solidarity.

The entire session for the study abroad L2 group lasted 34 minutes. For the first two minutes, there was no interaction at all, only silence. During this time, Eva and Gail waited for Betty to read the instructions in silence. At the two-minute mark, Eva and Betty began to have a conversation with each other about the rules and appeared to mutually confirm that the other understood the game. Gail remained quiet. At around the four-minute mark, the group finally began to play the game. Between the four-minute mark and the 15-minute mark, it is indistinguishable whose turn it was; all three worked together on each turn and continuously communicated about each turn. There is very little extralinguistic communication; they remained in the target language and focused on the rules of the game. Perhaps, given that they already knew each other, it was unnecessary to engage in small talk. There was no self-deprecating (extra)linguistic behavior; there were no patterns of affiliating as L2 speakers, specifically; and there were no patterns of deference to each other, maintaining a very informal context. Unlike the at-home group, the study-abroad L2 group did not appear to co-construct a hierarchy based on L2 proficiency level or varying levels of expertise of the game's rules. Rather, this group's interaction showed all of the characteristics of solidarity, such as talking over each other, collaborating on specific moves, and, like the at-home group, clapping and cheering for each other. This could have been due to the fact that they were all rated with the same proficiency level. Given their emphasis on collaboration, we consider their group identity to be that of solidarity, predominantly consisting of involvement strategies. Excerpt 4 provides an example of such solidarity.

Excerpt 4.
Bettie: *Yo quiero compartir contigo porque tú puedes ...* [makes a turn-taking gesture] –
        'I want to share with you because you can ...'
Eva: – *Sí y me das tres tarjetas...*
        'Yes and you give me three cards...'
Bettie: [Laughing] *ok-*
Eva: [looking and pointing at Gail] *Y tú también puedes.*
        'And you can too.'
Gail: *Oh, sí* [moves her pieces]
        'Oh, yes.'

Discussion

In their concluding chapter, Malovrh and Moreno (2023) hypothesized that L2 speaker identity assumes the status of "learner" or "nonexpert" because L2 learners reported their preference to exercise deference when communicating with native speakers and reported that they avoid using the target language with native speakers if the topic of conversation is important and/or sensitive, as a strategy to avoid misunderstandings. The authors concluded that such self-perceived identity and behavior exhibits a lack of intercultural competence and contradicts the tenets of global citizenship due to its lack of active engagement. The results of the present study reveal a much more complex pattern of behavior and sophistication among L2 speakers that varies according to situational context regarding the microsocial-pragmatic factors of power and distance (Barron & Schneider, 2009). Our observations yield two important findings. One is that L2 proficiency level is a main contributor to L2 identity but more so when L2 learners are communicating with other L2 learners. The other is that the identity co-indexed by L2 learners is variable and sensitive to relationships of power and distance among members of a group and that the strategies used to negotiate power are not based solely on L2 proficiency level but may also involve other forms of expertise beyond nativelike-speaking status. A L2 learner may adopt different politeness strategies according to the sociopragmatic variation of factors like power and distance, such as deference to group members with a higher power status (Scollon et al., 2012), to co-index their L2 identity within their situational context. These differences in identity indexation are reflected in a L2 learner's variable language behavior as they become aware of microsocial changes in their group setting. Our L2 learner revealed a level of sophisticated language use that adapted to each situation she was in.

Research question #1

The first research question asked whether a L2 learner would use aspects of language play as a strategy to foster involvement with, or independence from, their interlocutors. Over the course of the six game-playing sessions, Eva made several attempts to use smiling, laughter, and self-deprecating language to foster involvement with the other players. During Phase I, we see that anytime Eva stalled linguistically, she signaled that she needed help from the others by going silent, smiling, and then laughing. This strategy appeared successful with the other L2 learners during all three sessions of Phase I. Additionally, she utilized clapping and cheering during her and others' turns to foster collaboration with the group, situating herself as a group participant rather than observer, while inviting others to do the same.

However, during Phase II, when Eva was in Spain playing with the native Spanish speakers, the strategy of utilizing language play to foster involvement and index herself as a group participant was unsuccessful. Eva initially attempted to utilize language play (smiling) in Turn 3 of her first session during Phase II, but the intended audience (Paula) did not reciprocate. Eva repeated similar attempts throughout the next few turns, yet the L1 Spanish speakers did not engage with or respond to Eva's attempts to utilize language play as an involvement strategy. While Eva was hoping to foster involvement and affiliation with the Andalusian Spanish speakers, the end result was that the other players quickly situated her as a non-group member. While independence was not Eva's goal during Phase II, she was quickly forced into that role through the rejection of her attempts at language play. During Session II of Phase II, we noticed that Eva only attempted to utilize language play once, during her first turn, before leaning into an independence strategy and accepting her role as non-group member. Interestingly, this led to Eva (consciously or unconsciously) shifting her role within the group from novice linguistic ability to expert game-playing ability, possibly attempting to shift the power dynamic back in her favor.

When Eva played the game with a new group of L2 Spanish speakers (who had also been playing with L1 Spanish speakers) during Phase III, there was little to no language play. Rather, the players fostered group involvement through collaboration and mutual support of each other through clapping and cheering. This was surprising, given how much language play was utilized to foster involvement with the L2 Spanish speakers when playing at-home. This invites speculation as to whether the study-abroad L2 Spanish speakers reduced their language play, such as the smiling, laughter, and self-deprecation because the group was more equal in terms of linguistic and game-playing ability or because the group had adopted the cultural norms regarding rejection of language play that had been experienced when playing the game with the L1 Spanish speakers. Quantitative analyses of a more robust set of data could help distinguish between the two possibilities.

Research question #2

To answer RQ2, we compared the hierarchical face systems between all sessions of game-play and found that Eva clearly co-constructed her identity depending not only on her interlocutors but also on the face systems constructed during each session. During Phase I, Eva very quickly indexed herself as linguistically inferior to the other group members, deferring to her communicative partners to fill gaps in her linguistic and game-playing knowledge. This seems to have led to a clearly hierarchical (+P, +D) face system by the second session of Phase I, where Eva continuously co-indexed her identity as a novice speaker, which simultaneously led to Annie's indexing as linguistic expert. Even as the social distance decreased by the end of Phase I (−D), Eva continued to index herself as a novice to Annie's linguistic expertise, reinforcing the hierarchical face system, though the dynamic had shifted from +P, +D to +P, −D.

Eva's attempts to foster involvement with the Andalusian participants fell flat, instead reinforcing social distance between group members and the power dynamic of Eva as less powerful than other group members in terms of linguistic ability. However, by the end of Phase II, Session I, Eva shifted her strategy from involvement to independence and began to co-index herself as an expert, not in terms of linguistic ability but of game-play knowledge as compared to her group members. Eva began to index herself as autonomous because she knew how to play the game whereas her partners were still learning the rules. Throughout her turns during Phase II, Session II, Eva redefined the +Power dynamic as game-play knowledge, rather than linguistic abilities. She showed many instances of involvement by directing others' moves during the game while also co-indexing her identity as expert game player to her group members' identities of novice game players. Surprisingly, the Andalusian Spanish speakers accepted this change by listening and following her instructions during their own turns.

Research question #3

Was Eva's behavior during the different phases explainable by a variationist SLA framework? We saw great variation in Eva's sociopragmatic behavior (language play) when interacting with the other L2 learners versus when interacting with the L1 Spanish speakers. When working with other L2 speakers, Eva successfully used language play to co-construct her identity as novice in terms of linguistic abilities alongside Annie's development of expert linguistic abilities. This strategy was not successful with the L1 Spanish speakers, so Eva had to quickly adapt and vary her sociopragmatic behavior to match that of the Andalusians in an attempt to index involvement and group membership. In this regard, we conclude that Eva's interaction varied according to the power relationship with her interlocutors but that the constituents of power varied between L2 and native-speaking groups. Based on our case study of Eva, we hypothesize that L2 learners' preoccupation with, and sensitivity toward, their own level of L2 proficiency is greater when comparing themselves with other L2 learners than it is when comparing themselves to native speakers of the target language. In that regard, the co-indexing of nonexpert status based on language use is not a constant characteristic of L2 identity but may in fact be predicted by group membership status. When Eva was an insider, she appeared more self-conscious about her linguistic abilities, becoming completely deferential. When she was an outsider, she utilized her expertise of the game and co-indexed her identity as an active and important participant within the interaction.

While a larger dataset, along with more nuanced quantitative analyses would be needed to confirm it, we speculate that the behavioral norms of the native speakers in the present study influenced those of our L2 learners to the extent that they (the L2 learners) adapted accordingly. With regard to Eva, she possessed the sociopragmatic competence and awareness of each situation and of her interlocutors to interact in such a way to achieve a desirable outcome. Most interestingly, her ability to do so was not limited to language ability but included her knowledge of the topic of interaction.

Conclusion

The use of language play among L2 learners is an effective strategy to co-index speaker identity and to establish involvement with interlocutors, but it is used differently according to sociopragmatic contexts. L2 learners' level of awareness of changes in power and distance across different contexts is essential to their ability to effect positive change; whereas language play may help to do so in some contexts, it does not in all contexts. In the present study, we observed a L2 learner's variable behavior pattern in relation to contextual variation in group membership and topical expertise and to the attributes of identifying as a L2 learner. We found that such patterns are dependent on both and that they are constrained by the L2 learner's awareness of their own self and of others'. We conclude that L2 learner identity is not defined only by L2 proficiency level but also by expertise in particular foci of specific interactions and that language play is an important strategy in the co-indexing of L2 identity among other L2 speakers but not necessarily when interacting with specific native-speaking groups. We invite future research to empirically test our conclusions by examining the behavior of more participants and with a larger dataset.

References

ACTFL. (2012). *ACTFL Proficiency Guidelines 2012*. White Plains, NY: ACTFL.
Bachman, L. F. (1990). *Fundamental considerations in language testing*. Oxford University Press.
Barron, A. (2005). Variational pragmatics in the foreign language classroom. *System, 33*(3), 519–536.
Barron, A., & Schneider, K. P. (2009). Variational pragmatics: Studying the impact of social factors on language use in interaction. *Intercultural Pragmatics, 6*(4), 425–442.
Bateson, G. (1953). The position of humor in human communication. In H. von Foerster (Ed.), *Transactions of the Ninth Conference on Cybernetics* (pp. 1–47). Macy Foundation.
Bell, N. (2015). *We are not amused: Failed humor in interaction*. De Gruyter Mouton.
Bell, N., & Attardo, S. (2010). Failed humor: Issue in non-native speakers' appreciation and understanding of humor. *Intercultural Pragmatics, 7*, 423–447.
Bennett, M. J. (1986). A developmental approach to training for intercultural sensitivity. *International Journal of Intercultural Relations, 10*(2), 179–196.
Bennett, M. J. (1993). Towards ethnorelativism: A developmental model of intercultural sensitivity. In M. Paige (Ed.), *Education for the Intercultural Experience* (pp. 21–71). Intercultural Press.
Boxer, D., & Cortés-Conde, F. (1997). From bonding to biting: Conversational joking and identity display, *Journal of Pragmatics, 27*, 275–294.
Bravo, D. (1996). La risa en el regateo: estudio sobre el estilo comunicativo de negociadores españoles y suecos [Doctoral dissertation, Stockholm University]. Retrieved from https://urn.kb.se/resolve?urn=urn:nbn:se:su:diva-153012
Brecht, R. D., Rivers, W. P., Robinson, J. P., & Davidson, D. E. (2017). Professional language skills: Unprecedented demands and supply. In T. Brown & J. Bown (Eds.), *To advanced proficiency and beyond: Theory and methods for developing superior second language ability* (pp. 171–184). Georgetown University Press.

Cantos-Delgado, C. & Maíz-Arévalo, C. (2023). "I hear you like bad girls? I'm bad at everything": A British-Spanish cross-cultural analysis of humour as a self-presentation strategy in Tinder profiles. *The European Journal of Humour Research*, 11(3), 31–53.

Colcher, D. (2022). Corrective feedback and the ideological co-construction of expertise. In L. Czerwionka, R. Showstack, & J. Liskin-Gasparro (Eds.), *Contexts of co-constructed discourse: Interaction, pragmatics, and second language acquisition* (pp. 68–90). Routledge.

Czerwionka, L. (2021). Using the L2 to express intercultural competence. In M. R. Menke & P. A. Malovrh (Eds.), *Advancedness in second language Spanish: Definitions, challenges, and possibilities*, (pp. 273–298). John Benjamins.

Czerwionka, L., Showstack, R., & Liskin-Gasparro, J. (Eds.) (2022). *Contexts of co-constructed discourse: Interaction, pragmatics, and second language applications*. Routledge.

Geeslin, K. (2020). Variationist perspective(s) on interlocutor individual differences. In L. Gurzynski-Weiss (Ed.), *Cross-theoretical explorations of interlocutors and their individual differences* (pp. 128–157). John Benjamins.

Geeslin, K. (2021). Sophisticated language use in context: The contributions of variationist approaches to the study of advanced learners of Spanish. In M. R. Menke & P. A. Malovrh, (Eds.), *Advancedness in second language Spanish: Definitions, challenges, and possibilities* (pp. 219–243). John Benjamins.

Geeslin, K., Gudmestad, A., Kanwit, M., Linford, B., Long, A., Schmidt, L., & Solon, M. (2018). Sociolinguistic competence and the acquisition of speaking. In R. A. Alonso (Ed.), *Speaking in a second language* (pp. 1–25). John Benjamins.

Geeslin, K., & Hanson, S. (2022). Sociolinguistic approaches to communicative competence. In M. Kanwit & M. Solon (Eds.), *Communicative competence in a second language* (pp. 40–59). Routledge.

Geeslin, K., with Long, A. (2014). *Introduction to sociolinguistic variation. Sociolinguistics and second language acquisition: Learning to use language in context* (pp. 27–47). New York: Routledge.

Gumperz, J. (1992). Contextualization and understanding. In A. Duranti & C. Goodwin (Eds.), *Rethinking context: Language as an interactive phenomenon* (pp. 229–252). Cambridge University Press.

Hay, J. (1995). Only teasing! *New Zealand English Newsletter*, 9, 32–35.

Hymes, D. (1972). On communicative competence. In J. B. Pride & J. Holmes (Eds.), *Sociolinguistics: Selected readings* (pp. 269–293). Penguin.

Malovrh, P. A., & Moreno, N. (2018). Meeting the demands of globalization: One goal of ISLA research. In P. A. Malovrh & A. G. Benati (Eds.), *The handbook of advanced proficiency in second language acquisition* (pp. 199–218). John Wiley & Sons, Inc.

Menke, M. & Malovrh, P. A., (Eds.) (2021). *Advancedness in second language Spanish: Definitions, challenges, and possibilities*. John Benjamins.

Malovrh, P. A., & Moreno, N. (2023). *Second language identity: Awareness, ideology and assessment in higher education*. Cambridge University Press.

Priego-Valverde, B., Bigi, B., Attardo, S., Pickering, L., & Gironzetti, E. (2018). Is smiling during humor so obvious? A cross-cultural comparison of smiling behavior in humorous sequences in American English and French interactions. *Intercultural Pragmatics*, 15(4), 563–591.

Sampietro, A. (2019). Emoji and rapport management in Spanish WhatsApp chats. *Journal of Pragmatics, 143*, 109–120.

Schneider, K. P., & Barron, A. (Eds.) (2008). *Variational pragmatics: A focus on regional varieties in pluricentric languages*. John Benjamins.

Scollon, R., Scollon, S. W., & Jones, R. H. (2012). *Intercultural communication: A discourse approach* (3rd ed.).Wiley.

Shively, R. (2018). *Learning and using conversational humor in a second language during study abroad*. De Gruyter Mouton.

Spencer-Oatey, H. (2005). (Im)politeness, face and perceptions of rapport: Unpackaging their biases and interrelationships. *Journal of Politeness Research, 1*, 95–119.

Trudgill, P. (1972). Sex, covert prestige and linguistic change in the urban British English of Norwich. *Language in Society, 1*(2), 179–195.

CHAPTER 9

Dialectal variation in secondary Spanish classrooms in the United States
A sociolinguistically informed pedagogical approach to teaching and learning the *usted, tú,* and *vos* forms of address

Francisco Salgado-Robles, Angela George
& Brisilda Ndreka
City University of New York | University of Calgary | University of Connecticut

> This study examines the development of the second-person singular pronouns (*usted, tú,* and *vos*) by adolescent learners of Spanish, both heritage- and second-language speakers, participating in a beginner-level Early College Program located on the East Coast of the United States. Learners received input and instruction on all three pronouns through a sociolinguistically informed pedagogical approach. The results of the written fill-in-the-blank task and the oral discourse completion task show increased usage of all three forms from the beginning to the end of the semester by both learner groups with variations by task type (oral vs. written). These findings suggest benefits of the pedagogical approach and the addition of *vos* in beginner-level Spanish courses for second and heritage language learners.
>
> **Keywords:** adolescent learners, forms of address, heritage speakers, sociolinguistically informed pedagogy, sociolinguistic competence, Spanish, *voseo*

This study investigates the awareness and use of Spanish second-person singular forms of address (*usted, tú,* and *vos*) among adolescent second-language (L2) and heritage-language (HL) learners in introductory Spanish courses. Given the diverse linguistic background of students in such courses, particularly HL learners from regions where *vos* is predominant, this research sheds light on how both L2 and HL learners develop these forms of address. This analysis among high school Spanish learners underscores the need for language education that reflects the authentic diversity of the Spanish language, paving the way for more inclusive and effective teaching strategies. This study seeks to address how the second-person singular forms of address (*usted, tú,* and *vos*) differ in two types of tasks (oral and written) among two groups of Spanish learners (L2 and HL) throughout the course of one semester. By examining variation in learners' usage, this study highlights the importance of incorporating sociolinguistic elements into language education, addressing the need for a more inclusive and comprehensive approach that mirrors the authentic use of Spanish in various contexts. This study not only fills existing research needs by providing insights into the sociolinguistic strategies employed by learners, but also underscores the critical role of pedagogical practices in fostering effective communication skills in a L2 (Geeslin & Hanson, 2023).

Background

The sociolinguistic competence of Spanish learners

Sociolinguistic competence is a complex concept that encompasses the knowledge and skills necessary to address the social dimension of language use, linguistic markers of social relationships, norms of common courtesy, proverbial phrases (sayings, idioms, etc.), differences in register, turn-taking, dialectal variation, and accent. The concept of sociolinguistic competence originally proposed by Canale and Swain (1980) has been developed further to include not only sociolinguistic or sociocultural competence but also discursive or textual competence and pragmatic or actional competence. A widely held belief by second language acquisition (SLA) scholars is that sociolinguistic competence is necessary for effective communication in the target language (Geeslin & Hanson, 2023).

Labov (1966) defined sociolinguistic variation as choosing between two or more forms to fulfill the same or similar function. Regarding L2 acquisition, Geeslin and Garrett (2018) noted that "variation between forms can fall along two axes" (p. 18): vertical and horizontal. While in vertical variation learners vary between two or more forms, at least one of which is nontargetlike, horizontal variation is, conversely, when speakers choose between two or more forms that are both targetlike (Adamson & Regan, 1991). For example, vertical variation would be choosing between 1a and 1b, while horizontal variation would be choosing among 2a, 2b, and 2c:

(1) a. *(yo) *sabí*
      knowed.PST.1SG
      'I knew'
   b. *(yo) supe*
      knew.PST.1SG
      'I knew'

(2) a. *(tú) sabes*
      know.PRS.2SG
      'you know'
   b. *(vos) sabés*
      know.PRS.FAM.2SG
      'you know'
   c. *(usted) sabe*
      know.PRS.EXAL.2SG
      'you know'

To date, there has been a wealth of research conducted on the acquisition of sociolinguistic variation by learners of Spanish. However, most of these studies that examine the sociolinguistic competence of adult L2 or HL learners of Spanish focus on students who have spent some time in a Spanish-speaking environment during their academic studies. This field of research examines how learners can benefit directly from interactions with first-language (L1) speakers abroad. These studies have focused on measuring the linguistic and extralinguistic factors that account for such a development. While linguistic factors are specific to the feature under study, extralinguistic variables include — but are not limited to — language learner profiles (e.g., L2 learner, HL learner, etc.), language learner characteristics (e.g., attitude, gender, identity, intercultural competence, motivation, language proficiency level, social class, etc.), language contact with L1 speakers (e.g., social networks), length of program (e.g., short-term summer or winter program, 12–16-week semester, academic year, etc.), and programmatic features (e.g., experiential learning, internship, service-learning, volunteer experience, etc.). Research on the acquisition of sociolinguistic variation by learners of Spanish abroad has focused on the development of phonological, morphosyntactic, and pragmatic features (see Geeslin & Garrett, 2018 for a comprehensive review of the research pertaining to these areas).

Dialectal feature under investigation

With nearly 60 million Spanish speakers (including L1, L2, and HL speakers), the United States has the second largest Spanish-speaking population in the world after Mexico. The vast majority of the U.S. Hispanic population comes from Latin America (U.S. Census Bureau, 2023). A common feature among Latin American Spanish speakers is the use of *vos* as the second-person singular pronoun, present across most Spanish-speaking countries and territories in the region. Using census data and official estimates, Morgan et al. (2017) concluded that *vos* is used by 150 million *voseantes* in Latin America out of a Spanish-speaking population of 400 million, which indicates that one third of the region's Spanish-speakers use *voseo*. Additionally, *vos* may also coexist with the use of *usted* and *tú* in many regions. This three-tiered system is used in Central American Spanish to indicate the degree of respect or familiarity: one formal pronoun, *usted*, and two informal pronouns, *tú* and *vos*. *Usted* expresses distance and respect; *tú* corresponds to an intermediate level of familiarity, but not deep trust; and *vos* is the pronoun of maximum familiarity and solidarity (Carricaburo, 2015; Quesada-Pacheco, 2023). *Voseo* is prevalent in at least eight Latin America countries: five in Central America (Costa Rica, El Salvador, Guatemala, Honduras, and Nicaragua) and three in South America (Argentina, Paraguay, and Uruguay). Furthermore, *voseo* is also deeply ingrained in everyday language and cultural identity and present in regional locations in several Latin American countries (e.g., Bolivia, Colombia, Chile, Ecuador, Mexico, and Peru; Benavides, 2003; Carricaburo, 2015).

Table 1 shows the three-tiered system of the regular verb paradigm typical in two Central American countries: El Salvador and Honduras. In comparing the *tú* and *vos* verb forms, in all cases, *vos* forms, unlike *tú* forms, are stressed on the final syllable. Furthermore, while regular present indicative *tú* forms use the morpheme -*es* with both -*er* and -*ir* verbs, *vos* forms distinguish between these verb classes, employing -*és* and -*ís*, respectively. Similarly, while regular *tú* imperative forms use the suffix -*e* with both -*er* and -*ir* verbs, *vos* conjugations also maintain a distinction between these verb classes: -*é* with -*er* verbs, and -*í* with -*ir* verbs.

Table 2 shows the three-tiered system of stem-changing verbs typically evidenced in two Central American countries: El Salvador and Honduras. In comparing the *tú* and *vos* verb forms *vos* forms, unlike *tú* forms, do not undergo a stem change. Additionally, the *vos* forms maintain the distinction between verb classes indicated in Table 1.

The *voseo* paradigm consists of three types: authentic *voseo* and two types of mixed *voseo* (Félix-Brasdefer, 2019, p. 222). Authentic *voseo* refers to the use of the pronoun *vos* and its *voseante* verbal form, as in (1).

Table 1. Three-tiered system of verbal paradigm in Central American (El Salvador and Honduras) Spanish (Carricaburo, 2015)

Pronoun	Present indicative	Imperative
usted	habla speak.PRS.EXAL.2SG 'you speak' come eat.PRS.EXAL.2SG 'you eat' escribe write.PRS.EXAL.2SG 'you write'	hable speak.IMP.EXAL.2SG 'speak' coma eat.IMP.EXAL.2SG 'eat' escriba write.IMP.EXAL.2SG 'write'
tú	hablas speak.PRS.2SG 'you speak' comes eat.PRS.2SG 'you eat' escribes write.PRS.2SG 'you write'	habla speak.IMP.2SG 'speak' come eat.IMP.2SG 'eat' escribe write.IMP.2SG 'write'
vos	hablás speak.PRS.FAM.2SG 'you speak' comés eat.PRS.FAM.2SG 'you eat' escribís write.PRS.FAM.2SG 'you write'	hablá speak.IMP.FAM.2SG 'speak' comé eat.IMP.FAM.2SG 'eat' escribí write.IMP.FAM.2SG 'write'

(1) *Y vos, ¿cómo te llamás* (you are named.PRS.2SG, 'you are named')? 'And you, what is your name?
Cerrá (close.IMP.FAM.2SG, 'close') *la puerta, no te quedés* (stay.IMP.FAM.2SG, 'stay') *afuera.* 'Close the door. Don't wait outside.'

Mixed pronominal *voseo* consists of the use of the pronoun *vos* with verbal morphology corresponding to *tú*, as in (2):

(2) *Y vos, ¿dónde vives* (you live.PRS.2SG, 'you live')? 'And you, where do you live?'
Cierra (close.IMP.2SG, 'close') *la puerta, vos.* 'Close the door.'

Table 2. Three-tiered system of stem-changing verb paradigm in Central American (El Salvador and Honduras) Spanish (Carricaburo, 2015)

Pronoun	Present indicative	Imperative
usted	*cierra* close.PRS.EXAL.2SG 'you close' *quiere* wish.PRS.EXAL.2SG 'you wish' *prefiere* prefer.PRS.EXAL.2SG 'you prefer'	*cierre* close.IMP.EXAL.2SG 'close' *quiera* wish.IMP.EXAL.2SG 'wish' *prefiera* prefer.IMP.EXAL.2SG 'prefer'
tú	*cierras* close.PRS.2SG 'you close' *quieres* wish.PRS.2SG 'you wish' *prefieres* prefer.PRS.2SG 'you prefer'	*cierra* close.IMP.2SG 'close' *quiere* wish.IMP.2SG 'wish' *prefiere* prefer.IMP.2SG 'prefer'
vos	*cerrás* close.PRS.FAM.2SG 'you close' *querés* wish.PRS.FAM.2SG 'you wish' *preferís* prefer.PRS.FAM.2SG 'you prefer'	*cerrá* close.IMP.FAM.2SG 'close' *queré* wish.IMP.FAM.2SG 'wish' *prefirí* prefer.IMP.FAM.2SG 'prefer'

Mixed verbal *voseo* corresponds to the use of the pronoun *tú* (together with its forms *te, ti, tu, tuyo*) with verbal morphology corresponding to *vos*, as in (3):

(3) *Y tú, ¿dónde vivís* (you live.PRS.FAM.2SG, 'you live')? 'And you, where do you live?'

Y tú, ¿te querés (you wish.PRS.FAM.2SG, 'you wish') *dormir con tus primos? O ¿preferís* (you prefer.PRS.FAM.2SG, 'you prefer') *quedarte en tu casa?* 'And you, do you wish to sleep with your cousins? Or do you prefer to stay at home?'

Uber (2008) offered some strategies for learners who wish to employ *voseo*, which help further explain the feature under study. The research first explained that forms of address are used to express relationships and social norms. On the one hand, between people of similar social levels, informal symmetrical treatment (the *tú* or the *vos* forms of address) is used to express solidarity and intimacy. On the other hand, between people from different social positions, asymmetric treatment is used (some use the *tú/vos* forms of address; others use the *tú* form only) to demonstrate and maintain social distance between interlocutors based on the discrepancy of power. A formal symmetrical address (the *usted* form of address) can also be used to express social distance, respect, or courtesy. Because the morphology and nuances of *voseo* can be complex for a Spanish learner, the author also offered a series of practical tips to be considered at the workplace. For instance, nonnative speakers of a *voseo* variety should always use *usted* with all the interlocutors and, to change to *tú* or *vos*, they should wait for the interlocutor to start talking to them informally or wait for the interlocutor to encourage addressing them informally.

Empirical studies examining morphosyntactic development by Spanish language learners

Research on the acquisition of morphosyntactic variation by L2 and HL Spanish learners abroad has focused on the production of clitics (Geeslin et al., 2010; Salgado-Robles, 2011, 2014, 2018, 2020), subject expression (Denbaum, 2020; Linford, 2016; Linford et at., 2018; Salgado-Robles, 2017), verb tenses (Geeslin et al., 2012; Geeslin et al., 2013; Kanwit & Solon, 2013; Whatley, 2013), and forms of address (George, 2018, 2019; George & Salgado-Robles, 2021; Hoffman-González, 2015; Pozzi, 2017, 2021; Pozzi et al., 2023; Reynolds-Case, 2013; Ringer-Hilfinger, 2013; Salgado-Robles & George, 2019, 2023). Among the research on the acquisition of address forms, studies by Hoffman-González (2015), Pozzi (2017), Pozzi (2021), and Pozzi et al. (2023) investigated the development and use of *vos* by university learners studying abroad in Argentina. The other studies on the acquisition of forms of address have focused on the informal second-person plural, *vosotros*, while studying in Spain.

Hoffman-González (2015) reported low overall use of *voseo* forms compared to other dialectal features among her seven participants (two Spanish HL speakers of Mexican descent and five L2 learners of Spanish), despite an increase from 46.1% rate of production of *voseo* pre-study abroad to 59.6% post-study abroad. Moreover, Hoffman-González attributed this small change over time to the administration of one of the *vos* elicitation tasks at the end of the interviews, which the author suggested may have resulted in participant fatigue. Pozzi (2017,

2021) investigated the development of *voseo* among 23 L2 learners of Spanish during a five-month semester in Buenos Aires. The findings from the multivariate analysis of over 1200 tokens of *tú* and *vos* indicated that learners used *vos* verb forms in semi-spontaneous speech from 0% to 65% mid-semester and over 70% by the end of the sojourn. Two of the author's conclusions were that the stronger the learners' social networks and the higher their Spanish proficiency level, the more they used *vos* verb forms. In another study, Pozzi et al. (2023) presented a case study on the pragmatic development of a U.S.-based Spanish HL speaker of Mexican descent, Juan, during an 11-week study abroad program in Argentina. Juan decreased his use of *vos* in favor of *usted* and increased his metapragmatic awareness while reflecting on his bicultural identity and participation in the host community. These four studies represent the first accounts of the acquisition of a widespread morphosyntactic feature of Latin American Spanish.

The integration of sociolinguistics into the Spanish classroom

To better understand the influence of educational input on the sociolinguistic competence of language learners, approaches that foster the development of critical language awareness (CLA) have been proposed (Loza & Beaudrie, 2022). Regarding CLA, Leeman (2018) states that:

> rather than serving primarily as a means to acquire prestige norms and assimilate students to the status quo, the incorporation of sociolinguistics should be designed to help students develop an understanding of how language and linguistic variation work, not just at the formal (i.e., linguistic) level but also with regard to social, political and aesthetic concerns. (p. 351)

Scholars have long solicited calls for a sociolinguistically informed pedagogy in language classes that raises and hones students' critical awareness of issues related to language attitudes, language ideologies, language variation, and multilingualism (Klee & Lacorte, 2021; Leeman, 2014, 2018; Martínez, 2003; Moreno-Fernández, 2023). In the CLA vein, Geeslin with Long (2014) discussed how language teachers can effectively integrate sociolinguistics into their classrooms. They emphasized five key points about language variation: all speakers vary their language, language varies at all grammar levels, language choices reflect identity, context influences language use, and politeness involves appropriate language variation (pp. 258–260). The authors recommended that teachers be aware of target selection, create effective course materials, set reasonable expectations, and include a range of language varieties in their teaching (pp. 260–270). They stressed the importance of using evidence-based sociolinguistic information and activities to raise students' awareness and competence, considering students' language proficiency and individual needs. Additionally, the authors highlighted the need for teachers to stay current with pedagogical practices and research. They suggested that when creating new teaching materials, teachers should remember foundational principles, focus on learner goals and communication, develop all aspects of competence, consider individual learning styles, and adapt existing practices to new objectives (pp. 270–275). By doing so, teachers can help students develop comprehensive communicative competence, including sociolinguistic competence. This approach also involves sensitivity to and knowledge of specific linguistic forms like *vos*.

Despite the importance of addressing *vos* in the language classroom, *voseo* is strikingly absent from U.S. Spanish instructional curricula, which prevents language learners from being exposed to this form of address. Most Spanish learners at the secondary and postsecondary levels are unaware of the fact that *voseo* is prevalent in Latin America. The consistent omission of *vos* in U.S. education has been reported in the literature (Cameron, 2012; Griffin, 2019).

Although *vos* is largely absent from most Spanish textbooks and curricula in the U.S., a few studies indicate that the form has been addressed in various ways in specific Spanish classrooms. First, Pearson (2006) described the use of digital audio technology in a class on Spanish dialectology to develop students' awareness of language variation and specifically *voseo*. Similarly, Kingsbury (2011) had students analyze specific fragments of an adapted version of Marco Denevi's novel *Rosaura a las diez* (1955) by drawing their attention to the contextual uses of different forms of address (*usted, tú,* and *vos*) by different characters. This type of classroom-based dialect awareness helps students question common beliefs about sociolinguistic variation. The author also recommended having students research *voseo* as an extension activity in the teaching of Argentine literature.

A thorough analysis of *vos* variants and how teachers can incorporate them into the classroom is offered by Shenk (2014). The author promoted the teaching of *vos* mainly due to sociolinguistic reasons and supported her claim with the world-readiness standards for learning languages (i.e., the five "C" goal areas: Communication, Cultures, Connections, Comparisons, and Communities) established by the American Council on the Teaching of Foreign Languages. Regarding the areas of communication and community, learners improve their ability to communicate by recognizing and responding appropriately to *voseo*. Moreover, the presentation of evidence-based sociolinguistic information about language variation contributes to establishing connections because such awareness reinforces students' knowledge of other disciplines through the foreign language. Finally, within the culture and comparison goals, students better understand the relationships and linguistic practices with respect to the pronouns *usted, tú,* and *vos* in a community and compare how they themselves express formality, intimacy, and solidarity in their L1. To that end, the author suggested a series of activities designed to raise students' sociolinguistic awareness in the Spanish classroom. Shenk (2014) concluded that it is imperative to start teaching *vos* in the Spanish classrooms (or at least to pay more attention to it) to better prepare students to communicate in the diverse Spanish-speaking world. Moreover, Cameron (2017) argued that, regardless of the millions of *voseo* users, "the twentieth century did not see a single article published in *Hispania* that suggested incorporating instruction on *voseo* into the language classroom" (p. 67). Additionally, the author highlighted rising trends in study abroad destinations and immigration in the United States from *voseante* nations. These precedents serve as a call for inclusion of the *voseo* in the 21st century Spanish curriculum.

Furthermore, LeLoup and Schmidt-Rinehart (2018), Griffin (2019), and Potvin (2022) found that *voseo* is disregarded in textbooks. LeLoup and Schmidt-Rinehart (2018) showed that teachers do not offer instruction that includes the use of *vos*. Therefore, we can conclude that students are not learning *vos* through classroom instruction. Griffin (2019) argued for three reasons why this informal second-person singular pronoun should be integrated into the classroom: the number of U.S. college students studying abroad in *voseante* regions, the large immigrant population from Central American countries in the United States, and the millions of *voseo* speakers throughout Latin America.

These studies indicate that sensitivity toward and knowledge of dialectal variation (e.g., the incorporation of *voseo* into the Spanish classroom and curricula) in the target language is an important component of sociolinguistic competence, and ultimately, communicative competence. Moreover, adopting a CLA approach in the language classroom would be conducive to creating "inclusive and transformative learning spaces for (…) students" (Beaudrie & Loza, 2023, p. 154). With this in mind, the present study seeks to answer two main research questions (RQs):

RQ1: How does the use of the singular forms of address (*usted, tú,* and *vos*) among L2 and HL participants change from the beginning (T1) to the end (T2) of the semester on an oral and a written task?

RQ2: How do the rates of use of singular forms of address differ between L2 and HL participants?

Method

Participants

Fifty-three American English-speaking students were recruited from two separate Spanish classes in a large public Hispanic serving university (i.e., over 25% of full-time, undergraduate students identify as Hispanic) located in the U.S. northeast to participate in the current study. Based on their sociolinguistic background, participants were divided into two groups. The L2 Spanish group ($n=35$; 14 men and 21 women) was comprised of native-English-speaking L2 learners of Spanish, and the HL Spanish group ($n=18$; 7 men and 11 women) consisted of high school students of Guatemalan ($n=4$), Honduran ($n=8$), and Salvadoran ($n=6$) descent. All participants were enrolled in the Early College Program — that is, they were high school students who aspired to attend college and who took strategically sequenced university classes during their regular high school days at no cost to themselves or their families.

Participants were enrolled in a first-semester Spanish language course. They completed an online consent form, a language background questionnaire, and a placement test designed by the department. The language background questionnaire aimed to elicit information about participants' self-perception as language learners; their experiences using Spanish at home, in their community, or abroad; their linguistic history; their formal education in Spanish; and their learning goals.

Explicit instruction of *vos*

Formal classroom instruction consisted of three 90-minute classes on a weekly basis throughout the semester (16 weeks). A sociolinguistically informed pedagogy (Beaudrie et al., 2014; Geeslin with Long, 2014) was implemented to teach students how to differentiate between and use *usted, tú,* and *vos* based on the communicative context in both written and oral registers. This approach involved assessing students' prior knowledge of the use of *vos*, tailoring the curriculum to meet students' needs, examining the norms within their Spanish-speaking communities, and imparting sociolinguistic knowledge, especially regarding forms of address. Additionally, it emphasized respecting students' language varieties and enhancing their language repertoire by providing more opportunities to use their language both within their communities and in broader contexts. This approach aimed to raise students' awareness of the sociolinguistic significance of *vos*, illustrating its reflection of social relationships, cultural identity, and regional diversity (Klee & Lacorte, 2021). These critical reflections prompted students to investigate the linguistic practices within their own communities and question widely accepted beliefs and values about language that frequently lead to the negative depiction of specific dialectal varieties. Equally important were instructional strategies, like using authentic materials and conducting role-playing and simulations, as well as classroom activities that encouraged dialogue, interaction, and comparative analysis. Incorporating these elements helped create a rich, sociolinguistically informed learning environment that enhanced students' understanding and use of *vos*, thereby contributing to their overall communicative competence in Spanish (Geeslin with Long, 2014). Both classes were taught by the same instructor, who was trained in communicative and sociolinguistic approaches to teaching Spanish. The instructor was a *voseante* speaker from El Salvador.

Elicitation tasks

To measure participants' sociolinguistic competence in the use of the three-tiered system (*usted, tú,* and *vos*), all participants completed two distinct tasks: a fill-in-the-blank task (FBT) and an oral discourse completion task (ODCT). In an effort to minimize the possible effect of language exposure on participants' responses and to avoid affecting the participants' verb use, the tasks were administered on different days in the order of FBT and ODCT, respectively. Both tasks were completed at two different points in time (week 3 and week 15) during the semester.

The FBT required that the participants fill in the gaps of five short written conversations with the appropriate verb forms in the present tense based on context. While three of the missing verbs were expected to be conjugated in one of the three second-person singular forms (*usted, tú,* and *vos*) under investigation, the remaining six were expected to be conjugated in other persons (*yo, ella, ustedes,* etc.) and used as fillers. The FBT was completed by each participant on a computer in the language lab. For each of the five short conversations on the FBT, participants had nine minutes (maximum) to fill in the nine blanks with the conjugation of the missing verbs. Intentionally, the system did not allow participants to return to a previous conversation for modification purposes. The participants took between 35–45 minutes to complete this task. What follows is an example from the FBT featuring one of the five short conversations which includes nine blanks for filling in the missing verb conjugations.

"Luis and his wife Patricia, both from Honduras, are in a Mexican restaurant with their friend Macarena, from Spain. Luis and Patricia work and live in New York City. Macarena is visiting them for a few days only."

Note: Image generated using the prompt "A photo of Luis, Patricia and Macarena at a Mexican restaurant," by Imagined-with AI, 2023 (https://imagined-with.ai/)

Camarera: ¡Buenas tardes y bienvenidos al restaurante Taquería Coyoacán! _____ (Llamarse) Marta y voy a ser quien les atienda hoy.
'Waitress: Good afternoon and welcome to Taquería Coyoacán! _____ (To be called) Marta, and I will be serving you today.'

Luis: Buenas tardes, Marta. Patricia, para beber, ¿qué _____ (querer) tomar?
'Luis: Good afternoon, Marta. Patricia, what _____ (to want) to drink?'

Patricia: No _____ (estar) segura. ¿Qué es el piznate?
'Patricia: _____ (not / to be) sure. What is piznate?'

Camarera: Es una bebida tradicional mexicana. Es fría y dulce a base de maíz con un toque de canela. Es muy rica y popular en el estado de Nayarit.
'Waitress: It's a traditional Mexican drink. It's cold and sweet, made with corn and a touch of cinnamon. It's very delicious and popular in the state of Nayarit.'

Patricia: Pues piznate para mí.
'Patricia: Well, piznate for me.'

Luis: ¿Y tú, Macarena?
'Luis: And you, Macarena?'

Macarena: _____ (Querer) agua de jamaica.
'Macarena: _____ (To want) hibiscus water.'

Luis: Para mí, agua de horchata, por favor.
'Luis: For me, horchata water, please.'

Camarera: Y para comer, ¿qué _____(desear) ordenar, señora?
'Waitress: And for food, what _____ (to wish) to order, ma'am?'

Patricia: Para mí, primero sopa de tortilla y, después, arrachera con puré de papa.
'Patricia: For me, first tortilla soup, and then, flank steak with mashed potatoes.'

Camarera: ¿Y para usted, señor?
'Waitress: And for you, sir?'

Luis: Para empezar, yo quiero pozole y, luego, un bistec con papas.
'Luis: To start, I want pozole, and then a steak with potatoes.'

Macarena: Patricia, ¿qué me _____ (recomendar): carne o pescado?
'Macarena: Patricia, what _____ (to recommend): meat or fish?'

Patricia: Me _____ (gustar) ambos, pero prefiero la carne.
'Patricia: _____ (To like) both, but I prefer meat.'

Macarena: Bien, entonces, _____ (ir) a pedir crema de flor de calabaza y filete de res con salsa de chocolate.
'Macarena: Okay, then _____ (to go) to order pumpkin flower cream soup and beef fillet with chocolate sauce.'

Camarera: Muy bien. _____ (Regresar) enseguida con las bebidas.
'Waitress: Very well. _____ (To return) right away with the drinks.'

In this conversation, the use of *usted* (*desea*) was expected when the waitress asked Patricia what she would like to order for food; the use of *tú* (*recomiendas*) was expected in the question asked by Macarena to Patricia; and the use of *vos* (*querés*) was expected when Luis asked his wife Patricia what she would like to order for drink. The remaining six verbs were expected to be conjugated in other persons (*yo, ellos,* etc.) used as fillers.

The ODCT required that the participants respond to five written scenarios, each comprised of nine situations, recording their answers into a digital recorder. Each scenario consisted of three target and six distractor situations. All participants read the prompts in their L1 (English) and responded in their L2 or HL (Spanish) at two different points in time (week 3 and week 15) during the semester. The ODCT was completed by each participant on a computer in the language lab. The participants were provided up to one minute (maximum) to read the prompt and answer the situation to the best of their ability. Intentionally, the system did not allow participants to return to a previous question for modification purposes. The participants took between 35–45 minutes to complete this task. An example of a scenario accompanied by its situations (a-i) used on the ODCT is shown below.

"Samuel and Victoria, seated on the sofa in the image, are international students from El Salvador, and Michelle, behind them on the phone, is originally from Mexico. The three of them met at their school's new student orientation last month in New York City, and today they are hanging out in the dorm lounge."

Note: Image generated using the prompt "A photo of Samuel, Victoria, and Michelle hanging out in the dorm lounge," by Imagined-with AI, 2023 (https://imagined-with.ai/)

a. Michelle asks Samuel and Victoria if they know where there is a pharmacy near campus.
b. Samuel tells Victoria that The Yankees are his favorite baseball team.
c. Michelle is on the phone with Dr. Villar, a professor at her university in Mexico, whom she asks if she knows how many credits she needs to take next semester.
d. Victoria tells Michelle that she and Samuel are hungry.

e. Samuel tells Michelle and Victoria that their math teacher is very funny.
f. Michelle asks Samuel if he knows what time English class is.
g. Victoria tells Samuel that she and Michelle want to go to Central Park next Sunday.
h. Victoria tells Samuel and Michelle that her older sister is a famous singer from El Salvador.
i. Samuel asks Victoria if she wants to go to the movies next weekend.

In this scenario, the use of *usted* was expected in situation C; the use of *tú* was expected in the question asked by Michelle to Samuel (situation F); and the use of *vos* was expected in situation I. The distractors are A, B, D, E, G, and H, where none of the three second-person singular forms (*usted, tú,* or *vos*) was expected.

Data coding and analysis

In order to determine how the two groups of learners (L2 and HL learners) differed on the two tasks (FBT and ODCT), the data were analyzed in R (R Core Team, 2024). The number of expected uses of *usted, tú,* and *vos* were recorded. For example, if a participant did not use *vos* where expected that was recorded as a 0, and if a participant used *vos* where expected that was recorded as a 1. There were five expected uses of *vos* in the written task at both T1 and T2, and similarly five possible uses in the oral task at T1 and T2. There were the same number of possible uses for *tú* and *usted*. In summary, the dependent variables were the expected uses of each of the three second-person singular pronouns, and the independent variables were the task type and the time. Because the data were not normally distributed, the Wilcoxon signed-rank test was used for paired data (measuring changes over time in pronoun usage in the same group of participants), and the Wilcoxon rank-sum test (i.e., Mann-Whitney U test) was used for independent samples (measuring differences in pronoun usages between the two groups of participants at both times).

Results

In this section, we present the results as they are relevant to each research question. To this end, we first explore the changes in L2 and HL learners' use of the singular forms of address (*usted, tú,* and *vos*) from T1 to T2, as measured through both oral and written tasks. We aim to understand how instructional interventions may have influenced the learners' command of these pronouns. We then compare the performance of L2 learners with that of HL learners to highlight any differential progress between the two groups.

To address how the use of the singular forms of address (*usted, tú,* and *vos*) among L2 and HL participants change from the beginning to the end of the semester on an oral and a written task, Table 3 shows the mean (*M*) and standard deviation (*SD*) at T1 (pretest) and T2 (posttest) of the three forms for the L2 and HL learners. The highest possible score on each task was 5.

Table 3. Average number of uses of second-person singular verb forms for each task

Pronoun	Task	L2 learners Pretest M	SD	Posttest M	SD	HL learners Pretest M	SD	Posttest M	SD
usted	FBT	3.51	1.58	4.34	1.35	2.61	2.03	3.83	1.79
	ODCT	3.69	1.86	4.49	1.27	3.67	1.75	4.72	0.57
tú	FBT	2.46	2.13	3.57	1.91	2.06	2.18	3.94	1.73
	ODCT	2.34	2.25	3.34	2.10	1.94	2.01	3.89	1.45
vos	FBT	0.00	0.00	2.17	2.15	2.94	2.21	4.22	1.44
	ODCT	0.00	0.00	1.57	2.13	4.06	1.70	4.67	0.97

We then conducted a statistical analysis to determine if the increase in L2 and HL learners' use of all three second-person forms throughout the semester was significant. Because the data did not meet the normality assumptions for parametric tests, a Wilcoxon signed-rank test, a nonparametric test, was used to assess differences between pretest and posttest scores. The null hypothesis assumed no difference between the pretest and posttest scores (the median of the differences is zero), while the alternative hypothesis suggested a difference (the median of the differences is not zero). At a significance level of a *p* value below .05 led to rejecting the null hypothesis, indicating a significant difference between the pretest and posttest scores.

The bar plots in Figure 1–3 represents the distribution of pretest and posttest scores for the L2 learners for the three forms: *usted* (Figure 1), *tú* (Figure 2), and *vos* (Figure 3). The yellow line represents the oral task (FBT), and the black line represents the written task (ODCT). Each vertical line serves as an error bar, with the top and bottom of the line representing the first and third quartiles, respectively, and the fixed dot indicating the data mean, which provides a visual representation of the variability and spread of the data.

As shown in Figure 1 and Table 3, the mean score test level of the L2 students for *usted* in the written and oral tasks, at the beginning of the semester was 3.51 and 3.69, respectively. After the semester, the posttest mean score rose to 4.34 and 4.49, respectively, indicating the effectiveness of the semester in the increased use

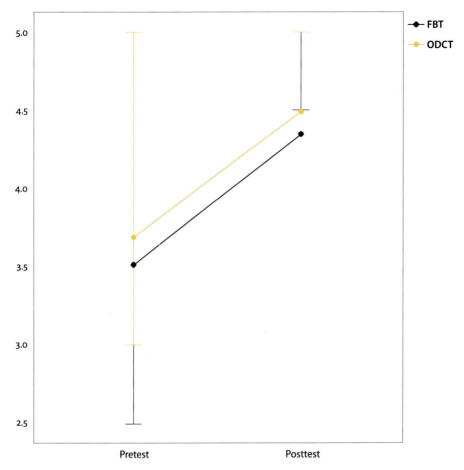

Figure 1. Use of singular forms of address *usted* throughout the semester in two different tasks by L2 learners

of the *usted* form. To statistically support this observation, a Wilcoxon signed-rank test ($W=271.5$; $p=.003$) resulted in a significant increase in the contextually correct use of *usted*. Additionally, Figure 1 shows the same increasing score rate for the two types of tasks, as indicated by the parallelism between the two lines. A Wilcoxon signed-rank result ($W=23$; $p=.340$) reveals that the L2 learners similarly increased their contextually appropriate use of *usted* in both writing and speaking.

The increased use of *tú* as shown in Figure 2 is confirmed by the Wilcoxon signed-rank test results ($W=230.5$; $p<.001$). Furthermore, a Wilcoxon signed-rank test comparing scores at T2 for writing and oral performance revealed no significant difference in the expected use of the *tú* form between the two tasks ($W=82$; $p=.776$).

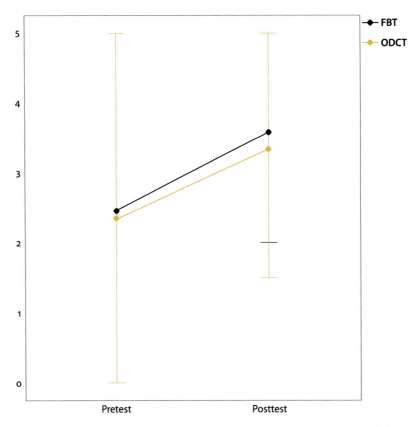

Figure 2. Use of singular forms of address *tú* throughout the semester in two different tasks by L2 learners

Even though students initially had the same low score for *vos* (for both tasks at T1, the mean score equals 0), the graph in Figure 3 suggests an increased command of *vos* particularly in the written task. A Wilcoxon signed-rank test statistically confirmed what was indicated by the graph in Figure 3 ($W=0$, $p<.001$). Regarding the use of *vos* at T2, no significant difference was observed between the written and oral tasks ($W=113.5$; $p=.992$).

Figures 4–6 shows the results for the HL learners. The use of all three forms in contextually appropriate places increased throughout the semester. More specifically, the results revealed significant increases in the use of *usted* ($W=0$; $p<.001$), *tú* ($W=0$; $p<.001$), and *vos* ($W=9$; $p=.001$) throughout the semester. There were differences found in the use of these forms depending on the type of task, written or oral. As illustrated in Figures 4–6, at the end of the semester, HL learners produced these address forms in contextually appropriate places significantly more in

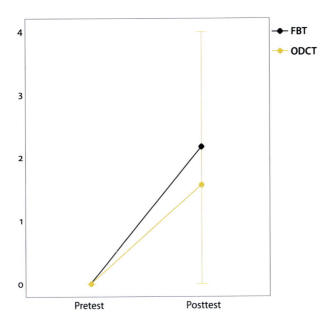

Figure 3. Use of singular forms of address *vos* throughout the Semester in two different tasks by L2 learners

the oral task compared to the written task for *usted* ($W=10.5$; $p=.046$), but not for *tú* ($W=29.5$; $p=.602$) or *vos* ($W=0$; p value $=1.00$).

To analyze differences between the L2 and HL groups, test scores for each task were visualized using boxplots for the two time periods, as shown in Figure 7. In the boxplot, the yellow color represents the performance of the HL learners throughout the semester, while the black color indicates the performance of the L2 learners.

For the *usted* form of address at the beginning of the semester, Figure 7 shows that, within the group of L2 learners, most students demonstrated a higher command than the HL learners for the written task. However, empirical analysis concluded that the two groups had the same performance ($W=393.5$; $p=.938$). They also exhibited almost the same performance in the speaking task ($W=319$; $p=.537$). This pattern persisted even at the end of the semester (T2) ($W=349.5$ and $p=.796$ in the written task; $W=314.5$ and $p=.500$ in the oral task). Both groups increased their usage of *usted* throughout the semester. Similarly, both groups showed higher usage of *usted* in the oral task compared to the written task.

Regarding the test score for *tú*, the following conclusions can be drawn. At the beginning of the semester, both groups exhibited nearly identical performance using this form of address. The statistical test results failed to reject the null

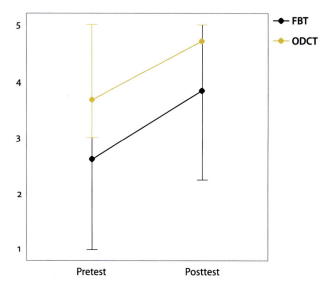

Figure 4. Use of singular forms of address *usted* throughout the semester in two different tasks by HL learners

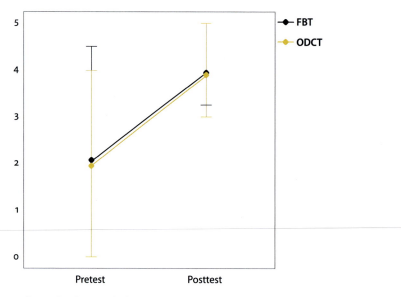

Figure 5. Use of singular forms of address *tú* throughout the semester in two different tasks by HL learners

hypothesis, which suggests that the median difference between the two groups is equal to zero. Both the written and oral tasks resulted in p values greater than .05 ($W = 353.5$, $p = .777$ in the written task; $W = 336.5$, $p = .667$ in the oral task). How-

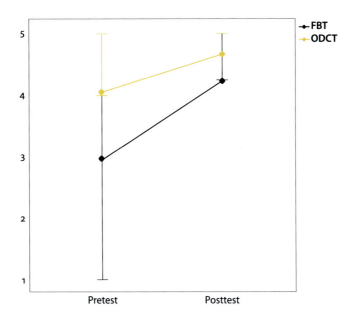

Figure 6. Use of singular forms of address *vos* throughout the semester in two different tasks by HL learners

ever, by the end of the semester (T2), the slight increase in the use of *tú* by the HL learners on both oral (ODCT) and written (FBT) tasks was not significant ($W = 281.5$, $p = .248$ in the oral task; $W = 287.5$, $p = .280$ in the written task).

Lastly, both groups of learners increased their use of *vos* throughout the semester. However, by the end of the semester, the HL learners produced significantly more *vos* forms than the L2 learners. A Wilcoxon signed-rank test was conducted to assess whether the HL group had greater usage of the correct *vos* form compared to the L2 learners. The results did support this hypothesis in both tasks, with the following outcomes in oral task: $W = 83$ and $p < .001$; and written task: $W = 132.5$ and $p < .001$.

When students were retested at the end of the semester, some increases were observed in both groups. For the L2 learners, although the usage of *vos* forms increased over time, it remained relatively low at the end of the semester, compared to the other two forms. At T2, the boxplot corresponding to *vos* is shifted downward compared to those for *tú* and *usted*. This indicates that, on average, the values for *vos* are lower than those for *tú* and *usted*. A different pattern emerged in the HL learners, where the development of the *vos* form of address revealed an increase in usage. Notably, the black boxplot for *vos* is upwardly shifted compared to the other forms.

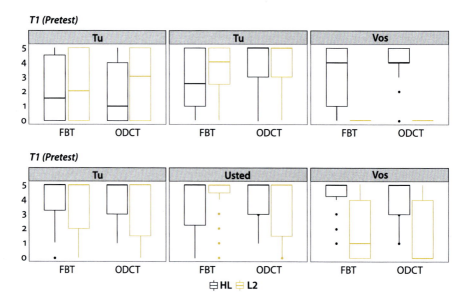

Figure 7. Use of singular forms of address produced by the L2 and HL learners by task

Discussion

Our study's examination of the pedagogical impact on the use of second-person singular forms of address — *usted, tú,* and *vos* — provides insights into language acquisition dynamics of both L2 and HL learners in Spanish language courses within Early College Programs offered to U.S. high school students. The comparison of both types of learners across a semester illuminated how Spanish instruction can influence language usage, particularly the adoption of formal and informal address forms. The results indicate a positive trajectory in the L2 and HL learners' command of all three forms of address, with a significant increase in the correct contextual use of *usted*. The upward parallel trends for *usted* in both written and oral tasks suggest that the teaching methods effectively addressed the formality aspect of the language. Similarly, the increased use of *tú* suggests enhanced familiarity and comfort with this form for the L2 and HL learners, potentially reflecting the influence of the instruction. The *vos* form, initially unfamiliar to the L2 learners, showed progress for L2 and HL learners, especially in written tasks, which could reflect the structured nature of written exercises in language learning.

Comparing the L2 learners to the HL learners, there were no significant differences in the usage of *tú*, which could be due to the fact that both groups understood from classroom instruction when and where to employ *tú*. For *usted*, the L2 learners initially showed a higher command than the HL learners in writing but the two groups were similar in speaking. Both groups improved over time, with the oral task showing more significant gains compared to the written task. Recall that in Figures 4–6, nearly every boxplot for the oral task is shifted upward from T1 to T2, suggesting that, on average, the values increased over time. This could suggest that oral practice, perhaps through conversation and direct interaction, reinforces formal address more effectively than written tasks. The *vos* form showcased the clearest distinction between participant groups. The HL learners, familiar with *vos* due to their linguistic background, consistently scored higher, suggesting that heritage exposure plays a crucial role in mastering less formally taught language aspects. The L2 learners' lower scores for *vos* at T2, despite increases, highlight the ongoing challenge *vos* presents for learners without prior exposure.

Hoffman-González (2015) observed modest increases in the use of *voseo* among a small cohort, which may have been influenced by factors such as participant fatigue, suggesting the need for careful task design in elicitation studies. Pozzi (2017) demonstrated that learners' engagement with local speech communities and their overall proficiency were instrumental in increasing the use of *voseo*. Our study's results resonate with these findings, showing a marked improvement in the use of *vos* among the L2 learners, likely due to the inclusion of classroom instruction on when, where, and how to use *vos*.

The importance of integrating sociolinguistics into language instruction was highlighted by Geeslin with Long (2014), who provided a framework for enhancing learners' sociolinguistic competence. The incorporation of sociolinguistic content in the classroom, as advocated by Loza and Beaudrie (2022), aligns with our study's approach, where a CLA pedagogy was used to inform learners about language variation and to foster their ability to use language appropriately in various contexts. The fact that the participants in the study, who were explicitly taught about *vos*, increased their use of *vos* on both tasks throughout the semester suggests that including *vos* in the curriculum can be effective.

The surveys conducted by LeLoup and Schmidt-Rinehart (2018) and the textbook analyses by Griffin (2019) and Potvin (2022) revealed the scant presence of *vos* in educational materials. Our study's implication is clear: There is a pressing need for textbooks and instructional materials to reflect the linguistic realities of the Spanish-speaking world, thereby equipping learners with a more comprehensive communicative competence (Geeslin & Hanson, 2023).

Conclusion

Summary of key findings

When examining the use of the three forms under study throughout the semester by both L2 and HL learners, the *usted* form was overused at T1, where *tú* or *vos* forms would have been more contextually appropriate. However, there was a marked increase in its appropriate use by T2, signifying increased sociolinguistic competence. Initially, the *tú* form was not employed as much as expected despite its common presence in textbooks, but at T2 there was a notable increase in its use, reflecting increased sociolinguistic competence due to it being used more frequently as expected in the context. At the outset, there appears to be a lack of or limited sociolinguistic knowledge or competence with the *vos* form, but at T2, an increased use of this form of address is found for both participant groups.

Upon comparing usage across the two task types (oral versus written), at T2, participants exhibited more appropriate use of *usted* on the ODCT and showed greater aptitude with *tú* and *vos* on the FBT. This pattern suggests that participants' sociolinguistic command is higher in the semi-spontaneous oral production, while they are still developing their sociolinguistic competence in the production of *tú* and *vos*. Conversely, results from the FBT indicate that students' sociolinguistic competence of *tú* and *vos* is higher at T2 when compared to the results from ODCT.

Study contributions

By focusing on *voseo*, seldom included in the U.S. Spanish curricula, this study addresses a critical area of the teaching of dialectal variation. It underscores the need for curricular changes that reflect the linguistic realities of the Spanish-speaking world, advocating for the inclusion of *voseo* in educational materials to prepare students for communication in diverse Spanish-speaking environments (Geeslin & Hanson, 2023). The study also provides insight into the nuanced effects of heritage exposure on language learning. It shows that HL learners maintain a slight advantage in language retention or acquisition, likely due to extracurricular exposure, which is a significant consideration for language educators (Carreira & Chik, 2018).

Limitations and future directions

The current study has some limitations that future research can take into consideration. First, while the investigation presented in this chapter paints a picture of *voseo* usage among adolescent L2 and HL learners, subsequent research could incorporate L1 monolingual Spanish data (and potentially family members from the HL participants) employing the same tasks as used in the present study. Second, further investigations could include a control group comprising students who did not receive instruction on *vos*, compared to an experimental group consisting of students who did receive explicit instruction, to assess the effect of instruction more directly. Additionally, different types of instruction could be examined to determine which approach works best for teaching awareness and use of the forms (Klee & Lacorte, 2021). Such instruction could include a series of short virtual exchanges throughout the semester with speakers who employ *vos* to determine the impact on awareness and usage of this type of activity. Finally, extending the length of data collection and testing the same participants a semester later, a year later, or even five years later would show the long-term trajectory of the development of these forms of address to determine how they change over time.

Concluding insights

In conclusion, this study confirms the positive impact of targeted pedagogy on adolescent L2 learners' grasp of dialectal variation, with significant advancements in understanding and using *usted, tú*, and *vos*. It also reveals the nuanced effects of heritage exposure and the necessity of incorporating diverse linguistic forms into language curricula (Geeslin with Long, 2014). The improvements in the L2 learners underscore the possible effectiveness of including *vos* in classroom instruction, while the sustained performance of the HL learners highlights the advantages of HL experience. The positive outcomes observed in the L2 learners point to potential benefits of a sociolinguistically informed pedagogy that embraces dialectal variation (Klee & Lacorte, 2021; Leeman, 2014, 2018; Martínez, 2003; Moreno-Fernández, 2023). This study contributes to the broader discourse in SLA, emphasizing the importance of sociolinguistic competence and the potential benefits of integrating formal education with the informal, lived experience of language. We would like to conclude with a quote related to our study that also honors the life and work of Kim Geeslin (2021), "Put simply, competent language users are not just grammatically accurate, they are situationally appropriate too" (p. 879).

References

Adamson, H., & Regan, V. (1991). The acquisition of community speech norms by Asian immigrants learning English as a second language: A preliminary study. *Studies in Second Language Acquisition, 13*(1), 1–22.

Beaudrie, S., Ducar, C., & Potowski, K. (2014). *Heritage language teaching: Research and practice*. McGraw-Hill.

Beaudrie, S., & Loza, S. (2023). *Heritage language program direction: Research into practice*. Routledge.

Benavides, C. (2003). La distribución del voseo en Hispanoamérica. *Hispania, 86*(3), 612–623.

Cameron, R. D. (2012). Why it's time to teach *voseo* and how to start. *Academic Exchange Quarterly, 16*(3), 72–77.

Cameron, R. D. (2017). Study abroad, immigration, and "voseo" in the twenty-first-century classroom. *Hispania, 100*(5), 67–73.

Canale, M., & Swain, M. (1980). Theoretical bases of communicative approaches to second language teaching and Testing. *Applied Linguistics, 1*(1), 1–47.

Carreira, M., & Chik, C. H. (2018). Differentiated teaching: A primer for heritage and mixed classes. In K. Potowski (Ed.), *The Routledge handbook of Spanish as a heritage language* (pp. 359–374). Routledge.

Carricaburo, N. (2015). *Las fórmulas de tratamiento en el español actual* (2nd ed.). Arco Libros.

Denbaum, K. (2020). Role of social interaction abroad in the L2 acquisition of sociolinguistic variation: The case of subject expression in the Dominican Republic. In D. Pascual y Cabo & I. Elola (Eds.), *Current theoretical and applied perspectives on Hispanic and Lusophone linguistics* (pp. 63–84). John Benjamins.

Denevi, M. (1955). *Rosaura a las diez*. Editorial Sudamericana.

Félix-Brasdefer, J. C. (2019). *Pragmática del español: contexto, uso y variación*. Routledge.

Geeslin, K. L. (2021). Sociolinguistic competence in second languages. In H. Mohebbi & C. Coombe (Eds.), *Research questions in language education and applied linguistics: A reference guide* (pp. 879–883). Springer.

Geeslin, K. L., Fafulas, S., & Kanwit, M. (2013). Acquiring geographically-variable norms of use: The case of the present perfect in Mexico and Spain. In C. Howe, M. Lubbers, & S. Blackwell (Eds.), *Selected proceedings of the 15th Hispanic linguistics symposium* (pp. 205–220). Cascadilla Proceedings Project.

Geeslin, K. L., García-Amaya, L. J., Hasler-Barker, M., Henriksen, N., & Killam, J. (2010). The SLA of direct object pronouns in a study abroad immersion environment where use is variable. In C. Borgonovo, M. Español-Echevarría, & P. Prévost (Eds.), *Selected proceedings of the 12th Hispanic Linguistics Symposium* (pp. 246–259). Cascadilla Proceedings Project.

Geeslin, K. L., García-Amaya, L. J., Hasler-Barker, M., Henriksen, N. C., & Killam, J. (2012). The L2 acquisition of variable perfective past time reference in Spanish in an overseas immersion setting. In K. L. Geeslin & M. Díaz-Campos (Eds.), *Selected proceedings of the 14th Hispanic Linguistics Symposium* (pp. 197–213). Cascadilla Proceedings Project.

Geeslin, K. L., & Garrett, J. (2018). Variationist research methods and the analysis of second language data in the study abroad context. In C. Sanz & A. Morales-Front (Eds.), *The Routledge handbook of study abroad research and practice* (pp. 17–35). Routledge.

Geeslin, K. L., & Hanson, S. (2023). Sociolinguistic approaches to communicative competence. In M. Kanwit & M. Solon (Eds.), *Communicative competence in a second language: Theory, method, and applications* (pp. 40–59). Routledge.

Geeslin, K. L., with Long, A. Y. (2014). *Sociolinguistics and second language acquisition: Learning to use language in context*. Routledge.

George, A. (2018). The development of regional morphosyntactic features by learners of Spanish in a study abroad setting: The case of *vosotros*. *Hispanic Studies Review, 3*(1), 101–125.

George, A. (2019). Study abroad homestay versus dormitory: Extralinguistic factors and regional features. *Spanish in Context, 16*(1), 77–103.

George, A., & Salgado-Robles, F. (2021). The long-term impact of a sojourn abroad by heritage language learners of Spanish: The case of *vosotros* vs. *ustedes*. In R. Pozzi, C. Escalante, & T. Quan (Eds.), *Heritage speakers of Spanish in study abroad* (pp. 33–50). Routledge.

Griffin, M. (2019). Evidencias a favor de la enseñanza del voseo en las clases de español. *Spanish and Portuguese Review, 5*, 45–56.

Hoffman-González, A. C. (2015). *Language use or non-use in study abroad as an indicator of community membership* [Unpublished doctoral dissertation]. University of Wisconsin-Madison.

Imagined-with AI. (2023). [Artificial intelligence system]. https://imagined-with.ai/

Kanwit, M., & Solon, M. (2013). Acquiring variation in future time expression abroad in Spain and Mexico. In J. Cabrelli Amaro, G. Lord, A. Prada Pérez, & J. E. Aaron (Eds.), *Selected proceedings of the 16th Hispanic Linguistics Symposium* (pp. 206–222). Cascadilla Proceedings Project.

Kingsbury, K. C. (2011). *Rosaura a las diez en el aula*: La gramática a través de la literatura. *Hispania, 94*(2), 329–347.

Klee, C. A., & Lacorte, M. (2021). La sociolingüística en la enseñanza del español como lengua segunda y lengua de herencia. *Journal of Spanish Language Teaching, 8*(2), 182–194.

Labov, W. (1966). *The social stratification of English in New York City*. Center for Applied Linguistics.

Leeman, J. (2014). Critical approaches to teaching Spanish as a local/foreign language. In M. Lacorte (Ed.), *Routledge handbook of Hispanic applied linguistics* (pp. 275–292). Routledge.

Leeman, J. (2018). Critical language awareness and Spanish as a heritage language: Challenging the linguistic subordination of US Latinxs. In K. Potowski (Ed.), *The Routledge handbook of Spanish as a heritage language* (pp. 345–358). Routledge.

LeLoup, J. W., & Schmidt-Rinehart, B. C. (2018). Forms of address in the Spanish language curriculum in the United States: Actualities and aspirations. *Hispania, 101*(1), 10–24.

Linford, B. G. (2016). *The second-language development of dialect-specific morpho-syntactic variation in Spanish during study abroad* [Unpublished doctoral dissertation]. Indiana University.

Linford, B., Zahler, S., & Whatley, M. (2018). Acquisition, study abroad and individual differences: The case of subject pronoun variation in L2 Spanish. *Study Abroad in Second Language Acquisition and International Education*, 3(2), 243–274.

Loza, S., & Beaudrie, S. (Eds.). (2022). *Heritage language teaching: Critical language awareness perspectives for research and pedagogy*. Routledge.

Martínez, G. (2003). Classroom based dialect awareness in heritage language instruction: A critical applied linguistic approach. *Heritage Language Journal*, 1(1), 44–57.

Moreno-Fernández, F. (2023). *Las variedades de la lengua española y su enseñanza* (3rd ed.). Arco Libros.

Morgan, T.A., López-Alonzo, K., Potowski, K., & Ramos, Z. (2017, July). El primer y único censo del voseo. Presented at the XVIII Congreso Internacional de la Asociación de Lingüística y Filología de América Latina, Universidad Nacional de Colombia, Bogotá, Colombia.

Pearson, L. (2006). Teaching Spanish dialectology with digital audio technology. *Hispania*, 89(2), 323–330.

Potvin, C. (2022). Tuteo, voseo y ustedeo en los manuales de ELE: Estado de la cuestión. *MarcoELE: Revista de Didáctica Español Lengua Extranjera*, 34, 1–22.

Pozzi, R. (2017). The acquisition of regional features during a semester abroad in Buenos Aires, Argentina [Unpublished doctoral dissertation]. University of California, Davis.

Pozzi, R. (2021). Learner development of a morphosyntactic feature in Argentina: The case of *vos*. *Languages*, 6, 1–18.

Pozzi, R., Escalante, C., & Quan, T. (2023). "Being Myself in Spanish": A heritage speaker's evolving pragmatic choices and awareness during study abroad. *Study Abroad Research in Second Language Acquisition and International Education*, 8(2), 230–259.

Quesada-Pacheco, M.A. (2023). El español en las repúblicas centroamericanas. In F. Moreno-Fernández & R. Caravedo (Eds.), *Dialectología hispánica: The Routledge handbook of Spanish dialectology* (pp. 371–382). Routledge.

R Core Team. (2024). *R: A language and environment for statistical computing*. R Foundation for Statistical Computing.

Reynolds-Case, A. (2013). The value of short-term study abroad: An increase in students' cultural and pragmatic competency. *Foreign Language Annals*, 42(2), 311–322.

Ringer-Hilfinger, K. (2013). The acquisition of sociolinguistic variation by study abroad students: The case of American students in Madrid [Unpublished doctoral dissertation]. University at Albany–State University of New York.

Salgado-Robles, F. (2011). The acquisition of sociolinguistic variation by learners of Spanish in a study abroad context [Unpublished doctoral dissertation]. University of Florida.

Salgado-Robles, F. (2014). Los efectos del aprendizaje-servicio en la adquisición de la variación regional por aprendices de español en un contexto de inmersión: El caso del leísmo vallisoletano. *Revista Electrónica de Lingüística Aplicada*, 1, 233–258.

Salgado-Robles, F. (2017). Los efectos del contexto educativo en el desarrollo del uso del pronombre personal sujeto en español como segunda lengua. *Revista Internacional de Lenguas Extranjeras*, 7, 85–119.

Salgado-Robles, F. (2018). *Desarrollo de la competencia sociolingüística por aprendices de español en un contexto de inmersión en el extranjero*. Peter Lang.

Salgado-Robles, F. (2020). Relación entre tipo de programa académico en el extranjero, competencia intercultural y adquisición del leísmo por aprendices de español como lengua de herencia. In P. Taboada-de-Zúñiga Romero & R. Barros Romero (Eds.), *Actas del XXIX Congreso Internacional de ASELE: Perfiles, factores y contextos en la enseñanza y el aprendizaje de ELE/EL2* (pp. 1013–1026). Santiago de Compostela University Press.

Salgado-Robles, F., & George, A. (2019). The sociolinguistic impact of service-learning on heritage learners sojourning in Spain: *Vosotros* versus *ustedes*. *Heritage Language Journal*, 16(1), 71–98.

Salgado-Robles, F., & George, A. (2023). Relationship between external factors and development of regional variation (*vosotros* vs. *ustedes*) by L2 learners of Spanish in Spain. In S. L. Zahler, A. Y. Long, & B. Linford (Eds.), *Study abroad and the second language acquisition of sociolinguistic variation in Spanish* (pp. 20–53). John Benjamins.

Shenk, E. (2014). Teaching sociolinguistic variation in the intermediate language classroom: *Voseo* in Latin America. *Hispania*, 97(3), 368–381.

Uber, D. R. (2008). Creo que entiendo el uso de *tú, usted, ustedes*, y *vosotros*. Pero, ¿qué hago con *vos*? In J. Ewald & A. Edstrom (Eds.), *El español a través de la lingüística: Preguntas y respuestas* (pp. 50–60). Cascadilla Press.

U.S. Census Bureau. (2023). 2023 Census of Population: The Hispanic Population. Retrieved from https://www.census.gov/quickfacts/fact/table/US/RHI725219

Whatley, M. (2013). The acquisition of past tense variation by L2 learners of Spanish in an abroad context. In J. Cabrelli Amaro, G. Lord, A. Prada Pérez, & J. E. Aaron (Eds.), *Selected proceedings of the 16th Hispanic linguistics symposium* (pp. 190–205). Cascadilla Proceedings Project.

CHAPTER 10

Acquisition of sociolinguistic variation
The case of filled pauses in L2 Spanish

Megan Solon, Travis Evans-Sago & Kaitlin Moen
Indiana University | Graded – The American School of São Paulo | University at Albany, SUNY

This study explored filled pauses in second language (L2) Spanish from a sociolinguistic perspective. Eighty-two L2 learners and seven native Spanish speakers were recorded during three brief monologic tasks. Filled pauses ($K = 2{,}707$) were identified, labeled as lexical or phonological, and coded for several linguistic factors. Measurements for duration and formant values were taken from phonological filled pauses. The data underwent two stages of analysis: (1) examining the choice between phonological and lexical pauses and (2) analyses for each type. Results indicated an increase in lexical filled pauses and a shift in the vocalic quality of phonological filled pauses at higher learner proficiency levels. This research contributes new information to our overall understanding of L2 sociolinguistic variation and its development.

Keywords: filled pauses, lexical fillers, sociophonetic variation, *um*, L2 variation

Acquisition of sociolinguistic variation: The case of filled pauses in L2 Spanish

Filled pauses are hesitation phenomena in speech marked by the insertion of lexical or phonological elements. Lexical pauses involve the use of filler words such as *well, you know, I mean,* or *like* in English or *bueno* 'ok', *entonces* 'so/then', *pues* 'well', *como* 'like', *o sea* 'I mean', and *este* 'this' in Spanish. Phonological filled pauses include non-lexical elements, such as *um, uh, em,* and *eh*.[1] Research on

---

[1]. Regarding nomenclature, the present study aligns with Erker and Bruso (2017) in adopting the term "filled pauses" to encompass both lexical and phonological elements and in distinguishing between lexical filled pauses and phonological filled pauses. Laserna et al. (2014), in contrast, describe a category "filler words," which include discourse markers (lexical) and filled

filled pauses in second language (L2) speech has typically focused on the relationship between filled pauses and fluency in the L2 (e.g., Freed et al., 2004; García-Amaya, 2015; Lennon, 1990; Towell et al., 1996). In contrast, recent first language (L1) sociolinguistic research has focused on the potential of studying filled pauses to enhance our understanding of sociolinguistic phenomena and processes, such as contact-induced change (i.e., innovation resulting from the interaction of two or more languages; Erker & Bruso, 2017; Michnowicz et al., 2023; see also Fruehwald, 2016). The present study combines these two lines of inquiry, adopting a sociolinguistic approach to the study of L2 Spanish filled pauses to explore whether investigating the use of filled pauses in L2 speech can contribute to our understanding of the acquisition of sociolinguistic and, particularly, sociophonetic variation in the L2.

Existing research on sociophonetic variation in the production of L2 Spanish has predominantly focused on phonetic phenomena that are regionally constrained but not typically socially variable (e.g., use of /θ/; Ringer-Hilfinger, 2012), or on socially constrained and perhaps stigmatized aspects of phonetic variation (e.g., /s/ weakening, Geeslin & Gudmestad, 2008). Findings often indicate very little adoption of regional and non-standard variants (e.g., 2.8% /θ/ use overall in Ringer-Hilfinger, 2012; only five of 130 learners exhibiting any /s/ weakening in Geeslin & Gudmestad, 2008), even among learners who have spent significant time abroad or who possess extensive L2 experience (though see an exception in learners' adoption of Buenos Aires *sheísmo/zheísmo* in Pozzi & Bayley, 2021). The present study aimed to investigate whether filled pauses, considered "intrinsic component[s] of natural speech" (Erker & Bruso, 2017, p. 205) that are also systematically variable, can provide an additional, rich context for the study of L2 sociolinguistic and sociophonetic acquisition.

Background

Filled pauses, such as *uh* and *um*, have garnered significant attention in linguistic research. Chomsky (1965) regarded these phenomena as performance errors unrelated to linguistic knowledge. This stance was challenged by empirical studies like Goldman-Eisler (1968), which acknowledged the value of filled pauses in contributing to our understanding of linguistic performance. Later, Schegloff et al. (1977) argued that filled pauses, alongside related phenomena such as self-

---

pauses (phonological). Readers may also see Clark and Fox Tree (2002) and Kosmala and Crible (2021) for more about the debate regarding the lexical or non-lexical status of "phonological" filled pauses.

repairs, are integral components of language, governed by linguistic principles and conventionalized patterns. Clark and Fox Tree (2002) further refined this perspective by proposing that *uh* and *um* in English serve as intentional signals of speech planning and/or performance difficulties, with *uh* typically signaling minor delays and *um* indicating more substantial ones. Corpus-based evidence reinforced filled pauses' function as deliberate "signals, not symptoms" of speech performance (Clark & Fox Tree, 2002, p. 104).

Production-based evidence from Dutch and Japanese has highlighted filled pauses as markers of discourse transitions and indicators of complex content. Swerts (1998) explored how Dutch speakers strategically employ filled pauses to manage discourse structure, highlighting their role beyond mere hesitation markers. Watanabe et al. (2004) established a noteworthy correlation between the presence of filled pauses and the number of lexically rich items in Japanese clauses, suggesting that filled pauses serve as cues for the presence of more complex linguistic content. From a listener-oriented perspective, Fox Tree (2001) examined how *uh* and *um* affect word recognition in English and Dutch, finding *uh* to enhance word recognition, while *um* did not exhibit the same effect. Psycholinguistic studies (e.g., Corley et al., 2007) have further demonstrated that specific filled pauses, like *er*, reduce processing difficulty for less predictable words and enhance memory retention. Moreover, Watanabe et al. (2008) showed that pauses, regardless of type, improve responsiveness among Japanese listeners, particularly with more complex descriptions.

Thus, L1 research has shown that filled pauses serve a crucial function in both the production and comprehension of language. They signal speech planning, mark transition to complex content, and aid comprehension across different linguistic contexts. This study builds upon prior research to advance our understanding of how filled pauses function within language, aiming to contribute new insights into their (variable) form and patterns of usage, particularly for L2 learners.

L2 filled pauses

In the field of second language acquisition (SLA), research on filled pauses has often centered on their relationship to speaker fluency and proficiency. For instance, hesitation phenomena have been used as measures of oral fluency by analyzing metrics such as the number of words spoken without disfluencies (Freed et al., 2004) or the frequency of filled pauses per speech turn and the ratio of filled pauses to syllables (García-Amaya, 2009). Research on L2 pause patterns has found that more proficient learners tend to use fewer unfilled pauses (Shea & Leonard, 2019) and that increased frequency and duration of pauses in speech can lead to perceptions of reduced fluency (Pinget et al., 2014). García-Amaya (2015), however, offered an alternative perspective on the connection between filled pauses and language development. His study, which examined L2 learners of Spanish in at-home and immersion contexts, found that as learners advanced to using more complex syntactic structures and speaking at faster rates, their use of filled pauses actually increased. This finding challenges the view that filled pauses merely indicate level of fluency and suggests they may instead (or also) reflect developmental stages in language acquisition.

Finally, specifically related to L2 Spanish filled pauses, one study has also explored their phonetic form. Machuca (2022) examined vocalic fillers used by learners of Spanish whose L1s (English, French, and Russian) have vocalic fillers that are distinct from what her study assumed as the most common vocalic filler in Spanish — [e]. Machuca first categorized vocalic fillers as /e/-like or not /e/-like. She then extracted first and second formant (F1 and F2) values from the midpoint of all identified vocalic fillers — both /e/-like and non-/e/-like. She found that, across all three learner L1 backgrounds, advanced learners used a higher percentage of (L1 Spanish-like) /e/ fillers than intermediate-level learners. She also found that, across all three L1 background groups, formant values of learners' Spanish fillers categorized as /e/ matched those of the L1 Spanish speakers. However, formant values of non-/e/ fillers differed by L1 background. Taken together, the findings suggest that learners' filled pause patterns reflect L1 norms and also that, as L2 proficiency increases, learners' Spanish filled pauses more closely resemble those of L1 Spanish speakers.

In sum, research on L2 filled pauses has primarily employed pauses as a metric for operationalizing L2 fluency; the relationship between L2 proficiency and pausing behavior has also been explored. In Spanish, specifically, some work has explored the vocalic properties of L2 Spanish realizations (and suggested that the acoustic properties of filled pauses more closely approximate those of L1 Spanish speakers at higher L2 proficiencies). Nevertheless, L2 filled pause research to date has largely ignored a growing body of sociolinguistic research that documents the inherent and systematic variability of filled pause behavior. The present study aims to combine L2 and sociolinguistic perspectives to examines whether L2 filled pauses are a fruitful locus of investigation for understanding the acquisition of L2 sociolinguistic (and, specifically, sociophonetic) variation. We next turn to existing research on filled pauses from a sociolinguistic perspective.

Sociolinguistic perspectives on filled pauses

Sociolinguistic research has revealed that filled pause use is shaped by linguistic and social factors. Fruehwald (2016) documented generational shifts in English filled pause patterns, with *um* replacing *uh*. Gender- and age-related effects have also been identified for filled pause patterns. Liberman (2014), analyzing the Fisher Corpus, observed that men preferred *uh*, whereas women favored *um*, with usage rates varying based on the conversation partner's gender. Laserna et al. (2014) found an age effect for both lexical and phonological fillers in spontaneous speech recorded in the daily lives of participants. However, gender effects were observed only for lexical fillers, with young speakers and women as well as young women exhibiting greater rates of use of lexical fillers. Tottie (2011, 2014) demonstrated variation in *uh* and *um* usage between American and British English, with higher rates of these filled pauses observed in the speech of British English speakers, particularly among older, upper-class speakers in non-private settings.

In Spanish, Soler Arechalde (2008) found that *este* production in Mexico City speech is constrained by context and gender, as it is produced more frequently in informal contexts and by women speakers. In a cross-city analysis of the use of *este* versus *eh* in four varieties of Spanish, Graham (2018) found rates of *este* use above 60% in Mexico City, San Juan, and Montevideo, while speakers in Medellín used *este* in only 3% of relevant contexts. He also found that the choice between *este* and *eh* was influenced by factors such as speakers' age, level of education, and gender as well as the position of the filled pause in the turn and that the influence of these factors differed across Spanish varieties. Graham asserted that uses of these markers can often be viewed as "strategies of cultural self-identification" (p. 2).

Erker and Bruso (2017) adopted an exploratory, variationist approach to investigate possible effects of language contact on pausing behavior among Mexican and Peruvian Spanish speakers in Boston. Adopting a broad definition of filled pause — including both lexical and non-lexical or phonological elements — Erker and Bruso explored filled pause patterns across speaker groups and examined the influence of numerous factors. Notably, they found that speakers of Mexican Spanish in Boston preferred lexical filled pauses (e.g., *este, como*), whereas Peruvian Spanish speakers in Boston preferred phonological filled pauses (e.g., *eh, em*). Additionally, speakers with more extensive experience living in the United States, more frequent English use, and higher self-perception of English proficiency exhibited phonological filled pauses that shifted towards increased use of centralized variants, such as *a(m)* and *uh(m)*, at the expense of *eh(m)*. Erker and Bruso's study, as well as more recent studies also examining bilingual filled pause behavior from a sociolinguistic perspective (e.g., Michnowicz et al., 2023), serve as a model and point of departure for a similar broad and exploratory look at filled pauses in L2 Spanish from a variationist perspective. Variation in L2 hesitation phenomena offers an intriguing avenue to explore the intersection of sociolinguistics and SLA. By investigating L2 Spanish filled pause use through a variationist lens, this study takes a first step in understanding whether and how learners may systematically vary lexical and phonological filled pauses in their L2, what contextual factors may constrain L2 pausing behavior, and the ways in which such patterns compare to those of other bilingual speakers of the target language with differing backgrounds.

Present study

The present study explores the overarching question of whether filled pause use can provide insight into the acquisition of sociolinguistic (and particularly sociophonetic) variation. More specifically, in line with the exploratory approach of Erker and Bruso (2017), we examine the use of filled pauses in L2 Spanish, guided by the following research questions:

1. With what frequency do L2 learners use lexical and phonological filled pauses, and what factors influence L2 Spanish learners' choice between lexical and phonological filled pauses?
2. What lexical filled pauses are used by L2 Spanish learners and with what frequency?
3. What are the characteristics of phonological filled pauses used by L2 Spanish learners, and what factors condition their form?

We also compare L2 Spanish filled pause patterns to that of a small sample of bilingual L1 speakers of Spanish from the same institutional context to provide a point of reference (in addition to that provided by previous research on L1 Spanish filled pause behavior) against which to compare and understand L2 patterns. To be clear, we do not consider this L1 group or their pausing patterns to represent the L2 group's target, but we do believe that they offer a helpful metric to understand how the Spanish pausing patterns of L2 Spanish speakers compare to those of other speakers of Spanish.[2]

---

2. For further discussion of the caveats of L1 comparison groups, see Ortega (2013).

Method

Participants

A total of 89 participants, recruited from three US universities, completed the requisite tasks for the present study. The 82 L2 learners of Spanish were recruited from Spanish language courses ranging from first-semester basic language through graduate levels as well as from Spanish instructors at these locations. These participants were divided into three proficiency levels using cluster analysis based on their performance on a Spanish elicited imitation task (EIT) as described in more detail in the next subsection; for ease of exposition, we will refer to these L2 proficiency levels as low, mid, and high. Table 1 summarizes the EIT score and language learning characteristics of these three learner groups.

Table 1. Summary of participants' language background by proficiency group

L2 proficiency group	n	M EIT score (out of 144)	Course level[a]	M age of onset	M months immersion
Low	24	23.92 (SD=11.61, range=5–47)	1.46 (SD=0.51)	15.38 (SD=9.92)	0.05 (SD=0.10)
Mid	27	77.30 (SD=13.52; range=53–102)	3.22 (SD=1.12)	12.48 (SD=2.99)	1.74 (SD=4.48)
High	31	123.19 (SD=10.64; range=107–143)	5.32 (SD=0.87)	12.03 (SD=3.70)	10.63 (SD=8.52)
Total	82	79.02 (SD=42.27; range: 5–143)	3.5 (SD=1.81)	13.16 (SD=6.16)	4.61 (SD=7.49)

a. For course level, 1=100-level class, 2=200-level class, 3=300-level class, 4=400-level class, 5=graduate coursework, 6=beyond graduate coursework

Data were also collected from seven native speakers of Spanish (all of whom were also bilingual in English) attending or working at the same US universities as the L2 participants. These participants ranged in age from 25–40 years old (M age=31.29; SD=5.28) and were from a variety of regional and national origins (i.e., Argentine, Chilean, Colombian, Mexican, Puerto Rican, and Spanish). These data were collected to provide a point of comparison against which to understand L2 pausing behavior. This comparison both provides readers without knowledge of L1 Spanish pausing patterns a baseline point of reference but also responds to Ortega's (2013) call for SLA to reach across disciplinary boundaries and contribute, for example, to the larger discussion of human language by providing a picture of late bi/multilingualism, here with reference to other bilingual speakers of the same two languages but with differing language learning backgrounds.

Tasks and procedures

All participants completed a background questionnaire, the Spanish EIT previously mentioned, and three oral production tasks. The background questionnaire asked participants about several demographic characteristics and their language backgrounds. A summary of participant information elicited from the background questionnaire was provided in Table 1.

As an independent measure of language proficiency, participants completed Solon et al.'s (2019) extended version of Bowden's (2016) and Ortega et al.'s (1999) 30-item Spanish EIT. For this task, participants listened to and repeated 36 unrelated Spanish sentences that ranged in length from 7–27 syllables. The sentences, which increased in length as the task progressed, were presented aurally, one at a time. Each sentence was followed by a 2-second pause and then a ringtone to cue participants to repeat exactly what they heard. Participants were audio-recorded during the task, and repetitions were then scored using a 5-point rubric (Ortega, 2000) ranging from 0 (Silence, unintelligible content, or only one content word) to 4 (Perfect repetition), with a focus on the re-creation of meaning. Thus, scores on the EIT ranged from 0 to a possible maximum of 144.

Finally, participants completed three short oral production prompts. For each one, students were given a context and topic on which to talk as well as a suggested time for preparation and for speaking. For example, the first prompt instructed participants in this way:

> Your school newspaper is doing a story on how students spend their time during the week, and you've been asked to give a short interview. Take 30 seconds to think about your answer and then give the interviewer a response (~1 minute) in which you describe what you do on a typical weekday during the school year.

After completing the first prompt, students progressed to the second (involving giving their opinion to a friend trying to make a tough decision) and third (in which participants recounted the events of a neighborhood running race to someone who missed the event using pictures).[3] All prompts involved imaginary interlocutors but were completed in monologic form using written instructions. Participants were audio recorded throughout the completion of the oral production task.

---

3. The oral production task was designed for a different study, for which the data were originally collected. For the present study, no differences in filled pause behavior were hypothesized or anticipated between the three prompts. Thus, prompt was not included as a variable of interest in the statistical analyses reported in this chapter.

Coding and analysis

To code our data, we first identified the variable context following Erker and Bruso (2017). The variable context was defined as including both lexical (e.g., *bueno, este, como*) and phonological forms (e.g., *um, uh, eh*) used to fill a pause. As Erker and Bruso (2017, p.218) contend, although these forms are not variants of one underlying phonetic representation or lexical item, from a functional perspective, they are "variable ways of saying the same thing" (Labov, 1978, p.6) or functionally equivalent (Sankoff & Thibault, 1981). In these contexts, their function is to communicate that the speaker intends to hold the floor (e.g., sending a message akin to 'Hold on, I'm thinking'). Erker and Bruso also contend that, when used for this turn-extending function, these forms tend to share certain properties including that they are "semantically and syntactically independent from the surrounding utterance" and that they "tend to contain at least one vowel that is relatively long in duration and spectrally stable" (p.218). Figure 1 demonstrates the difference between the lexical item *y* 'and', when used for its standard function as a conjunction (the first instance marked on the 2nd tier in the text grid) and when it is used as a filled pause (the second instance, marked with _FP). The second instance of *y*—that is, *y* used as a lexical filled pause — has a visually noticeable longer duration and is set off from the surrounding utterance.

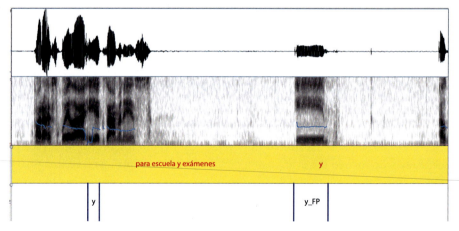

Figure 1. Spectrographic illustration of y used as a conjunction and y used as a filled pause

All data were coded by the first and third authors.[4] Using Praat (Boersma & Weenink, 2018), we identified and marked all filled pauses and coded each for filled pause type (lexical or phonological) as well as position with respect to the word (word internal versus at word boundary) and position with respect to the utterance (utterance internal versus at utterance boundary). We also measured the duration of each filled pause as well as the time or delay after the filled pause until speech continued. For phonological filled pauses, we further coded each case categorically according to the vocalic portion (e.g., *uh* vs. *eh*, determined auditorily), and coded each case according to whether it was only a vowel or also included a nasal component (e.g., *uh* or *eh* vs. *um* or *em*). Finally, formant measurements were taken from the midpoint of each vocalic portion using a script in Praat; settings included a window length of 0.025 s for all tokens and five formants estimated under 5500 Hz for women and under 5000 Hz for men.[5]

Given the exploratory nature of the present study, we describe the data descriptively to examine filled pause behavior in various ways. We used logistic mixed models to explore the factors constraining the use of a lexical versus a phonological filled pause and the choice between only a vocalic filled pause (e.g., *uh*) versus a vocalic pause with a nasal component (e.g., *um*). Linear mixed models were used to examine more closely the relationship between various factors and the acoustic realization (i.e., formant values) of phonological filled pauses.

---

4. Prior to initiating coding, the first and third researchers established a clear coding procedure and met to confer about coding practices and review coding examples. A subset of the data was then coded by both coders who met to review coding and discuss all discrepancies. Following this, the data were divided and coded by the two researchers.

5. We chose not to normalize the vowel measurements for several reasons, the principal one being that the main purpose of this acoustical analysis was to explore the production qualities of these filled pauses separate from any categorical analysis. That is, we saw the classification of these productions into *eh* and *uh* categories as a first step at exploring how these speakers fill pauses phonologically. This second step was meant to explore the phonological data in a "rawer" sense, without applying vowel categories to the data (which is required for normalization in, for example, the NORM suite, Thomas & Kendall, 2007). We do acknowledge that these data, thus, have not been adjusted to account for physiological differences in, for example, speaker vocal tract size. While this is a limitation, we believe that the extraction of the formant data using gender-specific settings and the inclusion of participant as a random factor in our statistical models help to mitigate some of the participant-specific variation that normalization addresses.

Results

In total, the participants produced 2,707 filled pauses across the three narrative tasks. Table 2 provides a summary of filled pause use across speaker level.

Table 2. Summary of filled pause use by participant group

Level/Group	k	M FPs/participant	M Time on task (min)	M FP/minute
Low	527	21.96 (SD=26.28; range=1–107)	3.96 (SD=1.95; range=0.63–9.21)	4.96 (SD=3.80; range=0.75–12.16)
Mid	938	34.74 (SD=15.59; range=7–64)	4.23 (SD=0.84; range=2.72–5.97)	8.19 (SD=3.14; range=1.77–12.49)
High	1078	34.77 (SD=19.79; range=2–83)	4.26 (SD=1.29; range=2.81–9.83)	8.25 (SD=4.15; range=0.57–18.01)
NS	164	23.43 (SD=18.68; range=3–56)	3.84 (SD=1.67; range=1.57–6.44)	6.06 (SD=3.37; range=0.94–10.07)

Note. FP = filled pause; NS = native (L1 Spanish) speaker.

Lexical versus phonological filled pause use

To explore our first research question, we examined learners' use of lexical versus phonological filled pauses. Table 3 summarizes the number and percentage of filled pauses of each type by speaker level or group.

Table 3. Number and percentage of lexical versus phonological filled pause use by group

Level/Group	Lexical FP k	Lexical FP %	Phonological FP k	Phonological FP %	Total FP
Low	71	13.47	456	86.53	527
Mid	172	18.34	766	81.66	938
High	221	20.50	857	79.50	1078
NS	53	32.32	111	67.68	164

As can be seen in Table 3, all speaker groups filled pauses with phonological fillers (e.g., *um, eh*) more often than with lexical fillers (e.g., *como, entonces*). As learner level increased, so too did the percentage of filled pauses that were lexical (increasing from 13.5% at the low level to 20.5% at the high learner level). However, each learner group, descriptively, preferred phonological filled pauses at a higher rate than did the L1 Spanish speaker group.

We next considered how many speakers at each level used each filled pause type. Table 4 summarizes the number and percentage of speakers at each level who used both lexical and phonological filled pauses, those who used only lexical filled pauses, and those who used only phonological filled pauses.

Table 4. Number and percentage of participants who used each type of filled pause by level

Level/Group	Use both n	Use both %	Lexical FPs only n	Lexical FPs only %	Phon FPs only n	Phon FPs only %
Low ($n=24$)	16	66.67	1	4.17	7	29.17
Mid ($n=27$)	24	88.89	0	0	3	11.11
High ($n=31$)	31	100	0	0	0	0
NS ($n=7$)	7	100	0	0	0	0

As can be seen in Table 4, at each level, most speakers used both lexical and phonological filled pauses. Nevertheless, nearly 30% of low-level learners used only phonological filled pauses (e.g., *um, eh*). This rate decreased to 11% of mid-level learners. At the high learner level and in the native speaker group, all speakers employed both lexical and phonological filled pauses in their speech.

Next, to explore the role of several predictors in the choice between a lexical and a phonological filled pause, we ran a logistic mixed effects model using the glmerMod function in R (R Core Team, 2023). The filled pause type (lexical vs. phonological) was the dependent variable. We considered the following fixed effects: speaker group/level, position with respect to the word, position with respect to the utterance, duration, and delay until speech continues as well as interactions between speaker group/level and all other fixed effects. However, position with respect to the word and its interaction with speaker group/level were removed from the model due to an extreme imbalance in the sample (with very few filled pause tokens occurring word internally). Participant was entered as a random effect. Table 5 summarizes the model output, predicting use of a lexical filled pause.

As shown in Table 5, the model showed significant main effects for level and position with respect to the utterance. Mid-level learners were significantly more likely to produce a phonological filled pause as compared to the L1 Spanish group (the reference category) and a phonological filled pause was significantly more likely utterance internally than at utterance boundaries. Several factors exhibited interaction effects with speaker group/level in predicting the choice between a lexical or a phonological filled pause. For the mid-level group, the odds of pro-

Table 5. Results of logistic mixed effect model predicting use of lexical versus phonological filled pause (reference category: Lexical)

Effect	Estimate	SE	95% CE	z	p
(Intercept)	1.44	0.71	[0.05, 2.81]	2.04	.042
Level					
NS	Reference				
Low	0.50	0.87	[−1.20, 2.20]	0.58	.564
Mid	1.92	0.80	[0.25, 3.50]	2.39	.017
High	−0.10	0.76	[−1.60, 1.39]	−0.14	.892
Position: Utterance					
Utterance boundary	Reference				
Utterance internal	1.50	0.44	[0.64, 2.35]	3.41	<.001
Duration (continuous)	−1.49	0.96	[−3.37, 0.39]	−1.55	.121
Delay until speech continues (continuous)	−0.14	0.44	[−1.00, 0.73]	−0.31	.757
Low Level × Duration	0.41	1.21	[−1.95, 2.77]	0.34	.757
Mid Level × Duration	−2.80	1.11	[−4.98, −0.62]	−2.52	.012
High Level × Duration	0.39	1.05	[−1.68, 2.46]	0.37	.713
Low Level × Utterance internal	1.18	0.69	[−0.18, 2.53]	1.70	.089
Mid Level × Utterance internal	1.46	0.62	[0.25, 2.67]	2.36	.018
High Level × Utterance internal	−0.02	0.51	[−.1.01, 0.97]	−0.04	.969
Low Level × Delay until speech continues	0.12	0.45	[−0.76, 0.99]	0.26	0.80
Mid Level × Delay until speech continues	0.18	0.45	[−0.71, 1.06]	0.39	.696
High Level × Delay until speech continues	0.77	0.50	[−0.21, 1.75]	1.55	.121
Random effect	Variance	SD	N		
Participant	0.83	0.91	89		

N = 2685, AIC = 2201.2

ducing a phonological filled pause (as opposed to a lexical filled pause) increased by 4.31 times (that is, exp(1.46)) when the pause was utterance internal as compared to when the pause was at an utterance boundary. Although phonological filled pauses were preferred over lexical filled pauses both at utterance boundaries and in utterance-internal position, lexical filled pauses (when used) were more likely to occur at utterance boundaries. To visualize this pattern, Figure 2 presents the proportion of lexical filled pause use in filled pauses at utterance boundaries versus in utterance-internal position by speaker group. Although all four speaker groups show similar patterns (with higher rates of lexical filled pause use at utterance boundaries than utterance internally), this interaction, as compared to the L1 Spanish speaker reference group, was only significant for the mid-level group.

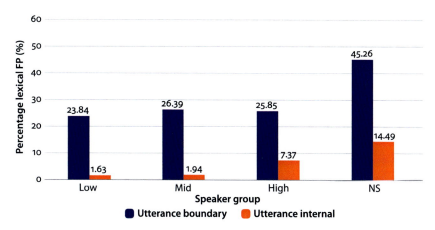

Figure 2. Percentage of lexical filled pause use utterance internally versus at utterance boundary by group

The mid-level group also exhibited a significant interaction for duration: As filled pause duration increased, the odds that mid-level learners would produce a phonological filled pause decreased; that is, longer filled pauses were more likely to be lexical in nature. Table 6 summarizes the duration of lexical and phonological filled pauses by speaker group.

Table 6. Mean duration (in seconds) of lexical and phonological filled pauses for each speaker group

Speaker group	Duration (s) of lexical FPs M (SD)	Duration (s) of phonological FPs M (SD)
Low	0.56 (0.14)	0.50 (0.20)
Mid	0.65 (0.24)	0.49 (0.19)
High	0.54 (0.25)	0.51 (0.19)
NS	0.57 (0.23)	0.48 (0.21)

As shown in Table 6, at each level, lexical filled pauses were longer in duration than phonological filled pauses, although this interaction effect was only significant for learners at the mid level.

Lexical filled pauses

Having explored the choice between a lexical and a phonological filled pause, our next research question asked specifically about lexical filled pause use. We explored what lexical items were used by our speakers to fill pauses and with what frequency. In total, eight lexical filled pauses were employed by our speaker sample: *bueno* 'OK', *como* 'like', *entonces* 'so', *este* 'this', *o* 'or', *o sea* 'I mean', *pues* 'well', and *y* 'and'. Figure 3 offers a visual display of the lexical filled pauses used by each speaker group.

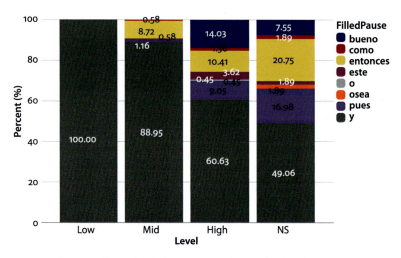

Figure 3. Distribution of lexical filled pause types by speaker level/group

As can be seen in Figure 3, the diversity of lexical filled pause types used and the frequency of use of various lexical filled pauses increased as level increased. Learners in the lowest level used only one type of lexical filled pause: *y* 'and.' Learners in the mid group used five different lexical filled pauses. Although *y* was still the most common (comprising 89% of all lexical filled pauses used by this group), mid-level learners also exhibited use of *entonces* (8.72%), *pues* (1.16%), *como* (0.58%), and *este* (0.58%) to fill pauses. At the high level, learners employed each of the same lexical filled pauses as the native speaker group (i.e., *bueno, como, entonces, este, o sea, pues, y*) plus one additional lexical filled pause that the native speakers did not employ in our tasks: *o* 'or.'

Phonological filled pauses

Overall, 2,190 of the filled pauses produced by the present study's participants were phonological filled pauses. As a reminder, these were first coded categorically based on the phonological filled pause produced, as determined impressionistically. There were various categories observed in the data (e.g., *um, eh, hmm, ah*); the four most common were *uh, um, eh,* and *em*. Table 7 presents a summary of the frequency of occurrence of these four phonological filled pauses as well as an "other" category by level. The "other" category included pauses categorized as other vocalic-sounding filled pauses (e.g., *oom, ahm*) as well as filled pauses categorized as *mm* or *hmm* (i.e., without a clear vocalic component). Percentages were calculated within the level (i.e., the percentage that each phonological filled pause comprised of the total number of phonological filled pauses for that speaker group).

Table 7. Percentage of occurrence of phonological filled pause type (out of total phonological filled pause use) by level

Level/Group	Uh k	Uh %	Um k	Um %	Eh k	Eh %	Em k	Em %	Other k	Other %	Total
Low	119	26.10	300	65.79	3	0.66	1	0.22	33	7.24	456
Mid	206	26.89	480	62.66	35	4.57	12	1.57	33	4.31	766
High	189	22.05	431	50.29	62	7.23	148	17.27	27	3.15	857
NS	10	9.01	10	9.01	58	52.25	19	17.12	14	12.61	111

As can be seen in Table 7, learners at the low and mid proficiency levels predominantly used *um* (66% of all phonological filled pauses for low-level learners and 63% for mid-level learners) followed by *uh* (26% and 27%, respectively). Learners in the high proficiency group still employed mostly *um* and *uh* (i.e., for a combined 72% of their phonological filled pauses), but an increase in the use of both *eh* and, especially, *em* was also observed. In comparison, *eh* and *em* were the two most common phonological fillers used by the Spanish native speakers in this study, constituting 69% of the phonological filled pauses they employed.

Next, we removed any phonological filled pauses that did not include a clear vowel sound (e.g., *mm, hmm*; $k=75$) and explored the choice between a purely vocalic phonological filled pause (e.g., *uh, eh*) versus a vowel + nasal (e.g., *um, em*). Table 8 presents the summary of vowel as opposed to vowel + nasal phonological filled pauses by speaker group.

As shown in Table 8, at all learner levels, the proportion of a vowel + nasal phonological filled pause (e.g., *um, em*) was descriptively higher than the use of just vocalic phonological filled pauses (e.g., *uh, eh*), whereas L1 Spanish speakers used higher rates of purely vocalic filled pauses.

Table 8. Percentage of vowel (e.g., uh, eh) versus vowel + nasal (e.g., um, em) phonological filled pause use by level

Level/Group	Vowel k	Vowel %	Vowel +Nasal k	Vowel +Nasal %	Total
Low	126	29.44	302	70.56	428
Mid	255	34.00	495	66.00	750
High	257	30.67	581	69.33	838
NS	69	69.70	30	30.30	99

To explore potential factors influencing speakers' use of a purely vocalic versus a vowel + nasal phonological filled pause, we ran a logistic mixed model including the same fixed effects examined for the choice of lexical versus phonological filled pauses: speaker group/level, position with respect to the word, position with respect to the utterance, duration, and delay until speech continues, as well as interactions between speaker level and all other fixed effects. Position with respect to the word was, again, excluded from the analysis due to extreme imbalance in the sample (i.e., very few word internal filled pauses). The model included a random effect for participant. Table 9 summarizes the significant effects by level for the choice between a purely vocalic versus a vowel + nasal phonological filled pause by speaker group.

As shown in Table 9, speaker level and duration of filled pause influenced the use of a purely vocalic versus a vowel + nasal phonological filled pause; there were no significant interactions between any predictor and speaker level. The mid-level learner group was significantly more likely than the L1 Spanish speaker group (the reference category) to produce a vowel + nasal phonological filled pause than a purely vocalic pause. With regard to duration, across the sample in general, as duration increased, so too did the odds of producing a vowel + nasal phonological filled pause (e.g., *um*) as opposed to a purely vocalic filled pause (e.g., *uh*). Figure 4 illustrates the duration of these two types of phonological filled pauses by speaker level/group, showing that vowel + nasal phonological filled pauses tended to be longer than purely vocalic phonological filled pauses across all groups.

Finally, to explore in more detail the vocalic quality of speakers' phonological filled pauses in Spanish, we examined formant measurements extracted from the midpoint of each vocalic portion of the phonological filled pauses (excluding those with no vocalic portion; e.g., *mm, hmm*). Although all phonological filled pauses were coded categorically (e.g., *uh, um, eh, em*), taking vowel measurements allowed us to explore more precisely where in the vowel space speakers produced these filled pauses. The first formant (F1) is regarded as an inverse index of

Table 9. Results of logistic mixed effect model predicting use of vowel versus vowel + nasal phonological filled pause (reference category: Vowel)

Effect	Estimate	SE	95% CE	z	p
(Intercept)	−4.36	1.25	[−6.93, −1.99]	−3.49	<.001
Level					
NS	Reference				
Low	1.57	1.44	[−1.14, 4.51]	1.10	.273
Mid	2.73	1.34	[0.17, 5.47]	2.03	.042
High	2.55	1.33	[0.02, 5.27]	1.91	.056
Position: Utterance					
Utterance boundary	Reference				
Utterance internal	−0.37	0.59	[−1.53, 0.77]	−0.62	.533
Duration (continuous)	6.24	1.83	[2.69, 9.88]	3.42	<.001
Delay until speech continues (continuous)	1.06	0.72	[−0.36, 2.49]	1.46	.145
Low Level × Duration	1.50	2.21	[−2.89, 5.79]	0.68	.497
Mid Level × Duration	−1.43	1.97	[−5.33, 2.43]	−0.73	.469
High Level × Duration	−.33	1.97	[−4.24, 3.50]	−0.17	.867
Low Level × Utterance internal	−0.44	0.66	[−1.73, 0.85]	−0.68	.497
Mid Level × Utterance internal	0.06	0.63	[−1.17, 1.31]	0.10	.925
High Level × Utterance internal	−0.27	0.64	[−1.50, 1.00]	−0.42	.675
Low Level × Delay until speech continues	−0.86	0.73	[−2.30, 0.57]	−1.18	.240
Mid Level × Delay until speech continues	−0.83	0.73	[−2.28, 0.61]	−1.13	.259
High Level × Delay until speech continues	−0.14	0.79	[−1.70, 1.43]	−0.17	.865
Random effect	**Variance**	**SD**	**N**		
Participant	2.69	1.64	86		

$k = 2102$, AIC = 1922.6

vowel height, with a lower F1 indexing a vocalic production that is higher in the vowel space. The second formant (F2) is considered an index of vowel frontness-backness, with a higher F2 indexing a more fronted vowel. Filled pauses that are more *eh*-like would be higher and more fronted in the vowel space than filled pauses that are more *uh*-like (and thus, *eh*-like filled pauses would be expected to have lower F1 values and higher F2 values than *uh*-like filled pauses). Figure 5 plots the F1 and F2 values for the vocalic portions of each phonological filled pause by speaker group, and Figures 6–9 show the same plots separated by speaker group/level.

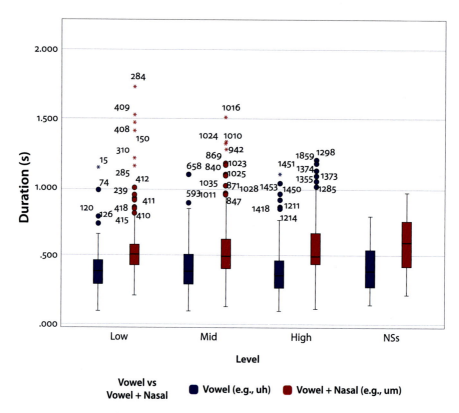

Figure 4. Duration of vowel versus vowel + nasal phonological filled pauses by group/level

Visually, Figures 5–9 demonstrate rather wide variability in the vowel sounds produced in phonological filled pauses by speakers within and across groups. Nevertheless, a visual comparison by speaker group suggests a gradual shift forward and perhaps slightly upward in the general location of the phonological filled pauses produced as speaker level increases, reflecting the results in the categorical coding that learners at the low and mid levels produced more *uh*-like filled pauses, learners at the high level started exhibiting some *eh*-like production, and L1 Spanish speakers produced phonological filled pauses that were more fronted still.

Two linear mixed effects models — one examining F1 and one examining F2—were run using the lmerTest package (Kuznetsova et al., 2017) in R (2023) to test the effect of five predictors on these two indices of vowel quality. In each model, fixed effects were speaker group/level, position with respect to the word, position with respect to the utterance, duration, and delay until speech continues. Participant was entered as a random effect. Tables 10 and 11 present the model summaries for F1 and F2 as the dependent variable, respectively.

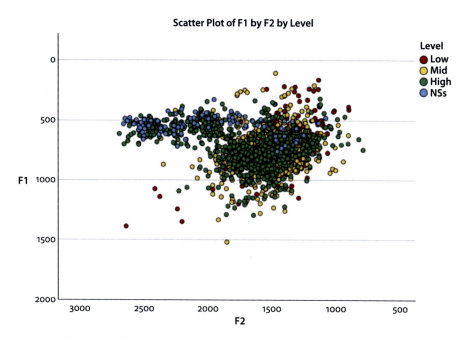

Figure 5. Plotted production of phonological filled pauses within the vowel space by group

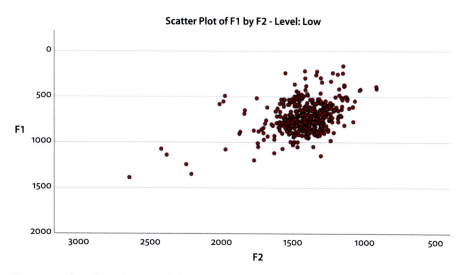

Figure 6. Plotted production of phonological filled pauses within the vowel space for low-level learners

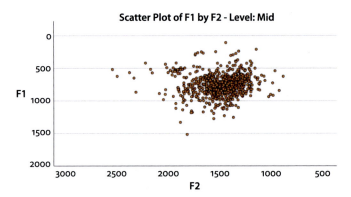

Figure 7. Plotted production of phonological filled pauses within the vowel space for mid-level learners

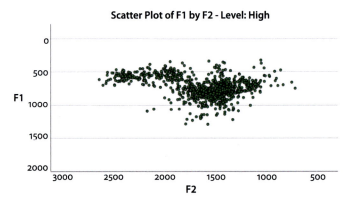

Figure 8. Plotted production of phonological filled pauses within the vowel space for high-level learners

All three learner groups exhibited F1 and F2 values that differed significantly from the L1 Spanish speaker reference group. Specifically, all three learner groups produced phonological filled pauses that were significantly lower in the mouth (i.e., had higher F1 values) and significantly further back in the mouth (i.e., had lower F2 values) than the L1 Spanish speaker group. Duration of the filled pause and the delay after the filled pause until speech continued also significantly constrained the acoustic properties of filled pauses: Overall, phonological filled pauses were higher in the mouth (i.e., had a significantly lower F1) and were more forward in the mouth (i.e., a significantly higher F2) when the duration of the filled pause was longer. They were also produced further back in the mouth (i.e., lower F2) with longer delays after the pause until speech continued.

Chapter 10. Filled pauses in L2 Spanish   281

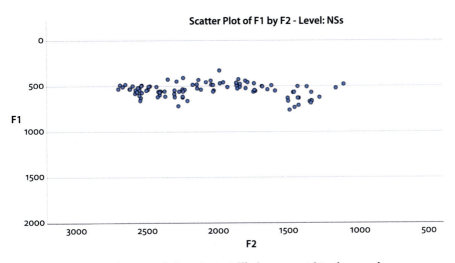

Figure 9. Plotted production of phonological filled pauses within the vowel space for NSs

Table 10. Summary of linear mixed model examining F1 as dependent variable

Effect	Estimate	SE	95% CE	t	p
(Intercept)	628.79	143.89	[346.58, 908.73]	4.37	< .001
Level					
NS	Reference				
Low	166.12	52.32	[64.92, 267.28]	3.18	.002
Mid	212.28	50.19	[115.24, 309.32]	4.23	<.001
High	179.26	49.66	[83.22, 275.29]	3.61	<.001
Position: Word					
Word boundary	Reference				
Word internal	−29.27	24.35	[−76.90, 18.46]	−1.20	.229
Position: Utterance					
Utterance boundary	Reference				
Utterance internal	−38.74	136.76	[−305.12, 230.37]	−0.28	.777
Duration	−0.12	0.02	[−0.16, −0.08]	−5.33	<.001
Delay until speech continues	−4.09	2.47	[−8.94, 0.74]	−1.65	.098
Random effect	**Variance**	**SD**	**N**		
Participant	12312	111.0	86		

Table 11. Summary of mixed effect model examining F2 as dependent variable

Effect	Estimate	SE	95% CE	t	p
(Intercept)	1856.71	207.57	[1450.96, 2260.70]	8.95	< .001
Level					
NS	Reference				
Low	−628.15	103.96	[−829.35, −426.94]	−6.04	<.001
Mid	−531.22	100.60	[−725.93, −336.49]	−5.30	<.001
High	−364.37	99.54	[−557.05, −171.67]	−3.66	<.001
Position: Word					
Word boundary	Reference				
Word internal	45.72	32.97	[−18.88, 110.24]	1.39	.166
Position: Utterance					
Utterance boundary	Reference				
Utterance internal	155.56	187.23	[−210.41, 522.63]	0.83	.406
Duration	0.11	0.03	[0.05, 0.17]	3.65	<.001
Delay until speech continues	−7.16	3.36	[−13.75, −0.59]	−2.13	.033
Random effect	**Variance**	**SD**	**N**		
Participant	53348	231.0	86		

Discussion

Inspired by Erker and Bruso's (2017) variationist research on the characteristics and patterns of filled pauses produced by bilingual Spanish speakers in Boston, our study investigated L2 Spanish filled pauses using variationist tools and explored the potential of filled pauses to serve as a rich source of data on L2 sociolinguistic development. The study's findings, affirming this potential, offer four key observations: (1) L2 learners showed variable filled pause behavior in Spanish; (2) filled pause repertoires and variability expanded with proficiency; (3) linguistic factors systematically shaped this variation; and (4) the L2 Spanish speakers' filled pause behaviors shifted as proficiency level increased. These shifts approximated the L1 Spanish filled pausing patterns in certain aspects, though demonstrated key differences as well.

Overall, the frequency and rate of filled pause use per participant increased with proficiency, a phenomenon echoing earlier research. For example, García-Amaya (2015) observed that learners with higher L2 proficiency used more filled pauses (cf. Segalowitz & Freed, 2004), possibly as they navigate more complex syntactic structures and develop quicker speech rates. In the present study, higher proficiency learners used more filled pauses not only than their less proficient L2 counterparts but also than the L1 Spanish speaker reference group, although broad individual variability within each level existed, as illustrated by the group-level ranges presented in Table 1.

The present study's findings also revealed that, like the L1 Spanish speaker group, most L2 learners employed both lexical and phonological elements to fill pauses, although phonological filled pauses appear to surface first and be the predominant option to fill pauses at lower proficiency levels. As learner level increased, the percentage of participants using both phonological and lexical filled pauses increased and so, too, did the rate of use of lexical fillers. Still, the present study's high-level L2 group's rate of lexical filled pause use (20.5%) was lower than the L1 speakers' group rate of 32.3% lexical (as compared to phonological) filled pause use.

The prevalence of phonological filled pauses among L1 Spanish speakers in our study stands in contrast to other research on Spanish filled pauses, where lexical variants predominated (Erker & Bruso, 2017; Graham, 2018; Soler Arechalde, 2008). For example, Erker and Bruso (2017) found that lexical filled pauses constituted 58% of their dataset from Spanish in Boston, and Graham's (2018) cross-variety study reported an overall preference for lexical filled pauses at a rate of 60.6%. These differences between our L1 Spanish speaker group and previous studies of L1 Spanish filled pause use are somewhat surprising. Nevertheless, we note that our study diverged from these referenced works in several ways. First, our study featured a smaller group of seven native speakers, which differs from the larger-scale studies of Erker and Bruso (24 participants) and Graham (293 speakers). Furthermore, our study included speakers from diverse origins, which may inflate or erase distinctions associated with variety-related differences. Importantly, our research also employed short monologic tasks, in contrast to the cited studies that retrieved tokens from sociolinguistic interviews. Task-related effects on filled pauses have been identified in prior research on other languages, whether tasks were monologic or dialogic (Rose, 2015), prepared or spontaneous (Kosmala & Crible, 2022), or task-oriented versus conversational (Tottie, 2014). The potential for task-related effects cannot be overlooked since, to the best of our knowledge, no study on Spanish filled pauses directly compares filled pause use across different tasks.

The present study's findings provide evidence that the variation observed in L2 Spanish filled pause use (considered in multiple ways) is systematic and constrained by linguistic factors. For example, the position at which the filled pause was produced with respect to the utterance and the filled pause duration significantly constrained the choice between a lexical and a phonological filled pause, especially for the mid-level learner group. Similarly, duration of the filled pause predicted the choice between a purely vocalic phonological filled pause (e.g., *uh, eh*) and a vowel + nasal (e.g., *um, em*), echoing Clark and Fox Tree's (2002) assertion that *uh* typically signals a minor delay and *um* suggests a more substantial hesitation.

Within lexical filled pauses, the diversity of lexical filled pause types and the frequency of use of more types increased with higher proficiency. At the lowest level, learners relied on a single type of lexical filled pause, specifically *y*. As learner proficiency advanced, this single variant gave way to a more varied repertoire, with five different lexical filled pauses in use at the mid proficiency level. Learners in the highest proficiency group exhibited comprehensive use of the same lexical filled pauses as the L1 Spanish speaker group (i.e., *bueno, como, entonces, este, o sea, pues,* and *y*) plus an additional form (*o*) not observed in the present L1 data. Similarly, within phonological filled pauses, learners' repertoires expanded at higher proficiencies as they added more use of *eh* and *em* to the lower levels' predominant use of *uh* and *um*.

Finally, this shift toward more /e/-like filled pauses is also reflected in the acoustic data, where we observed learners' phonological filled pauses shifting slightly up and forward in the vowel space as learner level increased. These findings parallel those of Machuca (2022), who identified a relationship between the language proficiency of her English, French, and Russian L2 speakers of Spanish and their use of the Spanish /e/ filler. In the present study, in addition to proficiency level, the vocalic quality of learners' filled pause productions was systematically influenced by linguistic factors. For example, phonological filled pauses had a significantly lower F_1 (i.e., were higher in the mouth) and a significantly higher F_2 (i.e., were more forward) when the duration of the filled pause was longer, suggesting that learners are more likely to implement "Spanish-like" phonological filled pauses during longer hesitations.

Although the present study examined only a small set of potential constraining factors, the findings point to the potential for filled pauses to offer a rich context for the study of L2 sociolinguistic development. Filled pauses encompass various language modules (e.g., lexical, phonological, phonetic, pragmatic), and the variation exhibited in filled pause production both crosses and exists within these levels. As demonstrated in the present study, L1 and L2 Spanish speakers varied in their choice between a lexical or a phonological filled pause, in the lexical or phonological type or item used, and in the phonetic form of the variant produced, allowing investigation of both categorical and gradient features. Similarly, as a natural component of human speech, filled pauses constitute a variable context that seems to appear earlier in learners' repertoires than do other sociolinguistic variables. For example, previous studies that explore the adoption of regional phonetic variants often uncover very low rates of adoption or variation at all (e.g., adoption of Spanish /θ/, Ringer-Hilfinger, 2012; or /s/-weakening, Geeslin & Gudmestad, 2008). The present study's findings, in contrast, suggest that filled pauses are a viable and prevalent variable context of interest in the speech of learners from relatively early stages of acquisition and a rich context for exploring learner development.

Thus, despite the exploratory nature of the present study, we argue that filled pauses constitute an interesting and valuable context for examining L2 sociolinguistic development. We encourage future investigation of the influence of a wide array extralinguistic and contextual factors on filled pause variation (including learner identity, social networks, interlocutor effects; e.g., Black, 2021; Kennedy Terry, 2023; Nance et al., 2016; Rindal, 2010). Future research that examines how L2 speakers' filled pause behavior changes in relation to particular contexts, interlocutors, or regional cues, could contribute to our understanding of, for example, Type III variation (or variation that accounts for L2 users' aims, motivation, and identity construction in defining their targets; Nance et al., 2016) or how learners studying in different regions adapt or not to the local filled pause patterns (with regard to both categorical and gradient measures). This research has the potential to contribute to the larger discussion of filled pauses as identity markers (e.g., Blondet, 2001; Graham, 2018) and to consider both variety-specific markers as well as learners' own goals and desires related to their L2 identity and sound (George & Hoffman-González, 2019; Nance et al., 2016). Similarly, research that examines pausing behavior across various elicitation tasks could offer valuable insights into task-related variation more broadly and into how task demands influence hesitation phenomena and whether such effects differ for L1 as compared to L2 speakers and/or how such effects change in relation to L2 proficiency. In-depth longitudinal studies tracking developmental trajectory of filled pause patterns among learners can show how proficiency and language experience shape hesitation phenomena over time. Likewise, attention to individual variability in L2 filled pause use and variation is a warranted next step.

Conclusion

This study explored L2 Spanish filled pauses from a variationist perspective. The broad look at L2 Spanish filled pausing behavior provided a descriptive account of the various and variable ways in which L2 users of Spanish signal their intention to continue speaking despite a hesitation (i.e., by filling a pause), how such behaviors are constrained by the linguistic context, and how patterns change as L2 proficiency develops. Though exploratory in nature, the present study offered a preliminary, foundational look at L2 Spanish filled pause behavior and the systematic variation therein at various levels. The present study also laid the groundwork for future variationist explorations of L2 filled pauses. We believe this variable context holds promise for offering insight into and new evidence for a wide range of topics of broader interest in research at the intersection of sociolinguistics and SLA.

References

Black, M. A. (2021). Interlocutor effects on sociolinguistic variation in L2 French (Unpublished doctoral dissertation). Indiana University, Bloomington.

Blondet, M. A. (2001). Las pausas llenas: marcas de duda e identidad lingüística. *Lingua Americana*, 8, 5–15.

Boersma, P., & Weenink, D. (2018). Praat: doing phonetics by computer [Computer program]. Version 6.0.30, retrieved from http://www.praat.org/

Bowden, H. W. (2016). Assessing second-language oral proficiency for research: The Spanish elicited imitation task. *Studies in Second Language Acquisition*, 38(4), 647–675.

Chomsky, N. (1965). Persistent topics in linguistic theory. *Diogenes*, 13(51), 13–20.

Clark, H. H., & Fox Tree, J. E. (2002). Using *uh* and *um* in spontaneous speaking. *Cognition*, 84, 73–111.

Corley, M., MacGregor, L. J., & Donaldson, D. I. (2007). It's the way that you, er, say it: Hesitations in speech affect language comprehension. *Cognition*, 105(3), 658–668.

Erker, D., & Bruso, J. (2017). *Uh, bueno, em...*: Filled pauses as a site of contact-induced change in Boston Spanish. *Language Variation and Change*, 29, 205–244.

Fox Tree, J. E. (2001). Listeners' uses of *um* and *uh* in speech comprehension. *Memory & Cognition*, 29, 320–326.

Freed, B. F., Segalowitz, N., & Dewey, D. (2004). Context of learning and second language fluency in French: Comparing regular classroom, study abroad, and intensive domestic immersion programs. *Studies in Second Language Acquisition*, 26, 275–301.

Fruehwald, J. (2016). Filled pause choice as a sociolinguistic variable. *University of Pennsylvania Working Papers*, 22, 41–49.

García-Amaya, L. (2009). New findings on fluency measures across three different learning contexts. In J. Collentine, M. García, B. Lafford, & F. Marcos Marín (Eds.), *Selected proceedings of the 11th Hispanic Linguistics Symposium* (pp. 68–80). Cascadilla Press.

García-Amaya, L. (2015). A longitudinal study of filled pauses and silent pauses in second language speech. In R. Eklund (Ed.), *Disfluency in spontaneous speech: DISS 2015* (pp. 23–27). https://diss2019.elte.hu/wp-content/uploads/2018/09/DiSS2015_Papers.pdf

Geeslin, K. L., & Gudmestad, A. (2008). The acquisition of variation in second-language Spanish: An agenda for integrating studies of the L2 sound system. *Journal of Applied Linguistics*, 5, 137–157.

George, A., & Hoffman-González, A. (2019). Dialect and identity: US heritage language learners of Spanish abroad. *Study Abroad Research in Second Language Acquisition and International Education*, 4(2), 252–279.

Goldman-Eisler, F. (1968). *Psycholinguistics: Experiments in spontaneous speech*. Academic Press.

Graham, L. A. (2018). Variation in hesitation: The case of *este* vs. *eh* in Latin American Spanish. *Spanish in Context*, 15, 1–26.

Kennedy Terry, K. (2023). Learning from locals: The impact of social networks with target-language speakers during study abroad. *L2 Journal*, 15(2), 92–109.

Kosmala, L., & Crible, L. (2022). The dual status of filled pauses: Evidence from genre, proficiency and co-occurrence. *Language and Speech*, 65, 216–239.

Kuznetsova, A., Brockhoff, P. B., & Christensen, R. H. B. (2017). lmerTest Package: Tests in linear mixed effects models. *Journal of Statistical Software*, 82(13), l1–26.

Labov, W. (1978). Where does the linguistic variable stop? A response to Beatriz Lavandera. *Working Papers in Sociolinguistics*, 44, 1–22.

Laserna, C. M., Seih, Y. T., & Pennebaker, J. W. (2014). Um… who like says you know: Filler word use as a function of age, gender, and personality. *Journal of Language and Social Psychology*, 33(3), 328–338.

Lennon, P. (1990). Investigating fluency in EFL: A quantitative approach. *Language Learning*, 40, 387–417.

Liberman, M. (2014, August 3). More on UM and UH. *Language Log*. https://languagelog.ldc.upenn.edu/nll/?p=13713

Machuca, M. J. (2022). An acoustic study on the use of fillers in Spanish as a foreign language acquisition. In T. Maqbool & L. Y. Lang (Eds.), *Second language acquisition — Learning theories and recent approaches* (pp. 1–15). IntechOpen.

Michnowicz, J., Ronquest, R., Chetty, S., Green, G., & Oliver, S. (2023). Spanish in the Southeast: What a swarm of variables can tell us about a newly forming bilingual community. *Languages*, 8(3), 168.

Nance, C., McLeod, W., O'Rourke, B., & Dunmore, S. (2016). Identity, accent aim, and motivation in second language users: New Scottish Gaelic speakers' use of phonetic variation. *Journal of Sociolinguistics*, 20(2), 164–191.

Ortega, L. (2000). Understanding syntactic complexity: The measurement of change in the syntax of instructed L2 Spanish learners [Unpublished doctoral dissertation]. University of Hawai'i at Manoa.

Ortega, L. (2013). SLA for the 21st century: Disciplinary progress, transdisciplinary relevance, and the bi/multilingual turn. *Language Learning*, 63(Supp. 1), 1–24.

Ortega, L., Iwashita, N., Rabie, S., & Norris, J. M. (1999). *A multilanguage comparison of measures of syntactic complexity [Funded project]*. Honolulu: University of Hawai'i, National Foreign Language Resource Center.

Pinget, A. F., Bosker, H. R., Quené, H., & De Jong, N. H. (2014). Native speakers' perceptions of fluency and accent in L2 speech. *Language Testing*, 31(3), 349–365.

Pozzi, R., & Bayley, R. (2021). The development of a regional phonological feature during a semester abroad in Argentina. *Studies in Second Language Acquisition*, 43(1), 109–132.

R Core Team. (2023). *R: A language and environment for statistical computing.* R Foundation for Statistical Computer, Vienna, Austria. https://www.R-project.org/

Rindal, U. (2010). Constructing identity with L2: Pronunciation and attitudes among Norwegian learners of English. *Journal of Sociolinguistics, 14*(2), 240–261.

Ringer-Hilfinger, K. (2012). Learner acquisition of dialect variation in a study abroad context: The case of the Spanish [θ]. *Foreign Language Annals, 45*, 430–446.

Rose, R. (2015). Um and uh as differential delay markers: The role of contextual factors. In R. Eklund (Ed.), *Disfluency in spontaneous speech: DISS 2005* (pp. 73–76). Edinburgh, Scotland.

Sankoff, D., & Thibault, P. (1981). Weak complementarity: Tense and aspect in Montreal French. In B. Strong Johns & D. Strong (Eds.), *Syntactic change* (pp. 206–216). University of Michigan Press.

Schegloff, E. A., Jefferson, G., & Sacks, H. (1977). The preference for self-correction in the organization of repair in conversation. *Language, 53*(2), 361–382.

Segalowitz, N., & Freed, B. F. (2004). Context, contact, and cognition in oral fluency acquisition: Learning Spanish at home and study abroad. *Studies in Second Language Acquisition, 26*, 173–199.

Shea, C., & Leonard, K. (2019). Evaluating measures of pausing for second language fluency research. *Canadian Modern Language Review, 75*(3), 216–235.

Soler Arechalde, M. A. (2008). Algunos factores determinantes y contextos de uso para el marcador discursivo 'este'… en el habla de la ciudad de México. *Anuario de Letras: Lingüística y Filología, 46*, 155–168.

Solon, M., Park, H. I., Henderson, C., & Dehghan-Chaleshtori, M. (2019). Revisiting the Spanish elicited imitation task: A tool for assessing advanced language learners? *Studies in Second Language Acquisition, 41*(5), 1027–1053.

Swerts, M. (1998). Filled pauses as markers of discourse structure. *Journal of Pragmatics, 30*(4), 485–496.

Thomas, E., & Kendall, T. (2007). NORM: The vowel normalization and plotting suite. [Online Resource: http://ncslaap.lib.ncsu.edu/tools/norm/]

Tottie, G. (2011). Uh and um as sociolinguistic markers in British English. *International Journal of Corpus Linguistics, 16*(2), 173–197.

Tottie, G. (2014). On the use of *uh* and *um* in American English. *Functions of Language, 21*(1), 6–29.

Towell, R., Hawkins, R., & Bazergui, N. (1996). The development of fluency in advanced learners of French. *Applied Linguistics, 17*, 84–119.

Watanabe, M., Den, Y., Hirose, K., & Minematsu, N. (2004). Clause types and filled pauses in Japanese spontaneous monologues. *Proceedings of the Eighth International Conference on Spoken Language Processing*, 905–908. Retrieved from: https://www.isca-archive.org/interspeech_2004/watanabe04c_interspeech.html

Watanabe, M., Hirose, K., Den, Y., & Minematsu, N. (2008). Filled pauses as cues to the complexity of upcoming phrases for native and non-native listeners. *Speech Communication, 50*(2), 81–94.

CHAPTER 11

An exploration of L1 attitudes and individual characteristics in the study of sociolinguistic perception in additional-language Spanish

Ian Michalski & Aarnes Gudmestad
Roanoke College | Virginia Polytechnic Institute and State University

This study takes as its foundation concerns about comparing learner language to that of native speakers in applied linguistics. Two possible avenues for alternative analyses include examinations of language users' full repertoires and their diverse language experiences. We explored participants' sociolinguistic perception in Spanish based on their sociolinguistic perception in English and other language-experience characteristics. The participants (first-language English speakers/additional-language learners of Spanish) completed two matched-guise tasks (one in each language) and a background questionnaire. The analysis uncovered preliminary evidence of limited connections between L1 attitudes and language-experience characteristics. We subsequently formulated hypotheses regarding additional-language sociolinguistic perception and offered concrete methodological recommendations for future research seeking to explain the acquisition of sociolinguistic perception without relying on comparisons with native speakers.

Keywords: sociolinguistic perception, SLA, variation, native-speaker bias, Spanish

A longstanding practice within the field of second language acquisition (SLA) has been to compare additional-language learners' language behavior to that of the native speaker (NS) and to make assessments of nativelikeness. However, this custom has not been without critique, with researchers such as Ortega (2013) and the Douglas Fir Group (2016) urging for reforms that move the field away from analyses that evaluate learner language through the lens of NS norms (see Background section). The debate about this issue (often called the NS or monolingual bias) is ongoing, and the field has yet to move away from its traditional

https://doi.org/10.1075/ihll.43.11mic
© 2025 John Benjamins Publishing Company

NS orientation (Ortega, 2016). The slow pace of change may be in part because, undoubtedly, this type of disciplinary shift is significant; it necessitates modifications both in the ways additional-language learning and behavior are conceptualized and in the methodological tools used to conduct research. The current study confronts these challenges as it seeks to consider how sociolinguistic perception of additional-language learners of Spanish could be examined without relying on a NS benchmark.

Like most subfields of second language acquisition (SLA), previous work on additional-language sociolinguistic perception has often included NS comparison groups (e.g., Schmidt, 2018; Michalski, 2023; see Schmidt & Geeslin, 2022, for an exception), and the analyses are usually built around assessments of targetlikeness that are based on NS benchmarks (e.g., Chappell & Kanwit, 2022). While these studies have contributed much to our understanding of how additional-language learners perceive and draw out social meaning from linguistic forms present within speech, there exists an opportunity, in light of calls for reform in SLA, to study the perceptions of additional-language users without relying on NS comparisons (cf. Grammon, 2022, 2024). Thus, in this chapter we take an exploratory approach to studying additional-language sociolinguistic perception without using a NS benchmark. Instead, we rely on the shared first language (L1) of participants (e.g., Cook, 2016) and various language-related experiences (e.g., Hall, 2016) to guide the analysis. We examine a dataset previously analyzed by Michalski (2023) that includes attitudinal perception data for all participants in L1 English (matched-guise perceptions of variable (ing)) and in additional-language Spanish (matched-guise perceptions of *para* versus *pa* and retention versus aspiration of syllable-final /s/). The participants also completed a background questionnaire in which they provided detailed information about previous language experiences. The objective of the present investigation is twofold. First, we make preliminary observations about the factors related to speakers' sociolinguistic perception of additional-language linguistic forms, without comparing learners to NSs. Second, we offer conceptual and methodological recommendations for future research that seeks to explain the acquisition of sociolinguistic perception in additional-language contexts without relying on NS baselines.

Background

NS comparisons in SLA

Although SLA is a diverse field, a commonality across investigations has been the focus on targetlikeness or accuracy (Cook, 2016). Detailed accounts of how learner behavior compares to NS or prescriptive benchmarks exist for many linguistic structures and various languages. Most research on grammatical gender in Spanish, for example, has centered on the errors that learners make in gender agreement between nouns and modifiers (e.g., *el*~masc~ *manzana*~fem~ *rojo*~masc~ 'the red apple') and on the developmental trajectory toward targetlike behavior (Alarcón, 2014; see Gudmestad et al., 2021, for an exception).

Despite how commonplace it has been in SLA to compare learner language to NS targets, this practice has been criticized. For instance, Bley-Vroman (1983) argued that comparing learner language to a NS target hinders the ability to understand interlanguage because these comparisons result in observations that fail to identify systematicity in learner language and suggest that interlanguage is "a degenerate form of the target system" (p. 4). Moreover, although Holliday's (2006) concerns were specifically about English, he used the term native-speakerism to refer to the ideology that holds the NS as the ideal standard and teacher of a language. He asserted that this perspective was problematic for various reasons, one of which was the way it marginalizes nonnative speakers. Cook (2016, inter alia), in another example, advocated for the multicompetence approach, defined as "the overall system of a mind or a community that uses more than one language" (p. 3). From this perspective, comparing bi/multilingual users to monolinguals is inherently inappropriate because it ignores the fact that multilinguals are not and will not be monolinguals. Ortega (2019, inter alia) has also sounded the alarm about the damage that native-speakerism and the NS bias have brought to SLA, in part because they have centered the field's scope of inquiry on language learners' shortcomings. In her calls for change, she has urged "SLA researchers to invest in future positive reframings of the late-learned, bi/multilingual nature of L2 acquisition" (Ortega, 2013, p. 14).

Given that NS, monolingual, and prescriptive benchmarks have played such a prominent role in analyses of learner language, it begs the question of how to investigate learner behavior and language development if comparisons to these baselines are no longer made. While there can be various responses to this issue, we highlight two possibilities put forth in previous literature that we adopt in the current study. First, Cook (2016, inter alia) and Ortega (2019, inter alia) have discussed the importance of examining language users' full language repertoires. Cook (2016) has argued that "SLA research that ignores the first language element is blind to the one inescapable feature of the L2 user's mind that distinguishes it from that of a monolingual – the first language system" (pp. 7–8). The examination of the L1 alongside other languages is also justified on empirical grounds because research has demonstrated that the languages in the mind of a user influence each other (Ortega, 2019, p. 25). We heed the call to more fully examine the linguistic repertoire of additional-language learners by investigating participants' sociolinguistic perception in additional-language Spanish and in English, the L1 of all participants in the present investigation.

The other avenue that we pursue in our investigation of sociolinguistic perception without comparing learners to NSs is to examine learners' language experiences in relationship to their sociolinguistic perception in additional-language Spanish. According to Hall (2016), individuals' diverse experiences shape language behavior, which means that language knowledge and use are not invariant as monolingual norms in particular suggest (see also Ortega, 2019). In this vein, learning languages beyond the first means that additional-language learners likely experience varied communicative contexts and linguistic practices in the different languages they use and learn (Hall et al., 2006, pp. 230–231).[1] Understanding how these experiences shape language and development, therefore, could help SLA retreat from NS benchmarks. In the current study, we conduct an initial examination of the potential relationship between sociolinguistic perception in additional-language Spanish and five characteristics of language experience — namely, length of university study of Spanish, length of time abroad in a Spanish-dominant country, experience with other languages, daily interaction in Spanish, and experience with linguistic courses.

Sociolinguistic competence and variationist SLA

Researchers working within the intersection of sociolinguistics and SLA seek to understand the development of sociolinguistic competence, one component of Canale and Swain (1980)'s communicative competence (see Geeslin & Hanson, 2023, for an overview of sociolinguistic approaches to communicative competence). Sociolinguistic competence refers to a speaker's ability to adhere to the rules of sociocultural and discourse appropriateness that condition language behavior. This construct inherently assumes that a norm or baseline of competence exists, and in much of the existing research, this baseline has been the language behavior of monolingual or bilingual NSs. For example, researchers working within variationist SLA have focused their examination of sociolinguistic competence on the acquisition of sociolinguistic variation, whereby they investigate instances of variability in the target language (see the Variable Structures subsection for examples) and analyze learners' developmental path toward targetlike or nativelike behavior of variable norms (Geeslin with Long, 2014). Learners are often compared to NSs in a region where they are studying abroad or to bilinguals whose L1 is the target language (e.g., Kanwit et al., 2015; Geeslin, 2003; see

---

1. Hall et al. (2006) raise concerns about languages as discrete systems (p. 225), which we do not address here.

Gudmestad & Edmonds, 2023, for an exception). Thus, in this area of scholarship, the benchmark for acquisition is a nativelike norm that is variable.

While a strength of variationist SLA is that learners are not compared to idealized monolinguals (as *idealized* is traditionally defined), the presence of a NS baseline could still be problematic for those concerned about NS biases in SLA for various reasons. For one, scholars have argued that the term NS tends to be connected to the privilege that comes with exposure to a language from birth (e.g., Davies, 2003; Rampton, 1990) and to ethnolinguistic nationalism (Bonfiglio, 2013). Another reason specifically addresses variationist SLA and sociolinguistic competence. Grammon (2022) has argued that the NS targets in this area of research are another form of an idealized NS norm because they are:

> based on an idealization of a culturally homogenous speech community comprised of NSs who perceive one another's normative sociolinguistic practices as inherently appropriate within that community regardless of differences in speakers' identities and social backgrounds. Sociolinguists have long critiqued similar definitions of speech community based on consensus models of sociolinguistic norms by revealing how the invocation of such norms obscures their status of successfully imposed ideologies which favor the interests of dominant social groups. (p. 2)

In addition to problematizing the NS target in variationist SLA, Grammon (2024) has raised questions about the appropriateness of employing these targets to evaluate learners' development of sociolinguistic competence. These concerns stem from two suppositions that variationist researchers seem to have made about learners. One assumption is that learners "objectively recognize native speakers in the host society as fully competent in the target language" and the other is that learners view NSs' language behavior as felicitous (pp. 1, 14). Grammon (2022, 2024) has challenged these assumptions and sought to better align research on sociolinguistic competence with scholarship that critiques NS targets by shifting the focus to ethnographic investigations of language ideologies. This pursuit is noteworthy because variationist SLA studies on language attitudes have not generally considered ideological components, despite how central they are when studying attitudes and sociolinguistic perception more generally (Garrett, 2010). While we see value in this work, we also believe that it is worth considering other approaches given that research on sociolinguistic competence without NS baselines is in nascent stages.

Before turning to scholarship on perception, we briefly examine variationist SLA research that has incorporated the L1 and other language-experience characteristics into their analysis. Beginning with the L1, early variationist SLA research hypothesized a role for the L1 by studying the permeability of the additional language relative to L1 norms governing stylistic variation in the interlanguage (Tarone, 1979). Beebe (1980), for example, tested this hypothesis and found that English learners whose L1 was Bangkok Thai transferred stylistic variation rules governing the L1 sound system into their use of English on formal and informal tasks. More recent work by Davydova et al. (2017) studied sociolinguistic awareness of German learners of English. They suggested that in forming social meanings in the additional language, learners engaged in *interlanguage ideological extension* by using knowledge about social meaning in the L1 to shape their sociolinguistic attitudes in the additional language, and they encouraged future research on this issue.

Variationist research has also investigated the role that various language-experience characteristics play in learners' use of variable structures. For instance, studies on the acquisition of regional features of Castilian Spanish like the interdental fricative /θ/ have shown that some learners choose not to incorporate the nativelike feature into their speech, often based on beliefs regarding norm-based rules and expectations of what is appropriate that are reinforced by experiences with instructors in language classes (Grammon, 2021). In another study on the interdental fricative, Knouse (2012) focused on the role of learning context (study abroad or at home) and other language-experience characteristics such as proficiency in Spanish and living situation abroad. She found that language-experience characteristics appeared to play a role in learners' limited acquisition of /θ/. Like variationist SLA work more generally, studies that have investigated the influence of language-experience characteristics on the acquisition of sociolinguistic variation have been interested in documenting whether learners acquire NS variable norms.

We center our remaining discussion in this subsection on sociolinguistic perception. Sociolinguistic perception is a process in which social information is extracted from language and used to make social meaning and form evaluative responses (i.e., attitudes) toward speakers (Campbell-Kibler, 2010). The tasks used to measure sociolinguistic perception often include the use of response scales constructed around speaker attributes (e.g., kindness, intelligence, formality) that are semantically linked to the social information and meaning associated with language. Research in this area includes perception of and attitudes toward linguistic variation and has shown that additional-language learners of Spanish can develop awareness of variable structures in the input and that they can learn to formulate attitudes toward speakers that use these variable features (e.g., Chappell & Kanwit, 2022; Geeslin & Schmidt, 2018; Michalski, 2023; Schmidt & Geeslin, 2022).

Variationist SLA research on perception, like that on language production, has made direct comparisons between learners and NSs (Chappell & Kanwit,

2022; Michalski, 2023). However, Schmidt and Geeslin (2022) made a point of not explicitly doing so and instead focused on examining how learner attitudes toward regional varieties of Spanish develop according to individual characteristics.[2] In so doing, Schmidt and Geeslin (2022) emphasized the fact that there is value in studying learner attitudes without drawing comparisons to NS norms, especially given that when it comes to attitudes toward regional variation, finding a single NS norm can be a challenge. The researchers instead looked to individual characteristics to describe the development of language attitudes in additional-language Spanish. Notably, some of these individual characteristics focused on language experience: proficiency, dialect awareness, and abroad experience. Their findings indicated that learners can distinguish between regional varieties of Spanish and evaluate them differentially. In particular, proficiency did not play a role in the development of perception of certain speaker traits, but exposure to a given dialect alongside increased proficiency was associated with an ability to distinguish among varieties of Spanish (Schmidt & Geeslin, 2022, p. 228). The authors offered an explanation by suggesting that perhaps when first forming attitudes about the additional language, learners begin with social norms in their L1, and later those attitudes change as proficiency, language experience, and interaction with the target culture and society increase (p. 228). Referencing Beebe (1980), Schmidt and Geeslin also considered that learners may transfer "social values of speech cues that are relevant in the L1 when making attitudinal judgments in the L2" (p. 226).

Although the role of the L1 in studies of additional-language perception has been acknowledged (Schmidt & Geeslin, 2022) and variationist SLA scholarship has investigated language-experience characteristics of learners (Geeslin with Long, 2014), we are not aware of a study on additional-language perception that has explicitly included both (i.e., the L1 and individual characteristics) into an investigation that has the goal of examining learner behavior without evaluating that behavior according to a NS norm.

Variable structures

The variable structures (termed linguistic variables in sociolinguistics) of focus in the current study come from Spanish and English but share some characteristics. Each of the three variable structures include variation between allophones that convey social meaning in target-language communities (see The Current Study section for a statement about the ways in which this exploratory investigation has

---

2. However, they structured their examination of development around proficiency level, where proficiency was based on prescriptive language norms, and in doing so made indirect comparisons to an idealized NS norm (see *The Current Study*).

and has not moved away from native-speaker norms and the Discussion for additional critical reflection on this issue). The variable structures are the English variable (ing), which consists of a velar nasal [ŋ] that is realized variably as an alveolar nasal variant [n] in specific contexts (Campbell-Kibler, 2007), the reduction of *para* 'for' to *pa* by way of the elision of /ɾ/ (Díaz-Campos et al., 2011), and the reduction or elision of /s/ to [h] or [Ø] in syllable-final positions (Nuñez-Méndez, 2022). Additionally, these variable structures all undergo stylistic variation and index a range of social meanings, making them good candidates for studying language attitudes (see Michalski, 2023, for an overview).

Previous research on (ing) has established a patterned association of social meaning and speaker attributes with each of the variants such that the velar variant [ŋ] is often associated with positive status attributes and negative solidarity attributes, while the inverse has been found for the alveolar variant [n] (Campbell-Kibler, 2011). Similarly, prior scholarship has examined the social meaning associated with the reduction of /s/ in Spanish varieties (e.g., Chappell, 2019; Walker et al., 2014). This work has confirmed that reduced /s/ variants for which production data have established a correlation with lower social class and education are, in fact, evaluated lower on scales of status attributes (i.e., professionalism, formality, education level, intelligence) and higher for solidarity attributes (i.e., kindness, sympathy) by most Spanish-speaking listeners. Although there is limited attitudinal research on the reduction of *para*, Díaz-Campos et al.'s (2011) analysis of production data revealed that the social stylistic correlations of the associated variants (*para, pa*) patterned similarly to other forms of consonant reduction, like /s/ reduction, thus suggesting that the two variable structures share similar social meanings. More recently, Michalski (2023) found that the status and solidarity attribute ratings of the reduction of *para* aligned with expectations based on the sociolinguistic distribution of *para* and *pa* in production data (e.g., *pa* is rated low for education level and formality).

The current study

In response to calls to find other ways of evaluating learner language and development, we conduct an exploratory analysis to identify possible relationships between additional-language sociolinguistic perception on the one hand and L1 sociolinguistic perception and language-experience characteristics on the other hand. We believe that the current study has moved away from NS norms in two ways. First, we depart from traditional analyses in variationist SLA because we do not explicitly evaluate learner behavior in terms of NSs' performance on the same task that learners completed (i.e., we do not compare learner attitudes to NS attitudes). Second, we do not discuss learner proficiency in terms of a metric that is rooted in prescriptive or idealized NS norms.[3]

We acknowledge, nevertheless, that the NS still plays a role in the present investigation. Our dataset was collected originally as part of a study that incorporated NS comparisons in various ways. For example, in the matched-guise tasks (see Method section), the variable structures of focus were presented within the task stimuli according to NS norms of variable occurrence, so as to present them as they naturally occur in NS speech (see also Schmidt & Geeslin, 2022). Additionally, the attributes that learners evaluated in the matched-guise tasks were rooted in NS perceptions of variants traditionally labeled as standard and vernacular (e.g., [s] and [h], respectively, for syllable-final /s/ in Spanish, Chappell, 2019). We see a possible advantage to these features of the current study. Moving away from NS benchmarks can result in notable changes in how we conduct research. However, the analysis of a dataset that can also be used for traditional analyses could serve as a bridge between different orientations in SLA because it can help to establish common ground. We return to this issue in the Discussion and consider the present chapter a valuable initial step in reconceiving research on sociolinguistic perception in additional languages.

To this end, the overarching objective of the current study is to conduct an exploratory, step-by-step analysis that enables us to begin to think about how learners' sociolinguistic perception, as measured by attitudinal ratings, can be examined without making comparisons to a NS benchmark. This objective can be separated into three specific goals as follows:

1. to explore the role that L1 attitudes may play in additional-language sociolinguistic perception,
2. to explore the ways in which language-experience characteristics may be connected to additional-language sociolinguistic perception, and
3. to offer hypotheses and recommendations for future scholarship that aims to investigate additional-language sociolinguistic perception without relying on NS baselines.

---

3. The participants completed a section of the DELE for the original study, but we do not consider the results in the present investigation.

Method

Participants

The participants included in this study ($n=90$) are a subset of participants reported on in Michalski (2023) and are all additional-language learners of Spanish for whom English is a L1. Eight participants reported another L1, in addition to English, and 23 participants reported additional languages other than Spanish (for details see *Supplemental Materials* available at https://osf.io/n9sx7/?view_only=f12073662bf8423cae8of0584c657d06). They ranged in age from 17 to 36 years ($M=21.14$, $SD=4.17$). Fifty-four identified as women, 32 as men, and four as non-binary. The undergraduate participants were enrolled in a second-year grammar course ($n=26$), a third-year culture course ($n=4$), a third-year Hispanic linguistics course ($n=35$), or a third-year literature course ($n=12$). The remaining 13 participants were graduate teaching assistants for undergraduate Spanish courses at one of three large midwestern universities. For two language-related characteristics that are relevant for the current study, 54 participants reported having taken a linguistics course, and 36 reported having traveled to a country where Spanish was a majority language for either vacation, study abroad, work, or other purposes ($M=6.25$ months, range $=0.25-66.25$, $SD=12.92$).

Tasks

All participants completed two modified matched-guise tasks (one in Spanish and one in English; see the Supplemental Materials for additional details) and a background questionnaire. The Spanish matched-guise task was constructed with digitally manipulated audio recordings of a written script. The script was comprised of 10 discrete, sentence-long items containing variants *para* or *pa* and two to three instances of syllable-final /s/. Both variable structures were presented in contexts in which variation is known to occur to represent the occurrence of these features as they may occur in the input. For syllable-final /s/, for example, the reduction is possible in syllable-final positions and most often before a consonant, whether in word-medial contexts such as *casta* [káh.ta] 'caste' or word-final contexts such as *los patos* [loh.pá.toh] 'ducks' and is also possible before vowels and even pauses (Núñez-Méndez, 2022). For *para* and *pa*, the variation is conditioned by the semantic meaning (e.g., goal or direction oriented), grammatical category of the following word (e.g., preposition, adverb), and the articulation of the following segment (e.g., obstruent, back vowel) (Díaz-Campos et al., 2012). A phrase such as *Ella se viene para (pa) Caracas* ('she comes to Caracas') includes directionality and an obstruent in the following segment, and both are contexts where reduction to *pa* could occur. The Spanish audio recordings were presented as part of a contextualized task in which participants were told they would be listening to and evaluating recordings made by candidates applying to become newscasters for a local public radio station.

The English-language audio stimuli were constructed in similar fashion, using a script with a series of sentences each containing progressive verb constructions comprised of copula + gerund (e.g., 'is carrying') to study the (ing) variants of [ŋ] and [n]. This variation occurs in words across a range of grammatical categories (e.g., gerunds, prepositions, progressive) and can be conditioned by the following phonological environment (e.g., front or back consonant, vowel, pause) such that progressive constructions followed by a fronted consonant would show higher rates of variability between [ŋ] and [n] (Kiesling, 1998). The script was written as a public radio segment about daily home and work routines and divided into 10 segments, each containing two instances (ing) variation.

Five male speakers of Spanish provided the recordings of the stimuli for the Spanish matched-guise task. These recordings were then used to create the short (3–5 seconds) audio stimuli for the matched-guise task. Using PRAAT and a copy and splice methodology (Campbell-Kibler, 2007), the linguistic variant (either *para/pa*, [s]/[h]) was removed and replaced with either the same variant or an alternate to create matched pairs or quadruplets.[4] The different combinations of linguistic variants were represented in the matched pairs and quadruplets and all audio files were digitally manipulated. The English task was constructed using the same process. However, instead of male voices, the recordings were made by five women.[5] The speakers recorded multiple versions of the scripted stimuli and linguistic variants, using alveolar and velar variants, from which matched pairs were created using a copy and slice method (Campbell-Kibler, 2007). Additional details on the creation of the stimuli, their organization within the tasks, and Table A, which provides the items from each task, are available in the Supplemental Materials.

---

4. While it is common to only manipulate one variable structure in this type of matched-guise experiment, we included combinations of variants in the present investigation because variable structures do not exist in isolation and together can communicate social meaning (see D'Onofrio, 2020).

5. We recognize that (a) the gender of both the speaker and listener plays a role in perception and attitudes, (b) the English and Spanish tasks differ in that they used voices of different genders, and (c) differing genders between tasks is not methodologically ideal. However, we believe that while the L1 English task was not originally designed to be used in this way, the unique advantage of having L1 and additional-language attitude data for all participants warrants the comparisons despite the mismatch in gender, especially given the exploratory nature of the present investigation.

Each stimulus within both tasks was followed by six semantic differential scales that placed a single attribute at a positive and negative pole. The selection of attributes was based on previous research relative to the social correlates of the Spanish linguistic structures under study (e.g., Díaz-Campos et al., 2011; Núñez-Méndez, 2022) and previous work studying language attitudes toward English (ing) (e.g., Campbell-Kibler, 2007). For the Spanish matched-guise task, listeners rated speakers according to *amabilidad* (kindness), *profesionalismo* (professionalism), *formalidad* (formality), *nivel de estudios* (education level), *inteligencia* (intelligence), and *simpatía* (sympathy).[6] Likewise, for the English matched-guise task, listeners rated speakers according to kindness, professionalism, formality, education level, intelligence, femininity. Each participant rated all 10 Spanish-speaker and English-speaker voices according to all social attributes. The resulting ratings represent a measure of listener evaluation (i.e., attitudinal response) to the speaker voice.

The third task consisted of a background questionnaire that gathered information from participants regarding a variety of individual characteristics (e.g., age, gender expression, L1s, travel experiences). It also asked for information about participants' educational experiences, such as number of semesters studying Spanish and experience with courses in linguistics. The items included in this questionnaire appeared in Spanish and English side-by-side translations. For details on the data-collection procedure, see Supplemental Materials.

Data coding and analysis

We designed a data-analysis procedure that enabled us to begin to examine the relationship between learners' sociolinguistic perception in Spanish and, on the one hand, their sociolinguistic perception in English and, on the other hand, several language-experience characteristics. Table B in the Supplemental Materials offers an overview of each step in the analysis.

The first two steps of the analysis focused on the relationship between L1 and additional-language attitudes. For the first step, the raw scores that each participant provided as ratings were averaged so that there was a single value for each participant, each attribute (e.g., *amabilidad*/kindness), and each linguistic variant (e.g., [h]) for both English and Spanish tasks. We focused on the five attributes that the two tasks had in common: kindness, professionalism, formality, education level, and intelligence. These mean attitudinal ratings were then analyzed using R (R Core Team, 2023) and following the two-part process described. The first part of the analysis aimed to explore the general relationship between

---

6. The English translations provided here are identical to those provided to the participants.

sociolinguistic perception in the L1 (English) compared to the additional language (Spanish). This was accomplished by first running bivariate correlations between the mean attitude ratings for each linguistic variant from the English matched-guise task and the mean attitude ratings for each linguistic variant from the Spanish matched-guise task for each attribute. For example, one correlation explored the possible relationship between [n] in English and [h] in Spanish for the kindness attribute. The second step involved creating learner profiles based on the distribution of participants' ratings of English (ing). Two groups were identified based on their ratings. Ultimately, the groups were comprised of participants who rated [n] in English either consistently high or consistently low for both professionalism and formality (see the Results section for a discussion of why other attributes were not used to create learner profiles). We considered these two groups to have differing sociolinguistic perception. Using these profiles, we then turned to their ratings of the Spanish guises, and we conducted a comparison of means to determine whether there appeared to be any differences in the attitudes that these two groups had toward the Spanish variants *para* versus *pa* and the variants of syllable-final /s/.

The final two steps in the analysis centered on the Spanish matched-guise task data only and five individual characteristics pertaining to experiences with language (i.e., semesters studying Spanish, travel in a Spanish-dominant country, linguistics classes, daily interaction in Spanish, speaking an additional language). The third step in the analysis involved using mean ratings for each participant, attribute, and linguistic variant. The relationships between each language-related characteristic and attitudes were first explored by way of bivariate correlations for numeric variables (e.g., semesters studying Spanish) and comparisons of means for categorical variables (e.g., speaking an additional language), again looking at all combinations of attributes and linguistic variants separately. Thus, the third part of the analysis served to explore relationships between perception of Spanish variants and language experiences. For the final step, we used the observations from the third step to create two learner profiles. The profiles distinguished between learners with more and less language experience (see Results). These profiles were then used to determine if there appeared to be differences (again by comparing means) in how participants fitting these profiles rated the Spanish guises containing variable *para* versus *pa* and the variants of syllable-final /s/.

Given the exploratory nature of our study, we do not engage in null hypothesis significance testing (NHST). Thus, instead of using p values to determine which relationships are important, we rely on effect sizes to guide our analysis (r for correlations and d for means; see Plonsky, 2015). We then use the preliminary observations that emerge from our analysis to propose hypotheses that could be investigated in future research (see Discussion).

Results

Step 1

The first step in the analysis consisted of a series of correlation analyses between attitude ratings that participants gave for English stimuli and the attitude ratings participants gave for the Spanish stimuli.[7] The goal was to determine whether there appeared to be a linear relationship between attitude ratings in the L1 and the additional language and to assess the relative strength of this relationship. To interpret the correlation coefficients, we draw on Plonsky (2015), who offered recommendations for interpreting r effect sizes; the benchmark for a small correlation effect size is 0.25 (p. 38). Given the exploratory nature of the current study, we opted to be less restrictive in our selection of correlations to examine with data visualization compared to benchmarks used in more well-established areas of research. Thus, we identified any correlations with an effect size of .3 or greater to explore further (i.e., greater than the .25 baseline for small effect sizes). Of the 40 correlations performed (Table C, Supplemental Materials), three correlations met the criterion for further exploration. First, kindness ratings for [n] and [pa.ɾa] were positively correlated ($r(70) = .3$). Second, intelligence ratings for [n] and [h] were positively correlated ($r(45) = .3$). Third, kindness ratings for [ŋ] and [h] were positively correlated ($r(45) = .4$). The plots for these correlations are in Figure 1. Generally speaking, we can say that in these three cases, learners who rated the English guises positively also rated the Spanish guises positively. The strength, or magnitude, of the relationship between these English and Spanish ratings appears to be greater than small. Furthermore, the correlation between [ŋ] and [h] for kindness is the strongest, reaching a medium effect size (Plonsky, 2015).

Step 2

To continue exploring the potential relationship between L1 and additional-language attitudes of variable structures, we categorized learner responses with the goal of creating groups of learners who rated English stimuli similarly across various attribute categories. This process entailed calculating average ratings of each linguistic variant and attribute combination (e.g., kindness + [n]) for each participant, resulting in 10 values per participant (i.e., five attributes × two English variants). Next, the mean ratings for [n] were compared across all attribute categories to determine if an individual participant on average rated the guise consis-

---

7. The ratings were not normalized or standardized. Given that the response scales for all attributes were of the same format (six-point semantic differential scales) and were not combined with another response scale, like perceived age, normalization or standardization is not necessary (Rosseel et al., 2019; Levon & Fox, 2014).

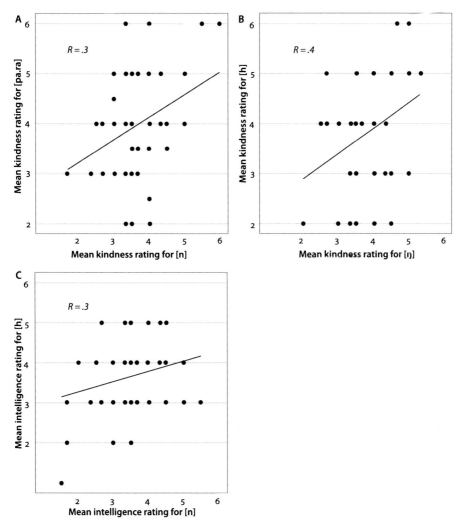

Figure 1. Correlation plots for mean kindness and intelligence ratings

tently high (above 4.33 on the six-point scale) or consistently low (below 3). While no groups of participants rated [n] consistently high or low across all attribute categories, there were some who did so collectively for two of the attributes — formality and professionalism. We subsequently identified two profile groups consisting of individuals who rated [n] guises in English consistently high ($n=13$) or consistently low ($n=30$) for formality and professionalism. The details of their ratings are in Supplemental Materials Table D. We name these groups the high and low L1 attitude profile groups, respectively. The remaining attributes were not included in the profiles as no common group of participants gave similar ratings for kindness, intelligence, or education level.

Next, we examined each L1 attitude profile group separately, focusing now on their perception of variable structures in Spanish and the formality and professionalism attributes. A summary of their ratings is in Figure 2, which contains a series of boxplots for the two groups organized by each variable structure in Spanish and the two attributes. When comparing the two groups and all of the variants and attributes collectively, we see that the high L1 attitude profile group shows more variability and less grouping, as indicated by the greater interquartile range for certain variants (i.e., [h] and [pa] for professionalism), than the low L1 attitude profile group. We then compared the two groups' ratings for each variant using effect-size comparisons of means to determine the strength of the differences between each group's mean rating for the combination of linguistic variant and attribute (Table E, Supplemental Materials). Similar to our examination of correlations, we used Plonsky (2015) to guide our analysis, where the benchmark for small effect sizes for a between-group mean difference is 0.4 (p. 38). Thus, we identified any effect sizes that were at least 0.5 as potentially important and explored them further (i.e., larger than the 0.4 benchmark for small effect sizes). The effect size for the comparison of mean ratings of [pa.ra] for professionalism between the high L1 attitude group ($M=3.75$) and low L1 attitude group ($M=3.34$) was $d=0.5$, indicating a greater than small magnitude of difference and suggesting that this difference may be more important than the other comparisons. Figure 2 also demonstrates that the high L1 attitude group, compared to the low L1 attitude group, has a higher, more restricted range, and less dispersion, which may suggest a tendency for the high L1 attitude group to rate Spanish variants higher for formality and professionalism.

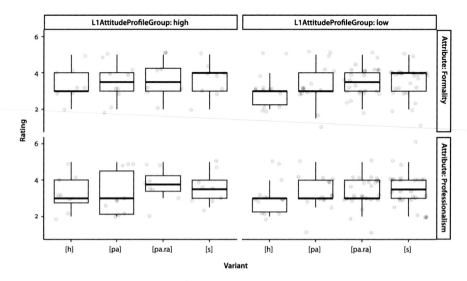

Figure 2. Mean formality and professionalism ratings in Spanish for L1 profile groups

Step 3

Like the first data-analysis phase, the third step explored all possible relationships between various language-experience characteristics (i.e., number of semesters studying Spanish, travel time abroad in a Spanish-dominant country, experience with linguistics classes, daily interaction in Spanish, and speaking additional languages) and perceptions of variable structures by learners of Spanish. For those characteristics that were measured with a numeric variable, 40 Pearson's product-moment correlations were performed, and for those that were measured with binary categories, two groups were created, allowing for 60 effect-size comparisons of means. We used the same effect-size thresholds that we established for Steps 1 and 2.

Two positive correlations were identified as potentially important (see Table F, Supplemental Materials). For semesters of study and [h], there were positive correlations for ratings of professionalism (r(34)=.3) and education level (r(45)=.4). Figure 3 shows that participants rated [h] higher on professionalism and education-level scales with more semesters of Spanish study. A comparison of the two plots also suggests that this effect may be stronger for education level, an observation that is strengthened by the finding that the effect size reaches the benchmark for a medium effect size (Plonsky, 2015). No correlations for travel time abroad reached the .3 threshold.

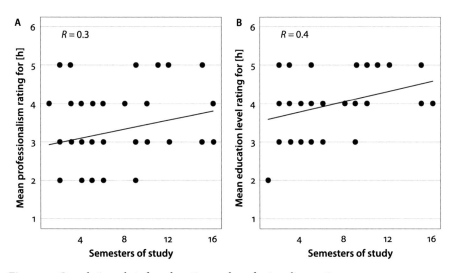

Figure 3. Correlation plots for education and professionalism ratings

The effect-size comparisons of means for the remaining language-experience characteristics resulted in nine comparisons that reached our 0.5 threshold for Cohen's *d*, indicating at least a small effect size (see Table 1 for these nine comparisons; see Tables G-I, Supplemental Materials, for all comparisons). Whether a learner had taken a linguistics course showed two potential differences: Those who had studied linguistics rated [s] as more professional and [pa.ɾa] as more formal than those who had not studied linguistics.

For the variable concerning daily interaction with Spanish, three comparisons appeared to merit further exploration. First, those who interacted with Spanish daily rated [pa.ɾa] for kindness higher than those who did not. Similarly, those with daily interaction rated [s] and [pa] higher for education level than those without daily interaction.

For the final language-experience variable of speaking languages in addition to Spanish and English, four comparisons of means reached the .5 threshold. Participants who had experience with other languages rated [pa] higher for professionalism, formality, and education compared to those who did not speak other languages. They also rated [h] higher for education level.

Table 1. Language-experience characteristics with at least a 0.5 effect size

Variant	Attribute	d	M	n	SD	M	n	SD
Experience with linguistics courses			Yes ling. courses			No ling. courses		
[s]	professionalism	0.5	3.67	47	0.92	3.22	29	0.83
[pa.ɾa]	formality	0.6	3.76	44	0.73	3.25	28	1.00
Daily interaction in Spanish			Yes daily interaction			No daily interaction		
[pa.ɾa]	kindness	0.6	4.39	18	0.83	3.84	54	1.03
[pa]	education level	0.5	4.50	12	0.67	4.05	37	0.91
[s]	education level	0.5	4.39	18	0.63	4.00	58	0.77
Speaking additional languages			Yes languages			No languages		
[pa]	professionalism	0.5	3.65	10	0.82	3.22	39	0.95
[pa]	formality	0.8	3.90	10	0.88	3.17	39	1.00
[pa]	education level	0.6	4.55	10	0.76	4.06	39	0.88
[h]	education level	0.5	4.20	10	0.63	3.86	37	0.75

Figure 4 contains a series of boxplots that complement the effect-size comparisons by showing other characteristics of the data, such as the distribution, dispersion, and range of ratings. Due to space constraints, we highlight here what we see as the most notable observation for each of the three language-experience char-

Chapter 11. L1 attitudes and individual characteristics in perception 307

acteristics based on the magnitude of difference as indicated by Cohen's *d*. In Plot B, the median ratings of formality for [pa.ɾa] by those who had studied linguistics was higher than those who did not, but the overall range of ratings were similar.

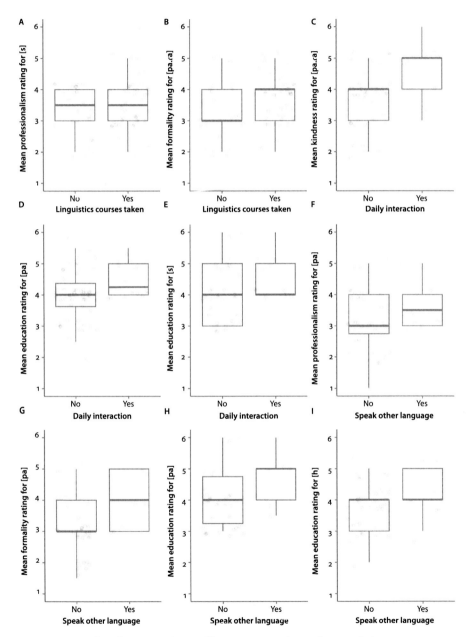

Figure 4. Boxplots for comparisons of language-experience characteristic and perceptions of Spanish

We also see that those with daily interaction with Spanish speakers had a higher median kindness rating for [pa.ɾa], and the range did not extend to the lower half of the rating scale compared to participants who did not interact in Spanish daily (Plot C). Finally, Plot G shows that those who speak an additional language provided ratings of formality for [pa] that were more dispersed and within a greater interquartile range compared to those who speak only English and Spanish.

Step 4. Language-experience profiles and perceptions of Spanish

Finally, we created two profiles of learners based on two of the language-experience characteristics for which we found at least small effect-size differences for some of the comparisons of means (speaking additional languages and daily interaction in Spanish). Although there appeared to be two potential differences for the language-experience characteristic pertaining to linguistics courses, this factor was ultimately not used in the creation of the learner profiles. This is because, when we compiled profiles based on all three variables, we found that too few participants were in the group with a higher degree of language experience (i.e., had taken linguistics courses, had daily interaction with Spanish, and spoke a language other than English and Spanish). To have groups comprised of a larger number of participants, we set aside the having taken linguistics courses characteristic. We thus created a group who reported speaking a language other than Spanish or English and had interacted daily with Spanish speakers ($n=8$) and a group who did not report speaking a language other than Spanish or English and did not interact daily with Spanish speakers ($n=57$). In this way, there were two groups, one with a higher degree of language experience and one with a lower degree of language experience, respectively. With these two groups established, we performed a series of effect-size comparisons of means to explore potential differences in terms of how the members of these groups rated the Spanish guises containing [pa.ɾa], [pa], [s] and [h] according to the five attributes, for a total of 20 comparisons.

The two profile groups showed differences that appeared to have a greater than small effect size in their ratings of seven attribute/variant combinations, as determined by comparisons of means and the calculation of Cohen's d (see Table 2 for these seven comparisons; see Table J, Supplemental Materials, for all comparisons). First, in terms of how the high and low experience groups rated [pa.ɾa], the differences in mean ratings showed a medium effect for ratings of education level and a greater than small effect for ratings of kindness. Second, the differences in ratings of kindness for [s] showed a greater than small effect size. Third, for ratings of [pa], there was a greater than small effect size for professionalism and a medium effect size for formality and education level. Finally, there was a greater than small effect size for ratings of [h] and education level. In all of these cases, the group with more language experience rated the Spanish variant higher on the attribute scale than the group with less language experience. Finally, in Figure 5 we display boxplots for all comparisons between the language-experience profile groups. Notably, across all four plots we can see that the high-experience group tended to provide ratings of three and higher on the rating scale, while the low-experience group's ratings included the full range of the scale.

Table 2. Effect-size comparisons for language-experience profiles with at least a 0.5 effect size

Variant	Attribute	d	M	n	SD	M	n	SD
			High-experience group			Low-experience group		
[pa.ɾa]	kindness	0.6	4.50	7	1.04	3.85	47	1.02
[s]	kindness	0.5	4.38	8	1.06	3.92	52	0.91
[pa]	professionalism	0.6	3.70	5	0.83	3.84	54	1.03
[pa]	formality	0.5	4.50	12	0.84	3.16	32	0.88
[pa.ɾa]	education level	0.5	4.36	7	0.63	3.97	47	0.82
[pa]	education level	0.7	4.60	5	0.89	3.98	32	0.93
[h]	education level	0.6	4.25	4	0.50	3.85	26	0.73

Discussion

We begin with our first two research goals, which focus on the results of our analysis, and then we turn to our third goal, which is more reflective in nature and offers an opportunity to think critically about the research process and how the field could approach research on perception differently to avoid comparing learners to NS benchmarks. We note that because the current study is exploratory and does not engage in NHST, our discussion of the first two research goals centers on formulating hypotheses for future investigations, rather than interpreting the results (as is common with NHST studies), and on methodological reflections.

L1 and sociolinguistic perception

The first goal was to explore the relationship between L1 and additional-language sociolinguistic perception. We found positive correlations between L1 ratings of [n], on the one hand, and additional-language ratings of [pa.ɾa] for kindness and [h] for intelligence, on the other hand. We also found a positive correlation

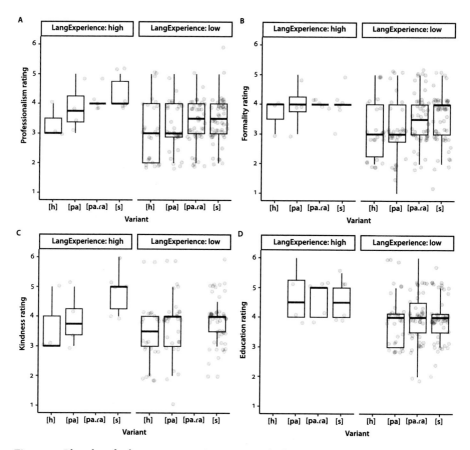

Figure 5. Bloxplots for language-experience groups by linguistic variant and attribute

between L1 ratings of [ŋ] and additional-language ratings of [h] for kindness. These results point to the general hypothesis that learners' attitudes toward L1 and additional-language linguistic forms can be connected, which relates to Davydova et al.'s (2017) *interlanguage ideological extension* construct that refers specifically to connections between L1 and additional-language attitudes. This type of analysis also supports the value of considering language users' full linguistic repertoires when seeking to understand additional-language behavior (Cook, 2016; Ortega, 2019). We then created L1 profiles based on participants' attitudes toward [n] and the attributes of professionalism and formality. While just one effect-size comparison appeared to be greater than small ([pa.ra] ratings for professionalism), descriptively, we observed that the group that rated [n] in English higher for professionalism and formality tended to rate Spanish variants higher for the same attributes. These observations suggest a second hypothesis: Additional-language learners who rate variants in their L1 higher (i.e., more strongly associate variants with status attributes) may be more open to additional-language variants also indexing status. We believe this hypothesis aligns with Grammon (2021), who has shown that learners demonstrate a degree of agency when assigning meaning to sociolinguistic variation. Thus, this methodological approach seems worthy of further exploration, particularly with studies that are originally designed to investigate the relationship between L1 and additional-language attitudes because they can examine the relationship more thoroughly than we have been able to do here. In pursuing this first goal, we have found preliminary evidence, albeit limited, that L1 and additional-language attitudes toward linguistic forms are related and that the use of learner profile groups could be one way to incorporate the L1 into an analysis that investigates learner behavior in its own right.

Language experience and sociolinguistic perception

The second goal was to explore how learner characteristics related to language experience could be leveraged to better understand sociolinguistic perception in additional-language contexts. We first conducted a series of correlations and effect-size comparison of means to explore relationships between language-experience characteristics and attitudes toward [pa.ɾa]/[pa] and [s]/[h]. The findings suggested several possible relationships between Spanish variants and status attributes for most language-experience characteristics. We then utilized two of these individual characteristics to create language-experience profiles to analyze further. For the status attributes of professionalism, formality, and education level, our preliminary observations from the fourth analysis step suggest the hypothesis that the way in which learners rate speaker guises can differ depending on their degree of language experience, such that those with more language experience rate variants as more emblematic of status attributes. When we reflect collectively on all variants and attributes under investigation, we see that learners' attitudes are not restricted to a subset of variants or attributes. Thus, we hypothesize that language experience can influence the range and types of social meanings drawn from the variable structures. Our results resonate with Schmidt and Geeslin's (2022) findings in that they also considered aspects of language experience (dialect awareness and abroad experience) in studying attitudes toward regional varieties of Spanish. Thus, language profiles pertaining to differences in language experience also seem to be a worthy methodological pursuit for investigating sociolinguistic perception when NS benchmarks are not part of the research design.

Recommendations for future study

The third goal of this chapter was to offer recommendations for how to approach the design of investigations on additional-language perception that, from the outset, seek to move beyond the NS bias. To make observations about additional-language behavior and development without NS comparisons, we believe that it is worthwhile to start from the ground up, beginning with the individuals we choose as participants and the tasks we design. We also believe that existing analyses in variationist SLA can still be valuable without a NS comparison group.

In the current study, we responded to the call for including the L1 of participants as an object of study in additional-language perception (Cook, 2016), and we recommend that future investigations continue to pursue this avenue of research by taking a principled approach that begins with the selection and grouping of the participants. For example, a study design could include balanced subgroups of participants with different linguistic repertoires that share a common additional language but have distinct L1 backgrounds (e.g., L1 English only + additional-language Spanish, L1 Mandarin only + additional-language Spanish, L1 English/Hindi + additional-language Spanish, L1 English/Arabic + additional-language Spanish). By adopting this approach to participant selection, we would be able to compare L1 groups and may be able to learn more about the ways in which L1 language attitudes shape additional-language sociolinguistic perception.

Moreover, the current study was not originally designed as a study seeking to avoid the role of the NS. Nevertheless, we think that much stands to be gained by purposefully designing matched-guise tasks with the NS bias in mind. For example, it would be quite valuable to develop stimuli using voices that come from a range of language users, including, for instance, advanced additional-language speakers and heritage speakers, rather than focusing exclusively on speakers who are dominant in the language under study (as we have done in the present investigation). This task feature would better represent the diversity of language users who exist and would not privilege a certain group.

The current application of matched-guise tasks, in which the recorded stimuli are manipulated by the researcher to create matched pairs, is a tool that we believe is valuable for studying additional-language perception, regardless of whether learners are compared to NSs. We suggest that future matched-guise tasks include a wider range of linguistic structures than we examined in the present study. Tasks that include multiple linguistic structures in both the L1 and additional language and structures in different domains of language would allow for more detailed examinations of how language attitudes are related across the linguistic repertoire. However, the decision of which linguistic structures to study is challenging, as it can be difficult to completely avoid the influence of NS expectations. Some linguistic variants are deemed standard, while others are considered to be vernacular, and even the way in which the forms vary or, in the case of perception, the way in which they are perceived is often understood in the literature through the NS lens. Therefore, we suggest that future scholarship make use of a research process that has traditionally been used to develop matched-guise tasks in sociolinguistics. With this process, the researcher uses focus groups (Campbell-Kibler, 2007) not only to identify a wide range of speaker attributes that listeners associate with linguistic variation but to also identify the linguistic variation itself. In this way, the linguistic variants of study and the creation of stimuli emerge from what additional-language users themselves notice, whether on their own or with the guidance of the research, and not simply from literature on NSs.

In terms of analysis, we recognize that the current analysis was exploratory in nature, given our objective to offer a potential process for developing learner profiles that would facilitate the investigation of additional-language perception without comparing learners to NSs. We suggest that the creation of experience-based profiles could prove useful as an alternative to prescriptive proficiency measures or direct comparisons to NSs when analyzing learner development of sociolinguistic perception. Rather than analyze developmental changes in perception as prescriptive proficiency increases, researchers could analyze development of perception as the components of experience-based learner profiles change or expand. We also believe that these learner profiles can complement well-established quantitative analyses in variationist SLA that seek to simultaneously consider a range of factors that condition additional-language behavior. Schmidt and Geeslin (2022) serves as a good example of how various factors related to language experience can be incorporated into a more advanced statistical model (i.e., general linear mixed models) that also does not rely on explicit comparisons with NSs. Additionally, if our suggestion of using focus groups to identify a range of attributes that listeners associate with a given linguistic form were implemented, it would allow for the use of a factor analysis. Previous SLA research on sociolinguistic perception has used this to confirm the reduction of attributes into more manageable categories for subsequent analysis (e.g., Chappell & Kanwit, 2022; Michalski, 2023), and extending its application to limit NS bias could be a valuable addition to this line of research.

Conclusion

We have responded to a call for more research on additional-language behavior that does not rely on NS benchmarks by conducting an analysis of additional-language sociolinguistic perception that drew on the larger linguistic repertoire of learners (their L1 attitudes) and their diverse language experiences (e.g., semesters of study, linguistics courses, daily interaction in the target language), rather than through comparison with NSs. In conducting our exploratory analysis, we were able to find connections between L1 attitudes and language-experience characteristics on the one hand and additional-language perception on the other. We also put forth hypotheses and recommendations to guide future SLA research that seeks to investigate language attitudes while minimizing the influence of the NS bias.

References

Alarcón, I. (2014). Grammatical gender in second language Spanish. In K. L. Geeslin (Ed.), *The handbook of Spanish second language acquisition* (pp. 202–218). Wiley.

Beebe, L. (1980). Sociolinguistic variation and style shifting in SLA. *Language Learning*, 30(2), 433–447.

Bley-Vroman, R. (1983). The comparative fallacy in interlanguage studies: The case of systematicity. *Language Learning*, 33(1), 1–17.

Bonfiglio, T. P. (2013). Inventing the native speaker. *Critical Multilingual Studies*, 1(2), 29–58.

Campbell-Kibler, K. (2007). Accent, (ING), and the social logic of listener perceptions. *American Speech*, 82(1), 32–64.

Campbell-Kibler, K. (2010). Sociolinguistics and perception. *Language and Linguistics Compass*, 4(6), 377–389.

Campbell-Kibler, K. (2011). The sociolinguistic variant as a carrier of social meaning. *Language Variation and Change*, 22(3), 423–441.

Canale, M., & Swain, M. (1980). Theoretical bases of communicative approaches to Second language teaching and testing. *Applied Linguistics*, 1, 1–47.

Chappell, W. (2019). Caribeño or mexicano, profesionista or albañil?: Mexican listener's evaluations of /s/ aspiration and maintenance in Mexican and Puerto Rican voices. *Sociolinguistic Studies*, 12(3–4), 367–393.

Chappell, W., & Kanwit, M. (2022). Do learners connect sociophonetic variation with regional and social characteristics? *Studies in Second Language Acquisition*, 44(1), 185–209.

Cook, V. (2016). Premises of multi-competence. In V. Cook & L. Wei (Eds.), The Cambridge handbook of linguistic multi-competence (pp. 1–25). Cambridge University Press.

Davies, A. (2003). *The native speaker: Myth and reality*. Multilingual Matters.

Davydova, J., Tytus, A. E., & Schleef, E. (2017). Acquisition of sociolinguistic awareness by German learners of English: A study in perceptions of quotative *be like*. *Linguistics*, 55(4), 783–812.

Díaz-Campos, M., Fafulas, S., & Gradoville, M. (2011). [pa.ra] the interplay between socioeconomic class and age in Caracas Spanish. In J. Michnowicz & R. Dodsworth (Eds.), *Selected proceedings of the 5th Workshop on Spanish Sociolinguistics* (pp. 65–78). Cascadilla Proceedings Project.

Díaz-Campos, M., Fafulas, S., & Gradoville, M. (2012). Variable degrees of constituency: Frequency effects in the alternation of *pa* vs. *para* in spoken discourse. In K. Geeslin & M. Diaz-Campos (Eds.), *Selected Proceedings of the 14th Hispanic Linguistics Symposium* (pp. 75–87). Cascadilla Proceedings Project.

D'Onofrio, A. (2020). Personae in sociolinguistic variation. *WIREs Cogn Sci*, *11*, e1543.

The Douglas Fir Group. (2016). A transdisciplinary framework for SLA in a multilingual world. *The Modern Language Journal*, *100* (S1), 19–47.

Garrett, P. (2010). *Attitudes to language*. Cambridge University Press.

Geeslin, K. L. (2003). A comparison of copula choice: Native Spanish speakers and advanced learners. *Language Learning*, *53*(4), 703–764.

Geeslin, K., & Hanson, S. (2023). Sociolinguistic approaches to communicative competence. In Kanwit, M. & Solon, M. (Eds), *Communicative competence in a second language: Theory, method, and applications* (pp. 40–59). John Benjamins.

Geeslin, K. L. with Long, A. Y. (2014). *Sociolinguistics and second language acquisition: Learning to use language in context*. Routledge.

Geeslin, K. L., & Schmidt, L. B. (2018). Study abroad and L2 learner attitudes. In C. Sanz & A. Morales-Front (Eds.), *The Routledge handbook of study abroad research and practice* (pp. 385–405). Routledge.

Grammon, D. (2021). Consequential choices: A language ideological perspective on learners' (non-)adoption of a dialect variant. *Foreign Language Annals*, *54*(3), 607–625.

Grammon, D. (2022). *Es un mal castellano cuando decimos 'su'*: Language instruction, raciolinguistics ideologies and study abroad in Peru. *Linguistics and Education*, *71*, 1–10.

Grammon, D. (2024). Inappropriate identities: Racialized language ideologies and sociolinguistic competence in a study abroad context. *Applied Linguistics*. Advance online publication.

Gudmestad, A., & Edmonds, A. (2023). The variable use of first-person-singular subject forms during an academic year abroad. In S. L. Zahler, A. Y. Long, & B. Linford (Eds.), *Study abroad and the second language acquisition of sociolinguistic variation in Spanish* (pp. 266–290). John Benjamins.

Gudmestad, A., Edmonds, A., & Metzger, T. (2021). Moving beyond the native-speaker bias in the analysis of variable gender marking. *Frontiers in Communication*, *6*, 165.

Hall, J. K. (2016). A usage-based account of multi-competence. In V. Cook & L. Wei (Eds.), *The Cambridge handbook of linguistic multi-competence* (pp. 183–205). Cambridge University Press.

Hall, J. K., Cheng, A., & Carlson, M. T. (2006). Reconceptualizing multicompetence as a theory of language knowledge. *Applied Linguistics*, *27*(2), 220–240.

Holliday, A. (2006). Native-speakerism. *ELT Journal*, *60*(4), 385–387.

Kanwit, M., Geeslin, K. L., & Fafulas, S. (2015). Study abroad and the SLA of variable structures: A look at the present perfect, the copula contrast and the present progressive in Mexico and Spain. *Probus*, *27*(2), 307–348.

Kiesling, S. (1998). Men's identities and sociolinguistic variation: The case of fraternity men. *Journal of Sociolinguistics*, *2*(1), 69–99.

Knouse, S. (2012). The acquisition of dialectal phonemes in a study abroad context: The case of the Castilian theta. *Foreign Language Annals*, *45*(4), 512–542.

Levon, E., & Fox, S. (2014). Social Salience and the Sociolinguistic Monitor: A case study of ING and TH-fronting in Britain. *Journal of English Linguistics, 42*(3), 185–217.

Michalski, I. (2023). L2 sociolinguistic perception of stylistic variation: Attitudes toward two variable linguistic features of Spanish. In S. Fernández Cuenca, T. Judy & L. Miller (Eds.), *Innovative approaches to research in Hispanic linguistics: Diachronic, regional, and learner profile variation.* (pp. 225–247). John Benjamins.

Núñez-Méndez, E. (2022). Variation in Spanish /s/: Overview and new perspectives. *Languages, 7*(77), 1–50.

Ortega, L. (2013). SLA for the 21st century: Disciplinary progress, transdisciplinary relevance, and the bi/multilingual turn. *Language Learning, 63*(Supplement 1), 1–24.

Ortega, L. (2016). Multi-competence in second language acquisition: Inroads into the mainstream? In V. Cook & L. Wei (Eds.), *The Cambridge handbook of multi-competence* (pp. 50–76). Cambridge University Press.

Ortega, L. (2019). SLA and the study of equitable multilingualism. *The Modern Language Journal, 103*(Supplement), 23–38.

Plonsky, L. (2015). Statistical power, *p* values, descriptive statistics, and effect sizes: A "back-to-basics" approach to advancing quantitative methods in L2 research. In L. Plonsky (Ed.), *Advancing quantitative methods in second language research* (pp. 23–45). Routledge.

R Core Team. (2023). R: A Language environment for statistical computing. *R Foundation for Statistical Computing, Vienna, Austria.* URL https://www.R-project.org/

Rampton, M. B. H. (1990). Displacing the 'native speaker': Expertise, affiliation, and inheritance. *ELT Journal, 44*(2), 97–101.

Rosseel, L., Speelman, D., & Geeraerts, D. (2019). Measuring language attitudes in context: Exploring the potential of the Personalized Implicit Association Test. *Language in Society, 48*(3), 429–461.

Schmidt, L. B. (2018). L2 development of perceptual categorization of dialectal sounds: A study in Spanish. *Studies in Second Language Acquisition, 40*(4), 857–882.

Schmidt, L. B., & K. L. Geeslin. (2022). Acquisition of linguistic competence: Development of sociolinguistic evaluations of regional varieties in a second language. *Revista Española de Lingüística Aplicada/Spanish Journal of Applied Linguistics, 35*(1), 206–235.

Tarone, E. (1979). Interlanguage as chameleon. *Language Learning, 29*(1), 181–191.

Walker, A., García, C., Cortés, Y., Campbell-Kibler, K. (2014). Comparing social meanings across listener and speaker groups: The indexical field of Spanish /s/. *Language Variation and Change, 26*(2), 169–189.

CHAPTER 12

Theoretical, methodological, and computational perspectives on immersive virtual reality in variationist SLA
Insights from user experience

Mason A. Wirtz & Simone E. Pfenninger
University of Zurich

> This study contributes to the methodological debate regarding the development of innovative data collection methods such as immersive virtual reality (VR) technology to investigate second-language (L2) learners' acquisition of sociolinguistic variation. Questionnaire data were collected from 32 L2 German learners (first-language English) regarding their VR user experience. We home in on participants' subjective judgements of system usability, workload, VR sickness, spatial presence, and satisfaction. Quantitative analyses revealed that the VR tasks did not disadvantage learners in terms of their user experience as a function of individual differences in age, L2 varietal proficiency, or exposure. We conclude with potential ways to exploit the strengths of VR in the expanding field of variationist SLA.
>
> **Keywords:** virtual reality, variationist SLA, user experience, generalized additive modeling

At the intersection of sociolinguistic and psycholinguistic lines of research, there is a growing need for experimental procedures that can reconcile ecological validity and experimental control (Peeters, 2019; Wirtz, 2022). In variationist second language acquisition (SLA), this requirement is exacerbated as a function of the field's critical focus on when, how, and why second language (L2) learners acquire sociolinguistic competence, that is, "the capacity to recognize and produce socially appropriate speech in *context*" (Lyster, 1994, p. 263, italics by authors; see also Geeslin & Hanson, 2023). Because social contexts are the byproducts of real-world interactions, highly controlled experimental data are often criticized for neglecting much of the multimodal richness and complexity of everyday communication (Taguchi, 2021). On the flip side, (semi-directed) interview methods typically retain high ecological validity and so "respect[s] the dynamics of everyday placed communication" (Peeters, 2019, p. 895). However, they do not proffer researchers much control over the behavior of the observed participant and can restrict generalizability due to differences in settings of data collection, interviewer-interviewee relationships, interactional or conversational roles, turn-taking rights, etc.

In light of the contextually grounded nature of sociolinguistic competence, and thus the need to capture the patterns of variable behavior *in context*, there exist continued appeals in variationist SLA to "expand methodologically beyond what currently exists" (Geeslin, 2010, p. 514). Given such calls to action, virtual reality (VR), as a novel experimental method, has been positioned as an instrument with the unique potential to capture learner behavior across interlocutors, contexts, and formalities in a controlled yet realistic three-dimensional setting (Peeters, 2019; Taguchi, 2021; Vanrell et al., 2018). Indeed, VR has been shown to afford a highly immersive, interactive, and emotionally engaging environment for first-language (L1) speakers (Wirtz, 2022), and this study expands on these results by addressing the issue of L2 learners' user experiences when engaging with a sociolinguistically oriented task, one involving interactive, conversational tasks between VR interlocutor and participant.

It is important to stress that our study constitutes a methodological contribution to this volume. Thus, although the primary focus of our study lies in analyzing data collected from L2 learners of German, it is crucial to recognize that the methodological insights garnered from our research possess a breadth of relevance that transcends this specific linguistic context. Indeed, the universal applicability of our findings extends across a spectrum of domains within the field of SLA, offering valuable insights that can be extrapolated to diverse language-learning scenarios. Notably, our methodological framework holds particular significance for variationist SLA in general, where nuanced examinations of linguistic variability are paramount. In this regard, our study offers a unique lens through which to explore variationist SLA, including variationist SLA with a focus on L2 Spanish. By acknowledging the transferability of our results and methodologies beyond the confines of German language acquisition, we underscore the broader implications of our research for understanding and advancing the study of SLA in various learning contexts.

Background

Early L2 variationist studies focused predominantly on the acquisition of L2 French or English (e.g., Adamson & Regan, 1991; Rehner, 2002). However, the past two decades have seen immense growth in applying variationist approaches to the acquisition of L2 Spanish (e.g., Geeslin, 2003; Geeslin & Gudmestad, 2008; Kanwit & Geeslin, 2014), especially as concerns expanding the methodological inventory of tasks to elicit how and why L2 learners (do not) employ variation typical of L1 speakers. As we will argue, however, many of these instruments emphasize *either* ecological validity *or* experimental control, rather than attempting to reconcile the two. In the following sections, we pay tribute to the methodological innovation variationist approaches to SLA have brought to the table and argue that sustaining this momentum entails integrating new digital methods such as VR into our methodological repertoire in order to conceive of experimentally controlled tasks that still respect the multimodal dynamics of everyday communicative interactions.

Task design and administration in variationist SLA

Lines of inquiry in the field of variationist SLA are typically interested in L2 learners' ability to comprehend and convey sociolinguistic meaning; vary speech across settings to indicate group membership, friendliness, and authority; and interpret socio-indexical meaning communicated via variable use of variants and varieties, to name a few (Geeslin & Hanson, 2023; Gudmestad, 2022). For example, a speaker of Spanish in Venezuela who never omits or aspirates a syllable-final /s/ (e.g., *listo* versus *lihto* or *lito* 'smart') or a speaker of Spanish who never omits the subject pronoun (e.g., *yo hablo español* versus *hablo español* 'I speak Spanish') may sound excessively formal or "even just odd" (Geeslin, 2018, p. 548; see also Schmidt, 2018). Thus, along with grammatical knowledge, L2 learners must acquire the ability to demonstrate familiarity, solidarity, politeness and so forth in order to form alliances, make friendships, and assert authority in an additional language. In other words, L2 learners are challenged to develop knowledge about the context-dependent use of language.

Consequently, the issue of *context* is central to variationist approaches to SLA: A major goal in variationist SLA is to draw on variationist sociolinguistic conceptual and methodological tools in order to explore L2 learners' acquisition of structures and forms that are variable in the target language community, homing in on both their contextually sensitive production and perception of these forms (Geeslin, 2022) – classically referred to as horizontal variation (Adamson & Regan, 1991) or Type II variation (Rehner, 2002). In light of the centrality of context in variationist-centered issues, Taguchi (2021) underscored the necessity to develop context-rich instruments in order to better observe the ecological nature of learner behavior. That said, context is notoriously difficult to capture, and Ushioda (2015, p. 47) lamented the challenge in "how to define, delimit and empirically capture what is meant by context." In order to contextualize learner responses to sociolinguistic tasks, a variety of data collection methods have emerged.

Among oral production tasks, the sociolinguistic/semi-directed interview (Geeslin with Long, 2014; Schilling-Estes, 2008), adapted from the study of variationist sociolinguistics in L1 communities (see Labov, 1966), has a long tradition in variationist approaches to SLA to capture L2 learners' use of stylistic variation in free speech. This method aims to provide a naturalistic, communicative setting for participants to respond meaningfully, and it may include the traditional interviewer-interviewee design, a group design where the interviewer is absent and learners are left with a list of questions/topics to discuss, or pair interviewers who conduct the interview simultaneously (for more detailed discussions, see Kanwit, 2022; Wirtz, 2022). For example, Gudmestad et al. (2013) conducted 30-minute sociolinguistic interviews in which both L1 and L2 speakers of Spanish spoke with two L1 Spanish speakers. The interviewers asked a series of questions covering topics such as plans for the future, past experiences, and opinions, with the goal being to collect free speech in order to investigate subject expression among speakers of L1 and L2 Spanish. Specifically, Gudmestad et al. (2013) focused on the subject form of any third-person verb form (e.g., null subject Ø *canta* '[She] sings', lexical noun phrase *Inés canta*, 'Inés sings', or overt personal pronominal *Ella canta*, 'She sings'). The method provided these authors with a sizable number ($N=6,342$) of tokens in an interactional context intended to "gain access to less formal and less monitored speech" (Geeslin with Long, 2014, p. 33) and thus represent learners' linguistic behavior in casual, everyday communicative interactions.

Variationist SLA scholars have also developed slightly more structured methods to elicit certain structures that may occur less often in purely open-ended dialogue. One example of this is Solon and Kanwit's (2014) use of story squares. In this method, pairs of participants are provided with an information gap activity that includes relevant pictures alongside information gaps. The goal is to guide oral conversations between partners via story squares that have been designed to elicit discussions in which participants need to produce certain (sociolinguistic) forms to achieve the task goals. Solon and Kanwit (2014), for instance, employed this method to explore variation in future-time expression in Spanish by L2 learners and recorded productions of a number of verbal forms used in future-time contexts (e.g., periphrastic future, morphological future, lexical future, etc.). This method comes with the particular advantage that it can facilitate a relatively informal setting and thus mimic more natural conversation, especially when the experiment is conducted among peers, but it allows the researcher more control in targeting structures of interest and helps to guarantee that each participant provides enough data to subject to statistical analyses.

In order to explore (extra-)linguistic constraints on variants that are more difficult to elicit or are otherwise unlikely to occur a sufficient number of times in open-ended dialogue, written contextualized tasks can be particularly useful. These provide participants with 3–5 contextualization sentences and require learners to select their preference among responses that differ according to the structure in question. Importantly, these tasks do not require learners to produce language themselves. Instead, they tap into learners' sociolinguistic knowledge about the linguistic and social contexts in which a variant is likely to be used. For example, Geeslin (2003) explored whether variation in copula choice in Spanish (*ser* and *estar* 'to be') is constrained by certain linguistic factors, such as adjective class (e.g., age, mental state). While the high degree of experimental control provided by the task ensures comparable data across participants and also facilitates efficiency in data collection, it does come at the cost of both loss in ecological validity and a narrower analytical focus (i.e., the tasks are typically used to explore only one variable structure at a time).

Similar arguments concerning the trade-off between ecological validity and experimental control can be made for instruments eliciting data on, for example, L2 perception of sociolinguistic or sociophonetic variation, for example via matched-guise tasks. These focus on how learners interpret or 'judge' sociolinguistically variable structures, and what indexical value listeners attach to them. Matched-guise tasks include matched pairs of language samples (i.e., 'guises' of the same speaker using different varieties/variants) and require participants to judge speakers on personal or affective traits such as likability or intelligence. In variationist studies on the acquisition of L2 Spanish, the matched-guise method, or variations thereof such as a verbal guise in which different individuals provide the guises, have been used to investigate learners' attitudes toward and attachment of social meaning to Spanish regional varieties such as Castilian Spanish, Rioplatense Spanish, etc. (Geeslin & Schmidt, 2018) and also the social capital learners attach to different sociophonetic variants such as coda /s/ (realized as [s] or debuccalized [h]; Chappell & Kanwit, 2022). Matched-guise tasks proffer the researcher a high degree of experimental control, but the degree of ecological validity can vary, depending on the choice of stimuli. In order to maximize the ecological validity of their matched-guise task, Walker et al. (2014), for instance, ensured that the stimuli sounded as natural as possible to naïve listeners via expert reviews by trained linguists.

In a similar vein, tasks that enrich the contextual detail provided to participants have the potential to increase ecological validity without jeopardizing experimental control. One example of this is Solon and Kanwit's (2022) contextualized preference task with an aural component. This was developed to tap into learners' knowledge of sociolinguistically variable phenomena (in their case, realized versus deleted /d/), regardless of their production of these variants in speech. In this task, participants imagined themselves as film directors who first read a contextualized dialogue presented as a film script. For each item, participants listened to two aural stimuli that varied in the realization of the final syllabus (i.e., realized or deleted /d/) and were asked to decide which 'take' fit best within a movie scene. The context comprising the movie scenes (i.e., the contextualized dialogues) was systematically manipulated to reflect differences in gender, grammatical category, lexical frequencies, etc. Solon and Kanwit (2022) maintain that data from this type of task should be seen as complementary to production data, in that it provides valuable information on learners' developing sociolinguistic repertoire as concerns knowledge of sociophonetic variants prior to available evidence in production.

As we have outlined, variationist SLA has a wide range of instruments geared towards eliciting variable behavior and interpretations of variation patterns in a certain linguistic or social context. However, many of these tasks fall victim to the 'ecological validity – experimental control continuum', in that they facilitate one extreme or the other. Oral interviews, for example, respect the dynamics of commonplace communication, but are subject to confounding factors such as power asymmetries, different interactional situations across participants as a result of interlocutor/interviewer idiosyncrasy, and/or unintentional interviewer accommodation (Milroy & Gordon, 2003; Schilling-Estes, 2008; Wirtz, 2022). Other tasks (e.g., matched-guise, written contextualized tasks) indeed proffer the researcher experimental control but ignore much of the richness of everyday communication. Tasks such as story squares fall somewhere between the two extremes on the continuum, given that they allow for more content and context control against a more ecological backdrop of, for instance, a partner discussion. That said, as Peeters (2019) argued, it may be time to neglect the notion of an ecological validity – experimental control *continuum* in favor of considering "experimental control and ecological validity [...] as two orthogonal factors" (p. 895).

This is where VR comes in: Technological advances in VR task design and administration now allow for designs combining experimental control and ecological validity in an unprecedented way (e.g., Peeters, 2019; Taguchi, 2021). Specifically, with VR, it is possible to conceive of three-dimensional virtual environments that mimic the dynamism and complexity of everyday situations (Peeters, 2019), all the while facilitating experimental control over how we define, delimit, and empirically capture what is meant by context. As Fox et al. (2018) argued, such a VR-based method is suitable to study psychological, behavioral, and social phenomena and, by extension, to more carefully explore contextual factors that are part of the environmental frame of reference for the system in question, its dynamic actions, and its patterned outcomes.

Applying VR to data collection in variationist SLA: What are we missing?

As is the case with many, primarily experimental, highly controlled elicitation instruments in variationist SLA, contextual information is condensed into a brief scenario involving only a single or a few sentences, as is the case in the written contextualized task and contextualized preference task (among others). One way to overcome challenges concerning the ecological validity of such tasks is to employ VR technology to develop a three-dimensional environment that simulates real-life experiences by replacing the cues of the real-world environment with digital ones (Fox et al., 2018). By "blocking of sensory impressions from physical reality," immersing the senses in the virtual world, and entrusting "the body […] to a reality engine" (Biocca & Levy, 1995, p.135), it is possible to 'transport' participants into immersive, context-rich environments in order to examine and observe how L2 learners behave in interaction.

Taguchi's (2022b) analysis of L1 and L2 speaker fluency in computer-based versus VR-based tasks is a prime example of the advantages VR offers, as opposed to using purely video or audio material. She found social-interpersonal demands to be higher in the VR-based tasks, in that participants appeared to be more attentive to the potential impact their linguistic behavior may have on the interlocutor. Along similar lines, Taguchi (2022a) noted that the realistic nature of VR likely invoked stronger affective responses in participants, which goes to support the immersiveness of VR and its effectiveness in simulating the multimodal nature and (socioaffective) dynamics of everyday communication (see also Wirtz, 2022).

That said, studies that capitalize on the strengths of VR in variationist SLA lines of inquiry are still rare. Even rarer are variationist SLA studies targeting participants' user experience to assess whether VR tasks hinder certain participants more than others based on individual differences in proficiency, exposure, or age. This is a particular research lacuna in both SLA and sociolinguistics: Regarding the latter individual-difference variable, the recent uptake in research investigating SLA by understudied age groups (e.g., L2 learners in middle-age and later life; see Pfenninger & Singleton, 2019; Singleton & Pfenninger, 2019) necessitates a (re-)assessment of the suitability, feasibility, and potential challenges associated with data-collection methods for populations beyond the traditional adolescent and college-aged demographic (Andringa & Godfroid, 2020). Relatedly, variationist approaches to SLA often include multiple proficiency levels to explore cross-sectional sociolinguistic developmental trajectories (e.g., Kanwit, 2017). This brings with it the question as to how susceptible tasks targeting complex language use (e.g., use of sociolinguistic variation) are to proficiency- and/or exposure-related variation. In other words, by incorporating individual differences in proficiency, exposure, and age into analyses addressing whether elicitation instruments disproportionately profit/hinder certain learners over others, we can better ensure that our research designs (whether innovative or conventionally utilized) do not fall victim to unintended age-, proficiency-, or exposure-related biases.

The present study

The goal of the present study is not to address L2 learners' varietal behavior in the VR (for this, see Wirtz, 2023; Wirtz & Pfenninger, 2023), but rather to explore L2 learners' user experience with a complex and immersive set of VR tasks. In so doing, we contribute empirical data to the debate concerning whether, and the extent to which, VR is suitable for use with L2 learners in terms of task and modality demands. The results should moreover add to the discourse regarding the unique potential and unprecedented advantages of VR in research design and rigor. In this spirit, the present study is novel in several regards: Whilst VR has seen a recent rise in assessing pragmatic competence in the L2 (Taguchi, 2021, 2022a, 2022b), this is the first study to examine L2 learners' subjective user experiences in an interactive socio-/psycholinguistic VR task in which learners must actively engage in conversational exchange with VR agents. Moreover, this is the first study to our knowledge that specifically investigates whether the sociolinguistically oriented VR task demands favor certain participants more than others based on individual differences in age, exposure, and proficiency. These novelties make the present study a strong methodological contribution, and will serve as useful insights concerning VR as a tool in future (variationist) SLA elicitation instrument development and application.

Method

Participants

A total of 32 L2 German learners (13 women, 18 men, 1 gender diverse), all of whom were native English speakers currently living/working/studying in Bavarian-speaking Austria (Salzburg or Upper Austria; one participant lived in Vienna but worked in Salzburg), completed a user experience questionnaire. Fifteen participants were born in the United States, 10 in the United Kingdom, two each in Canada and New Zealand, and one each in South Africa and Australia. One participant was born in Peru to English-speaking parents but moved to the United States during their childhood. The participant pool was drawn via convenience sampling using flyers and word-of-mouth. Our sample pool comprises young and middle-aged adults ($M_{age} = 30.5$; $SD = 8.10$; range = 20–57). Participants varied in terms of self-reported proficiency for reading, writing, speaking, and listening on a 100-point scale in standard German ($M_{S.G.prof.} = 60.0$, $SD = 21.2$, range = 16–100) and Austro-Bavarian dialect ($M_{dial.prof.} = 24.1$, $SD = 21.1$, range = 0–78.8). Participants were also diverse regarding their self-reported exposure (see the description of the Multilingual Language Profile below) to standard German ($M_{S.G.exp.} = 33.5$, $SD = 24.3$, range = 4.90–103) and Austro-Bavarian dialect ($M_{dial.exp.} = 24.1$, $SD = 22.8$, range = 0–92.1), the highest attainable score for each variety being 163.5. Participants were heterogeneous in terms of occupational status, including, for example, students, human resource specialists, teachers, translators, etc. Because this questionnaire was voluntary during the experimental procedure (due to time constraints), the responses of only 32 participants are analyzed, as opposed to the 40 participants from whom data was collected for the cross-sectional study (see Wirtz, 2023; Wirtz & Pfenninger, 2023). For reasons of space, we refer interested readers to the Open Science Framework (https://osf.io/sbtae/) for additional information regarding the participant pool.

VR tasks

The VR test battery comprised a Virtual Reality Oral Dialogue Construction Discourse Completion Task and a Virtual Reality Open Item-Verbal Response Discourse Completion Task. In the former, participants interacted with a female, standard German-speaking interlocutor and a female Austrian dialect-speaking interlocutor. To ensure participants clearly understood the social-situational context and also to mitigate risks of power asymmetries, each VR set began with explicit contextual information presented verbally in English in virtual space. During the VR tasks and in the spirit of a Labovian sociolinguistic interview (see Schilling-Estes, 2008), the standard German-speaking and dialect-speaking virtual interlocutor asked the participant a series of conversational questions (in total lasting approximately 15 minutes). The goal here was to elicit learners' sociolinguistic ability to adapt their varietal behavior to the respective variety of the interlocutor (i.e., inter*personal* varietal behavior; for more details, see Wirtz, 2022, 2023). In the latter task, we were interested in participants' differential use of standard German, dialect, and mixture varieties across situations with different constellations of social distance and dominance (i.e., their inter*situational* varietal behavior). Participants were shown six item-verbal response discourse completion tasks, loosely adapted from select open item-verbal response discourse completion tasks used in Safont-Jordà (2003). Participants were immersed sequentially in six audio-visual situations (each lasting between 2 and 4 minutes) while being read detailed social-contextualizing information in English about the present situation, after which participants were prompted to perform a task in the virtual environment (e.g., ask for a ride home). Two situations simulated social distance/formality, two neutrality, and two social closeness/informality. Although there is an 'interlocutor' visible in each task, they do not speak and function as a 'prop' to facilitate a more realistic environment (for more details, see Wirtz, 2023).

The VR configuration consisted of a Shinecon (model: FIYAPOO) headset for smartphones. The smartphone was an iPhone 11 (software version 14.4.2) with a 6.06" full HD screen, 4 GB RAM and a gyroscope sensor. The VR videos were shown using the pro-version VRPlayer app, which was configured with a profile created for a headset — smartphone combination. The VR-based tasks included pre-recorded videos with a field of vision of approximately 180 degrees (refresh rate of 60 Hz), and participants saw and 'interacted' with a real-life person in the VR rather than with an avatar. Importantly, while previous VR studies have employed more expensive and more advanced VR hardware configurations, low-cost VR headsets for smartphones have been found to produce similar results in terms of user experience (Amin et al., 2016; Papachristos et al., 2017). Given this, the low-cost configuration was chosen.

User experience battery

The user experience questionnaire (approximately 5 minutes) was adapted from Papachristos et al. (2017) and Wirtz (2022) and aims to address the extent to which the VR configuration provides an immersive environment in terms of spatial presence, usability, workload, VR sickness, and satisfaction. Spatial presence refers to the immersiveness of new technology and targets factors such as field of view and visual quality. Given the axiom that "enhanced sense of presence is central to the use, and therefore the usefulness and profitability, of the new technologies" (Lombard & Ditton, 1997), spatial presence represents a necessary metric in evaluating L2 user experiences with VR. It was measured using an abridged version of the Temple Presence Inventory (Lombard et al., 2009) comprising four items on 7-point scales (Cronbach's $\alpha = 0.82$). To measure the ease with which the instrument can be used, the metric usability was included, which was measured by the System Usability Scale (Brooke, 1996). This scale comprises a 10-item dimension with a range from 0 to 100 (Cronbach's α = 0.76). Scores above approximately 70 represent adequate usability (Bangor et al., 2009).

Arguably the most important metric was VR sickness, which was measured using the Virtual Reality Sickness Questionnaire (Kim et al., 2018). This questionnaire consists of a nine-item dimension containing questions targeting possible oculomotor and disorientation symptoms (Cronbach's α = 0.88). Responses were provided on a 4-point scale. Following Kim et al. (2018), the total score, letting o be the total number of oculomotor symptoms and d the total number of disorientation symptoms, was calculated using the following formula:

$$((o/12) * 100 + (d/15) * 100) / 2$$

This resulted in scores between 0 and 100, with 0 representing 'no symptoms'. Admittedly, there does not appear to be an agreed upon cutoff for adequately low VR sickness, but scores under 25 tend to represent few to no symptoms.

Workload was measured using the Task Load Index (Hart, 2006) and was included to evaluate the degree of physical and mental effort required in the VR task. This dimension comprised six items (performance, mental demand, physical demand, temporal demand, effort, frustration), and participants could obtain scores between 0 and 100, with lower scores indicating a lower workload index (Cronbach's α = 0.80). Finally, following Papachristos et al. (2017), participants also reported on their overall satisfaction with the VR instrument, which was a single-scale item on a seven-point scale.

Biodata, proficiency, and exposure battery

All participants completed a questionnaire called the Multilingual Language Profile (MLP; Wirtz & Pfenninger, 2023; approximately 10 minutes). The MLP assessed participants' self-reported language history, use, contact, and proficiency with respect to the standard German and Austro-Bavarian varieties. We used participants' scores from the modules language history, use, and contact to operationalize standard German and dialect exposure. Participants could reach a total of 163.5 points per variety. Self-reported proficiency in standard German and Austro-Bavarian dialect was assessed on 100-point slider scales for the dimensions reading, writing, listening, and speaking, which were aggregated so that participants could achieve a maximum score of 100 for each variety. Subsequently, participants completed an online biodata questionnaire, which collected data on relevant sociodemographic variables such as age, gender, and occupation.

Data analyses

First, all continuous outcome (user experience scores) and predictor variables (age, varietal proficiency, varietal exposure) were z-transformed to convert scales into standard units (i.e., standard deviations). All analyses were conducted in R, and generalized additive modeling (GAM; Wood, 2006) was performed using the *mgcv* package and visualized using the *gratia* package. Five models were computed in which each user experience metric was entered respectively as the outcome variable as a nonlinear function of age, varietal proficiency, and varietal exposure. The rationale behind a GAM approach was to account for potential between-participant predictor – outcome nonlinearity. For example, if there is a steep downward curve in age's predictive power of better user experience only at older ages, GAM allows us to capture this complex nonlinear relationship. In GAM, such relationships between the response and predictor variables are modeled by smooth (basis) functions, and the amount of nonlinearity (i.e., the 'wiggliness') of each predictor variable is controlled by penalizing more complicated basis functions more strongly than simpler ones. Since GAMs do not include straightforwardly interpretable coefficients, visualization of model fits is essential.

Results and discussion

Overall user experience

Figure 1 visualizes the descriptive data concerning the participant-subjective user experience responses. Overall, the VR headset appears to provide a positive user experience in terms of spatial presence, usability, simulator sickness, workload, and satisfaction. Based on the results, the following observations can be made. First, the spatial presence scores are relatively moderate ($M=4.41$, $SD=1.13$, range = 2.25–6.5). Given the 'immersive' nature of VR, we initially expected higher scores. That said, even with more extensive VR configurations (e.g., with the Oculus), the spatial presence metric tends to remain within this vicinity (Papachristos et al., 2017, p. 479). It is plausible that the moderate scores in this experimental setting may be due to the fact that participants could not navigate the environment freely but rather were 'ushered' from interlocutor to interlocutor and setting to setting. That is, participants could not agentively decide their VR trajectory. Similarly, the moderate scores may also be an artifact of the relatively short amount of time spent in each VR sequence.

As it concerns system usability, scores were comparatively high ($M=73.2$, $SD=13.9$, range = 32.5–97.5; i.e., higher than the ~50-point threshold to represent "adequate" or "OK" usability). Specifically, according to the Adjective Rating Scale developed in Bangor et al. (2009, pp. 119–121) to assess system usability (a 7-point scale from "worst imaginable" to "best imaginable"), the mean score for this metric can be categorized as "good" (i.e., 5/7). The relatively high score may be attributed to the fact that the VR was rather passive (i.e., the participants were not required to navigate any obstacles other than engaging in conversation with the virtual interlocutors).

The results for the task load index indicate a moderate score ($M = 36.7$, $SD = 16.5$, range = 0–77), with the items 'mental demand' and 'effort' contributing the most to overall workload (see Figure 2). Plausibly, the slightly higher workload in terms of mental rather than physical demand is likely attributable to the degree of spontaneity required to react to the questions in the interactive, conversational virtual environment. Participants otherwise conveyed feeling confident in completing the tasks in the VR ('performance,' noting the variable is reverse-coded) and moreover reported low scores of physical and temporal demand alongside low scores of frustration with the VR tasks.

Overall, the VR sickness metric evinces that participants experienced few to no symptoms during the experimental procedure ($M = 21.0$, $SD = 19.3$, range = 0–72.5). At most, participants reported very low scores for oculomotor symptoms (eyestrain, difficulty focusing, general discomfort), although again, as Figure 3 shows, the means for each of these hovered around 1 on a scale from 0–3 (before weights and data transformation were applied for the overall VR sickness score). Finally, participants reported moderately high levels of satisfaction with the VR instrument on the single-item 7-point scale ($M = 4.81$, $SD = 1.55$, range = 1–7).

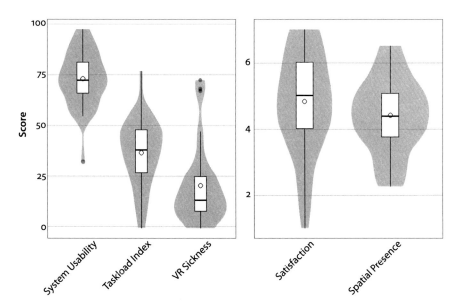

Figure 1. Descriptive data for user experience

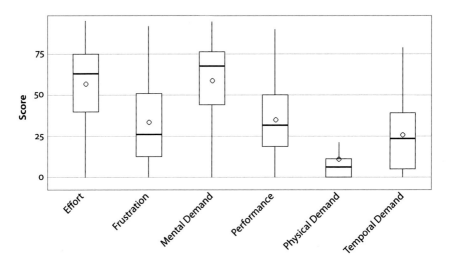

Figure 2. Descriptive item-level data for task load index

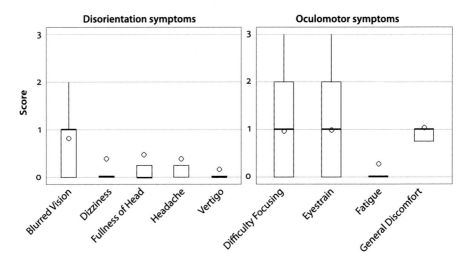

Figure 3. Descriptive item-level data for VR sickness

Individual differences in user experience

In order to explore whether the VR task demands favor or hinder certain participants based on select individual differences, we investigated not only whether participant age may impact user experience, but also whether the proficiency in and exposure to the specific varieties participants are confronted with in the VR (standard German and Austro-Bavarian dialect) may differentially impact user experience.

The GAM analyses in Figure 4 assessing the inter-individual effects of the aforementioned individual differences on participants' user experience scores illustrate marked nonlinearity in the respective associations. As the numeric model summaries in Tables B1–B5 in Appendix B (https://osf.io/sbtae/) show, however, none of these relationships reached significance at an $\alpha \leq .01$ or $\alpha \leq .05$ level. At most, there appears to be a slight association between participants' subjective judgements of task load index and standard German proficiency ($F = 3.41$, $edf = 2.32$, $p = .067$). Specifically, as Figure 4 visualizes, there is a plateau effect until the group-level average of standard German proficiency, after which the task load index falls (i.e., reduced workload during the VR for participants with higher standard German proficiency).

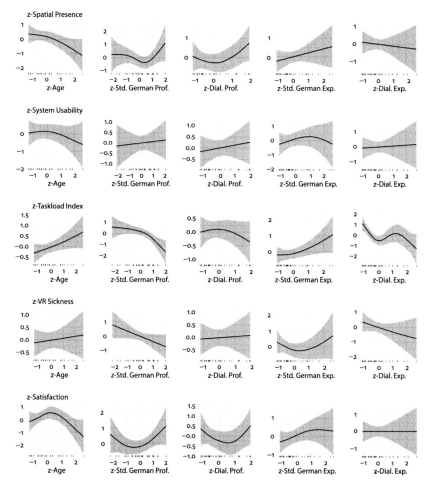

Figure 4. Fixed effects of between-participant variance in the z-transformed predictors age, varietal proficiency, and varietal exposure

Note. Each row represents a separate model, and the title of each row indicates the respective z-scored outcome variable. Std. = Standard, Dial. = Dialect, Exp. = Exposure.

Importantly, as concerns the relationship between task administration, design, and sample choice, age did not emerge as significant in any model. That said, while the task does not seem to systematically discriminate against learners at the interindividual level, an (albeit nonsignificant) negative trend does indicate a slightly lower satisfaction for older learners ($F=0.18$, $edf=2.48$, $p=.85$). In light of this, alongside (a) the recent rise in research investigating L2 acquisition by learners beyond the adolescent and college-aged demographic (Pfenninger & Singleton, 2019; Singleton & Pfenninger, 2019) and (b) the increase in tasks incorporating digital designs (Hampel, 2006), it seems prudent to test for potential age effects during task development and when addressing topics concerning human computer interaction, particularly as concerns affective engagement with and the acceptance of technology. In so doing, we can also better do justice to the goals of inter alia Europe's Digital Decade (Thierry Breton, European Commissioner for the Internal Market), which mobilizes research endeavors to ensure that citizens in Europe — of *all* ages — have access to state-of-the-art technologies with a view to enhancing self-development, social inclusion, and competitiveness.

Discussion and future directions

As we have discussed both from a theoretical and an empirical angle, VR is a time-efficient method and also, according to our results, appears to be for the most part an age-independent task that proffers us the unique potential to delve into the 'nitty gritty' of how we can better define, delimit, and capture what is meant by context. The results of this contribution go to underscore that even low-cost VR technology (i.e., VR designs accessible for 'the average researcher on the street') can immerse L2 learners in a realistic environment primed to elicit data more representative of the multimodal richness and complexity of everyday communication. Additionally, the user experience metrics explored here (system usability, workload, VR sickness, spatial presence, and satisfaction) did not provide any indications that the VR task demands hinder certain participants based on individual differences in age, exposure, or proficiency. While noting that the sample size (32 L2 German learners) was comparatively limited, these initial results are encouraging and in line with previous investigations (Taguchi, 2021, 2022a, b) underscoring VR as a suitable elicitation method in variationist SLA research.

In light of the aforementioned promising results, we use the remainder of this article to outline an array of new avenues that may stir interest and inspire future variationist SLA investigations, placing special emphasis on theoretical, methodological, and computational perspectives concerning how VR may be exploited to continue exploring the nuances of inter- and intraindividual variation in L2 sociolinguistic development. Specifically, we present potential methods that can reconcile experimental control and ecological validity using VR while retaining and indeed emphasizing a focus on the individual learner.

Theoretical perspectives

The variationist enterprise has hitherto primarily explored quantitative patterning of inter- and intra-speaker variation and documented the sensitivity of this variation to social factors (e.g., class, gender) and, especially in variationist SLA analyses of L2 Spanish, to socioaffective variables as well (e.g., George, 2014; Ringer-Hilfinger, 2012). Work in this vein has produced a wealth of information on linguistic, situational, social, and affective parameters that characterize L2 learners' use of one sociolinguistic variant over another. That said, most analyzes have focused on the aggregate distribution of linguistic features across different learner groups, proficiency levels, or, though more rarely, across time. By contrast, questions relating to the dynamics of variation within the speech of an individual has largely been put on the backburner, as Tamminga, MacKenzie et al. (2016) pointed out. For instance, it may be that two L2 learners of Spanish arrive at similar rates of subject pronoun omission in free speech, but the temporal structuring of the realization or omission of the subject pronoun may differ drastically (e.g., speaker 1 may produce variants X and Y as XXXYYY, while speaker 2 produces XYXYYX). In traditional quantitative variationist approaches, such temporal-sequential properties of the variable observations (by which we refer to which variants are produced when, relative to other variants, following Tamminga, MacKenzie et al., 2016) are lost. This is particularly disappointing, especially seeing as L2 learners' sociolinguistic repertoires are subject to prominent idiosyncratic, individual-level variability (e.g., Geeslin et al., 2013).

Thus, as Tamminga, Ahern et al. (2016) and Tamminga, MacKenzie et al. (2016) argued, there is a pressing need in variationist sociolinguistics and SLA to employ methods that better allow us to examine the scales of temporal variability that accompany individuals and identify factors that predict not only overall rates of variant usage, but also, for example, which variants were produced when, relative to other variants. Such questions require a more tailored focus on intra-individual variation (IAV), defined as "differences in the level of a developmental variable within individuals," and potentially also between repeated measures (van Geert & van Dijk, 2002, p. 341). This is especially because IAV is regarded as better representative of the level of the individual, their meaningful idiosyncrasies, and developmental pathways than means-based analyses (de Bot et al., 2007). IAV and related temporal variability is thus not merely white noise (Ellis & Larsen-Freeman, 2006).

To be clear, traditional group-level statistical practices are in no way inadequate and indeed answer important research questions (Kanwit, 2022). A focus on IAV should be thought of as complementary to means-based analyses. This is because it can answer additional research questions concerning which factors predict the temporal-sequential properties of sociolinguistic variant usage, and how these factors may differ between, for example, learners and/or proficiency levels. As has been lamented, however, analyzing within-person temporal dynamics can be complex (e.g., Tamminga, MacKenzie et al., 2016), and there are few methods that can ensure the contextual stability needed to draw reliable comparisons between multiple speakers/learners as concerns predictors of temporal variability. It is thus important to continue expanding our purview to encompass new questions, new methods, and a wider bandwidth of operational measures tailored to both methodologically and computationally capturing the IAV and variability in sociolinguistic resources in the L2. In the following sections, we therefore focus not only on how VR can do justice to Geeslin's (2010) words to "expand methodologically beyond what currently exists" (p. 514), but also on how VR can be exploited to more carefully address issues relating to IAV and thus variability measures that are able to provide additional information to that of mean performance.

Methodological perspectives

With the previous theoretical notes in mind, we now offer several proposals for improving/advancing task design and administration using VR for variationist SLA lines of inquiry. Note that only in the subsequent section do we discuss how the task design advances detailed below can be coupled with computational methods geared towards capturing the meaningfulness of IAV.

Among one of the most notable tasks in variationist SLA and sociolinguistics, the sociolinguistic interview, characterized as a semidirected, informal interview, has enjoyed wide use to elicit relatively spontaneous, unmonitored, and informal speech. Given its nature as an open-ended task, however, "each participant does not produce either the same number of instances of the variable structure or identical contexts for the variable structure" (Gudmestad, 2022, p. 226), which can make between-participant comparisons difficult. A logical next step is thus to develop and employ methods that can introduce higher experimental control to the sociolinguistic interview without fatally undermining the method's ecological validity. To this end, VR has been proposed (e.g., Peeters, 2019) and employed in a successful manner to simulate a sociolinguistic, semidirected interview, both for L1 speakers (Wirtz, 2022) and L2 learners (Wirtz & Pfenninger, 2023). In this procedure, participants engage in informal conversations with a VR interlocutor.

Notably, the drawback here is that the VR interlocutor's speech cannot be tailored to individual participants, in that the VR agent cannot answer questions or react differently to participant responses. Instead, the VR interlocutor's pre-recorded speech (e.g., reactions to participant responses, asking follow-up questions, segueing to new conversational topics) must be general enough so as not to appear salient to participants in the respective context. Planning VR interlocutors' responses, while difficult, is the aspect that allows the greatest experimental control. For instance, the VR interlocutor's pre-recorded speech can be (a) held consistent across all participants, which is hardly possible for live interviewers, and (b) experimentally manipulated in any number of ways to observe whether and how participants react differently to the use of, for example, different sociolinguistic variants. What is more, a VR task may include (sequential) interactions with multiple VR interlocutors with different varieties of Spanish and across different contexts (e.g., in a coffee house, at a friendly gathering, when working on a group project). In other words, this type of VR experimental procedure allows contextual variables to be freely manipulated during task design depending on the research question, and the visual information can be tailored to equate the social-spatial and temporal context (e.g., by recording the videos in the respective settings; see Taguchi, 2022a, for an example and necessary equipment). In addition to collecting spontaneous, unmonitored, and informal speech in the spirit of a traditional sociolinguistic interview, the experimenter may also consider including formal contexts as well (e.g., a job interview, meeting with a professor) to explore how learners vary their language in relation to the situational (in)formality.

As opposed to tasks that have inherent ecological validity (e.g., live interviews), other tasks are designed to facilitate experimental control. These can also profit from VR, specifically as regards maximizing their ecological validity without jeopardizing their controlled nature. As an example, let us consider Solon and Kanwit's (2022) contextualized preference task with an aural component. Recall that this task aims to tap into learners' knowledge of sociolinguistically variable phenomena, regardless of their production of these variants in speech. The contextual detail and task directions in which participants take on the role of a film director and are required to choose the best take enriches the ecological validity of the otherwise very controlled experimental conditions. Employing VR in such a procedure would allow future experimenters to further augment the contextual and situational detail of the task. For example, if the goal is to observe differences in form preference as a function of formality, the VR setting may be situated in an office with an editorial assistant. The VR assistant shows the participant (in the VR) the two takes (contextualized via the [audio]visual surroundings and personal demographics of the virtual speaker) and then asks which take the participant would prefer (for an example, see Table 1). The participant may then be prompted to explain their choice in order to also glean qualitative data on participants' preference(s). Such a VR task offers the added benefit of creating an experimental environment conducive to iteratively capturing both quantitative and qualitative aspects of learners' preferences for sociolinguistic variants, and the task may have the additional advantage of facilitating learner engagement with the experiment (e.g., Taguchi, 2021).

Formal context (e.g., interview)	VR Assistant: *We're trying to choose which take works best for our short film. It's the interview scene where the protagonist is trying to get her first job. Let me show you the two takes.* Take 1: 'Estoy dispuesto a trabajar muy duro para conseguir este trabajo.' Take 2: 'E'toy di'pue'to a trabajar muy duro para conseguir e'te trabajo.' VR Assistant: *Which one do you think works better here?* [PARTICIPANT RESPONSE] VR Assistant: *Ah, I see, good point. Could you explain a little bit more while I take some notes?*

Figure 5. Example of a VR contextualized preference task for /s/-retention or /s/-omission on the basis of Spanish 'I'm willing to work really hard for this job'

Whereas the first VR task implementation discussed above focused on oral production and the second on differences in preference, it is also feasible to draw on VR as a potential method to investigate learners' interpretations of variable structures. Specifically, we propose that a form of 'idiodynamic evaluative judgment task' may have wide-reaching implications for variationist sociolinguistics and SLA. Idiodynamic methods (MacIntyre, 2012) aim to uncover fluctuations over time and the possible reasons underlying them, allowing the researcher to "subject the phenomenon to sharp focus within a short timescale, using procedures that focus on the time-dependent variation within a single individual or unit" (Hiver & Al-Hoorie, 2020, p. 226). Traditionally, the idiodynamic method involves videotaping the participant and then showing them the video to solicit ratings about their own performance. The video is then directly loaded into a specialized software (e.g., Anion Variable Tester) using which participants provide ratings on a specific variable (e.g., motivation) for every second of the task. Drawing on VR, it would be feasible to present participants with an audiovisual conversational setting in which the participant is a third-person viewer. To ascertain how, when, and why L2 learners' evaluative judgements of certain variants or even entire varieties are prone to dynamic fluctuations over time, participants can provide evaluative judgements on different indexical domains (e.g., intelligence, friendliness, etc.) for the entirety of the (preferably brief) interactional instance. From a quantitative angle, this would allow us to localize how different features or varieties based on their contextual location in the stimulus and the personal demographics of the speaker contribute to fluctuations in sociolinguistic evaluative judgements. Using stimulated recall, the participant may then also provide qualitative data to facilitate explanations for their ratings and rating trajectory.

On the whole, these proposals offer unique ways to home in on individual variability and time-dependent variation, albeit notably on comparatively short timescales. However, given their contextual and temporal stability, the tasks may be included in longitudinal investigations over longer time periods. Specifically, these methods have the potential to produce rich IAV which can be systematically, both quantitatively and qualitatively, analyzed to better home in on the meaningfulness of participant-level idiosyncrasy and within- and between-task variance. In the final section, we direct our focus to quantitative methods that can capture and adequately handle such intra-individual fluctuations without relegating them to white noise or generalizing over potentially significant "'messy little details' that make up the 'here and now' of real time" (Larsen-Freeman & Cameron, 2008, p.159).

Computational perspectives

Recent rises in more sophisticated statistical modeling procedures (e.g., mixed-effects regression) allow us to control for non-independence arising due to multiple data points per individual but comes with the drawback that such statistical practices are typically used to generalize over individual-level variation. Under the conceptual notion of IAV as a source of information, such practices are tricky, as this would smooth away the very variability that may provide further information on the temporal dynamics of stylistic variation (Tamminga, Ahern et al., 2016; Larsen-Freeman & Cameron, 2008). This necessitates modeling procedures that strike the right balance between "over-simplification distorting reality and under-simplification presenting an overwhelming amount of unmanageable information" (Pallotti, 2022, p.691), and GAM has been proposed as a method that has the potential to generate multifactorial, nonlinear, probabilistic models with a better fit to the data than those currently available (Pfenninger & Wirtz, 2024). As we illustrated in the cross-sectional analysis above, GAMs can capture nonlinear relationships in group-level studies and have thus also been used informally to suggest the functional form for the association between two continuous covariates (Hastie & Tibshirani, 1986).

For this reason, Tamminga, Ahern et al. (2016) suggested that a GAM approach may be a fruitful avenue for exploring potential sociolinguistic and psycholinguistic sources of temporal clustering within an oral interview situation. In a variationist SLA framework, such analytic methods translate to investigating why and when deflections from baseline varietal behavior emerge. Using VR as the experimental elicitation method, it is possible to generate the stability in context needed to address such research questions (Peeters, 2019; Taguchi, 2021, 2022a, 2022b; Wirtz, 2022). In so doing, we can investigate issues regarding whether and even at which points contextual factors (operationalized as the time-dependent audiovisual VR material at the time[s] of baseline deflection) impact learners' varietal behavior, the insights from which would have promise in speaking to the temporal dynamics of stylistic practice in the L2. Combining group- and individual-level analyses of this would then break new ground as to the level of individuality not only within the group, but the systematicity of behavior in individuals and in function of which VR contextual aspects.

In the case of VR semidirected interviews (e.g., including both formal and informal settings, interlocutors with different varieties), analyses (such as GAM) tailored to capturing learner-level IAV within a particular context, in addition to differences in varietal behavior or sociolinguistic variant choice between contexts, have the potential to provide rich information concerning participants' developing sociolinguistic resources. For example, what is the temporal structuring of the production of sociolinguistic variants, and are there any contextual aspects of the VR that contribute to observed variability in participants' interlanguage? Similar questions may be applied to future investigations employing the proposed idiodynamic sociolinguistic evaluative judgment task. That is, in the perceptual/interpretive domain, how can we correlate sociolinguistic form use and varietal behavior by VR agents with shifting dynamics of L2 learners' perceptions of socio-indexical variation? Which multimodal contextual factors of the VR agents (e.g., varietal use, gesture, eye gaze, facial expressions) impact changes in varietal perception and evaluative judgements, and to what extent do such changes relate to individual learner differences in socioaffect, cognition, and proficiency? In terms of computational practices, and in line with Tamminga, Ahern et al. (2016), we argue that GAM in combination with VR task design and administration has promise for extracting and further investigating the temporal, context-dependent dynamics of stylistic practice and multidimensional interpretations thereof in the L2.

Conclusion

The present study argued from a theoretical and empirical angle the unique potential VR proffers variationist SLA research and beyond. Even low-cost VR headsets can immerse L2 learners in realistic environments that both facilitate experimental control on the side of the researcher and, at the same time, are more representative of the multimodal richness and complexity of everyday communication. Importantly, the user experience metrics explored here did not suggest that the VR tasks come at a disadvantage to certain participants as a function of individual differences in age, exposure, or proficiency. While these results must be replicated with larger samples in additional contexts and in the presence of different VR tasks, we used these findings as a springboard to detail a range of new avenues that may inspire future variationist SLA investigations. The hope is that these theoretical, methodological, and computational perspectives stir interest among variationist SLA scholars concerning the extensive possibilities for exploiting the strengths of VR to continue exploring, in a context-dependent way, the nuances involved in the development of sociolinguistic competence in the L2.

References

Adamson, D. H., & Regan, V. (1991). The acquisition of community speech norms by Asian immigrants learning English as a second language: A preliminary study. *Studies in Second Language Acquisition*, *13*(1), 1–22.

Amin, A., Gromala, D., Tong, X., & Shaw, C. (2016). Immersion in cardboard VR compared to a traditional head-mounted display. In S. Lackey & R. Shumaker (Eds.), *Virtual, augmented and mixed reality* (pp. 269–276). Springer.

Andringa, S., & Godfroid, A. (2020). Sampling bias and the problem of generalizability in applied linguistics. *Annual Review of Applied Linguistics*, *40*, 134–142.

Bangor, A., Kortum, P., & Miller, J. (2009). Determining what individual SUS scores mean: adding an adjective rating scale. *Journal of Usability Studies*, *4*(3), 114–123.

Biocca, F., & Levy, M. R. (1995). Communication applications of virtual reality. In F. Biocca & M. R. Levy (Eds.), *Communication in the age of virtual reality* (pp. 127–157). Erlbaum.

Brooke, J. (1996). SUS – A quick and dirty usability scale. In P. W. Jordan, B. Thomas, I. L. McClelland, & B. Weerdmeester (Eds.), *Usability evaluation in industry* (pp. 189–194). Taylor & Francis.

Chappell, W., & Kanwit, M. (2022). Do learners connect sociophonetic variation with regional and social characteristics?: The case of L2 perception of Spanish aspiration. *Studies in Second Language Acquisition*, *44*(1), 185–209.

de Bot, K., Lowie, W. M., & Verspoor, M. H. (2007). A dynamic systems theory approach to second language acquisition. *Bilingualism: Language and Cognition*, *10*(1), 7–21.

Ellis, N. C., & Larsen-Freeman, D. (2006). Language emergence: Implications for applied linguistics – Introduction to the special issue. *Applied Linguistics, 27*(1), 558–589.

Fox, J., Arena, D., & Bailenson, J. N. (2018). Virtual reality: A survival guide for the social scientist. *Behavior Research Methods, 50*(2), 862–869.

Geeslin, K. L. (2003). A comparison of copula choice: Native Spanish speakers and advanced learners. *Language Learning, 53*(4), 703–764.

Geeslin, K. L. (2010). Beyond "naturalistic": On the role of task characteristics and the importance of multiple elicitation methods. *Studies in Hispanic and Lusophone Linguistics, 3*(2), 501–520.

Geeslin, K. L. (2018). Variable structures and sociolinguistic variation. In P. A. Malovrh & A. G. Benati (Eds.), *The handbook of advanced proficiency in second language acquisition* (pp. 547–565). Wiley-Blackwell.

Geeslin, K. L. (2022). Introduction. In K. L. Geeslin (Ed.), *The Routledge Handbook of second language acquisition and sociolinguistics* (pp. xix–xxvi). Routledge.

Geeslin, K. L., & Gudmestad, A. (2008). Comparing interview and written elicitation tasks in native and non-native data: Do speakers do what we think they do? In J. B. de Garavito & E. Valenzuela (Eds.), *Selected proceedings of the 10th Hispanic linguistics symposium* (pp. 64–88). Cascadilla Proceedings Project.

Geeslin, K. L., & Hanson, S. (2023). Sociolinguistic approaches to communicative competence. In M. Kanwit & M. Solon (Eds.), *Communicative competence in a second language. Theory, method, and applications* (pp. 40–59). Routledge.

Geeslin, K. L., Linford, B., Fafulas, S., Long, A. Y., & Díaz-Campos, M. (2013). The L2 development of subject form variation in Spanish: The individual vs. the group. In J. Cabrelli, G. Lord, A. De Prada Pérez, & J. Aaron (Eds.), *Selected proceedings of the 16th Hispanic Linguistics Symposium* (pp. 156–174). Cascadilla Proceedings Project.

Geeslin, K. L., with Long, A. Y. (2014). *Sociolinguistics and second language acquisition. learning to use language in context*. Routledge.

Geeslin, K. L., & Schmidt, L. B. (2018). Study abroad and L2 learner attitudes. In C. Sanz & A. Morales-Front (Eds.), *The Routledge Handbook of study abroad research and practice* (pp. 387–405). Routledge.

George, A. (2014). Study abroad in Central Spain: The development of regional phonological features. *Foreign Language Annals, 47*(1), 97–114.

Gudmestad, A. (2022). Eliciting variable structures across tasks. In K. L. Geeslin (Ed.), *The Routledge Handbook of second language acquisition and sociolinguistics* (pp. 224–236). Routledge.

Gudmestad, A., House, L., & Geeslin, K. L. (2013). What a Bayesian analysis can do for SLA: New tools for the sociolinguistic study of subject expression in L2 Spanish. *Language Learning, 63*(3), 371–399.

Hampel, R. (2006). Rethinking task design for the digital age: A framework for language teaching and learning in a synchronous online environment. *ReCALL, 18*(1), 105–121.

Hart, S. G. (2006). Nasa-Task Load Index (NASA-TLX); 20 Years Later. *Proceedings of the Human Factors and Ergonomics Society annual meeting, 50*(9), 904–908.

Hastie, T., & Tibshirani, R. (1986). Generalized additive models. *Statistical Science, 1*(3), 297–310. https://www.jstor.org/stable/2245459.

Hiver, P., & Al-Hoorie, A. H. (2020). *Research methods for complexity theory in applied linguistics*. Multilingual Matters.

Kanwit, M. (2017). What we gain by combining variationist and concept-oriented approaches: The case of acquiring Spanish future-time expression. *Language Learning*, 67(2), 461–498.

Kanwit, M. (2022). Sociolinguistic competence: What we know so far and where we're heading. In K. L. Geeslin (Ed.), *The Routledge Handbook of second language acquisition and sociolinguistics* (pp. 30–44). Routledge.

Kanwit, M., & Geeslin, K. L. (2014). The interpretation of Spanish subjunctive and indicative forms in adverbial clauses: A cross-sectional study. *Studies in Second Language Acquisition*, 36(3), 487–533.

Kim, H. K., Park, J., Choi, Y., & Choe, M. (2018). Virtual reality sickness questionnaire (VRSQ): Motion sickness measurement index in a virtual reality environment. *Applied Ergonomics*, 69(1), 66–73.

Labov, W. (1966). *The social stratification of English in New York City*. Center for Applied Linguistics.

Larsen-Freeman, D., & Cameron, L. (2008). *Complex systems and applied linguistics*. Oxford University Press.

Lombard, M., & Ditton, T. (1997). At the heart of it all: The concept of presence. *Journal of Computer-Mediated Communication*, 3(2). https://onlinelibrary.wiley.com/doi/full/10.1111/j.1083-6101.1997.tb00072.x.

Lombard, M., Ditton, T. B., & Weinstein, L. (2009). Measuring presence: The temple presence inventory. *Twelfth International Workshop on Presence*, 1–15.

Lyster, R. (1994). The effect of functional-analytic teaching on aspects of French immersion students' sociolinguistic competence. *Applied Linguistics*, 15(1), 263–287.

MacIntyre, P. D. (2012). The idiodynamic method: A closer look at the dynamics of communication traits. *Communication Research Reports*, 29(4), 361–367.

Milroy, L., & Gordon, M. (2003). *Sociolinguistics: Method and interpretation*. Blackwell.

Pallotti, G. (2022). Cratylus' silence: On the philosophy and methodology of Complex Dynamic Systems Theory in SLA. *Second Language Research*, 38(3), 689–701.

Papachristos, N. M., Vrellis, I., & Mikropoulos, T. A. (2017). A comparison between Oculus Rift and a low-cost smartphone VR Headset: Immersive user experience and learning. *IEEE 17th International Conference on Advanced Learning Technologies*, 477–481.

Peeters, D. (2019). Virtual reality: A game-changing method for the language sciences. *Psychonomic Bulletin & Review*, 26(3), 894–900.

Pfenninger, S. E., & Singleton, D. (2019). A critical review of research relating to the learning, use and effects of additional and multiple languages in later life. *Language Teaching*, 52(4), 419–449.

Pfenninger, S. E., & Wirtz, M. A. (2024). Reconciling the divides: A dynamic integrative analysis of variability and commonality in (pre)primary school English development in Switzerland. *Language Teaching Research Quarterly*, 46(1), 145–173.

Rehner, K. (2002). *The development of aspects of linguistic and discourse competence by advanced second language learners of French* [Doctoral Dissertation]. OISE/University of Toronto.

Ringer-Hilfinger, K. (2012). Learner acquisition of dialect variation in a study abroad context: The case of the Spanish [θ]. *Foreign Language Annals*, 45(1), 430–446.

Safont-Jordà, M. P. (2003). Metapragmatic awareness and pragmatic production of third language learners of English: A focus on request acts realizations. *The International Journal of Bilingualism*, 7(1), 43–69.

Schilling-Estes, N. (2008). Stylistic variation and the sociolinguistic interview: A reconsideration. *25 Years Os Applied Linguistics in Spain: Milestones and Challenges*, 971–986.

Schmidt, L. B. (2018). L2 development of perceptual categorization of dialectal sounds. A study in Spanish. *Studies in Second Language Acquisition*, 40(4), 857–882.

Singleton, D., & Pfenninger, S. E. (2019). Bilingualism in midlife. In A. De Houwer & L. Ortega (Eds.), *The Cambridge Handbook of bilingualism* (pp. 76–100). Cambridge University Press.

Solon, M., & Kanwit, M. (2014). The emergence of future verbal morphology in Spanish as a foreign language. *Studies in Hispanic and Lusophone Linguistics*, 7(1), 115–147.

Solon, M., & Kanwit, M. (2022). New methods for tracking development of sociophonetic competence: Exploring a preference task for Spanish /d/ deletion. *Applied Linguistics*, 1–21.

Taguchi, N. (2021). Application of immersive virtual reality to pragmatics data collection methods: Insights from interviews. *CALICO Journal*, 38(2), 181–201.

Taguchi, N. (2022a). Dispreferred speech acts in virtual reality: Analysis of tone choices and hesitations. *System*, 106, 102793.

Taguchi, N. (2022b). Immersive virtual reality for pragmatics task development. *TESOL Quarterly*, 56(1), 308–335.

Tamminga, M., Ahern, C., & Ecay, A. (2016). Generalized additive mixed models for intraspeaker variation. *Linguistics Vanguard*, 2(s1).

Tamminga, M., MacKenzie, L., & Embick, D. (2016). The dynamics of variation in individuals. *Linguistic Variation*, 16(2), 300–336.

Ushioda, E. (2015). Context and Complex Dynamic Systems Theory. In Z. Dörnyei, P. D. MacIntyre, & A. Henry (Eds.), *Motivational dynamics in language learning* (pp. 47–54). Multilingual Matters.

van Geert, P., & van Dijk, M. (2002). Focus on variability: New tools to study intra-individual variability in developmental data. *Infant Behavior and Development*, 25(4), 340–374.

Vanrell, M. del M., Feldhausen, I., & Astruc, L. (2018). The Discourse Completion Task in Romance prosody research: Status quo and outlook. In I. Feldhausen, J. Fliessbach, & M. del M. Vanrell (Eds.), *Methods in prosody: A Romance language perspective*, (pp. 191–227). Language Science Press.

Walker, A., García, C., Cortés, Y., & Campbell-Kibler, K. (2014). Comparing social meanings across listener and speaker groups: The indexical field of Spanish /s/. *Language Variation and Change*, 26(2), 169–189.

Wirtz, M. A. (2022). Discourse completion tasks meet virtual reality: A pilot study on virtual reality as an elicitation instrument. *Research Methods in Applied Linguistics*, 1(3), 1–12.

Wirtz, M. A. (2023). Inter- and intra-individual variation in adult L2 sociolinguistic repertoires. Dynamics of linguistic, socioaffective and cognitive factors [Doctoral Dissertation]. University of Salzburg.

Wirtz, M. A., & Pfenninger, S. E. (2023). Capturing thresholds and continuities: Individual differences as predictors of L2 sociolinguistic repertoires in adult migrant learners in Austria. *Applied Linguistics*, 1–23.

Wood, S. (2006). *Generalized additive models: An introduction with R*. CRC Press.

EPILOGUE

Kimberly Geeslin's contributions to second language acquisition, sociolinguistics, and Hispanic linguistics and her role as a mentor and academic leader

Robert Bayley[1], Kristen Kennedy Terry[2], Laura Gurzynski-Weiss[3] & Eliza Pavalko[3]
[1] University of California, Davis | [2] Arizona State University | [3] Indiana University

This epilogue reviews the extraordinary career of Kimberly Geeslin as a scholar, mentor, and academic leader. The chapter first examines her numerous contributions to the fields of second language acquisition, sociolinguistics, and Hispanic linguistics. We then discuss her role as a mentor, not only to numerous students at her home institution of Indiana University but to many early-career scholars whose professional development she fostered. Finally, the chapter examines Professor Geeslin's contributions as an academic leader, including her role in building the graduate program in Hispanic Linguistics and her overall contributions to her university, with particular attention to her role in promoting the careers of women in academia.

Keywords: second language acquisition, variation, sociolinguistics, Hispanic linguistics mentor, colleague

Kimberly Geeslin lived a full and multi-dimensional life not only as a scholar, editor, mentor, and academic administrator, but also as a devoted mother and spouse, amateur athlete, involved community member, and steadfast friend to many. This epilogue offers an overview of a few of the aspects of her remarkable life: her many contributions to the fields of second language acquisition (SLA), sociolinguistics, and Hispanic linguistics and her roles as an academic mentor and university leader. As noted in the announcement of her receipt of the 2024 Susan Gass Award for Impact in Second Language Acquisition, "her scholarly work over the last three decades was absolutely foundational in advancing our understanding of the intersection of SLA and sociolinguistics." Moreover, as attested in the award announcement, "Kim was a role model for all who aspired to success in academia and in applied linguistics, and she did so while always recognizing the human side of being a scholar" ("Announcing", 2024, p. 1). In this epilogue we will try to do justice to the legacy of our colleague, friend, and mentor by first considering Professor Geeslin's extraordinary studies, many conducted with colleagues and former or current students, that serve as models for those who wish to conduct research that combines the insights of variationist sociolinguistics with SLA. We then focus on Professor Geeslin's roles as an editor and book author. We also provide an overview of her role as a mentor, not only to her own students, of whom there were many, but also to numerous scholars who have become more widely recognized thanks in no small part to her role in promoting their work and inviting them to participate in various projects. Finally, we provide a perspective on her important roles as a university colleague and administrator.

Contributions to the interdisciplinary study of second language acquisition and sociolinguistics

The modern study of language variation and change began in the 1960s with William Labov's studies on the island of Martha's Vineyard off the coast of Massachusetts and later in New York City's Lower East Side and Harlem (Labov, 1963, 1966, 1972). This work was based on the insight that the variation that we observe in all linguistic levels is not random, or free. Rather, it is constrained by linguistic influences, such as the influence of the following phonological environment on consonant cluster reduction in English or the grammatical status of the form containing the cluster, as well as the speaker's social characteristics such as gender, class, and ethnicity. For example, final -t/-d is more likely to be deleted from a word like "mist" when it is followed by another consonant rather than a vowel, and /t/ is more likely to be deleted from a monomorpheme like "mist" than when the /t/ serves as a past-tense marker in "missed" (Guy, 1980; Labov, 1989). That is, variation in language is usually not random. Rather, it is characterized by "orderly heterogeneity" (Weinreich et al., 1968, p. 100).

In his work on the Lower East Side, Labov developed methods that have become standard in sociolinguistics. These include the sociolinguistic interview, a set of questions in modules designed to elicit relatively informal speech (Labov, 1966, 1984). Questions deal with topics such as childhood games, characteristics of young men or women in the neighborhood, and most famously, whether interviewees had ever been in a situation where they thought they might die (i.e., danger of death scenarios). In addition, interviews often included a number of tasks designed to promote style shifting such as a reading passage, a word list, and a list of minimal pairs.

As noted above, a fundamental insight of variationist sociolinguistics is that a speaker's choice of one or another variant is affected not only by one, but by multiple factors. For example, consider the well-known case of variation between null and overt subject pronouns in Spanish and other languages (e.g., *yo/Ø hablo* 'I speak'). A speaker's choice to use or to omit a subject pronoun is conditioned by numerous factors including whether there is a change from the subject of the preceding finite verb; the person and number of the verb; and the tense, mood, and aspect of the verb, among others (see e.g., Barrenechea & Alonso, 1973; Guy et al., forthcoming; Otheguy & Zentella, 2012; Silva-Corvalán, 1994).

In studies of both mono- and multilingual communities, systematic variation has been found at all linguistic levels, ranging from phonological variation, such as /s/-aspiration and deletion in Spanish (File-Muriel & Brown, 2011; Lynch, 2009; Terrell, 1979) to grammatical variation, such as the aforementioned variation between overt and null subject pronouns or variation between the morphological and periphrastic future (Orozco, 2018), to variation in patterns of code-switching (Torres Cacoullos & Travis, 2019; Zentella, 1997). The question, though, is whether systematic variation, or orderly heterogeneity, is also characteristic of learner language and, if so, what the study of such variation can tell us about the process of acquisition.

The modern study of SLA began around the same time as the modern study of language variation and change, or variationist sociolinguistics. Among the key insights of early SLA was that learner language constituted a system, or interlanguage (Selinker, 1972), characterized by features of the target language and the learner's first language (L1), but fully explainable by neither. Further, among the most obvious characteristics of learner language is its variability. For example, sometimes learners will use a correct verbal inflection and sometimes they will not, or sometimes they will correctly use a form of the Spanish copula *ser* to refer to a permanent characteristic and sometimes they will use a form of the copula *estar*. The question arises, then, when are learners more likely to use the correct form of the verb or when are they more likely to choose the appropriate copula? Is the variation that characterizes learner production systematic, like variation in native speech? That is, given sufficient data, can we predict, in a probabilistic sense, when learners are likely to choose one form and when they are likely to choose another? While a number of early second language (L2) studies used variationist methods to attempt to answer such questions (e.g., Adamson & Kovac, 1981; Dickerson, 1975; Tarone, 1985; Wolfram, 1985; Young, 1988), until the late 1990s and early 2000s, studies of variation in L2 speech were relatively unusual, and most dealt with English or French. For example, in their edited volume on SLA and linguistic variation, Bayley and Preston (1996) were only able to include a single paper on variation in a language other than English: Regan's (1996) study of variable *ne* deletion (the first particle of negation) by Irish learners of French. The situation today is quite different, in part due to the very substantial body of research by Geeslin and her students on variation in L2 Spanish, as well as Geeslin's efforts to promote the work of scholars working on other languages such as L2 Chinese and French (e.g., Li, 2010, 2014; Li et al., 2022 for L2 Chinese; Kennedy Terry, 2017, 2022 for L2 French).

Kimberly Geeslin's contributions to SLA and sociolinguistics

Kimberly Geeslin advanced the fields of SLA and sociolinguistics in numerous ways beginning with her University of Arizona dissertation (1999), which examined variation in the use of the copulas *ser* and *estar* with adjectives by 77 high school students of Spanish in Durham, New Hampshire. The students, representing four different levels, had minimal or no contact with native speakers of Spanish and had similar experiences in learning Spanish. The dissertation was among the first to examine a structure that is not only complex but that is also undergoing change in the target language. Specifically, the acquisition of the Spanish copular forms is complicated by an ongoing change occurring throughout the Spanish-speaking world, where *estar* is being used in contexts that were previously restricted to *ser*, a change that Silva-Corvalán (1986, 1994) argues is accelerated in situations of language contact such as the United States, where Spanish is in contact with English. In her dissertation, Geeslin addressed Preston's (1993) argument that L2 learners are on a "fast track" of language change, and, in contrast to native speakers, they are less likely to be affected by social evaluations of incoming forms. She thus innovatively combined the study of an ongoing change in Spanish with the study of the acquisition of a complex feature by L2 learners.

As would become characteristic of her later work, in the dissertation, Geeslin used multiple means of data elicitation, including a semi-structured interview with questions designed to elicit copulas, a picture description task, and a contextualized preference task. As is typical in sociolinguistic research, she used regression analysis to test the effect of multiple constraints on students' choice of *estar* or *ser*. Constraints ranged from grammatical accuracy (i.e., accuracy in person, number, and tense) to susceptibility of the characteristic to change (i.e., whether the attribute is susceptible to change, e.g., fat vs. tall) to aspectual categories of dynamicity and telicity. Importantly, the results showed a clear relationship between the stages of language change in monolingual communities and language acquisition.

Geeslin published the most important results of the study in a 2002 article in *Studies in Second Language Acquisition*, and, in a 2003 article in *Language Learning*, she extended her work on copula choice through a direct comparison of contextualized questionnaire data from advanced L2 learners with data from native Spanish speakers. Results from the comparative study showed that the choice of the copula *estar* is predicted by the interaction of semantic and pragmatic features but that there are important differences between the learners and native Spanish speakers. Semantic features included characteristics such as size, age, status, etc., while pragmatic features included frame of reference (i.e., whether a comparison was implied and dependent on direct experience with the situation described). Specifically, she found that advanced learners apply pragmatic constraints in contexts where native speakers do not, while native speakers are more affected by lexical and semantic constraints.

Geeslin went on to study the acquisition of many other features of Spanish, as well as to conduct important research on variation in the language varieties of the Iberian Peninsula, but the study of copula choice remained a focus of considerable work. Studies include work on copula choice in steady-state L2 grammars (Geeslin & Guijarro Fuentes, 2003); the acquisition of Spanish copula choice by Portuguese speakers (Geeslin & Guijarro-Fuentes, 2006); variation in the use of *estar* in the Spanish of bilingual Galicians (Guijarro-Fuentes & Geeslin, 2006); copula choice in the Spanish of speakers of Basque, Catalan, Galician, and Valencian (Geeslin & Guijarro-Fuentes, 2008); and a study of copula choice in Venezuelan Spanish (Díaz-Campos & Geeslin, 2011). Although all of these studies are models of rigorous research and contribute to our understanding of an ongoing change, the 2008 paper in *Bilingualism: Language and Cognition* that compares copula choice in four different language contact situations, is perhaps the most important. Results showed that, contrary to what Guijarro-Fuentes and Geeslin (2006) found for Galician Spanish, greater selection of *estar* does not occur in all contact situations. That is, bilingualism does not necessarily lead to more rapid language change. Moreover, their results showed that the predictors of copula choice are stable across different groups of bilinguals even though the rates of selection of *ser* or *estar* vary considerably.

Geeslin's final study of copula choice, conducted with her former student and one of the editors of this volume, Matthew Kanwit (Kanwit & Geeslin, 2020) is part of a newer strand of L2 research that focuses on learners' interpretation of variable linguistic forms. Specifically, they asked how learners interpret the copulas *ser* and *estar* with adjectives, and, as is typical of Geeslin's studies of language learners, they included learners at multiple levels and compared learners' responses with those of native speakers. Their results showed how learners' interpretation of the copula plus adjective structure developed as their proficiency increased. Moreover, like their earlier studies of learners' interpretation of subjunctive and indicative verb forms (Kanwit & Geeslin, 2014, 2018), the 2020 study of copula choice provides an insight into how learners interpret variable structures, an important component of sociolinguistic competence.

Although Kimberly Geeslin studied many other aspects of language variation and language learning, we have spent considerable time on her studies of the copula contrast for several reasons. First, these studies illustrate the skill with which she was able to take a single linguistic feature that is undergoing change and show how detailed examination of that feature in a wide range of contexts could enhance our understanding of language change generally, as well as the processes involved in language learning. As noted above, for example, her research on copula choice in different bilingual contexts with Guijarro-Fuentes (2008) showed that bilingualism did not have a uniform effect on a structure undergoing change, but rather, that rates differed according to the context. Second, like her studies with former student Matthew Kanwit of learners' interpretation of verbal mood (Kanwit & Geeslin, 2014, 2018), their later study (2020) of copula choice advanced our understanding of how learners acquire a relatively understudied aspect of sociolinguistic competence: the ability to interpret the meaning and social implications of variation in grammatical structures.

Like many variationists, Geeslin tended to study particular sociolinguistic variables from multiple perspectives, as shown in her work on copula choice as well as in several other areas, including subject pronoun expression (SPE). In formal linguistics, SPE has been the object of intense study for decades, beginning with Chomsky's (1981) discussion of the pro-drop parameter. Discussions of SPE have also figured prominently in Spanish sociolinguistics, beginning with Barrenechea and Alonso's (1973) study of SPE in Buenos Aires. Thanks to five decades of research, the constraints on speakers' choices to use or omit a subject pronoun are well known (Carvalho et al., 2015; Otheguy & Zentella, 2012). For example, as mentioned in the introduction to this epilogue, speakers are more likely to use an overt pronoun when there is a change in subject. As well, speakers are more likely to choose the overt option with singular than with plural verbs (Guy et al., forthcoming; Otheguy & Zentella, 2012). In addition, like copula choice, SPE has been a focus of sociolinguists studying the effects of language contact. Thus, Otheguy and Zentella (2012), in a study of several generations of speakers of six national Spanish dialects in New York City, report that speakers born in the United States tend to use more overt pronouns than more recent migrants. Moreover, Guy et al. (forthcoming) based on the Otheguy and Zentella corpus as well as data from California, Massachusetts, and Texas, show a correlation between the percentage of their life that speakers have lived in the United States and rates of overt pronoun use.

Because SPE has been so extensively studied and the constraints in monolingual speech are so well understood, it presents an ideal structure to study whether and how L2 learners acquire the constraints on variation that have been identified in native speech. Geeslin's research in the area extends over several decades and, as in her studies of copula choice, she often brought in current and former students as collaborators. These important collaborations with graduate students and faculty are discussed in detail in a later section.

In her research with Aarnes Gudmestad and other former students, Geeslin sought to go beyond the formal focus that had characterized previous research on subject expression in SLA to compare the patterns observed in L2 speech with the patterns in native Spanish that had been found in the extensive sociolinguistic literature on this variable. Geeslin and Gudmestad (2008c), for example, compared the performance of 16 advanced speakers of L2 Spanish with 16 native speakers from a range of Spanish-speaking countries. In addition to a background questionnaire, participants completed a multiple-choice grammar test and a 30-minute sociolinguistic interview conducted by native speaker interviewers.

Overall results from this initial study showed similarities between native and nonnative speakers. Thus, as found in other studies, in the sociolinguistic interviews, speakers in both groups used more overt pronouns with first- and third-person singular verbs than with the corresponding plurals. However, in contrast to the usual practice in sociolinguistic studies, Geeslin and Gudmestad suggest that the full range of subjects needs to be explored, including lexical noun phrases, null subjects, and overt pronouns, as well as indefinite, interrogative, and demonstrative pronouns. Of course, the inclusion of multiple variants of the dependent variable complicates the analysis as well as defining the envelope of variation. However, as the authors contend, there is no reason to think that L2 learners limit variation to the context where native speech allows variation.

Geeslin, Gudmestad, and other students and colleagues continued to examine the acquisition of subject expression from a wide variety of perspectives. Studies included work that relied on sociolinguistic interviews and related methods (e.g., Geeslin & Gudmestad, 2011; Gudmestad & Geeslin, 2010, 2011) as well as studies focusing on subject selection using written contextualized preference tasks (WCPTs), also known as written contextualized tasks (WCTs) (Geeslin et al., 2015; Geeslin et al., 2023; Linford & Geeslin, 2022). Much of this work is discussed in Escalante et al. (Chapter 5, this volume) and will not be covered in detail here. Suffice it to say that, as with her studies of copula choice, Geeslin explored the acquisition of SPE from multiple perspectives and compared learner performance with native speaker performance on a wide range of tasks.

Geeslin went on to produce important studies of the acquisition and use of a number of other grammatical features including, for example, habitual and progressive aspectual marking (Geeslin & Fafulas, 2022) and variation in the use of the present perfect in Mexico and Spain (Geeslin et al., 2013), and, along with former and current students, she investigated the acquisition of these structures by different groups of students in different contexts, including study abroad. For example, in a 2015 article in *Probus*, Kanwit, Geeslin, and Fafulas expanded their previous work on the present perfect and examined copula contrast and selection of the present progressive by students studying abroad in Mexico and Spain. And, as is typical in Geeslin's work, she and her collaborators also included data from native speakers in each country to establish appropriate regional targets.

In addition to producing numerous meticulously crafted studies of the acquisition of particular variable features, Geeslin addressed a variety of theoretical and methodological issues. These include an agenda for integrating studies of the L2 sound system in L2 variation research and an overview of the state of research on variation in L2 Spanish (Geeslin, 2011), a study of the possible contribution of Bayesian statistics to SLA (Gudmestad et al., 2013), an important chapter on the role of the interlocutor in L2 variation research (Geeslin, 2020), an overview of the acquisition of sociolinguistic competence by heritage learners studying abroad (Geeslin, Gudmestad et al., 2021), and an account of how variationist research can contribute to our understanding of advanced learners of L2 Spanish (Geeslin, 2021), among many other book chapters and review articles. Space does not permit discussion of the full range of papers cited here. Hence, we will examine in detail two of the more important papers (Geeslin, 2020, 2021), which will serve as examples of the quality and significance of Geeslin's methodological and theoretical studies.

Geeslin (2020) addresses the important but often neglected role of the interlocutor in L2 variation research. Studies of both L1 and L2 variation have shown that the social characteristics of the interviewer or conversational partner can affect the type of language used in sociolinguistic interviews (see, e.g., Bayley, 1994; Rickford & McNair-Knox, 1994; Schilling-Estes, 2004). Bayley (1994) for example, found that Chinese learners of English used more correct past-tense forms when interviewed with a fellow Chinese interlocutor present than when interviewed alone by the researcher, a white male graduate student. Rickford and McNair-Knox reported that the number of African American English variants used by a young woman changed based on the race of the interviewer. Additionally, Schilling-Estes (2004) offers a detailed analysis of conversations between an African American male graduate student and a Lumbee male undergraduate in North Carolina. She found that the speakers' language use changed depending on the topic of the conversation and whether speakers were highlighting their identities as minority students in a predominantly white environment or focusing more particularly on their specific ethnic identity.

Despite considerable evidence of the effect of the interlocutor's social characteristics and the importance of the input learners receive, the interviewer's social characteristics have seldom been taken into account in SLA studies nor has the language of the interviewer been analyzed in detail. Based on an extensive review of the role of the interlocutor in sociolinguistics, Geeslin (2020) notes that speech (the input for L2 learners) varies in multiple ways and summarizes two important implications of this fact for L2s: "The first is that second language learners must also acquire the ability to manage these tools in order to accurately interpret and express facts about their own identities and the second is that the input to which learners have access is neither constant nor the same for all learners" (2020, p. 137).

Geeslin proposes a model, based on Preston's (1993, 1996, 2000; Fasold & Preston, 2007) psycholinguistic model of inherent variability for incorporating interlocutor characteristics and features of the learning situation into researchers' analyses. Crucially, the model incorporates the insight that learners are active participants in language use and that learner participation is influenced by both cognitive (e.g., working memory) and experiential factors (e.g., opportunities for interaction with native speakers of the target language). Both the learner and the interlocutor participate in the developing interactional context. Geeslin concludes: "As we build our understanding of the variable nature of learner-directed speech across contexts, the variability in learner-produced language as it reflects social, situational, and acquisitional facts about the learner and the interaction, and the manner in which many of these factors change over time, we must also continue to incorporate these insights into a dynamic model of contextually-situated, co-constructed interactions between learners and interlocutors" (2020, p. 146).

In another study of a sometimes-neglected area, Geeslin (2021) outlines the possible contributions of a variationist perspective to our understanding of sophisticated language use by advanced learners. She uses an extended example from a study of variable intervocalic /d/ deletion, a feature of many Spanish dialects, by advanced L2 learners and native Spanish speakers. In the exemplified study, Solon, Linford, and Geeslin (2018) found that native speakers' choice of a variant of /d/ was conditioned by preceding and following vowels, grammatical category, and stress. In contrast, the production of the advanced L2 learners was conditioned primarily by lexical frequency, suggesting that the learners had acquired lexical items with /d/ prototypically deleted (e.g. *todo* 'all' or *nada* 'nothing').

This example illustrates how Geeslin used the results of studies of L2 variation to address larger questions. We know, for instance, that children begin to acquire the constraints on variable forms before they have mastered many of the basic rules of the grammar (Labov, 1989), and we know that most variable forms are subject to a range of linguistic constraints at multiple levels. Detailed examination of variable features like /d/ deletion offers a way to understand how learners acquire variable structures. Moreover, in native speech, /d/ deletion is a mark of casualness and informality. Sophisticated language use involves not only correctness but also stylistic appropriateness. Studies of variable features, particularly those like /d/ deletion that are not stigmatized, provide a way to examine the paths learners take in acquiring the ability to style shift.

In addition to providing an example of how studies of the variation in the speech of advanced learners can help us understand subtle differences between advanced learners and native speakers, Geeslin (2021) suggests that variationist studies can provide a way to measure learners' interpretive abilities, which contributes to our understanding of sophisticated language use in context and to the relationship between acquisition and the input learners receive in the classroom.

In sum, in her research, Kimberly Geeslin explored many avenues and, thanks to her contributions and the contributions of the numerous students she trained directly, as well as the other scholars whose careers she fostered, work on L2 Spanish has become an important part of the variationist canon. Geeslin's studies have served as models of intellectual and methodological rigor for students and colleagues who study SLA and language variation and change.

Kimberly Geeslin as an editor and book author

In addition to her numerous studies of variation in L2 and L1 Spanish and related language varieties, Kimberly Geeslin contributed to linguistics and SLA more broadly through her extensive editorial work. She served as Associate Editor of *Studies in Second Language Acquisition* from 2015 until her untimely passing in 2023 and as Associate Editor of *Studies in Hispanic and Lusophone Linguistics* from its founding in 2008 until 2023. She was also Associate Editor of Routledge's Second Language Acquisition Research book series and co-editor of Benjamin's Issues in Hispanic and Lusophone Linguistics book series. In addition, she was the sole editor of three major handbooks, *The handbook of Spanish second language acquisition* (2014), *The Cambridge handbook of Spanish linguistics* (2018), and *The Routledge handbook of second language acquisition and sociolinguistics* (2022). Like many fields, linguistics has seen a proliferation of handbooks in recent decades, and leading scholars receive more invitations to contribute to such volumes than they can possibly manage. A look at the contributors' lists in the handbooks that Geeslin edited, however, provides a clear demonstration of the respect that she commanded in her field. The 30 chapters in *The handbook of Spanish second language acquisition*, for example, include work by noted scholars Robert DeKeyser ("Acquisition of grammar by instructed learners"), Silvina Montrul ("Ultimate attainment in Spanish L2 acquisition"), Kim Potowski ("Heritage learners of Spanish"), and Roumyana Slabakova ("Meaning in second language Spanish"), as well as many others.

Together, Geeslin's handbooks constitute a very significant contribution to the fields of Hispanic linguistics, sociolinguistics, and SLA. Indeed, considering the number of articles and chapters and the extensive organizational work involved in producing large reference works, it would not be surprising if that were all that Geeslin accomplished. However, that is not the case. In addition to a great many research studies and important reference works, she served the field by producing two important textbooks, one on sociolinguistics and SLA (Geeslin & Long, 2014) and the other on the acquisition of Spanish as a L2 (Geeslin, Long, & Solon, 2021).

Geeslin and Long (2014) fills a major gap in the literature. As is typical of much of Geeslin's work, it is co-authored with a former student, Avizia Long. While the book includes very substantial sections on the variationist approach, it provides an indication of Geeslin's breadth by incorporating clear accounts of a variety of perspectives including, for example, language socialization and socio-cognitive approaches as well as cognitive approaches to the acquisition of sociolinguistic competence.

While Geeslin and Long (2014) is directed to more advanced students of SLA, Geeslin, Long et al. (2021) is directed to students who intend to teach Spanish, but who have little familiarity with acquisition. Thus, in addition to providing rich examples of the acquisition of Spanish phonology and morphosyntax, Geeslin and her co-authors also outline the development of SLA as a field, including a section on behaviorist and generative approaches and the early morpheme studies as well as Krashen's (1982) Monitor Model. Geeslin et al. include discussions of the main issues in contemporary SLA research and conclude with a section of applications, with attention to study abroad and a discussion on insights for the classroom. Overall, the volume serves as a valuable resource for any student who wishes to teach Spanish, and the first section of the book on perspectives on SLA and research methods would be worthwhile reading to anyone who wishes to learn more about how languages are learned.

Kimberly Geeslin as a mentor

Kimberly Geeslin's contributions to the combined fields of SLA and sociolinguistics include not only her own significant scholarly production and the publication of a number of important edited volumes, but also the mentorship of early-career scholars and the promotion of their work as they entered and navigated the field. As previously noted, the respect that Geeslin commanded within the fields of SLA and sociolinguistics meant that many senior scholars were more than willing to contribute to the larger projects, such as handbooks, that Geeslin conceptualized and brought to fruition with her distinctive combination of enthusiasm, rigor, and dedication. At the same time, it is clear that Geeslin intentionally made use of these larger projects to bring together scholars at various stages of their careers, from tenured professors to graduate students. She also saw these larger projects as opportunities to mentor incoming and early-career faculty from many different institutions, not just her own, by offering them opportunities to publish their work in the company of some of the most well-respected researchers in the field. In this way, Geeslin repeatedly demonstrated another of her unique and outstanding qualities — her commitment to faculty mentorship at all levels of the discipline.

For example, Geeslin's most recent edited volume, *The Routledge handbook of second language acquisition and sociolinguistics* (2022), marks an important point in the evolution of two lines of inquiry that had been informing each other for decades but had not yet been established as an independent, yet wholly interdisciplinary, field within applied linguistics. As Geeslin wrote in the Introduction to the 2022 volume, "At present, many of the most widely read volumes on second language acquisition contain a chapter on social aspects of second language acquisition…and there are even textbooks that introduce students of applied linguistics to this field" (2022, p. xix). Yet, Geeslin also noted that "it is rare to find a unified volume that captures the range of approaches to social aspects of language learning and situated language use in dialogue" (2022, p. xix). Geeslin's 2022 handbook provided such a unified and state-of-the-art volume that included both the research of many pioneering scholars in the field of language variation and change while also showcasing recent research from over 40 scholars from around the world, many of whom were in the early stages of their academic careers.

Importantly, the list of contributors to the 2022 handbook attests to the strength and breadth of Geeslin's strong commitment to mentorship. First, many of the contributions to the 2022 handbook were among Geeslin's former graduate students from Indiana University who are now well established in their own careers. These nine contributors include the editors of the current volume, Aarnes Gudmestad (Ph.D., 2008), Matthew Kanwit (Ph.D., 2014), and Megan Solon (Ph.D., 2015), as well as Lauren B. Schmidt (Ph.D., 2011), Elena Schoonmaker-Gates (Ph.D., 2012), Stephen Fafulas (Ph.D., 2013), Bret Linford (Ph.D., 2016), Avizia Long (Ph.D., 2016), and Sara L. Zahler (Ph.D., 2018). What is readily apparent from this list of contributors is that Geeslin dedicated herself to faculty mentoring early in her career and never wavered from this mission. For example, Geeslin published in two sets of conference proceedings in 2008 with her then current student, Aarnes Gudmestad, *Selected proceedings of the 2007 Second Language Research Forum* (2008c) and *Selected proceedings of the 10th Hispanic Linguistics Symposium* (2008a), as well as a manuscript in the *Journal of Applied Linguistics* ("The acquisition of variation in second-language Spanish: An agenda for integrating studies of the L2 sound system", 2008b) in the same year. Geeslin and Gudmestad continued to publish together for the next 15 years with a focus on the acquisition of variation and sociolinguistic competence in L2 Spanish, as well as on comparisons of subject expression by native and nonnative Spanish speakers. Geeslin and Gudmestad's collaborations produced nearly 15 publications including manuscripts in well-known journals in the field of SLA, such as *Studies in Second Language Acquisition* (2010), *Studies in Hispanic and Lusophone Linguistics* (2011), and *Language Learning* (2013), as well as a co-authored chapter in *The Routledge handbook of variationist approaches to Spanish* (2021) and Gudmestad's chapter ("Eliciting variable structures across tasks") in Geeslin's 2022 edited volume, *The Routledge handbook of second language acquisition and sociolinguistics*. Geeslin and Gudmestad's collaborators also included numerous former graduate students whom Geeslin advised at Indiana University, including a co-authored chapter with Hasler-Barker, Kanwit, Long, and Solon in *Heritage speakers of Spanish and study abroad* (Pozzi et al., 2021) and a co-authored chapter with Kanwit, Linford, Long, Schmidt, and Solon in *Speaking in a second language* (Alonso, 2018). Geeslin and Gudmestad's collaborations from 2008–2022 exemplify a commitment to mentoring that did not end when Geeslin's students finished graduate school and moved into the professional world. In fact, this was often only the very beginning of many years of collaboration, guidance, support, and friendship that played a pivotal role in her former students' lives. In Gudmestad's words, "The gratitude I feel for everything that she did for me has continued to grow over the years as I have become more and more aware of how far-reaching her impact has been" (personal communication, June 12, 2024).

Geeslin's mentoring of many other graduate students who followed Gudmestad in the Ph.D. program at Indiana University demonstrates a similar commitment to the development of professional competence among early-career linguists during and following the completion of the Ph.D. program. For example, in 2013, Matthew Kanwit, another co-editor of the current volume, published a manuscript with Geeslin and a fellow graduate student, Stephen Fafulas, in the *Selected proceedings of the 15th Hispanic Linguistics Symposium*. In the following year, Kanwit and Geeslin published a manuscript comparing the interpretation of the Spanish subjunctive and indicative in adverbial clauses by native speakers and learners in the highly regarded journal, *Studies in Second Language Acquisition*, followed by a manuscript in *Probus* in 2015, on the acquisition of variation in L2 Spanish during study abroad, again co-authored with Fafulas. Similar to the relationship that Geeslin maintained with Gudmestad after graduation, Geeslin and Kanwit collaborated on multiple projects in the 10 years following Kanwit's departure from Indiana University, including the previously mentioned chapters in *Speaking in a second language* (Alonso, 2018) and *Heritage speakers of Spanish and study abroad* (Pozzi et al., 2021), co-authored by Geeslin, Gudmestad, and other former graduate students of Geeslin's, two additional manuscripts published in *Studies in Second Language Acquisition* (2018, 2020), and Kanwit's chapter ("Sociolinguistic competence: What we know so far and where we're heading") in Geeslin's 2022 edited handbook. Similar to Gudmestad, Kanwit has expressed that Geeslin's impact on his life and career extended far beyond his years in graduate school and included both professional and personal mentorship for which Geeslin always made herself available. About Geeslin's role in his life, Kanwit wrote, "You've given us the ultimate standard for how to be in life and work… Always doing everything for everyone and yet somehow never too busy for others. I can't think of an important decision in any aspect of life over the past 10 years where you didn't have exactly the right thing to say" (personal communication, June 12, 2024).

Similar to both Gudmestad and Kanwit, the lead editor of the current volume, Megan Solon, completed her Ph.D. under Geeslin's direction in 2015 and collaborated extensively with Geeslin as a graduate student and in her professional career until Geeslin's death in 2023. Of her experience, Solon wrote that Geeslin was "The most incredible mentor and role model who taught us how to be scholars but also just let us be people" (personal communication, June 12, 2024). Solon first collaborated with Geeslin in 2016 on a chapter ("Measuring lexical frequency: Comparison groups and subject expression in L2 Spanish"; Linford et al., 2016) published in the volume *The usage-based study of language learning and multilingualism* (Ortega et al., 2016). This chapter was co-authored with two other graduate students, Bret Linford and Avizia Long, both of whom completed a Ph.D. in 2016 under Geeslin's direction. In the same year, Solon published another chapter co-authored with Geeslin, Linford, Long, and Whatley in *Spanish language and sociolinguistic analysis* (Sessarego & Tejedo-Herrero, 2016), followed by a manuscript published in 2018 in the *Revista Española de Lingüística Aplicada*, where Solon served as the lead author with both Linford and Geeslin. Also in 2018, Solon contributed to the chapter published in *Speaking in a second language* (Alonso, 2018), mentioned previously and co-authored by Geeslin, Gudmestad, Kanwit, Linford, Long, and Schmidt.

In this same year, 2018, Solon contributed to a chapter ("Examining multifaceted sources of input"; Gurzynski-Weiss et al., 2018) published in *Usage inspired L2 instruction: Researched pedagogy* (Tyler et al., 2018) which included two of Solon's contemporaries, Linford and Long, among the list of co-authors. Although this was certainly not Solon's last collaboration with Geeslin, this particular project provides an illustrative example of Geeslin's steadfast commitment to supporting linguists at all stages of their careers. The list of authors includes not only Geeslin's former graduate students, Solon, Linford, and Long, but also two of her then-current graduate students, Danielle Daidone (Ph.D., 2020) and Ian Michalski (Ph.D., 2019), as well as Dr. Laura Gurzynski-Weiss, the lead author on the project. Importantly, Geeslin was not only a mentor to her current and former students, but also to colleagues in the Department of Spanish and Portuguese like Gurzynski-Weiss, who wrote of Geeslin, "You always saw the kind, most innovative path forward in every difficult solution, and you taught me every day how one person can make a profound and lasting impact" (personal communication, June 17, 2024).

While the names of many scholars have become familiar over the preceding pages describing Geeslin's numerous collaborations, the appearance of new names in more recent years, such as Daidone and Michalski, both contributing authors to the current volume (Chapters 6 and 11, respectively), indicate that Geeslin's role as a mentor was never finished; it began anew each year with every incoming group of graduate students. Because of the ongoing life cycle of Geeslin's mentorship, while many of the contributors to the current volume benefitted from Geeslin's guidance for many years, some of the contributors only knew her for a short time and were not able to finish their work with her before she died. These contributors include Nicholas M. Blaker (Chapter 4), Travis Evans-Sago (Chapter 10), Thomas Goebel-Mahrle (Chapter 4), Jingyi Guo (Chapter 1), and Stacey Hanson (Chapter 7), many of whom published co-authored manuscripts with Geeslin posthumously in 2023. The inclusion of contributions from these authors who would, today, be Geeslin's current cohort of graduate students at Indiana University provides clear evidence that Geeslin's legacy of excellent, purposeful, and compassionate mentorship will persist through the work of those who were fortunate enough to learn from the very best.

Another important aspect of Geeslin's approach to faculty mentoring is that she did not restrict her mentorship and support to her own students or to her close colleagues and well-known peers. Instead, she generously shared it with many scholars who were just entering the field or who needed Geeslin's guidance and endorsement to develop their research profiles. For example, Geeslin's 2022 volume (*The Routledge handbook of second language acquisition and sociolinguistics*) not only includes contributions by nine of her own former students, but also includes six former students of Robert Bayley of the University of California, Davis, a close colleague of Geeslin's and contributor to the current volume, who shared Geeslin's commitment to active and purposeful mentoring at all stages and in all facets of the academic faculty journey. These contributors include Chelsea Escalante (Ph.D., 2018), Kristen Kennedy Terry (Ph.D., 2012), Kayla Palakurthy (NSF Postdoctoral Fellow, 2019), Rebecca Pozzi (Ph.D., 2017), and Xinye Zhang (Ph.D., 2023), who worked with Bayley at the University of California, Davis and Xiaoshi Li (Ph.D., 2007) who studied with Bayley at the University of Texas, San Antonio.

For many of Bayley's former students, Geeslin's support of their research, including but not limited to their contributions to her 2022 volume, was invaluable to both securing new faculty positions and to progressing toward tenure at their current institutions. For example, Pozzi, who first contacted Geeslin in 2018 with an invitation to contribute to a volume that she and her colleagues were editing, explained that "Kim has made a huge impact on my academic career through opening the door to numerous opportunities and connections, and going the extra mile to make me feel like I was capable not only of having a seat at the academic table, but also excelling in the academic world" (personal communication, June 21, 2024). Kennedy Terry tells a similar story about Geeslin's support that came at a time when Kennedy Terry was returning to her research after a break of many years and was wondering whether she had simply waited too long. In the fall of 2019, following Bayley's recommendation, Geeslin emailed Kennedy Terry to invite her to contribute a chapter on social networks to the 2022 volume (*The Routledge handbook of second language acquisition and sociolinguistics*). This invitation provided Kennedy Terry with "the motivation and confidence that I needed to keep going and to submit another manuscript to *The Modern Language Journal* (2022) that I had started many years before" (personal communication, June 15, 2024). Additionally, in the fall of 2020, Geeslin invited Kennedy Terry to develop the chapter on social networks from the 2022 volume into a monograph in the Routledge Second Language Acquisition Research series (*Social network analysis in second language research: Theory and methods*, Kennedy Terry & Bayley, 2024), and Geeslin enthusiastically supported Kennedy Terry as she subsequently pursued tenure-track faculty positions in French linguistics. Like so many others described in this chapter, Kennedy Terry's academic career was immeasurably impacted by the way that Geeslin generously shared her time, her energy, and her experience with scholars just entering the field, as well as with her former students, such as the editors of the current volume, who would someday need to be ready to step into Geeslin's shoes.

Geeslin's extensive publication and collaboration record described in this chapter is representative of the lasting impact that she has had, and will continue to have, on the combined fields of SLA and sociolinguistics — an impact made not only through the scope and rigor of her own research, but also through the research of all of those developing scholars who were fortunate enough to enter her sphere of influence and to benefit from her wisdom, her kindness, and her drive to expand and evolve the fields of applied linguistics, sociolinguistics, and Hispanic linguistics.

Kimberly L. Geeslin as an administrator and colleague

The dedication and passion that Kimberly L. Geeslin ("Kim," as she welcomed everyone to call her) brought to her scholarship and mentorship extended naturally to her growing administrative leadership in the Department of Spanish and Portuguese, Indiana University, and to national conversations about academic issues in higher education. Kim's administrative leadership was a natural extension of her mentorship, allowing her to mentor individual faculty of all ranks, career stages, and disciplines while also creating programs, policies, and practices to institutionalize those mechanisms of support. Rather than dreaming up top-down programs that can drain rather than generate faculty energy, her contributions evolved from listening closely to faculty needs and collaboratively developing creative forms of support to address those concerns. Kim's success creating institutional mechanisms for faculty support means that her work continues to enrich faculty in her department, Indiana University, and beyond.

In the Department of Spanish and Portuguese, which she joined in 1999, Kim served as Interim Chair (2015–2016), Associate Chair (2012–2015, 2017), and Director of Hispanic Linguistics (2004–2012). She was also a near constant fixture on the faculty-elected Chair's Advisory Committee (2001–2004, 2006–2007, 2008–2012, 2013–2015, 2018–2019, 2019–2020), among many others. In her roles as Interim/Associate Chair, Kim oversaw one of the largest departments in the College of Arts and Sciences, with more than 100 graduate students, 45 faculty and staff members, and offering more than 7,500 classes per year. Kim was responsible for many lasting impacts including the creation of two Hispanic Linguistics laboratories, dedicated to the many graduate students, faculty, and affiliate faculty. These laboratories quickly became a locus of connection for all. Kim secured funding for state-of-the-art equipment freely available to everyone, including soundproof booths for phonetic recordings, laptops, microphones for collecting data in the field, and an eye-tracker. She was also responsible for the creation of our Hispanic linguistics post-doctoral fellowship, which allowed regular engagement with diverse perspectives that mutually benefited our Indiana University Bloomington team and offered competitive opportunities to early-career scholars; those relationships are still felt today in mentorship that continues with current students, and through the publications used throughout the field that resulted from such collaborations. In her tenure as the Director of Hispanic Linguistics, Kim created mechanisms for active recruitment of potential students and was responsible for ensuring that a stipend and course release were made available to all future directors. Indeed, Kim always made sure that progress in our department was made for the good of all and in ways that increased inclusivity and access. She was, without exaggeration, the single most collegial member of our department, the one everyone turned to at the end of discussions for her opinion, for advice when faced with a problem, and for inspiration. Kim's mentorship of and fierce advocacy for her faculty, staff, and student colleagues was indefatigable and lasted well beyond their time at Indiana University.

Beyond the department, Kim dedicated her roles as Associate Vice Provost for Faculty and Academic Affairs (2017–2022), Director of the Initiative for the Advancement of Women (2020–2022), and ultimately, Vice Provost for Faculty and Academic Affairs (2022–2023) to supporting faculty and expanding recognition of their extraordinary work. She worked continuously during her various roles in academic affairs to ensure that all faculty had a transparent, fair, and rigorous campus system of review for promotion and tenure. Her efforts included co-leading dozens of workshops for faculty each year, myriad advising meetings with individuals going through promotion and tenure, oversight of the Campus Promotion and Tenure Committee, and working collaboratively with (then) Associate Vice Provost for Faculty and Academic Affairs Jamie Prenkert and the Bloomington Faculty Council on a major revision of the campus promotion and tenure standards. In response to data showing that mid-career faculty at Indiana and nationally faced challenges after being awarded tenure, Kim collaborated with the Institute for Advanced Studies at Indiana University to overhaul and expand mentoring for mid-career faculty, creating newly tenured working groups and a series of promotion workshops specifically designed for mid-career faculty.

Kim was instrumental in the creation and early direction of a critical resource supporting women's career advancement at Indiana, the Initiative for the Advancement of Women. This initiative has grown to include the Women in Leadership program she launched, as well as the Advocates and Allies for Equity program and the Women and Technology Series. The Initiative for the Advancement of Women grew out of survey data from faculty suggesting that women faculty had lower levels of satisfaction, recognition of their accomplishments, and retention, and that they faced a range of unique obstacles in career advancement. Kim led a faculty committee to investigate these concerns and to provide concrete recommendations, resulting in a report (Geeslin et al., 2019) to the Indiana University Bloomington campus. A key committee recommendation was to create a clearinghouse to link the many existing campus resources designed to support women faculty. The Initiative for the Advancement of Women Faculty was created in 2020 for this purpose, and Kim's vision for this initiative and her longstanding support of women made her the ideal inaugural director of this program. Since its inauguration in 2020, the scope of the Initiative has grown to provide career development resources for both faculty and staff, now named the Initiative for the Advancement of Women to reflect its continuing expansion.

Kim's creativity, dedication, and collaborative spirit were particularly valuable during the Covid-19 pandemic. While the pandemic interrupted faculty careers in varying ways, she quickly identified groups of faculty — such as recently hired and pre-tenure faculty, mid-career faculty, and faculty who had care responsibilities for children — who were at particular risk of career disruption. In addition to participating on numerous committees and working groups within Indiana University, she joined conversations with academic affairs officials across the Big Ten Academic Alliance and universities across the country to share information about career impacts and ways that universities could support faculty to minimize disruption. Kim's insights in these conversations shaped various programs designed to support Indiana faculty, including tenure clock extensions, small, easily attained grants to support faculty research, and innovative ways to integrate new faculty and to recognize faculty success at times when large faculty events were not possible. Not surprisingly, Kim quickly emerged as a leader in these national conversations, and her leadership included planning for the annual Faculty Affairs Retreat conducted by the Association of Public and Land-Grant Universities.

Kim cared deeply about her colleagues, and she was passionate about creating institutional structures and a culture where faculty would thrive. She listened carefully to faculty to understand the ways that the various organizational layers of the university (e.g., departments, schools, and campuses) supported or hindered their success, and she worked creatively and collaboratively to maximize support for faculty so they could do their best work. Her many contributions to supporting faculty careers are deeply woven into the institutional fabric of Indiana University, and her efforts continue to support and nurture faculty success.

Acknowledgements

Bayley and Kennedy Terry provided the reflections on Kim's research contributions and her roles as author/editor and mentor. Gurzynski-Weiss and Pavalko provided insights on Kim as an administrator and colleague at Indiana University.

References

Adamson, H. D., & Kovac, C. (1981). Variation theory and second language acquisition. In D. Sankoff & C. Cedergren (Eds.), *Variation omnibus* (pp. 285–293). Linguistic Research Inc.

Alonso, R. A. (Ed.). (2018). *Speaking in a second language*. John Benjamins.

Announcing the 2024 Susan Gass Award for Impact in SLA. (2024). *Studies in Second Language Acquisition*, 46(1), 1.

Barrenechea, A. M., & Alonso, A. (1973). Los pronombres personales sujetos en el español de Buenos Aires. In K. Karl-Hermann, & K. Rühl (Eds.), *Studia Iberica: Festschrift für Hans Flasche* (pp. 75–91). Francke.

Bayley, R. (1994). Interlanguage variation and the quantitative paradigm: Past tense marking in Chinese-English. In E. Tarone, S. M. Gass, & A. Cohen (Eds.), *Research methodology in second-language acquisition* (pp. 157–181). Lawrence Erlbaum.

Bayley, R., & Preston, D. R. (Eds.). (1996). *Second language acquisition and linguistic variation*. John Benjamins.

Carvalho, A. M., Orozco, R., & Shin, N. L. (Eds.). (2015). *Subject pronoun expression in Spanish: A cross-dialectal perspective*. Georgetown University Press.

Chomsky, N. (1981). Principles and parameters in syntactic theory. In N. Hornstein & D. Lightfoot (Eds.), *Explanation in linguistics: The logical problem of language acquisition* (pp. 32–75). Longman.

Díaz-Campos, M., & Geeslin, K. L. (2011). Copula use in the Spanish of Venezuela: Is the pattern indicative of stable variation or an ongoing change? *Spanish in Context*, 8(1), 73–94.

Dickerson, L. (1975). The learner's interlanguage as a system of variable rules. *TESOL Quarterly*, 9, 401–407.

Fasold, R. W., & Preston, D. R. (2007). A psycholinguistic model of inherent variability: Old Occam whips out his razor. In R. Bayley & C. Lucas (Eds.), *Sociolinguistic variation: Theories, methods, and applications* (pp. 45–69). Cambridge University Press.

File-Muriel, R. J., & Brown, E. K. (2011). The gradient nature of s-lention in Caleño Spanish. *Language Variation and Change*, 23, 223–243.

Geeslin, K. L. (1999). *The second language acquisition of copula choice in Spanish and its relationship to language change* [Unpublished doctoral dissertation]. University of Arizona.

Geeslin, K. L. (2002). The acquisition of Spanish copula choice and its relationship to language change. *Studies in Second Language Acquisition*, 24, 419–450.

Geeslin, K. L. (2003). A comparison of copula choice: Native Spanish speakers and advanced learners. *Language Learning*, 53(4), 703–764.

Geeslin, K. L. (2011). Variation in L2 Spanish: The state of the discipline. *Studies in Hispanic and Lusophone Linguistics*, 4(2), 461–517.

Geeslin, K. L. (Ed.). (2014). *The handbook of Spanish second language acquisition*. John Wiley & Sons.

Geeslin, K. L. (Ed.). (2018). *The Cambridge handbook of Spanish linguistics*. Cambridge University Press.

Geeslin, K. L. (2020). Variationist perspective(s) on interlocutor individual differences. In L. Gurzynski-Weiss (Ed.), *Cross-theoretical explorations of interlocutors and their individual differences* (pp. 129–195). John Benjamins.

Geeslin, K. L. (2021). Sophisticated language use in context: The contributions of variationist research to the study of advanced learners of Spanish. In M. R. Menke & P. Malovrh (Eds.), *Advances in second language Spanish: Definitions, challenges, and possibilities* (pp. 221–243). John Benjamins.

Geeslin, K. L. (Ed.). (2022). *The Routledge handbook of second language acquisition and sociolinguistics*. Routledge.

Geeslin, K. L., & Fafulas, S. (2022). Linguistic variation and second language Spanish: A study of progression and habitual marking by English-speaking learners. In R. Bayley, D. R. Preston, & X. Li (Eds.), *Variation in second and heritage languages: Crosslinguistic perspectives* (pp. 159–198). John Benjamins.

Geeslin, K. L., Fafulas, S., & Kanwit, M. (2013). Acquiring geographically-variable norms of use: The case of the present perfect in Mexico and Spain. In C. Howe, S. E. Blackwell, & M. Lubbers Quesada (Eds.), *Selected proceedings of the 15th Hispanic Linguistics Symposium* (pp. 205–220). Cascadilla Proceedings Project.

Geeslin, K. L., Goebel-Mahrle, T., Guo, J., & Linford, B. (2023). Variable subject expression in second language acquisition: The role of perseveration. In P. Posio & P. Herbeck (Eds.), *Referring to discourse participants in Ibero-Romance languages* (pp. 69–104). Language Sciences Press.

Geeslin, K. L., & Gudmestad, A. (2008a). Comparing interview and written elicitation tasks in native and non-native data: Do speakers do what we think they do? In J. Bruhn Garavito & E. Valenzuela (Eds.), *Selected proceedings of the 10th Hispanic Linguistics Symposium* (pp. 64–77). Cascadilla Proceedings Project.

Geeslin, K. L., & Gudmestad, A. (2008b). The acquisition of variation in second-language Spanish: An agenda for integrating studies of the L2 sound system. *Journal of Applied Linguistics*, 5, 137–157.

Geeslin, K. L., & Gudmestad, A. (2008c). Variable subject expression in second-language Spanish: A comparison of native and non-native speakers. In M. Bowles, R. Foote, S. Perpiñán, & R. Bhatt (Eds.), *Selected proceedings of the second language research forum* (pp. 69–85). Cascadilla Proceedings Project.

Geeslin, K. L., & Gudmestad, A. (2010). An exploration of the range and frequency of occurrence of forms in potentially variable structures in second-language Spanish. *Studies in Second Language Acquisition*, 32, 433–463.

Geeslin, K. L., & Gudmestad, A. (2011). Using sociolinguistic analyses of discourse-level features to expand research on L2 variation: Native and non-native contrasts in forms of Spanish subject expression. In L. Plonsky & M. Schierloh (Eds.), *Selected proceedings of the Second Language Research Forum* (pp. 16–30). Cascadilla Proceedings Project.

Geeslin, K. L., Gudmestad, A., Hasler-Barker, M., Kanwit, M., Long, A. Y., & Solon, M. (2021). Sociolinguistic competence among heritage speakers of Spanish abroad. In R. Pozzi, T. Quan, & C. Escalante (Eds.), *Heritage speakers of Spanish and study abroad* (pp. 13–32). Routledge.

Geeslin, K. L., Gudmestad, A., Kanwit, M., Linford, B., Long, A. Y., Schmidt, L., & Solon, M. (2018). Sociolinguistic competence and the acquisition of speaking. In R. Alonso Alonso (Ed.), *Speaking a second language* (pp. 1–25). John Benjamins.

Geeslin, K. L., & Guijarro-Fuentes, P. (2003). Age-related factors in copula choice in steady state L2 Spanish grammars. *Revista Española de la Lingüística Aplicada*, 2, 83–110

Geeslin, K. L., & Guijarro-Fuentes, P. (2006). Second language acquisition of variable structures in Spanish by Portuguese speakers. *Language Learning*, 56(1), 53–107.

Geeslin, K. L., & Guijarro-Fuentes, P. (2008). Variation in contemporary Spanish: Linguistic predictors of estar in four cases of language contact. *Bilingualism: Language and Cognition*, 11(3), 365–380.

Geeslin, K. L., Imhoff, S., James, T., Li, S., Liu, C., Marrone, M., Qi, W., & Widiss, D. (2019). Campus Assessment Committee on Gender and Faculty Satisfaction. Office of the Vice Provost for Faculty and Academic Affairs, Indiana University Bloomington. report-on-gender-and-faculty-satisfaction.coache2016.pdf (indiana.edu).

Geeslin, K. L., Linford, B., & Fafulas, S. (2015). Variable subject expression in second language Spanish: Uncovering the developmental sequence and predictive linguistic factors. In A. M. Carvalho, R. Orozco, & N. L. Shin (Eds.), *Subject pronoun expression in Spanish: A cross-dialectal perspective* (pp. 169–190). Georgetown University Press.

Geeslin, K. L., & Long, A. Y. (2014). *Sociolinguistics and second language acquisition: Learning to use language in context*. Routledge.

Geeslin, K. L., Long, A. Y., & Solon. (2021). *The acquisition of Spanish as a second language*. Routledge.

Gudmestad, A. (2022). Eliciting variable structures across tasks. In K. Geeslin (Ed.), *The Routledge handbook of second language acquisition and sociolinguistics* (pp. 224–236). Routledge.

Gudmestad, A., & Geeslin, K. L. (2010). Exploring the roles of redundancy and ambiguity in variable subject expression: A comparison of native and non-native speakers. In C. Borgonovo, M. Español-Echevarría, & P. Prévost (Eds.), *Selected proceedings of the 12th Hispanic Linguistics Symposium* (pp. 270–283). Cascadilla Proceedings Project.

Gudmestad, A., & Geeslin, K. (2011). Assessing the use of multiple forms in variable contexts: The relationship between linguistic factors and future-time reference in Spanish. *Studies in Hispanic and Lusophone Linguistics*, 4, 3–33.

Gudmestad, A., & Geeslin, K. L. (2021). Overlapping envelopes of variation: The case of lexical noun phrases and subject expression in Spanish. In M. Díaz-Campos (Ed.), *The Routledge handbook of variationist approaches to Spanish* (pp. 437–449). Routledge

Gudmestad, A., House, L., & Geeslin, K. L. (2013). What a Bayesian analysis can do for SLA: New tools for the sociolinguistic study of subject expression in L2 Spanish. *Language Learning*, 63, 372–399.

Guijarro-Fuentes, P., & Geeslin, K. L. (2006). Copula choice in the Spanish of Galicia: The effects of bilingualism on language use. *Spanish in Context*, 6(1), 63–83.

Gurzynski-Weiss, L., Geeslin, K. L., Daidone, D., Linford, B., Long, A. Y., Michalski, I., & Solon, M. (2018). Examining multifaceted sources of input. In A. E. Tyler, L. Ortega, M. Uno, & H. I. Park (Eds.), *Usage-inspired L2 instruction: Researched pedagogy* (pp. 291–311). John Benjamins.

Guy, G. R. (1980). Variation in the group and the individual: The case of final stop deletion. In W. Labov (Ed.), *Locating language in time and space* (pp. 1–36). Academic Press.

Guy, G. R., Adli, A., Bayley, R., Beaman, K. V., Erker, D., Orozco, R., & Zhang, X. (forthcoming). *Subject pronoun expression: A cross-linguistic variationist sociolinguistic study*. Cambridge University Press.

Kanwit, M. (2022). Sociolinguistic competence: What we know so far and where we're heading. In K. Geeslin (Ed.), *The Routledge handbook of second language acquisition and sociolinguistics* (pp. 30–44). Routledge.

Kanwit, M., & Geeslin, K. L. (2014). The interpretation of the Spanish subjunctive and indicative forms in adverbial clauses: A cross-sectional study. *Studies in Second Language Acquisition, 36*, 487–533.

Kanwit, M., & Geeslin, K. L. (2018). Exploring lexical effects in second language interpretation: The case of mood in Spanish adverbial clauses. *Studies in Second Language Acquisition, 40*, 579–603.

Kanwit, M., & Geeslin, K. L. (2020). Sociolinguistic competence and interpreting variable structures in a second language: A study of the copula contrast in native and second language Spanish. *Studies in Second Language Acquisition, 42*, 775–799.

Kanwit, M., Geeslin, K. L., & Fafulas, S. (2015). Study abroad and the SLA of variable structures: A look at the present perfect, copula contrast, and the present progressive in Mexico and Spain. *Probus, 27*, 308–348.

Kennedy Terry, K. (2017). Contact, context, and collocation: The emergence of sociostylistic variation in L2 French learners during study abroad. *Studies in Second Language Acquisition, 39*(3), 553–578.

Kennedy Terry, K. (2022). At the intersection of SLA and sociolinguistics: The predictive power of social networks during study abroad. *The Modern Language Journal, 106*(1), 245–266.

Kennedy Terry, K., & Bayley, R. (2024). *Social network analysis in second language research: Theory and methods*. Routledge.

Krashen, S. (1982). *Principles and practice in second language acquisition*. Pergamon.

Labov, W. (1963). The social motivation of a sound change. *Word. 19*, 273–309.

Labov, W. (1966). *The social stratification of English in New York City*. Center for Applied Linguistics.

Labov, W. (1972). *Language in the inner city: Studies in the Black English vernacular*. University of Pennsylvania Press.

Labov, W. (1984). Field methods of the project on linguistic change and variation. In J. Baugh & J. Sherzer (Eds.), *Language in use: Readings in sociolinguistics* (pp. 28–53). Prentice-Hall.

Labov, W. (1989). The child as linguistic historian *Language Variation and Change, 1*, 85–97.

Li, X. (2010). Sociolinguistic variation in the speech of learners of Chinese as a second language. *Language Learning, 60*(2), 366–408.

Li, X. (2014). Variation of subject pronominal expression in L2 Chinese. *Studies in Second Language Acquisition, 36*(1), 39–68.

Li, X., Bayley, R., Zhang, X., & Cui, Y. (2022). Sociolinguistic investigation of LE use by L2 Mandarin Chinese learners. In R. Bayley, D. Preston, & X. Li. (Eds.) *Variation and second language acquisition: Crosslinguistic perspectives* (pp. 15–41). John Benjamins.

Linford, B., & Geeslin, K. L. (2022). The role of referent cohesiveness in variable subject expression in L2 Spanish. *Spanish in Context, 19*(3), 508–536.

Linford, B., Long, A., Solon, M., & Geeslin, K. (2016). Measuring lexical frequency: Comparison groups and subject expression in L2 Spanish. In L. Ortega, A. E. Tyler, H. I. Park, & M. Uno (Eds.), *The usage-based study of language learning and multilingualism* (pp. 137–154). Georgetown University Press.

Linford, B., Long, A. Y., Solon, M., Whatley, M., & Geeslin, K. L. (2016). Lexical frequency and subject expression in native and non-native Spanish. In S. Sessarego & F. Tejedo-Herrero (Eds.), *Spanish language and sociolinguistic analysis* (pp. 197–216). John Benjamins.

Lynch, A. (2009). A sociolinguistic analysis of final /s/ in Miami Cuban Spanish. *Language Sciences*, 31(6), 766–790.

Orozco, R. (2018). *Spanish in Colombia and New York City*. John Benjamins.

Ortega, L., Tyler, A., Park, H. I., & Uno, M. (Eds.), *The usage-based study of language learning and multilingualism*. Georgetown University Press.

Otheguy, R., & Zentella, A. C. (2012). *Spanish in New York: Language contact, dialect leveling, and structural continuity*. Oxford University Press.

Pozzi, R., Quan, T., & Escalante, C. (Eds.). (2021). *Heritage speakers of Spanish and study abroad*. Routledge.

Preston, D. R. (1993). Variation linguistics and L2 acquisition. *Second Language Research*, 9(2), 153–172.

Preston, D. R. (1996). Variationist perspectives on second language acquisition. In R. Bayley & D. R. Preston (Eds.), *Second language acquisition and linguistic variation* (pp. 1–45). John Benjamins.

Preston, D. R. (2000). Three kinds of sociolinguistics and SLA: A psycholinguistic perspective. In B. Swierzbin, M. Anderson, C. Klee, & E. Tarone (Eds.), *Social and cognitive factors in SLA* (pp. 3–30). Cascadilla.

Regan, V. (1996). Variation in French interlanguage: A longitudinal study of sociolinguistic competence. In R. Bayley & D. R. Preston (Eds.), *Second language acquisition and linguistic variation* (pp. 177–201). John Benjamins.

Rickford, J. R., & McNair-Knox, F. (1994). Addressee- and topic- influenced style shift: A quantitative sociolinguistic study. In D. Biber & E. Finegan (Eds.), *Sociolinguistic perspectives on register* (pp. 235–276). Oxford University Press.

Schilling-Estes, N. (2004). Constructing identity in interaction. *Journal of Sociolinguistics*, 8, 163–195.

Selinker, L. (1972). Interlanguage. *International Review of Applied Linguistics in Language Teaching*, 10(3), 209–231.

Sessarego, S., & Tejedo-Herrero, F. (Eds.). (2016). *Spanish language and sociolinguistic analysis*. John Benjamins.

Silva-Corvalán, C. (1986). Bilingualism and language contact: The extension of *estar* in Los Angeles Spanish. *Language*, 62, 587–608.

Silva-Corvalán, C. (1994). *Language contact and change: Spanish in Los Angeles*. Clarendon Press.

Solon, M., Linford, B., & Geeslin, K. L. (2018). Acquisition of sociophonetic variation. *Revista Española de Lingüística Aplicada/Spanish Journal of Applied Linguistics*, 31(1), 309–344.

Tarone, E. (1985). Variability in interlanguage use: A study of style-shifting in morphology and syntax. *Language Learning*, 35, 373–403.

Terrell, T. D. (1979). Final /s/ in Cuban Spanish. *Hispania*, 62, 599–612.

Torres Cacoullos, R., & Travis, C. E. (2019). *Bilingualism in the community: Code-switching and grammars in contact*. Cambridge University Press.

Tyler, A. E., Ortega, L., Uno, M., & Park, H. I. (Eds.). (2018). *Usage-inspired L2 instruction: Researched pedagogy*. Georgetown University Press.

Weinreich, U., Labov, W., & Herzog, M. (1968). Empirical foundations for a theory of language change. In W. F. Lehmann & Y. Malkiel (Eds.), *Directions in historical linguistics* (pp. 98–195). University of Texas Press.

Wolfram, W. (1985). Variability in tense marking: A case for the obvious. *Language Learning, 35*, 229–253.

Young, R. (1988). Variation and the interlanguage hypothesis. *Studies in Second Language Acquisition, 10*, 281–302.

Zentella, A. C. (1997). *Growing up bilingual: Puerto Rican children in New York*. Blackwell.

Linford, B., Long, A. Y., Solon, M., Whatley, M., & Geeslin, K. L. (2016). Lexical frequency and subject expression in native and non-native Spanish. In S. Sessarego & F. Tejedo-Herrero (Eds.), *Spanish language and sociolinguistic analysis* (pp. 197–216). John Benjamins.

Lynch, A. (2009). A sociolinguistic analysis of final /s/ in Miami Cuban Spanish. *Language Sciences*, 31(6), 766–790.

Orozco, R. (2018). *Spanish in Colombia and New York City*. John Benjamins.

Ortega, L., Tyler, A., Park, H. I., & Uno, M. (Eds.), *The usage-based study of language learning and multilingualism*. Georgetown University Press.

Otheguy, R., & Zentella, A. C. (2012). *Spanish in New York: Language contact, dialect leveling, and structural continuity*. Oxford University Press.

Pozzi, R., Quan, T., & Escalante, C. (Eds.). (2021). *Heritage speakers of Spanish and study abroad*. Routledge.

Preston, D. R. (1993). Variation linguistics and L2 acquisition. *Second Language Research*, 9(2), 153–172.

Preston, D. R. (1996). Variationist perspectives on second language acquisition. In R. Bayley & D. R. Preston (Eds.), *Second language acquisition and linguistic variation* (pp. 1–45). John Benjamins.

Preston, D. R. (2000). Three kinds of sociolinguistics and SLA: A psycholinguistic perspective. In B. Swierzbin, M. Anderson, C. Klee, & E. Tarone (Eds.), *Social and cognitive factors in SLA* (pp. 3–30). Cascadilla.

Regan, V. (1996). Variation in French interlanguage: A longitudinal study of sociolinguistic competence. In R. Bayley & D. R. Preston (Eds.), *Second language acquisition and linguistic variation* (pp. 177–201). John Benjamins.

Rickford, J. R., & McNair-Knox, F. (1994). Addressee- and topic- influenced style shift: A quantitative sociolinguistic study. In D. Biber & E. Finegan (Eds.), *Sociolinguistic perspectives on register* (pp. 235–276). Oxford University Press.

Schilling-Estes, N. (2004). Constructing identity in interaction. *Journal of Sociolinguistics*, 8, 163–195.

Selinker, L. (1972). Interlanguage. *International Review of Applied Linguistics in Language Teaching*, 10(3), 209–231.

Sessarego, S., & Tejedo-Herrero, F. (Eds.). (2016). *Spanish language and sociolinguistic analysis*. John Benjamins.

Silva-Corvalán, C. (1986). Bilingualism and language contact: The extension of *estar* in Los Angeles Spanish. *Language*, 62, 587–608.

Silva-Corvalán, C. (1994). *Language contact and change: Spanish in Los Angeles*. Clarendon Press.

Solon, M., Linford, B., & Geeslin, K. L. (2018). Acquisition of sociophonetic variation. *Revista Española de Lingüística Aplicada/Spanish Journal of Applied Linguistics*, 31(1), 309–344.

Tarone, E. (1985). Variability in interlanguage use: A study of style-shifting in morphology and syntax. *Language Learning*, 35, 373–403.

Terrell, T. D. (1979). Final /s/ in Cuban Spanish. *Hispania*, 62, 599–612.

Torres Cacoullos, R., & Travis, C. E. (2019). *Bilingualism in the community: Code-switching and grammars in contact*. Cambridge University Press.

Tyler, A. E., Ortega, L., Uno, M., & Park, H. I. (Eds.). (2018). *Usage-inspired L2 instruction: Researched pedagogy*. Georgetown University Press.

Weinreich, U., Labov, W., & Herzog, M. (1968). Empirical foundations for a theory of language change. In W. F. Lehmann & Y. Malkiel (Eds.), *Directions in historical linguistics* (pp. 98–195). University of Texas Press.

Wolfram, W. (1985). Variability in tense marking: A case for the obvious. *Language Learning, 35*, 229–253.

Young, R. (1988). Variation and the interlanguage hypothesis. *Studies in Second Language Acquisition, 10*, 281–302.

Zentella, A. C. (1997). *Growing up bilingual: Puerto Rican children in New York*. Blackwell.

Index

A

adolescent 70, 230, 255, 323, 332
adverbial 12–19, 22, 25, 29, 36, 38, 43, 45–46, 49, 58, 94, 96, 346
address forms *See* forms of address
aspect: grammatical 3, 10–11, 14, 31, 42, 91, 110, 351
    Hypothesis 14, 28–29, 95
    lexical 12–19, 22–25, 27, 92, 95, 97, 99–100, 105–111, 347 *See also* tense-mood-aspect (TMA)
aspiration *See* /s/ weakening
attitudes 5, 57, 65–70, 72–73, 76–78, 80–83, 112, 180–182, 185, 195, 197–199, 232, 237, 293–297, 299–304, 310–314, 321

C

Caribbean Spanish 118, 181–182
Castilian Spanish 19–20, 65–67, 70–71, 74–78, 80–81, 83, 89, 93–94, 99, 108, 118, 148–149, 161, 178–182, 194–197, 199, 209, 212, 294, 321
Central American Spanish 181, 233–235, 239
Chinese *See* Mandarin
communication strategies (CSs) 37–38, 41–42, 58–59, 211, 215
communicative competence 12, 37, 41, 59, 238–241, 253, 292 *See also* sociolinguistic competence *and* strategic competence
comparison of means 301, 311
constraints: linguistic 11, 67, 90, 96–97, 116–121, 123–124, 129, 131, 136–138, 170, 173, 321, 347–350, 352
corpus 19, 29–31, 46–47, 124, 147, 262, 264
critical language awareness (CLA) 237, 239, 253
crosslinguistic influence 121, 136

D

dialect 66–68, 74, 77, 79, 81–83, 96, 149, 151, 185, 187, 189, 194, 238–240, 254–255, 295, 311, 325, 327, 349
didactic speech 144, 153, 172
distinción 181, 185, 197
duration 73, 75–79, 92, 260, 262, 268–269, 271–273, 276–278, 280–284
dynamics: of communication 319, 322–323
    of variation 333

E

ecological validity 5, 44, 317–319, 321–323, 333–335
effect size 25, 76, 165, 166, 301, 302, 304–306, 308–311
elicited imitation task (EIT) 266, 267
English: as first language (L1) 5, 13–14, 25, 43, 45, 70, 95–97, 116–117, 121–125, 128–138, 184–185, 195, 197–198, 243, 263, 290, 298, 301, 312, 317
    as second language (L2) 1, 41–42, 66, 123, 145, 319
European Spanish *See* Castilian Spanish
experimental control 5, 317, 319, 321, 322, 333–335, 339

F

filled pause 5, 260–265, 267, 268–286
form avoidance 3, 35, 37, 41, 42, 56–59
formant 149, 154, 260, 263, 269, 276, 277
forms of address 230, 231, 236, 238–240, 245–252, 255
frequency 3–4, 29, 35–37, 39–40, 42–43, 46–47, 49, 51–52, 55–59, 64, 68, 74, 90, 96–97, 100–102, 120, 145–146, 149–150, 161, 163, 166–169, 171, 206, 262, 265, 274–275, 282, 284, 352, 357
functional equivalence 268
future-time expression 3, 28, 35–37, 41–43, 45, 55, 58, 59, 320

G

generalized additive model/modeling (GAM) 21, 317, 328, 331, 337, 338

H

heritage-language (HL) learner *See* heritage learner
heritage learner 119, 122, 206, 230–233, 236–237, 239–240, 243, 245–246, 248–255, 351, 353
heritage speaker 4, 43, 117, 137, 230, 312, 356
hesitation 260, 262, 265, 284–285
hierarchical face systems 206, 225

I

identity 170, 198, 203–209, 211, 213, 215, 218–220, 222–227, 232–233, 237, 240, 285, 351
Implicit Association Test (IAT) 3, 65, 69, 70–74, 78–81, 83
implicit bias 3, 65, 69, 70, 73, 80–83
(ing) 1, 290, 296, 299–301
input 4, 15–16, 29–30, 39, 66, 97, 110, 121, 144–147, 149–150, 170, 172–173, 183, 198–199, 230, 237, 294, 298, 352–353, 357
interdental fricative /θ/ 3–4, 65–68, 70–81, 178–179, 181–185, 187–199, 261, 285, 294
interlocutor 1, 4 36, 42, 57, 147, 178–179, 183, 189 198, 196, 198–199, 203–209, 212–213, 215, 224–226, 236, 267, 285, 318, 322–323, 325–326, 328–329, 334–335, 338, 351–352

L

language attitudes *See* attitudes
language play 203, 207–210, 211, 217, 224–227
Latin American Spanish 68, 75–77, 93–94, 118, 181–184, 194–195, 233, 237 *See also* Central American Spanish *and* Caribbean Spanish
lexical aspect *See* aspect
lexical frequency *See* frequency

M

Mandarin 3, 116–125, 128–137, 144, 147, 312, 347, 351
matched guise 4, 67, 69, 70, 83, 178, 180, 185–186, 197, 290, 297–302, 312–313, 321–322
multilingual language profile (MLP) 327
multifunctionality 38, 43

N

native-speaker bias 5, 289, 291, 293, 312–314
naturalistic speech data 4, 100, 109, 120, 144, 146–147, 153, 185, 187, 205, 261, 284, 297, 320–321

P

pedagogy 29, 203, 230, 237, 240, 253, 255, 357 *See also* sociolinguistically informed pedagogy
Peninsular Spanish *See* Castilian Spanish
perception 3–4, 65, 67–70, 127, 129, 178–180, 182–184, 189–190, 194–199, 205–206, 240, 263–264, 289–290, 292–297, 299–301, 304–305, 307–309, 311–314
person/number 4, 30, 38, 43, 46–47, 49–51, 55, 57, 59, 66, 100, 111, 116–117, 119–121, 124–126, 129, 131, 133, 136–137, 216, 230–231, 233, 236, 239, 241, 243, 245–246, 252, 320, 346–347, 350
polarity 38, 46–51, 55
Praat 153, 269, 299
prestige 4, 82, 179, 182–187, 194–198, 237

R

reflexivity 116, 119, 125, 127, 129–133, 136–137
regional variation 4–5, 35, 65–67, 70, 82–83, 97, 178–185, 189, 194–199, 233, 240, 261, 266, 284–285, 294–295, 311, 321, 351
regularity 3, 35–37, 39–40, 42–43, 46–47, 49–53, 55–59, 64, 122, 233
rhotics 144, 150 *See also* trill

S

/s/ weakening 67, 162, 180, 261, 285, 290, 296–298, 319, 321, 336, 346
seseo 181, 185, 195, 197
sociolinguistic competence 12, 30, 57, 65, 68, 80, 82–83, 91, 111, 116, 121, 145, 205–206, 230–232, 237–239, 241, 253–255, 292–293, 317–318, 339, 349, 351, 354, 356–357 *See also* communicative competence
sociolinguistically informed pedagogy 230, 237, 240, 253, 255 *See also* pedagogy
sociophonetics 5, 144, 148, 150, 180, 197–198, 261, 263, 265, 321–322
sociopragmatics 4, 17, 203–206, 208–210, 212, 225–226
sophisticated language use 203–204, 206, 209, 224, 352–353

speech styles 147–148, 153, 169–173 *See also* style shifting
strategic competence 3, 12, 35–37, 41–42, 56–59 *See also* communicative competence
study abroad 3–4, 17, 66–69, 82–83, 89, 98, 180–182, 185–186, 194, 208–211, 213–215, 222, 225, 236–237, 239, 292, 294–295, 298, 311, 351, 354, 356
style shifting 346, 353
subject pronouns 3, 30, 116–138, 147, 319, 333, 346, 349
switch reference 116, 119–121, 125–126, 129–133, 136

T

teacher talk 144–150, 170
temporal distance *See* temporal reference
temporal reference 23–24, 35, 38, 43–46, 49, 51, 55, 57, 59, 89–90, 96–97, 99–105, 108–109, 111
temporal-sequential properties 333–335, 337–338
tense-aspect-mood (TAM) *See* tense-mood-aspect
tense-mood-aspect (TMA) 29, 111, 116, 119–120, 125–127, 129, 131
theta *See* interdental fricative /θ/
third language (L3) 117–118, 120–124, 129–130, 135–137
trill 4, 144–145, 148–150, 153–154, 161–166, 169–173

V

virtual reality (VR) 5, 317–319, 322–336, 338–339
voseo 233–239, 253–255

W

writing 35–36, 42, 44–45, 52, 117, 119–120, 124, 126, 137, 247